UNCOVERING THE
CONSTITUTION'S
MORAL DESIGN

UNCOVERING THE
CONSTITUTION'S
MORAL DESIGN

—— Paul R. DeHart ——

UNIVERSITY OF MISSOURI PRESS

COLUMBIA AND LONDON

Copyright © 2007 by
The Curators of the University of Missouri
University of Missouri Press, Columbia, Missouri 65201
Printed and bound in the United States of America
All rights reserved
5 4 3 2 1   11 10 09 08 07

Library of Congress Cataloging-in-Publication Data

DeHart, Paul R., 1975–
    Uncovering the constitution's moral design / Paul R. DeHart.
        p.   cm.
    Summary: "DeHart examines our constitution's normative frame-
work and moral meaning. He challenges the logical coherency of
modern moral philosophy, normative positivism, and other theories
that the constitution has been argued to embody and offers ground-
breaking methodology that can be applied to uncovering the normative
framework of other constitutions as well"—Provided by publisher.
    Includes bibliographical references and index.
    ISBN 978-0-8262-1760-8 (alk. paper)
    1. Constitutional law—Moral and ethical aspects—United States.
2. Constitutional law—Philosophy.   3. Constitutional law—
Methodology.   I. Title.
    KF4552.D44 2007
    342.7302—dc22

                                                    2007021033

⊗™ This paper meets the requirements of the
American National Standard for Permanence of Paper
for Printed Library Materials, Z39.48, 1984.

Designer: Kristie Lee
Typesetter: The Composing Room of Michigan, Inc.
Printer and binder: Thomson-Shore, Inc.
Typeface: Minion

The University of Missouri Press offers its grateful acknowledgment to
an anonymous donor whose generous grant in support of the publication of outstanding dissertations has assisted us with this volume.

For permissions, see p. 297.

To my parents, Bob and Marilyn DeHart,
for their unwavering support

To my wife, Robyn, for her undying love

To our beloved Cordelia

Contents

Acknowledgments

MOST OF THE CHAPTERS herein were presented at various conference meetings, in particular, at the annual meetings of the Midwest Political Science Association. I am grateful for the insightful comments and suggestions of the chairs, discussants, and fellow panelists.

A number of friends and colleagues offered listening ears, helpful insights, important criticisms, and encouragement along the way. Darrin Hanson provided a listening ear and helpful suggestions as I was putting together the methodology for this project. From the moment I entered graduate school to the present, conversations that ranged across the field of political philosophy with David Williams have never ceased to engage my mind or influence my thinking. I learned to admire the art of listening from Jason Pierce. I only hope I learned the art with sufficient skill to weave it into the very fabric of these pages. I doubt I have ever made an argument worthy of the name that has not benefited from discussion with Christian Esh. Certainly, the current project benefits tremendously from numerous discussions with this talented historian and good friend. My oldest friend, Jeff Combs, engaged in many a conversation about scientific reasoning and about the function of biological organisms that helped shape the second chapter of this book. My wife, Robyn, a very gifted writer, not only provided editorial advice but also offered suggestions that influenced the final shape of the argument on original intent. My work always draws from insights taken from many illuminating conversations with these wonderful people.

This work has been deeply influenced by Ronald J. Oakerson. He is the consummate political scientist. I first acquired my love of political philosophy under his tutelage. Every argument contained herein reflects the extent to which he has influenced my thinking about the Constitution and about politics more generally. This project originated as my dissertation. During the course of the project, H. W. Perry, Paul B. Woodruff, and Jeffrey K. Tulis asked probing questions and offered insightful suggestions that helped give the present project its particular shape. Robert C. Koons read multiple drafts of every chapter with great care. He asked challenging questions and offered insightful suggestions at every turn. There are few minds as penetrating as Rob's and perhaps none more so. Foremost acknowledgment must be given to J. Budziszewski, the supervisor of this project. All along the way he has posed the thorniest questions and offered the most penetrating of insights. Few are fortunate to count among their mentors one of the sages of our time. I am. I have no words to render thanks for the investment he has made not just in this project but also in my life. I probably owe J. and his wife, Sandra, more meals than I can count. At a later stage, this work benefitted from the sharp intellect and kind heart of Hadley Arkes. He not only offered insightful comments on the manuscript but has proven to be a boon of encouragement and a bulwark of support. I am compelled also to acknowledge the good people at the University of Missouri Press. It has been a privilege to work with such wonderful people, especially Gary Kass (the acquiring editor), who expressed so much enthusiasm for this project when it was still rather young.

My deepest debt of gratitude is owed to a select few: To my parents who have provided, in innumerable ways, unwavering support and encouragement from the very beginning of this long endeavor, I have no adequate words to express my gratitude. To my wife, Robyn, the love of my life and my inspiration, I never suspected that there was someone in the world who loves as deeply as you love. You take my breath away.

All that is good herein must be attributed to the wisdom of the kind souls just named as well as to others. All failing in fact or argument rests with the author alone.

UNCOVERING THE

CONSTITUTION'S

MORAL DESIGN

— 1 —

Constitutional Presuppositions

IS THE CONSTITUTION any good? Two logically prior questions lurk beneath this question. What does it mean to say of the Constitution, indeed of any constitution, that it is good? Further, just what sort of thing is the Constitution anyway? In this work I tackle these questions, while simultaneously taking seriously the old idea that constitutions are more than practical institutional arrangements. The institutional arrangements established by a constitution are shaped by a particular normative framework. Constitutions make normative assumptions and embody commitments to particular ends or purposes. They also reflect an understanding about where those ends come from. Roughly speaking, the normative assumptions made by the Constitution's institutional arrangement and the ultimate ends that arrangement aims to achieve constitute the Constitution's normative framework. Put another way, the Constitution's institutional framework entails a normative framework (i.e., it entails, whether right or wrong, that certain moral premises are true). The goal of this study is first to uncover and elaborate that framework and then to evaluate it. At day's end, the overriding question is this: Is the Constitution's normative framework philosophically sound? Does it make moral assumptions that correspond to moral reality, whatever that reality happens to be? It should be clear, then, that the descriptive question is asked for the sake of the evaluative question.

Intellectual History vs. Institutional Analysis: Two Approaches to Discerning the Constitution's Normative Framework

Ascertaining the Constitution's normative framework requires uncovering its moral assumptions and the ends for which it exists. As I see it, there are two approaches to ascertaining the Constitution's normative framework: the first is that of the intellectual historian and the second proceeds by the logical analysis of a particular institutional arrangement.[1]

The Intellectual Historian's Approach to the Constitution

There are two main aspects to approaching the Constitution's normative framework from the standpoint of intellectual history. The first tries to fit the Constitution into one of the categories employed by intellectual historians to sort the history of thought. These scholars craft categories, such as classical, modern, and positivist, to describe the modes of thinking *dominant* in different eras.[2] Applying this sorting to American constitutional thought, scholars argue over whether the Constitution's normative framework is classical, modern, or positivist (or whether it lacks a coherent framework). Each of these general normative frameworks takes a stand on the nature of sovereignty, the common good, natural law, and natural rights. Classical moral theory, for example, teaches that sovereigns are not free to command whatever they want. The commands of a sovereign only bind insofar as they aim at or are consistent with an objective common good, one that includes the constituent elements of human thriving. Further, humans exist for certain ends, and these ends are evident in the design of human nature. Humans are obliged to pursue these ends and to keep from acting in ways contrary to them. Finally, in classical theory natural rights derive from these natural duties and are protective spheres around them. One has a right to fulfill one's duty, a right with which no one else can legitimately interfere. In contrast, modernity posits a

---

1. I am not suggesting that these approaches are mutually exclusive. Nevertheless, one of these approaches will take priority in a particular study.

2. There are, of course, other categories (e.g., postmodern), but these are the ones most relevant to our inquiry. It also bears pointing out that "dominant" should *not* be taken to mean "only" in this sentence. Thrasymachus exists early in the classical period, and his thinking cannot be characterized as classical. When we characterize a mode of thinking as "dominant" within an era all that is meant is that the greatest and most influential thinkers of that period subscribed to that way of thinking. And no one puts Thrasymachus or Protagoras on par with Plato or Aristotle for weight of intellect or influence of thought in the classical period.

sovereign with unlimited power. The modernist's constitution recognizes a narrow common good that extends no further than peace or survival. Beyond the good of survival, people disagree about the nature of good and evil, which produces conflict. These opinions must therefore be set aside. Because all people share this one basic want, to live in peace with others, however, natural law consists of counsels of prudence that tell people to seek peace. This can only be done by setting aside private judgment in moral matters and by establishing a sovereign adequate to the task of securing peace, a sovereign that is absolute. Finally, modernists argue that all duties derive from natural rights. Positivists, like modernists, believe that the will of the sovereign is absolute. They go beyond modernists, however, in arguing that there is no common good. All beliefs about good and evil are mere matters of opinion or convention. Further, there are no natural laws pointing people to any common good. More, there are no natural rights. One only has a claim to anything insofar as the sovereign recognizes that claim. Scholars of a positivistic bent who write on the American Constitution frequently add that the people are sovereign and can therefore do whatever they want. With the foregoing modes of thinking in mind, scholars argue about which category the Constitution fits into best.

Second, in order to argue that the Constitution fits a particular category, scholars usually, though not always, treat the writings of key framers (e.g., *The Federalist*) as a proxy for the Constitution itself—or as the true exposition of the Constitution. The architects of the Constitution, however, failed to leave behind a systematic exposition of their work's normative framework. They did, however, rely on the works of various writers on morality, law, and regime design. Taking this under advisement, numerous scholars look to see whether the framers sound similar to writers of a classical or modernist bent. If the framers' exposition of the Constitution seems modern, then the normative framework of the Constitution must also be modern. The framers also made explicit reference to the moral theorists upon whom they drew. Thus, examining the works of these writers becomes key to uncovering the Constitution's moral meaning. This leads to using the normative framework contained in the works of the framers' intellectual resources as a proxy for the Constitution's normative framework. Scholars then move beyond description, making some sort of evaluative statement about the Constitution's normative framework. Such statements, however, are often made in an unsystematic way[3] and usual-

---

3. The normative cast of reflection on the Constitution's moral theory may be responsible for the frequency of such statements (which are sadly made more as assertions than as systematically de-

ly amount to an evaluation of the categories from intellectual history. The Constitution is classical and this is good; the Constitution is modern and this is bad, etc. What is key here is that both the descriptive and the evaluative enterprises are couched in terms of the categories of classical, modern, and positivist drawn from intellectual history.

Analyzing the Constitution Logically

The second approach to uncovering the Constitution's normative framework, the logical analysis of the Constitution's institutional arrangement, takes issue with the methodology used in the first approach.[4] To be sure, the writings of the framers and of those upon whose work they drew may be helpful in discovering the Constitution's moral meaning. After all, the framers were the architects of the Constitution. Nevertheless, the Constitution's meaning is distinguishable from the framers' meanings or intentions. I elaborate this later in this chapter. For now, it suffices to note that this distinction trades on the idea that the Constitution effects an objective, institutional arrangement that embodies normative presuppositions and ends. If we are to discern those presuppositions, then we must analyze the Constitution itself and not just consider what others, including its framers, say about it. Given this, the writings of the key framers cannot serve as a proxy for the Constitution.[5] It also follows that the normative framework contained in works the framers leaned upon cannot serve as a proxy for the Constitution's normative framework. If we are to identify the Constitution's moral framework, then we must do more than study the writings of the framers or the writings of those who influenced the framers.

---

fended propositions). However, it may be impossible to separate evaluation from description. As John Finnis says, "the development of modern jurisprudence suggests, and reflection on the methodology of any social science confirms, that a theorist cannot give a theoretical description and analysis of social facts unless he also participates in the work of evaluation, of understanding what is really good for human persons, and what is really required by practical reasonableness" (*Natural Law and Natural Rights*, 3). Indeed, how one chooses to describe something and the sort of distinctions that one sees as relevant all require one to engage in the work of evaluation. If engaging in the work of evaluation is inevitable, then it is better to be systematic in our evaluation.

4. Sotirios A. Barber's work provides an example of interpreting the Constitution through a logical analysis of its clauses and institutional framework. See his *On What the Constitution Means* and *Welfare and the Constitution*. Hadley Arkes's *Beyond the Constitution* also provides a logical analysis of the Constitution.

5. Although, again, we may certainly make use of them in constitutional analysis where those writings provide the best explanation of what the Constitution is. In short, I do not want to cast these writings aside, but rather to reframe how we put them to use.

The intellectual historians' approach makes another significant mistake by trying to fit the Constitution into general categories created by intellectual historians. As should be evident from the description of each category provided above, however, general categories such as classical, modern, or positivist bundle together *logically discrete* propositions concerning sovereignty, the common good, natural law, and natural rights.[6] Thus, for example, the classical idea that sovereigns should not be absolute is distinct from the classical idea that all constitutions should aim at an objective common good. The modernist notion that the common good is nothing more than peace is distinct from the modernist notion that natural rights are prior to duties and that duties derive from rights. But if the categories bundle together logically discrete propositions, then it becomes possible for the Constitution to embody a classical understanding of constrained sovereignty and a modern understanding of the priority of rights to duties. Or perhaps the Constitution embodies the classical idea of the common good with the modern notion of sovereignty—perhaps because an unconstrained sovereign is essential if any sort of common good is to be realized. And many such other combinations are possible. Thus it becomes necessary to separate our analysis of the Constitution's conception of sovereignty from its conception of the common good, natural law, or natural rights. We must take assumptions concerning sovereignty, the common good, natural law, and natural rights one at a time, something that I discuss later in this chapter and in chapter 2. So long as the foregoing is true, our analysis of the Constitution's normative framework must cast aside the general categories of intellectual history. Instead, we must turn our attention to uncovering that framework by analyzing the logic of and assumptions underlying the practical, institutional arrangements put into place by the Constitution. This method of argumentation proceeds by asking what moral propositions must be assumed to be true if we are to make sense of this institutional arrangement. What else must be true for this Constitution to make sense? We pose this question with respect to sovereignty, the common good, natural law, and natural rights. For instance, we inquire about what understanding of the common good best makes sense of this particular institutional arrangement. We then proceed to examine whether the Constitution's assumption about the common good is in fact good—and likewise with sovereignty, natural law, and natural rights.

6. This is not to say that the propositions in each category fail to cohere or that they are ontologically separable or even that some propositions from one historical category can be *coherently* combined with one or more propositions from a different category. That is a separate matter.

Describing and Evaluating the Constitution's Normative Framework

Previous Attempts to Describe the Constitution's Normative Framework

If we take the method for uncovering the Constitution's normative framework derived from the history of thought together with the assumption that the categories employed in that method stand or fall together, then we can generate a blueprint for sorting the relevant secondary literature:

1. *Classical constitutionalists* believe that the Constitution's normative structure corresponds to the category of classical moral theory. Thus the Constitution acknowledges the primacy of justice and the invalidity of laws that violate natural justice. Further, the Constitution aims at securing justice and the common good, by providing institutions that create and enforce laws conducive to these ends. *Classically inclined* scholars advance this interpretation and approve of a classical Constitution, usually because they think that classical moral theory is true or for whatever reason at least do not lament the Constitution's assumption of its truth. Although *classically disinclined* scholars subscribe to the classical interpretation of the framing, they lament that the framers drew on traditional moral theory. Natural law, they think, is a chimera.

2. *Modernists* say the Constitution aims to achieve the purpose of government as described by the philosophy of modernity—namely, the securing of peace in the face of religious and moral disagreement. Natural law in the modern sense simply tells people how to secure the good of peace. *Approving modernists* argue that modernity captures the truth in matters political and ethical, and therefore they delight in the Constitution's adherence to modernity. *Disenchanted modernists* believe modernity to be morally bankrupt. They are therefore disenchanted with the Constitution, because, as they see it, it adheres to modern moral teaching.

3. *Positivists* (the traditional sort) contend that law is whatever the sovereign commands. There is no natural law in the classical or modern sense pointing to any objective good. Thus, the sovereign is free to do whatever he pleases. As the people (i.e., a majority of the people) are sovereign in the United States, the Constitution is an instrument for effecting a popular (i.e., majority) will unconstrained by either justice or the common good. *Enthusiastic*

positivists relish the idea of a positivistic Constitution, for positivism posits that there is no such thing as natural law to constrain the will of the sovereign. Thus, if the people are sovereign, they *are* able to command anything they please. Many enthusiastic positivists, however, inconsistently turn this *are* into a *should,* suggesting that nothing *should* constrain the popular will. *Regretful positivists* subscribe to the positivistic interpretation of the Constitution but regret the influence of positivism upon the Constitution. Usually, regretful positivists think that at least some rights should be placed beyond popular reach. They do not believe that a majority should be able to do whatever it wants.

4. *Incoherentists* believe that the framers drew on incompatible thinkers in an incompatible way, rendering the Constitution essentially incoherent.

Now that we have this general blueprint, we can take a in-depth look at each of these groups. The first consists of *classical constitutionalists.* According to classical moral teaching, an objective and binding good overarches ruled and ruler alike. This objective good for human nature is evident in the very design of human nature. The obligations resulting from these purposes are natural laws. These obligations transcend all other obligations; therefore, no law contrary to natural law is valid. Concomitantly, as the *telos* (goal) of the law is the common good, no law contrary to the common good is binding. Natural law theory also holds that all or nearly all people know at least the basics of this law (i.e., its first principles and perhaps the immediate derivations from those principles) because its precepts are held in the practical reason, which arrives at its conclusions by reading natural inclinations (e.g., that things that exist have an inclination to go on existing points to the good of preservation for that which already exists).[7] To the extent that we can speak of rights in such a framework, these must be understood as logically dependent upon prior, natural duties. Finally, classical moral theory posits a constrained sovereign,

---

7. According to Edward S. Corwin,

> There are, it is predicated, certain principles of right and justice which are entitled to prevail of their own intrinsic excellence, altogether, regardless of the attitudes of those who wield the physical resources of the community. Such principles were made by no human hands; indeed, if they did not antedate deity itself, they still so express its nature as to bind and control it. They are external to all Will as such and interpenetrate all Reason as such. They are external and immutable. In relation to such principles, human laws are, when entitled to obedience save as to matters indifferent, merely a record or transcript, and their enactment an act not of will or power but one of discovery and declaration. (*The Higher Law Background of American Constitutional Law,* 4–5)

whether the sovereign be a monarch, aristocrats, the people, or some form of mixed sovereignty.[8]

The standard argument that the Constitution embodies classical moral assumption advances with the claim that the Constitution belongs to a homogenous classical tradition that unfolded from ancient through medieval to modern times. Those who framed the Constitution, say classical constitutionalists, belonged to and drew upon that tradition. We know this because certain structural features and certain textual provisions of the Constitution parallel the words and recommendations of classical authors.[9] According to Thomas Pangle,

> This "great tradition" was understood to have been initiated by Socrates, Plato and Aristotle. It was supposed to have undergone its most important change or advance at the hands of the Stoics, to whom was imputed (on very slender evidence) a doctrine of the moral equality of all men. More convincing was the observation that equality, humanity, and compassion had been most effectively introduced by the advent of Christ and the teachings of the New Testament. Though the idea of natural law was regarded as having been enriched and made more tidy by the medieval Christian and the later scholastic theorists (e.g., Thomas, Suarez, Hooker) the great tradition was thought to have acquired, during the Middle Ages, unfortunate encrustations of monkish prejudice and priestly claims to political power. A restoration was said to have been effected by the efforts of Calvinists and Separatist theologians and Enlightenment philosophers. The latter, especially Locke, were supposed to have drawn on the English common law as well as on Calvinist covenant theology in order to give a heightened—but not radically new stress to individual rights and especially property rights. In the final analysis, the very considerable apparent changes in the Great tradition were seen as of less moment than the basic continuities.[10]

8. In the *Republic,* Plato argues against placing constitutional constraints upon the philosopher-kings. However, in the *Laws,* he argues for constitutional constraints as well as for a mixed regime. Moreover, the *Republic* can be interpreted as a thought experiment about the nature of justice rather than as any recommendation—ideal or practical—concerning regime design. For an interesting discussion of Plato's position in the *Republic,* see Glenn Tinder's *Political Thinking: The Perennial Questions,* 130–38.

9. Thus, Corwin points out that

> The Ninth Amendment of the Constitution of the United States, in stipulating that "the enumeration of certain rights in this Constitution shall not prejudice other rights not so enumerated," illustrates this theory [of natural law] perfectly except that the principles of transcendental justice have been here translated into terms of personal and private rights. . . . They owe nothing to their recognition in the Constitution—such recognition was necessary if the Constitution was to be regarded as complete. (*Higher Law Background,* 5)

10. Pangle, *The Spirit of Modern Republicanism: The Moral Vision of the American Founders and the*

Classical moral theory begins in the ancient world with a collection of observations that become building blocks in the classical edifice. Thus Demosthenes observes that men discover rather than make law.[11] Sophocles' Antigone notes that these laws are the unwritten laws of heaven. Indeed, Antigone asserts that she can disregard Creon's edict because it is contrary to the unwritten laws.[12] Aristotle endorses this understanding, arguing for the general principle that commands or edicts that transgress the unwritten laws do not obligate us to obedience.[13] He also speaks of a natural and universally binding justice—that is, a justice not determined by convention.[14] Plato indicates that the goal of all law is the common good. Laws that fail to meet this goal are "bogus."[15] Cicero adds that this universal and natural justice is right reason. Thus the unwritten laws of heaven are connected to the human function of reasoning. They therefore have to do with human nature. Further, on Cicero's view, humans share right reason with God, thereby connecting the law of human nature to the divine nature.[16] Saint Paul points out that everyone knows this law as it is written on the heart.[17] These various aspects of classical moral theory reach a culmination point in the work of St. Thomas Aquinas. For Aquinas, God promulgates his eternal law in his design of human nature. Humans have natural inclinations, though they are disordered, to their proper ends. The practical reason reads these natural inclinations, discerning the basic requirements of the moral law and the immediate implications of those requirements (otherwise known as the Decalogue).[18]

This understanding, say classical constitutionalists, filtered down to the American framers through British jurists and through important continental philosophers of jurisprudence of the seventeenth century. The framers read the works of Edward Coke and William Blackstone who, according to classical constitutionalists, transmitted classical moral theory.[19] They also studied

---

Philosophy of John Locke, 8. In interpreting the Constitution, Benjamin F. Wright, *American Interpretations of Natural Law: A Study in the History of Political Thought,* Corwin, *Higher Law Background,* and Morton White, *The Philosophy of the American Revolution* and *Philosophy, "The Federalist," and the Constitution,* arguably do as Pangle suggests.

11. Demosthenes notoriously said, "Every law is a discovery, a gift of god—a precept of wise men" (cited in Corwin, *Higher Law Background,* 5–6).

12. Sophocles *Antigone* 490–500.

13. Aristotle *On Rhetoric* 1373b-1375b.

14. Aristotle *Nichomachean Ethics* 1134b.

15. Plato *Laws,* bk. 4, sec. 6, lines 715–716.

16. See Cicero *The Republic,* bk. 3, 33–34. See also Cicero *The Laws,* bk.1, 16–35, 42–46; and Romans (Epistle to) 2:14–15.

17. See Romans (Epistle to) 2:14–15.

18. See Aquinas, *Summa Theologica,* I–II, q. 90, art. 1–2; I–II, q. 91, art. 2; I–I I, q. 94; I–II, q. 91, art. 6.

19. According to Coke, "The law of nature is that which God at the time of Creation of the nature

Grotius, who recovered Cicero's identification of natural law with right reason and who argued that the moral law commands that which is intrinsically good and proscribes that which is intrinsically evil.[20] Additionally, America's constitutional architects read works on natural law by the likes of Pufendorf, Barbeyrac, Burlamaqui, and Vattel.[21] John Locke, the most important of the seventeenth-century writers on natural law, stood inside the classical tradition. Locke built on the British jurists and on the British divine, Richard Hooker.[22] Thus, Locke teaches that certain things are proper to human nature as such and that no laws contrary to the common good possess any validity.[23] Locke also points to the self-evidence of basic moral propositions, leading some scholars to endeavor to assimilate Locke's thought to that of Aquinas.[24] Final-

---

of man infused into his heart, for his preservation and direction; and this is *Lex aeterna,* the moral law, called also the law of nature. And by this law, written with the finger of God in the heart of man, were the people of god a long time governed before the law was written by Moses" (cited in Walter Berns, "Judicial Review and the Rights and Laws of Nature," 57). In fact, Coke goes on to note Aristotle's reference to natural justice in *Nichomachean Ethics* (see Corwin, *Higher Law Background,* 46). While Blackstone's belief in natural law is in dispute, at least some have taken him to subscribe to key elements of the traditional theory. Thus Blackstone says, "the law of nature, being coeval with mankind and dictated by God himself, is of course superior in obligation to any other. It is binding over all the globe in all countries, and at all times: no human laws have any validity if contrary to this." One should note that as prominent a scholar as Forrest McDonald believes that Blackstone can be interpreted as belonging to the classical tradition in key respects and that the rest of Blackstone's thought can be interpreted as being consistent with such a commitment (*Alexander Hamilton: A Biography,* 58, 60–61). In this judgment, Wright concurs (see his *American Interpretations of Natural Law*).

20. Hugo Grotius, *De iure belli ac pacis,* bk. 1, chap. 1, 20–21.

21. See White, *Philosophy of the American Revolution.* The framers drew on such works as Pufendorf's *De jure naturae et gentium* (1672); Barbeyrac's introduction to Pufendorf entitled "Historical and critical account of the science of morality" (1706); Burlamaqui's *Principles of Natural and Politic Law* (1747–1748); and Vattel's *The Law of Nations, or the Principles of Natural Law, Applied to the Conduct and the Affairs of Nations and of Sovereigns* (1758).

22. Locke famously drew on Richard Hooker's *Laws of Ecclesiastical Polity,* which first appeared in 1593–1597. Knud Haakonssen rightly notes, "Richard Hooker was a crucial link between scholasticism and English ideas of natural law" (*Natural Law and Moral Philosophy: From Grotius to the Scottish Enlightenment,* 49n64).

23. According to Locke, "truth and keeping faith belong to men, as men, and not as members of society" (*Second Treatise,* in *Two Treatises of Government,* 277). Concerning the connection of the law to the common good, Locke says that the legislative power is "limited to the public good of the Society. It is a power, that hath no other end but preservation, and therefore can never have a right to destroy, enslave, or designedly impoverish the Subjects" (357). Locke further maintains that the "Law of Nature stands as an Eternal Rule to Men, Legislators as well as others. The rules that they make for other Men's Actions, must, as well as their own and other Men's Actions, be conformable to the Law of Nature, i.e. to the Will of God" (358).

24. White endeavors to do just this in *Philosophy of the American Revolution,* 9–60. One might argue, however, that he misunderstands self-evidence in Aquinas and perhaps in Locke. White seems to think that Aquinas and Locke held that basic moral propositions might be unknown to certain persons whom Aquinas and Locke then view as less than fully human. After all, some things are self-

ly, Locke's understanding of rights is argued to be in keeping with the classical tradition, for he held that natural rights derive from natural duties. That is, natural rights are something like spheres of protection around natural duties—duties that no one has a right to infringe upon because they are between man and his Maker.[25]

These sources, according to the "old orthodoxy," transmitted classical moral and political thought to the American revolutionaries and then to the framers who incorporated classical moral commitments into the Constitution's institutional design (especially in the Ninth Amendment), an instrument designed to protect natural rights so that men could fulfill their natural duties.[26] While the framers drew upon an ancient tradition, however, advocates of the old orthodoxy emphasized that they had received this tradition through modern sources, without going back to the older ones.[27] The argument for the classical interpretation, therefore, amounts to the following: (1) the Constitution presumes the truth of classical moral theory; (2) we know (1) because the framers adhered to classical moral theory and drew on writers who were classical; and (3) we can tell these modern writers were classical because they drew on and echoed classical teaching.

Having fit the Constitution into the classical category, the classical constitutionalists then pass judgment on the category of classical moral thought as a whole. Some appraisal is made of one or more tenets of classical moral theory and then applied to the entire theory. Scholars of a classical bent therefore fall into two camps: those who are happy about the Constitution's classical background, the *classically inclined,* and those who are not, the *classically dis-*

---

evident only to the wise. This being true, dictators can then tyrannize over others in the name of self-evident truths to which they, as the wise, have special access. But both Locke and Aquinas held that basic moral truths and the immediate inferences from those truths are known to either everyone or most everyone. White, in other words, arguably restricts far too greatly the extent of moral knowledge that Aquinas and Locke believe the average person possesses.

25. As Haakonssen rightly says, "For Locke, as for Pufendorf, natural rights are powers to fulfill the fundamental duty of natural law" (*Natural Law and Moral Philosophy,* 55).

26. See Wright, *American Interpretations of Natural Law;* Corwin, *Higher Law Background;* and White, *Philosophy, "The Federalist," and the Constitution.*

27. Thus White refrains from tracing the origins of American moral theory "all the way back to Plato, Aristotle, or the Stoics because American thinkers were primarily influenced by modern theorists of natural law who had transformed ancient ideas of natural law before bequeathing them to American colonists" (*Philosophy of the American Revolution,* 143). White is almost certainly wrong. As Wright indicates, the Stoic conception of natural law presented through Cicero may in fact have been the primary conduit through which the doctrine was "transmitted to modern times" (*American Interpretations of Natural Law,* 5). But Pangle is also partly correct. The old orthodoxy did lean heavily on the idea that modern sources transmitted the doctrine to the framers. But Pangle and others overstate their case.

inclined. The classically inclined maintain that classical moral theory accurately describes moral reality.[28] As well, there are some from this camp who are at least content with the Constitution's classical background because they believe in the need for the concept of natural law, perhaps because political philosophy requires a set of standards of right and justice higher than the positive law or because such standards are viewed as necessary for appeals against the established legal order.[29] Yet, with perhaps one exception, those who argue that the Constitution is classical have failed to provide a systematic argument that the Constitution *should* be classical.[30] They seem to think it sufficient to note the desirability of some aspect or other of the Constitution's classical background. Likewise, those critical of the Constitution's classical background, the classically disinclined, seem to think that if they knock down some part or other of classical moral theory, then they've somehow destroyed the entire edifice.[31] For example, some think classical moral theory falls to the

28. Walter F. Murphy arguably belongs in this camp. He clearly subscribes to the classical interpretation, and his apparent sarcasm about the fact-value dichotomy that "besets modern social science" as well as his sarcasm about Holmesian positivism, something he debunks as cynical, belie a favoring of his natural law interpretation of the Constitution ("The Art of Constitutional Interpretation: A Preliminary Showing," 138–39).

29. According to Wright, "In order to prove that natural law is an outworn or harmful concept it is necessary to do more than demonstrate that it has sometimes been used harmfully, or in an overly intellectualistic manner. It is necessary to show that political philosophy has no need of a concept which is expressive of standards of right and justice other than, perhaps higher than, those set forth in the positive laws, or of a concept which attempts to state in general terms the principles of human nature and behavior in organized society." In connection with appeals against the established legal order, Wright argues that "natural law, and particularly the natural rights aspect thereof, will almost certainly be invoked in any case of appeal against the existing legal order. An appeal from that which is legally established to that which should be established almost invariably involves the assertion of principles of a higher validity than those made by human legislatures" (*American Interpretations of Natural Law,* 343, 341–42).

30. The exception here may be Hadley Arkes. I believe Arkes's *Beyond the Constitution* can be construed as arguing that the Constitution has a classical foundation or at least something that very nearly corresponds to a classical foundation. His work *First Things: An Inquiry into the First Principles of Morals and Justice,* written before *Beyond the Constitution,* provides a defense that such a foundation is good, though the moral system he advances is influenced by moderns such as Kant and Thomas Reid as well as by Aristotle and Aquinas. Of course, some have argued that Kant was quite classical in key respects, and Thomas Reid seems to share a certain affinity with certain elements of classical thought.

31. Quite a bit of the argument against classical moral theory is not really argument at all, but rather mere assertion. Frequently mockery replaces systematic analysis. Mocking the thinkers upon whom the framers drew, Thomas Cooper maintained, in 1826, that rights were nothing other than the creature of society. Listing some of the writers who proved influential to the framers—Grotius, Pufendorf, Barbeyrac, and Burlamaqui—Cooper asked when the law of nature had been enacted and by whom. He concluded, "What is called the law of nature, consists of systems fabricated by theoretical writers, on a contemplation of what might be usefully acknowledged among men as binding on each other." In keeping with this, John W. Burgess maintained that the eighteenth-century revolutionaries were completely wrong about nature being the source of individual liberties. The state was the true source (Wright, *American Interpretations of Natural Law,* 308–9, 311).

ground if the theory's notion of self-evidence can be shown problematic or if they simply assert that the notion of self-evident truth produces tyranny.[32] The point is that the critique is never systematic or precise. It turns on the idea that if one can vaguely point to some problems with classical moral teaching, then the game is over.

Modernists are the second group in our blueprint. This band of scholars believes that the Constitution embodies modern moral teaching, the *dominant* (though not singular) teaching of what is referred to as the "modern age." To see how the Constitution might embody modern moral thought, we must first understand the modern teaching. The paradigm case for such teaching is found in the political thought of Thomas Hobbes. The consummately modern moral teaching of Hobbes begins by flipping a key entailment of classical moral teaching on its head: the notion that natural moral duties are prior to rights and that natural rights derive from inalienable, natural duties. In contrast, the modern teaching begins with the claim that all people, by nature, possess a right to everything.[33] But people also live in a world of limited goods while possessing unlimited desires.[34] So long as people possess a right to everything and to do anything, conflict will arise. Human nature is therefore said to be basically conflictual.[35] Differing opinions about good and evil as well as about religious matters result from this conflictual nature. These disagreements also carry forward into conflict. The basic insight of modernity is that this conflict must be overcome if anyone is to survive. Survival therefore

32. In a self-referentially incoherent argument, Morton White claims that Locke's and Aquinas's teachings about self-evidence, because they allegedly teach that some things are self-evident only to the wise, can lead to tyranny and "haughty dictators." He clearly finds this morally abhorrent. But not everyone in history has found tyranny or haughty dictators to be morally abhorrent, so White must be among the few who know that it is. As he makes no systematic argument for the moral abhorrence of tyranny, he must take it to be self-evident or nearly so. Thus, his argument relies on the truth of propositions he wishes to deny (see *Philosophy of the American Revolution*, 268).

33. That is, in the state of nature, where there is no common power, there is no transcendent natural law that binds people to behave in particular ways. Referring to the state of nature, Hobbes asserts, "The notions of right and wrong, justice and injustice, have there no place. Where there is no common power, there is no law." Hobbes further notes that in the state of nature, which is a state of war, "every man has a right to everything, even to one another's body" (*Leviathan*, 78, 80).

34. In *Leviathan*, Hobbes seems to advocate this when he contends, "we are to consider that the felicity of this life consisteth not in the repose of a mind satisfied. For there is no such *Finis Ultimus* (utmost aim) nor *Summum Bonum* (greatest good) as is spoken of in the books of the old moral philosophers. Nor can a man any more live, whose desires are at an end, than he whose senses and imaginations are at a stand. Felicity is a continual progress of the desire, from one object to another, the attaining of the former being still but the way to the latter" (pt. 1, chap. 11, 57). Because people want to realize their desires and because this entails having the ability, or power, to do so, Hobbes adds that the all mankind has a "restless desire of power after power, that ceaseth only in death" (pt. 1, chap. 11, 58).

35. See Berns, "Judicial Review."

requires the seeking of peace with others, and this is the basic command of natural law. Peace is sought, practically speaking, in the transfer of rights from individual persons to an absolute sovereign capable of securing the good of peace (understood as survival). Finally, on the modern understanding, the sovereign is free to command however he sees fit. No unwritten laws of nature invalidate the commands of a sovereign that contradict them.

Adherents to the modern interpretation of the Constitution argue for their position in much the same way as proponents of the classical interpretation argue for theirs. To be sure, modernists make some mention of the structural features of the Constitution. Modern moral thought ends up justifying a government of powers, and the main thing about the Constitution is that its design establishes such a government. In fact, scholars holding this view suggest that the Constitution is a way of making a modern government of powers palatable to citizens. Nevertheless, these scholars argue that the Constitution is modern because the framers were modern. We can tell this because they sound like moderns and because they drew on works of modern philosophy.[36] Indeed, modernists rush into a breach created by classical constitutionalists in the building of the classical edifice. As noted, a number of classical constitutionalists have argued that the framers received classical teaching through modern writers. Modernists, however, claim that modern writers had an altogether different normative perspective from the classical world.[37] Writers such as Locke and Pufendorf were really moderns. The framers could not have gotten to Aristotle through Locke for these different thinkers embraced incompatible normative systems. Thus if the framers' writings echo Locke or Pufendorf or Grotius (or even Hobbes), then this indicates their basic modernity and therefore the modernity of the institutional structure they created. Once again the moral framework of the writers upon whom the framers drew serves as a proxy for the normative framework of the Constitution.

After proclaiming that the Constitution should be classified as modern, scholars then proceed to make some evaluative comments thought to reflect

---

36. According to Pangle, the framers were aware of their basic modernity. He therefore criticizes the old orthodoxy because "this appraisal quite failed to provide a basis for making sense of the Founders' strongly expressed awareness of their political modernism—their participation in radical innovation, both theoretical and practical" (*Spirit of Modern Republicanism*, 8).

37. According to Michael P. Zuckert, the old orthodoxy, described by Pangle, "has been too much undermined by subsequent research and reflection to be taken entirely seriously; the various elements have been shown to be more different and more hostile to each other than the consensus view allows" (*The Natural Rights Republic: Studies in the Foundation of the American Political Tradition*, 6). The hostility of the various elements is due to the lumping together of modern and classical authors.

on modern moral thought as a whole. Like the classical constitutionalists, the modernists can be divided into two camps: the *approving modernists* and the *disapproving modernists*. Approving modernists believe that modern writers correctly perceive the nature of moral reality. They advance their case by noting moral and religious disagreement and by asserting that good and evil have no basis in nature, by pointing out that human nature is conflictual and self-interested, and by noting that people can at least agree on seeking peace, though nothing else.[38] Disapproving modernists lament the Constitution's modern background. Modernity is morally bankrupt; therefore, if the Constitution is modern, it too is morally bankrupt. Why is the Constitution morally bankrupt? Here the main criticism seems to be that modernity brackets moral and religious questions in the name of peace. But moral questions are the most important questions of the day—the source of our conflict.[39] Modern conflicts are moral conflicts requiring moral resolution. But modern constitutions bracket moral questions and are therefore unfit to address the crisis of modernity. Indeed, it is doubtful that moral questions can be bracketed, making the modern project question begging. In all of this evaluation, the tendency is to fit the Constitution into the category of modernity and then to make some sort of statement about whether modernity is any good.

The third group in the blueprint, the *positivists,* generally contend that the Constitution embodies the moral teaching of normative positivism. Normative positivism denies that there is an objective good. There are no facts concerning good and evil, only opinions or conventions.[40] With this assumption

38. Thus Berns says,

> there is no basis in nature for opinions of good and bad, that men are certain to disagree about good and bad, but that men can agree on the need for peace. It is the only thing they can agree on, but, precisely because of that, civil society is possible. The peace of this civil society would be jeopardized, however, if men were permitted to dispute questions of good and bad, or to say the same thing, if men in their capacity as citizens were permitted to raise questions concerning the end or ends of civil society. Such questions must be suppressed in the modern liberal state.

Consequently, in the social contract, "Each man agrees that his opinions of good and bad, right and wrong, justice and injustice are just that—private opinions—and the principle of equality requires him to acknowledge that other opinions, even if contrary to his own, have as much (or as little) dignity as his own. What this means is that each man agrees to forgo his private judgment of the goodness or badness of the sovereign's laws." Berns approves of this: "Modern constitutionalism began when, for very good reasons indeed, they [Locke and Hobbes] sought a way to deny private judgment any role in politics" ("Judicial Review," 60, 83).

39. See H. Jefferson Powell, *The Moral Tradition of American Constitutionalism: A Theological Interpretation,* 2, 39.

40. Positivism famously asserts that statements only have truth value if they pass the criterion of

in hand, normative positivists also deny the existence of natural law. There are no naturally known principles to inform people about how they should live. This entails that there are no natural laws binding upon the sovereign, telling him what he can or cannot rightly command or telling him what ends he must pursue. Thus, in traditional (Austinian) positivism, law is nothing other than the command of the sovereign.[41] The Constitution recognizes these facts about moral reality by seeking to translate whatever the sovereign wants into public policy. Because the people are sovereign, the Constitution translates whatever the people want into public policy. As unanimity is impossible, the Constitution takes a majority as standing for the people.[42] The main thing about the Constitution, therefore, is that it is majoritarian.[43]

There are two versions of the positivistic interpretation of the Constitution. The argument for each is advanced quite differently from the arguments for the classical or modern interpretations. According to H. Jefferson Powell, the simplest version points out that "The Constitution's text is overwhelmingly concerned with process. Virtually all of the 1787 instrument deals with structuring the institutions of national government, all of which are majoritarian, or subject to majoritarian control."[44] This version is, however, overly simplis-

---

verifiability. Good and evil are, it is said, not verifiable, whereas opinions about good and evil are. This position is clearly incoherent. As I will argue in chapter 7, the criterion of verifiability is not itself verifiable. One has to cease being a positivist at the point of the foundational principle if one is to be a positivist about anything else. Further, opinions about the good, whether shared or differing, may indicate that there is a good to be opined about.

41. There is a different strain of positivism, à la H. L. A. Hart, that does not accept this Austinian definition. Law is, rather, the product of primary and secondary rules. But Hart's theory is notoriously difficult to classify. It can be viewed as an abstract Hobbesian, and therefore modern, theory or as thoroughly conventional. But if it is conventional, then there is a sovereign, and law is in fact determined by sovereign decree. The sovereign is the people or the society. The decrees of the sovereign are the acts of will that keep the conventions determining law in place. This will be further discussed in chapter 5.

42. I am not arguing that all positivists who study and write about the Constitution are in fact adherents to popular sovereignty or fans of majoritarianism. Rather, I am suggesting that scholars who interpret the Constitution as positivist, whether or not those scholars are positivists, tend to understand the Constitution as a mechanism for effecting the popular will.

43. Those who interpret the Constitution in this manner include Bruce Ackerman, *We the People: Foundations;* John Hart Ely, *Democracy and Distrust: A Theory of Judicial Review;* Robert Bork; and William Rehnquist. On these latter two, see Graham Walker, *Moral Foundations of Constitutional Thought: Current Problems, Augustinian Prospects,* 14. Archpositivist Oliver Wendell Holmes believed that his job as a judge under the Constitution was to help the people do whatever they want. In a letter to Harold Laski, he stated, "if my fellow citizens want to go to Hell I will help them. It's my job" (Michael J. Sandel *Democracy's Discontent: America in Search of a Public Philosophy,* 44). So saying, he revealed the connection of his positivism to his unbridled majoritarianism.

44. Powell, *Moral Tradition of American Constitutionalism,* 186. Here I am borrowing from Powell's apt summary of John Hart Ely's *Democracy and Distrust.* Interestingly, Ely's position is substantive-

tic. It identifies a principle of majoritarianism in the Constitution without paying sufficient attention to the features of the Constitution that are not majoritarian or to those that are antimajoritarian. Thus, a second version of the positivistic interpretation has developed to cope with the apparently antimajoritarian features of the Constitution. This interpretation, labeled *dualist democracy*,[45] recognizes that the people only speak, only articulate their will, on rare occasions. In these rare moments the people establish a constitution or a regime. This is called a constitutional moment. The other moments are those of normal politics and the routine functioning of the regime instituted by the people during constitutional moments. During normal politics, the people pay much less attention to politics. The legislature, during such times, is usually taken to be the primary conduit of the popular will. Advocates of dualist democracy, however, point out that the will of the legislature cannot be identified with the will of the people. Yet, so long as the popular will can be distinguished from the legislature's, we must seek ways to confine the legislature to the people's will as articulated in constitutional moments. Thus, apparently antimajoritarian elements of the Constitution such as the president's veto or judicial review can be understood as mechanisms for protecting the people's constitution or regime against legislative encroachments.[46] Dualist democracy, then, differs from simplistic positivism. Even so, it remains positivistic because the popular will, when it is expressed, is viewed as completely unconstrained.[47]

Note how both versions of this argument are made.[48] The intentions of the framers are set aside and an appeal is made to the design of the Constitution.[49] For some of these scholars, *The Federalist* serves as a proxy for the Constitution.[50] Still, the focus on institutional design as the path to understanding the

---

ly the same as Robert Bork's or Justice Rehnquist's (Walker, *Moral Foundations of Constitutional Thought*, 14).

45. Ackerman strongly advocates this position in *We the People*.

46. See ibid., 7.

47. Ackerman understands his interpretation of the Constitution to say just this. Thus, if the people want to establish a national religion, of any sort, nothing constrains the popular will. Powell, then, is correct in criticizing the theory as "naïve and thoroughgoing" in its positivism (*Moral Tradition of American Constitutionalism*, 199).

48. I am not suggesting that absolutely all positivists or that all those who interpret the Constitution proceed in the manner described in what follows. What follows, however, describes a dominant tendency.

49. While I disagree with the positivistic interpretation of the Constitution, I nevertheless concur with ascertaining the Constitution's moral meaning by an analysis of the institutional framework erected by the Constitution.

50. See, for example, Ackerman, *We the People*.

Constitution seems largely correct. At least some scholars of a positivistic bent are aware that the Constitution's framers adhered to a natural rights doctrine substantially at odds with positivism.[51] But the Constitution is not reducible to an aggregation of the framers' subjective intentions. Thus the framers' own writings and the writings upon which they drew do not enjoy a determinative status in ascertaining the meaning of the Constitution. Even so, the positivists share something with classical constitutionalists and modernists, because positivists have also chosen a category from intellectual history and then endeavored to argue that the Constitution as a whole fits that category. This is accomplished by showing the positivistic components of the Constitution and then by assuming that if it is positivistic in key respects, then the whole document must be. Thus, once one determines the Constitution is positivistic, then one goes about trying to accommodate institutional features that do not quite fit positivistic theory to the Constitution, all the while failing to take into account the possible validity of alternative explanations of those features.[52]

Having fit the Constitution into the category of positivism, scholars following this interpretive line then make an appraisal of the whole category of positivism. And once again we see two distinct groups: the *enthusiastic positivists* and the *regretful positivists.* The Constitution is positivistic and this is good or bad. That the tenets of positivism stand or fall together is assumed at the outset. Enthusiastic positivists point out that morality varies across cultures. There is no real morality "out there" of which we all have some knowledge; rather, morality is just a matter of subjective preferences or some sort of gratification in which people indulge.[53] The alleged variation of morality across cultures leads to moral skepticism. For the variation is taken to mean that there is no standard of right and wrong overarching all cultures, and, in turn, that the laws of each culture are just a matter of convention. But how does this lead to positivistic majoritarianism? The idea seems to be that since there is no objective constraint on the will of the people, the people should be able to will as they please. Because we cannot expect unanimity, the will of the majority is the best expression of the popular will. Therefore, the majority should be free to do whatever it wants.[54] Thankfully, say enthusiastic posi-

---

51. Ibid.

52. This, I would argue, is a fair characterization of what Ackerman does in *We the People.*

53. Rehnquist stands as a representative of the position that morality is nothing but subjective preference, and Bork, at least in earlier work, stands as a representative of the idea that morality is little more than some sort of gratification in which people indulge (Walker, *Moral Foundations of Constitutional Thought,* 14–15).

54. It is sometimes argued that *because* there is no real good, people should not be free to impose

tivists, the Constitution allows the majority to do just this. But some people lament the fact that the Constitution gives the majority the license to exercise such power. There are those who believe positivism to be a kindred spirit to modernity and morally bankrupt in the same way that modernity is morally bankrupt. Indeed, some consider positivism to be simplistic and morally naïve.[55] Others posit that positivism captures the truth about moral matters, but regret that the Constitution nevertheless fails to place some rights beyond the popular will. Because of this, they have grave fears of the injustices that might be committed by the popular will.[56] Of course, this is rather startling. Once one grants the truth of positivism, the possibility of calling any majority unjust in any meaningful sense has altogether vanished. Indeed, we might think such positivists are simply confused.

Our blueprint for sorting the secondary literature is rounded out by the *incoherentists*: those scholars who acknowledge both that the framers drew on classical and modern thinkers and that classical and modern thinkers do not fit together. The framers were influenced by the works of Xenophon, Aristotle, Cicero, Grotius, Pufendorf, Vattel, Sidney, Locke, and others. But these writers taught different and incompatible ideas. Because the framers drew on incompatible authors in the construction of the Constitution, it follows that the writings of the framers and the Constitution itself are incoherent.[57] On

---

their idea of the good on another individual or group. But to have a society, given human nature, we must agree on some laws. Since there is no agreement upon the good, the only way to find laws that will work is through democracy or the will of the people. And the only practical way to accomplish this is through the rule of the majority. The argument, of course, is self-referentially incoherent, but it keeps showing up in some guise or other.

55. See Powell, *Moral Tradition of American Constitutionalism*, 199.

56. Ackerman falls into this camp. In *We the People* he asks, "Must Americans be forced to endure a Holocaust before they follow the Germans in solemnly recognizing that there are some individual rights that a majority of the citizenry, however mobilized and deliberate, can never legitimately suppress?" (321). But in *Social Justice and the Liberal State* he asserts (without any argument whatsoever), "There is no moral meaning hidden in the bowels of the Universe" (368). Ackerman's positivism is therefore necessarily tragic. He has no grounds for claiming any exercise of popular will could ever be unjust, for there are no external constraints upon that will. Yet he simultaneously fears that this might lead to the unjust trampling of individual rights and potentially to holocaust.

57. Daniel T. Rodgers suggests that the founding discussion, generally speaking, was incoherent ("Republicanism: The Career of a Concept," 11–38). Forrest McDonald argues that the ingredients that went into the Constitution at the Philadelphia convention were "incompatible," thus suggesting that the Constitution is philosophically incoherent (*Novus Ordo Seclorum: The Intellectual Origins of the Constitution*, 8). To be sure, McDonald believes that there were some good ingredients, that the framers were wise to institutionalize pluralism (not meaning normative pluralism, but rather the embracing of many factions), and that the framers exercised wisdom in drawing the Constitution "loosely enough so that it might live and breathe and change with time." But the precariousness of the Constitution, constructed from incompatible ingredients, leaves him thinking that these reasons may not

the evaluative front, there do not seem to be advocates of incoherence and the charge that the Constitution is incoherent seems something of an implicit critique.

Problems with Previous Attempts to Describe the Constitution's Normative Framework

As can be imagined, given the complexity of the above, scholars who attempt to fit the Constitution into one of the categories employed by intellectual historians face numerous difficulties. These difficulties result less from the coherence or incoherence of these categories than from the method used to try to make the Constitution fit a particular category. In the end, the problems are significant enough that they suggest casting aside the usual method and starting from scratch. Further, because of the difficulties attendant to describing the Constitution in terms of these categories, it becomes impossible to use them to evaluate the Constitution. We must therefore seek a new way to discern the Constitution's normative framework, and we must give a more systematic evaluation of that framework.

As one delves into the details of the arguments for all the basic interpretive positions, fundamental historical problems emerge. The classical interpretation, for example, was built on the implausible assumption of the basic continuity of ancient and modern writers on natural law. Placing Xenophon, Aristotle, Cicero, Grotius, Pufendorf, Sidney, and Locke into one continuous stream, however, proves problematic. The old orthodoxy appears to place in one stream people who actually thought quite differently. Further, advocates of the great tradition assumed that if the framers drew upon classical resources, then they and their Constitution must be classical. The normative framework of the framers' background reading became identical with the Constitution's normative framework. Few, if any, engaged in serious, logical analysis of the Constitution's institutional structure. Instead, every now and then someone pointed to provisions in the Constitution that echoed recommendations contained in classical works.

So poorly constructed was the edifice known as the classical interpretation that modernists were able to break through its weak fortress walls and rush into the breach. They seized upon the assertion of some classical constitu-

---

explain why the Constitution has survived. "Perhaps," he notes, "as Bismarck is reported to have said, a special Providence takes care of fools, drunks, and the United States of America. Surely the Founders believed the last of these three" (293).

tionalists that the framers received their classical framework through modern sources and pointed to the philosophical modernity of those sources. Grotius, Pufendorf, and Locke were philosophical moderns hostile to classical thought. Locke, they contested, was really Hobbesian. Therefore, the framers' reliance on Locke, as well as on Grotius and Pufendorf, indicates their basic modernity. And it must be conceded that the framers did indeed draw on works of a modernist bent.

Still, modernists make two basic mistakes in their argument. First, they ignore the direct influence of classical writers upon the framers. The Constitution's architects read Xenophon, Plato, Aristotle, and Cicero, as well as Grotius, Pufendorf and Locke.[58] Second, modernists overstate the break of modern writers with classical moral thought.[59] Some writers in modern times did in

58. Thomas Pangle disagrees that ancient thinkers of a classical bent had any real relevance for the framers. He argues that Xenophon was important but not classical, whereas Aristotle was comparatively unimportant but classical (*Spirit of Modern Republicanism*, 29).

59. My position receives some support from the work of several historians. Paul A. Rahe, for example, believes that classical thought exercised at least some influence upon the framers. He wrote, "where American historians debate whether the regime produced by the American Revolution was republican or liberal, ancient or modern, or simply confused, I argue that it was a deliberately contrived mixed regime of sorts—liberal and modern first of all, but in its insistence that to vindicate human dignity one must demonstrate man's capacity for self-government, republican and classical as well" (*Republics Ancient and Modern: Classical Republicanism and the American Revolution*, x). Forrest McDonald (in both *Novus Ordo Seclorum* and *Alexander Hamilton*) gives stronger emphasis to the importance of classical ideas upon the American revolutionaries and the framers. In considering Jefferson's use of the idea of happiness in the Declaration, McDonald notes, "we can say, with measured confidence, that here was an Aristotelian idea which had figured in no major way in the classical revival in seventeenth-century England but was popularized by Burlamaqui and his followers amidst the eighteenth-century enthusiasm for natural law. We can also say that it somehow spread rapidly in America and that it was by 1776, in common currency among the patriots" (*Novus Ordo Seclorum*, x). The Aristotelian idea gained such currency because of its place in the work of Burlamaqui (a viewpoint popularized in the colonies in a pamphlet by James Wilson) and of Vattel, a significant influence in American thought. A number of revolutionaries also, it would seem, read Aristotle himself (not to mention Cicero). Turning to the Constitution's framers and defenders, one notes the apparent influence of the very classical Vattel upon Alexander Hamilton. Vattel suggested that the end of every human being is happiness in the Aristotelian sense and that natural laws were rules pointing the way to Aristotelian well-being. He also taught Hamilton the priority of duty to rights and that the purpose of government is greater than the mere securing of the natural rights of life, liberty, and property (McDonald, *Alexander Hamilton*, 52–57). Indeed, one might argue that Vattel's influence on Hamilton's constitutional thought was greater than Locke's and that Vattel's thought was simultaneously more thoroughly classical (which is not to say that Locke was fully modern). Moving beyond Hamilton, Madison's foremost biographer, Ralph Ketcham, suggests that this great American political thinker was influenced significantly by classical notions. Ketcham rejects the notion that Madison can be described as a "full" modern. He notes that Madison's education under Witherspoon "rested on an Aristotelian frame of seeing good or bad government possible whether rule was by one, the few, or the many. Quality of result, not numbers or process of government was crucial." This frame constitutes a "critically important aspect of Madison's political understanding" (*James Madison: A Biography*, viii). In fact, Madison was thoroughly acquainted with classical thought through his stud-

fact break away completely. Thomas Hobbes, for example, rejected the classical understanding of purpose (teleology), natural law, and the authority of the
sovereign.[60] Others broke away at the center of their thought and yet retained
some ideas consistent with classical teaching. Pufendorf, for instance, repudiated classical teleology,[61] but he advanced the idea that natural rights derive
from prior natural duties and constitute protective spheres around those duties.[62] Thus, he argued, we have a right to fulfill the obligations imposed upon
us by natural law. This understanding of natural rights fits nicely with the classical notion of natural law. Still others, such as Burlamaqui and Vattel, were,
arguably, thoroughly classical. Vattel, for instance, followed classical moral
theory in asserting that the goal of human life is happiness (or well-being) and
that natural laws are the rules of behavior, derived from the design plan for
human nature, discernible to human reason, and ordained by God.[63] Finally,
some, such as Locke and Blackstone, plausibly could be interpreted as belonging to the classical tradition, at least to some significant degree. Such a
claim, though defensible, is also controversial.[64] Granting all the foregoing

---

ies. He studied the works of both ancient and modern adherents of the classical doctrine. During his
political career, he leaned on the work of Vattel on more than one occasion (*James Madison: Writings*, 96, 443).

60. The subtitle to *Leviathan* mentions all of Aristotle's causes with one exception—final causation. The whole work can therefore be construed as an attempt to understand the formation and
function of the state, as well as natural law, without any recourse to classical teleology or any substantive notion of purpose. As Heinrich A. Rommen points out, with Hobbes, the very meanings of
"nature" and "natural" change (*The Natural Law: A Study in Legal and Social Philosophy*, 76).

61. Rommen notes that from Pufendorf forward "an anti-Aristotelian nominalism became, expressly or tacitly, the basis of philosophy" (ibid., 73).

62. See Haakonssen, *Natural Law and Moral Philosophy*, 41, and the discussion of Pufendorf's theory of rights in chapter 6 of this volume.

63. See McDonald, *Alexander Hamilton*, 53–54.

64. Regarding Locke, the modern interpretation is extremely problematic. If Locke is modern, he
should not believe that natural rights derive from prior natural duties. But he does (see Haakonssen,
Natural Law and Moral Philosophy, 55). Second, Locke maintains that man's natural condition is regulated by a natural law that is not created by human convention and that obligates ruled and rulers
in the condition of society (*Two Treatises*, 271 and 357–58). Indeed, in Locke's view, no ruler is absolutely sovereign. Some moderns have misunderstood Locke and have argued that his legislature is
absolutely sovereign, but this is clearly wrong. According to Locke, any "law" not in keeping with the
common good is not a law. He maintains that the legislative power is "limited to the good of the Society. It is a power, that hath no other end but preservation, and therefore can never have a right to
destroy, enslave, or designedly impoverish the subjects" (357). He adds, the "Law of Nature stands as
an Eternal Rule to Men, Legislators as well as others. The rules that they make for other Mens Actions, must, as well as their own and other Mens Actions, be conformable to the Law of Nature, i.e.
to the Will of God" (358). Additionally, Locke's doctrine of revolution means that he understands the
goal of society to be more than peace in the Hobbesian sense (i.e., survival). If mere survival is the
goal of society, his doctrine of revolution would be meaningless. Finally, humans, according to modern thought, are concerned with commodious self-preservation. But Locke follows the classical tra-

analysis, modernists correctly pointed to the incompatibility of a number of thinkers in the "great tradition." We must indeed account for this modernist insight, and we must also go beyond it. Not only is the modernist interpretation problematic from the standpoint of the history of thought, it also makes the same problematic assumption as the classical interpretation. It assumes that the Constitution must be modern because the framers' writings appear to have a modernist bent and because the framers relied on modern sources.

Contrary to both the old orthodoxy and the modernist interpretation, a close examination of the historical record indicates that the framers were influenced by thinkers from ancient and modern times, some classical, some not, who were in fact incompatible. The great virtue of the incoherentists' position lies in the admission of just this. But incoherentists wrongly assume that incompatible thinkers must be drawn upon in incompatible ways. It remains possible to draw on incompatible thinkers in ways consistent with a particular normative framework.[65] For example, one might be persuaded by the modernist Pufendorf's idea that rights are protective spheres around natural duties without ceasing to be classical. In fact, Pufendorf is more classical than modern in this particular. But reading the works of the framers or those that the framers read will not tell us whether the framers pulled off such a feat when constructing the Constitution.

Yet we must note that the correctness of the incoherentists' central insight is the tolling of the bells for the classical and modern interpretations as they have been presented. Works in moral philosophy, read by the framers, cannot provide a proxy for the Constitution's normative framework when those works contain mutually incompatible ways of thinking. This remains true even if the framers drew on incompatible thinkers in compatible ways, for the framers did not tell us how they drew on various thinkers. Indeed, disagreement over the Constitution's moral framework may be so persistent because one can argue

---

dition in arguing that people are obligated to pursue the preservation of humanity and to help one's neighbors. He contends, "Everyone as he is bound to preserve himself, and not quit his station willfully; so by like reason when his own Preservation comes not into competition, ought he, as much as he can, to preserve the rest of Mankind" (271). Further, "God the Lord and Father of all, has given no one of his children such a property, in his particular portion of the things of this world, but that he has given his needy brother a right to the surplusage of his goods; so that it cannot be justly denied him, when his pressing wants call for it" (*First Treatise*, 170). Concerning Blackstone, McDonald notes that Blackstone's own view of natural law came straight from Burlamaqui, meaning Aristotle may well lie behind Blackstone (*Novus Ordo Seclorum*, x–xi).

65. Donald S. Lutz wrote, "By the last half of the eighteenth century, the framing [of the colonists' mental disposition] had become so coherent and so mutually reinforcing that the colonists could borrow from disparate European thinkers and link what others viewed elsewhere as mutually incompatible ideas" (*The Origins of American Constitutionalism*, 68).

for quite different positions if one looks to the framers' intellectual backgrounds in order to find that framework. Thus while examining the works that influenced the framers and the framers' own writings may prove helpful, such research will not provide us with a determinative answer concerning the Constitution's normative framework. Rather, we need to analyze the Constitution itself. The great virtue of the positivist interpretation is that it does just this: it gives priority to the Constitution over the framers understanding of it. Therefore, it is possible that the framers were not positivistic. But the Constitution they created nevertheless is. Or perhaps they endeavored to design a modern constitution but ended up creating a classical one.

There are yet other problems with utilizing the categories taken from intellectual history. *The Federalist* serves as a proxy for the Constitution for a number of scholars on all sides.[66] Two problems, however, emerge. First, Publius—the shared pseudonym employed by the authors of *The Federalist*, Hamilton, Madison, and Jay—is notoriously difficult to categorize.[67] If he belongs to the classical camp he never tells us, and he repeatedly insists that he is up to something new. Further, he does not fit comfortably into modernist or positivist categories. Second, it is unclear whether Publius provides an acceptable proxy. I will elaborate the second problem in the following section. For now it suffices to address the first. Classical constitutionalists have a hard time relying on Publius because he does not provide a systematic statement of his own normative commitments. If we rely on Publius's intellectual resources, it becomes clear that he put various resources to use—from antiquity all the way to David Hume. A logical reconstruction of Publius might help us discover that Publius indeed had a particular normative framework. But that only tells us the Constitution's framework if Publius's understanding of that framework is identical to that document's framework. So long as we do not assume such an identification at the outset, however, we require more than a logical reconstruction of Publius.

---

66. Classical constitutionalist White, in *Philosophy, "The Federalist," and the Constitution,* modernist Pangle, in *Spirit of Modern of Republicanism,* and positivist Ackerman, in *We the People,* all lean heavily on interpretations of *The Federalist* to make their case about the Constitution.

67. Consider James Madison's words in that section of the *Detached Memoranda* that deals with *The Federalist* in this regard. According to Madison, while he and Hamilton communicated their respective papers to each other before sending them to press at the beginning of the effort to secure the election of delegates favorable to the Constitution to New York's ratifying convention, they stopped doing this for two reasons, one of which was "that it was found most agreeable to each, not to give a positive sanction to all the doctrines and sentiments of the other; there being a known difference in the general complexion of their political theories" (*James Madison: Writings,* 769).

We also need, as Publius does, to analyze the Constitution itself. Suppose we grant, however, that Publius is important and that he has not helped the classical position much. Even so, he is an even poorer ally for modernists and positivists. Modern political thought posits that people surrender their rights to the sovereign. In arguing that the Constitution does not require a list of reserved rights, however, Publius says, "Here, in strictness, the people surrender nothing, and as they retain everything, they have no need of particular reservations."[68] As well, modern governments aim only at securing peace or at mere preservation. But Publius says that the Constitution aims at securing justice.[69] Furthermore, modernists lean heavily on the idea that the Constitution establishes a government more powerful than that erected by the discarded Articles of Confederation and that it does so in such a way as to make a government of powers palatable. The modernist interpretation, however, finds insufficient support here because modern moral theory is arguably incompatible with any significant limitations on the government. Yet Publius is clearly concerned with limiting the national government. However, he does not want to do this in order to protect an unconstrained popular will. While the people are sovereign, Publius does not believe they are free to do anything they want. He argues that the Constitution exists to resist the popular will when that will is unjust. This is the express purpose of the Senate.[70] Publius only desires the governance of a just popular will. But any distinction among exercises of the popular will (e.g., favoring deliberate over nondeliberate, just over unjust popular will) is inconsistent with positivism.

Thus, Publius is neither entirely modern nor entirely positivist. Yet, this does not mean that he is entirely classical. The same is true of the Constitution. The categories of intellectual history have led us to *assume* that the Constitution fits neatly into one of these categories, and indeed it may.[71] But the *assumption* is unwarranted. It is logically possible that the Constitution is partly modern and partly classical. Or perhaps it is partly positivist and partly classical or perhaps some other combination. All this points to the unusability of the categories of intellectual history for unearthing the Constitution's moral commitments. It seems to follow that it is also problematic to evaluate the Constitution in terms of those categories. We need a new approach.

---

68. Alexander Hamilton, James Madison, and John Jay, *The Federalist* No. 84, 437.
69. "Justice is the end of government. It is the end of civil society" (Ibid., No. 51, 265).
70. See Ibid., No. 63, 320.
71. In fact, I will argue that it belongs to the classical category.

Logically Analyzing the Institutional Structure
Created by the Constitution

The approach I'm advocating begins by distinguishing the Constitution from the framers' understanding of the Constitution. Given this, the Constitution's normative framework is not simply identifiable with the one assumed in the writings of the framers (though they may turn out to be the same upon analysis). How then are we to uncover the Constitution's normative framework? We do this by considering various possible normative assumptions and inquiring as to which of them makes the best sense of why we have the particular institutions we have and why these institutions are arranged in the way that they are. Then we can contemplate whether the Constitution's normative assumptions are in fact good. But how do we come up with the assumptions to test both descriptively and normatively? While the approach of the intellectual historian has been discarded, we can still use the old categories to tease out plausible assumptions for testing. Classical, modern, and positivist moral thought all collect under their headings discrete propositions about sovereignty, the common good, natural law, and natural rights. Thus, instead of holding up the categories of classical, modernist, and positivist and asking, "Into which does the Constitution fit?" or "Into which should it fit?" we can say, "Here are various possible assumptions about the nature or reality of the common good. Which such assumption is most consistent with this institutional framework? Which assumption is the best one to have?" We can then approach sovereignty, natural law, and natural rights in the same way.

Before outlining my approach, it is appropriate to justify my distinction of the Constitution's meaning from the framers' understanding of its meaning, and I have two reasons for doing this. First, the framers themselves made this very distinction. Second, a constitution is an institutional structure and not just a collection of the intentions of its framers. That is, a constitution is an objective thing that can be considered on its own terms.

As for the first reason, originalist objectors to this distinction fail to notice that it was made by the framers themselves. In 1821, Madison wrote to John Jackson that we must distinguish between the Constitution's "true meaning" and "whatever might have been the opinions entertained in forming the Constitution." In fact, Madison always repudiated attempts to invoke the discussions of the constitutional convention in debates over constitutionality. Discussing his reasons for delaying the publication of his notes from the convention until after his death, he said, "As a guide in expounding and applying the provisions of the Constitution, the debates and incidental decisions of the Convention can have no authoritative character." The *Annals of Congress* attribute these words to Madison: "But, after all, whatever veneration might be entertained for the body of men who formed our Constitution, the sense of that body could never be regarded as the Oracular guide in expounding the Constitution." Madison even sounded a cautionary note to those who would employ *The Federalist* in constitutional discussions, arguing, "it is fair to keep in mind that the authors might be sometimes influenced by the zeal of advocates." Hamilton shared Madison's skepticism of the idea that the Constitution's meaning reduces to the subjective intentions of the framers. In the debate over the constitutionality of a congressional statute incorporating a national bank, Jefferson, in a "unusual resort to 'legislative history,'" noted that the Philadelphia convention had voted down a proposal that would have given Congress expressly delegated power to charter corporations. Hamilton responded,

> [W]hatever may have been the nature of the proposition or the reasons for rejecting it concludes nothing in respect to the real merits of the question. The Secretary of State will not deny, that whatever may have been the intention of the framers of a constitution, or of a law, that intention is to be sought for in the instrument itself, according to the usual & established rules of construction. Nothing is more common than for laws to *express* and *effect*, more or less than was intended. If then a power to erect a corporation, in any case, be deducible by fair inference from the whole or any part of the numerous provisions of the constitution of the United States, arguments drawn from extrinsic circumstances, regarding the intention of the convention, must be rejected.[72]

Now consider the implications of Madison's and Hamilton's words for the original intentionalist. The original intentionalist maintains (1) we can and ought only determine constitutionality by recourse to the framers' intentions. But we have seen (2) that the framers intend that we not recur to their intentions in determining constitutionality. What seems to follow is that a consistent originalist must hold (3) we ought to follow the framers' specific intention that we not recur to their intentions, which produces (4) we ought and

72. The quotations in this paragraph are cited in H. Jefferson Powell, "The Original Understanding of Original Intent," 83, 82, 82–83, 82, 101n53, and 69. Powell's presentation of Madison's rebuff of President Washington's attempt to invoke the Constitutional Convention in a memorandum to the House during the fourth Congress is on 71–74.

ought not take recourse in the framers' intentions in determining constitutionality. And (4) is clearly absurd (self-referentially incoherent at a minimum). The absurdity suggests that we reject (1). In keeping with this, if *The Federalist* is understood as an expression of the framers' intentions, then we ought not accord it an absolute authoritative status in determining what the Constitution means. Two things are *not* entailed by these observations. First, none of this requires setting *The Federalist* or other writings of the framers to the side. Rather, we should probe these writings to see whether they in fact contain the best account of our Constitution. And we should expect to find that works such as *The Federalist* do frequently (perhaps nearly all the time) contain such an account. After all, wise architects usually, though perhaps not always, understand their work better than do those who seek to comprehend it. Second, none of this entails the correctness of notions of a living constitution, which is really just another sort of intentionalism.[73] Hamilton's words, in particular, suggest that the Constitution has a meaning or intention of its own that is distinct from any person's or group's subjective intent, whether that group comprises the framers or the people as a whole at the present moment.

Concerning the second reason, it is pointless to ask whether the Constitution is any good without having some understanding of what a constitution is. The Constitution is not just writing on parchment. Rather, the Constitution effects a constitution.[74] That is, when I speak of the Constitution, I am referring to the practical institutional arrangement established by the document, the incentive patterns generated by that institutional arrangement, and the organization of the polity effected by those arrangements and incentives. On this understanding, the Constitution also includes the normative framework that is presupposed by its particular institutional arrangements, incentive patterns, and organization of the polity. A constitution's normative framework is that set of normative assumptions that makes the best sense of its particular institutional arrangement. Put another way, a constitution's normative framework includes those moral propositions that this particular institutional structure assumes to be true. We get at this set of assumptions by considering the different kinds of normative assumptions that any given constitution might take to be true. So considering one sees that there are various

73. The difference between original intentionalism and living constitutionalism is more a matter of whose intentions count in determining what the Constitution means rather than an alternative to an intentionalist theory of constitutional meaning. Arguments provided in chapter 2, by implication, will show why intentionalism as such, whether in the guise of original intentionalism or of living constitutionalism, fail.

74. I believe that I may owe this turn of phrase to Jeffrey K. Tulis.

possible assumptions about the nature of sovereignty (e.g., is it limited or unconstrained?); the common good (e.g., is there an objective common good or no?); natural law (e.g., does this constitution presuppose the know-ability of a natural law overarching ruled and rulers?); and natural rights (e.g., does this constitution presuppose priority of natural duties to natural rights or of natural rights to natural duties?). Possible normative assumptions that a constitution might make are discerned by listing plausible normative assumptions about sovereignty, the common good, natural law, and natural rights. In each case we use the history of political thought to generate an initial list of possible assumptions. That is, we disaggregate the categories—classical, modernist, and positivist—and reorganize the tenets in each of the categories, conceptually, under plausible assumptions about sovereignty, the common good, natural law, and natural rights. Then we approach the Constitution as an institutional arrangement and ask, in each instance, what understanding of sovereignty fits with this structure. We do likewise with the common good, natural law, and natural rights. What it means for a normative assumption to "fit" the Constitution will be discussed in chapter 2. For now I will simply illustrate the sort of conceptual reorganization I have in mind. If we disaggregate the logically discrete propositions contained in classical, modern, and positivistic thought and reorganize them conceptually, then we get the following lists:

The Constitutional Concept of Sovereignty

1. The Constitution presupposes that the people retain an unconstrained sovereignty. They authorize officials and institutions to carry out their will, and the people are free to command anything.

2. The Constitution presupposes that the people transfer sovereignty from themselves to the authority they establish. That authority is then free to command however it sees fit. The sovereignty of the governing authority, not that of the people, is unconstrained.

3. The Constitution presupposes that a sovereign is constrained by the dictates of justice, whether this sovereign be popular, mixed, or wholly unpopular.

The Constitutional Conception of the Common Good

1. The Constitution presumes that there is no objective common good toward which all laws must aim. All obligation derives from the command of the sovereign—in this case, the will of the people.

2. The Constitution's conception of the good is preservation or peace—a

peace attained by bracketing the questions that bring about violent dispute, such as those about religion or goods and evils other than the good of peace.

3. The Constitution presupposes the existence of an objective common good, which includes more than mere peace or preservation. It conceives a "thicker" common good that includes all of the dimensions of human well-being and rightly ordered relationships.

The Constitutional Concept of Natural Law

1. The Constitution presupposes that there is no common stock of knowledge about moral absolutes that derive from the purposes of human nature and that are ascertainable by reason. Rather, the Constitution presupposes that there is wide divergence on moral beliefs, that a moral consensus cannot be the basis of our governance, and that therefore we must be governed by the will of the majority.[75]

2. The Constitution presupposes that there is a stock of moral knowledge—of natural laws—available to all via instrumental reason. These "natural laws" are really mere counsels of prudence—or rules that people must follow if they are to avoid living in the "state of nature," the state in which everyone has a right to everything. These laws commend the seeking of peace and the doing of what is necessary for the realization of peace.

3. The Constitution presupposes that there is a common stock of moral knowledge—natural laws—known in their most basic requirements to all or nearly all, binding upon human beings and implicit in their nature or design. Further, humans have some natural inclination to obey them. No human enactment contrary to them has any validity.

The Constitutional Concept of Natural Rights

1. The Constitution presupposes that there are no natural rights. The only rights of citizens are those established by the Constitution itself. Thus, the positive law of the Constitution is the source of all rights.

2. The Constitution presupposes that there are natural rights, that they are prior to natural duties, and that natural laws are derivative from natural rights.

3. The Constitution presupposes that there are natural rights, but that nat-

75. Here I refer to that strain of positivism, represented by Ackerman, Ely, Oliver Wendell Holmes, and others, that is majoritarian. Most who categorize the Constitution as positivist describe it in terms of majoritarian positivism. I do not, however, mean to suggest that all positivists are majoritarian positivists.

ural duties are prior to natural rights and that natural rights are derivative from natural laws.

This list of possible constitutional presuppositions is not exhaustive. In the chapters that follow, I will expand the list of possible presuppositions under each of the headings above. For now I simply want to show what happens when we disaggregate the categories of the intellectual historian in favor of a conceptual organization of possible presuppositions.

Notice how this approach changes the initial question. The central concern herein is the reasonableness of the Constitution's normative framework. We ask the descriptive question for the sake of the normative question. We want to know what the Constitution's normative framework is so that we can determine if it is good. To ask the normative question, we had to find a new approach for uncovering the Constitution's normative framework. The old approach to the descriptive question would have left us wondering if the category into which the Constitution fit is a morally good one. In the new approach, we tackle normative assumptions arranged conceptually according to sovereignty, the common good, natural laws, and natural rights. In each area, we ask whether the Constitution's moral assumption is a good one. That is, we examine whether the Constitution's presupposition about the common good or about natural rights is in fact good. After addressing these particular questions, we can then ask if the Constitution is, on balance, good. But this question only arises after addressing the different ways in which the Constitution might or might not be good.

What Lies Ahead

In this chapter I have proposed disaggregating categories crafted by historians of thought and rearranging the normative premises in each of these under conceptual headings (or placing them in conceptual categories). I suggest that this approach will allow us to engage in a logical analysis of the Constitution's structure designed to uncover the Constitution's normative commitments. In chapter 2, I elucidate the methodology that is applied in later chapters to uncover the Constitution's moral assumptions. I recommend that we apply an argument form called inference to the best explanation in order to learn which proposition under each conceptual heading is most likely presupposed by the Constitution to be true. The methodology developed in chapter 2 is designed to ascertain the normative frameworks of constitutions in general, though I only apply it to the U.S. Constitution in this book. Chapter 3 analyzes the Constitution's theory of sovereignty. It concludes that the Constitution presupposes a constrained, wholly popular sovereign. I argue that the popular sovereign is constrained by a constitutional favoring of long-term preferences and desires over immediate ones and long-term popular will over short-term popular will and by a favoring of broadly distributed majorities over narrow ones. Chapter 4 takes up the Constitution's assumption about the common good, arguing that constrained popular sovereignty only makes sense on the assumption of a real common good, transcendent of and normative for human willing. I infer this because it is impossible, in any intelligible manner, to distinguish among different exercises of will on the basis of will alone or to distinguish among preferences on the basis of preference alone. In addition, I argue that the Constitution takes this good to be substantive and teleological—that is, the good in view has something to do with the proper functioning of the human design plan. Chapter 5 addresses the Constitution's theory of natural law and the nature of moral knowledge. I maintain that the Constitution presupposes that people come to know moral requirements through noninstrumental (or substantive) reason, rather than through sentiment or instrumental reasoning about how to obtain the objects of desire. Natural laws impose transcendent obligations rather than hypothetical imperatives. Chapter 6 argues that the Constitution presupposes the priority of natural duties to natural rights and that natural rights are protective spheres around natural duties. Each chapter contains not only a taxonomy of possible presupposition for the conceptual category under consideration, but also some normative assessment of many of the normative tenets considered. In chapter 7, I give specific focus to assessing the Constitution's normative framework, arguing that it rejects certain moral tenets for good reasons and that its moral theory as a whole is in fact coherent. Readers should be aware that in chapters 3–6 I elaborate the various moral premises that the Constitution might take to be true. I spend a good deal of time with particular moral theories because we can only understand why certain premises don't fit with our constitutional arrangement and why others do when we unpack and elucidate the moral premises or theories that constitute the set of possible constitutional presuppositions. It is only when we unpack these moral premises or theories that we see why some theories entail things contradicted by the Constitution's institutional arrangement and why others do not. There is no getting around the need to not only list possible moral presuppositions but also to explain them and to see what they entail.

2

Inferring Moral Assumptions

T H E   L A S T   C H A P T E R   asked how we should reason about the Constitution's normative framework. First, I argued that the Constitution should be considered as more than simply a text on parchment or the embodiment of the intentions of its framers. The Constitution, I maintained, should be treated as effecting a constitution—a pattern of institutional arrangements. Second, I argued that we need to think differently about the nature of constitutional moral assumptions—namely, that we need to disaggregate the categories of classical, modernist, and positivist. The upshot of all this is that we should consider the constitutional assumptions about sovereignty, the common good, natural law, and natural rights in terms of the institutional pattern effected by the Constitution. I also argued that there are good reasons for doing this without saying how such a task might be accomplished. In this chapter I will illustrate how we might infer moral assumptions from the Constitution by showing how to infer moral assumptions from constitutional structure more generally. This requires showing how inferences can be drawn from structures, generally speaking. Consequently, the methodology I will develop here can be applied to other constitutions, though I will apply it only to the U.S. Constitution. This chapter, therefore, will prove useful to those interested in constitutionalism more generally as well as to specialists in U.S. constitutional theory.

33

An Example of Reasoning from
Constitutional Structure

Before explaining how to infer specifically *moral* assumptions from constitutional structure, it is perhaps appropriate to consider how James Madison
reasoned about constitutional principles during the First Congress, not as an
appeal to original intent but as an illustration of the kind of structural reasoning I have in mind. One way of looking at this study, after all, is as the application of the methodology latent in Madison's own reasoning to the question of normative presuppositions (though the framers themselves never
made this precise application in a systematic way). Before proceeding, a brief
word of qualification is in order. In what follows my principal aim is not so
much to describe how the Constitution works in practice as it is to explicate
Madison's methodology for ascertaining constitutional principles from the
design pattern contained in the *formal* instrument. Still, I hope readers will
not simply dismiss Madison's description as wholly inaccurate if applied to the
operation of the Constitution in the present day.

Madison exhibits the sort of reasoning I have in mind in his discussion of
the presidential removal power. In the First Congress, it became a matter of
debate as to whether or not the president needs the concurrence of the Senate
to remove officials that, per the Constitution's requirement, he appoints with
the Senate's consent. An opinion had circulated through the Congress that the
president must secure the Senate's approval to remove such officials. Some
maintained that "it comports with the nature of things, that those who appoint, should have the power of removal." Madison, however, did not see how
the Constitution could warrant such sentiment.[1] This brings out an interesting point. The Constitution nowhere specifies how officials that must be appointed with the Senate's consent are to be removed. In the absence of clear
guidance from the text, Madison turned his attention to the institutional
structure that the Constitution puts into effect.

According to Madison, "It is one of the most prominent features of the constitution, a principle that pervades the whole system, that there should be the
highest possible degree of responsibility in all the executive officers thereof."[2]
Therefore, "any thing . . . that tends to lessen this responsibility is contrary to
its spirit and intention" except in that instance where the Constitution, in its

---

1. See *James Madison: Writings*, 435.
2. The responsibility in question is that of the chief executive to the body of the people.

letter, does so.[3] On these grounds, Madison opposes any legislative attempt to require a president to seek the Senate's approval to remove officials he appoints only with their consent. He reasons, "if the heads of the executive departments are subjected to the removal by the president alone, we have in him security for the good behavior of the officer." After all, if the officer appointed by the president "does not conform to the judgment of the president in doing the executive duties of his office, he can be displaced." This "makes [the officer] responsible to the great executive power, and makes the president responsible to the public for the conduct of the person he has nominated and appointed to aid him in the administration of his department." But if the president must secure the Senate's concurrence to remove those he appoints, then responsibility is destroyed: "if you take the other construction, and say, he shall not be displaced, but by and with the consent of the senate, the president is no longer answerable for the conduct of the officer; all will depend on the Senate. You here destroy a real responsibility without obtaining even a shadow; for no gentleman will pretend to say, the responsibility of the senate can be of such a nature as to afford substantial security." Madison then entertains the question of why the Senate's concurrence is required in the appointment of executive officials. He answers that the reason is simply so the Senate can provide advice. Yet, he points out, even here the president has primary responsibility for those who are appointed. After all, when it comes to nominating individuals for office, "no person can be forced upon him as an assistant by any other branch of the government."[4] The most the Senate can do is say no.

While Madison's arguments are not fully elaborated, the salient point is that Madison's reasoning involves making inferences from the Constitution's structure. He opens his argument by saying that he thinks it evident that the Constitution places the "highest degree of responsibility" in the executive officers—particularly on the president. But toward the end of his argument, he does give the reason that he thinks the primary responsibility in the appointment of officials lies with the president, and the reason is an institutional one. Madison argues that the Senate does not have the power to choose someone to be an assistant to the president if the president does not want that person to be appointed. Conversely, only the president determines who will be considered for these positions.

Some days after Madison made his argument, the issue resurfaced in the

---

3. The intention being referred to here is the Constitution's instead of that of the framers.
4. *James Madison: Writings,* 435–36.

First Congress, and Madison again noted, "It is evidently the intention of the constitution that the first magistrate should be responsible for the executive department; so far therefore as we do not make the officers who are to aid him in the duties of that department responsible to him, he is not responsible to his country." Madison did not explain how to ascertain this intention of responsibility. Perhaps he had in mind the point made above. For the sake of illustration, let us posit that Madison had those and other institutional reasons in mind. Say we can discern from the Constitution itself that it also has this goal of responsibility, particularly when it comes to the executive. The Constitution aims at making the executive responsible to the people. If this is true, then we can consider any scheme that undermines this responsibility to be inconsistent with the Constitution—in other words, to be unconstitutional. According to Madison, requiring the Senate's consent in removing officers appointed by the executive does just this. For such an arrangement makes executive officers dependent on the Senate in a way that may lead them to collude with the Senate. "And if it should happen that officers connect themselves with the senate, they may mutually support each other, and for want of efficacy reduce the power of the president to a mere vapor, in which his responsibility would be annihilated and the expectation of it unjust."[5]

Madison, therefore, determines the correct construction of the president's removal power by reasoning in terms of the institutional structure of the Constitution. He argues that requiring the Senate's consent in such matters creates a perverse incentive pattern that potentially undermines executive power altogether. Yet the Constitution clearly intends to create a real executive power. Requiring the Senate's consent for the removal of officers appointed by the president is unconstitutional, not only because it is inconsistent with the basic structure of the Constitution, but also because it undermines altogether a key feature of that structure—namely, the power and responsibility of the executive. Lurking beneath the surface of Madison's reasoning is an application of the law of noncontradiction. The Constitution creates a system designed to establish an executive who is responsible and responsible to the people. Making the president's removal power in this context dependent on the Senate removes responsibility and makes executive power virtually nonexistent.

Suppose that we allow R to stand for a responsible executive and E stand for the existence of a real executive power in the constitutional framework. Constructing the Constitution in a way that makes the removal power dependent on the agreement of the Senate is like saying R and not R (represented as ~R) and E and ~E.[6] The law of noncontradiction, however, precludes having R and ~R as well as having E and ~E. Because making the president's removal power dependent on Senate consent entails these contradictions, Madison rejects such an understanding of the Constitution or any attempt to institutionalize such an idea. In short, Madison has deduced a contradiction between the Constitution itself and a certain understanding of the Constitution (or, more aptly, between something entailed by the Constitution and something entailed by a certain understanding of it). He therefore rejects the problematic understanding.

Therefore, we have in hand the first point I wish to make about reasoning about constitutional structure. Understandings or constructions of the Constitution can be ruled out by deducing a contradiction with that understanding or something entailed by that understanding with some basic feature of the constitutional structure. Madison himself says that his examination of the Constitution in this instance is based on "what appears to be its true principles" and upon a consideration of "the great departments of the government in the relation they have to each other."[7] Yet in this citation we see that Madison's approach involves more than deducing contradictions in order to eliminate certain constructions of the Constitution. Part of Madison's reasoning relies on the basic principles of the Constitution that he discerns in its structure, apart from the elimination of contradictions with the Constitution.

Madison notes that "the constitution clearly intended to maintain a marked distinction between the legislative, executive, and judicial powers of the government."[8] That is, the Constitution aims at separating legislative, executive, and judicial power. How can we tell that this is a goal of the Constitution? Because the Constitution has a design that points in this direction. In other words, the constitutional structure has a discernible purpose. The main indication of this is the Constitution's creation of three distinct branches of government, each possessing the *lion's share* of power in a respective area: the Congress has the bulk of the legislative power, with two key exceptions; the executive branch has nearly all the executive power, with few exceptions; and the

---

6. The contradiction here is implicit. The premises that drive it are entailed by the nature of the Constitution and the nature of responsibility, taking into account some background knowledge of human motivation. All practical reasoning takes some amount of background knowledge into account. Consequently, the arguments contained herein will do so as well.

7. *James Madison: Writings*, 455.

8. Ibid., 458.

Supreme Court has nearly all the judicial power. The goal of keeping powers separate is manifest in a design plan that in fact separates power.[9]

But what about the indisputable fact that the Constitution also overlaps powers? After all, giving the president a veto gives him a share in legislative power. Further, requiring the consent of the Senate in the appointment of executive officers involves the legislative branch in the administration, or execution, of the government. One might take this fact of overlapping powers to show that the Constitution's intent is not to separate (and to maintain the separation of) powers. From the Madisonian perspective, two basic facts mitigate against such an understanding. First is the already noted fact that the written Constitution's tendency is not to overlap powers but to separate them. Exceptions to the separation of powers in the formal Constitution are few and far between. Second, one can look at the pattern the Constitution follows in overlapping power and discern very quickly that these instances of overlapping powers are designed to maintain a separation of powers rather than to paper over it. The first point has received some elaboration, but the second requires further comment.

One must take note of the way in which powers are overlapped. We already have one example of this: the Senate's consent is required in the appointment of executive officials. Yet the Senate's role in determining who will be appointed to specific positions is quite limited. They have no power to say, "We are appointing and confirming person x." Only the president can nominate, which gives him the preponderance of power in determining who shall serve under him, even where the Senate's consent is required. The Senate can provide advice and refuse to confirm a nominee, but it has only incidental or indirect control over the shape of the executive branch. The president's veto power is of the same nature. It is clearly of a legislative nature; yet the president isn't given a positive role in the legislative process. He cannot enact legislation. He can only say no to what the legislature proposes, and even then he can be overridden. The president's ability to shape legislation is, then, indirect

9. I am referring to the tendencies of the formal or written instrument. That is, the written Constitution gives the lion's share of legislative power to the Congress. However, I think careful reading of contemporary literature in political science reveals that this accurately describes how the Constitution works in practice as well. For instance, Richard E. Neustadt's famous book, *Presidential Power and the Modern Presidents: The Politics of Leadership from Roosevelt to Reagan*, reveals that presidents lack command power in the legislative arena. Presidential power, when it comes to this area, is ultimately the power to persuade. This concedes that the final say in legislative matters really does rest with the Congress.

and largely negative. The positive power of legislation rests primarily with the legislature.[10]

Now, requiring the Senate's consent in the appointment of certain executive officers and giving the president the power of the veto do create particular incentive patterns. Having to obtain the Senate's consent provides the president with an incentive to take into account the sort of person the Senate is likely to approve. But then he is not institutionally constrained to take this into account. He is not compelled to do so. He is provided with an incentive to do so that may or may not prove effective. Perhaps the president will appoint someone the Senate is not likely to approve and then lobby the Senate or appeal to the people in order to leverage the Senate. The president's veto over legislative action is similar. Because the president has the power of the veto, Congress, if it wants to pass legislation, has an incentive to take the president's policy preferences into account. Yet Congress is not compelled to do this. Indeed, if a majority is big enough, Congress can disregard the president's policy preferences altogether.

I have only examined two main areas of overlap, but the other instances fit this pattern. From our discussion we can see that the Constitution's overlapping of powers does not undermine the separation of powers. Rather, powers are overlapped in a way that is consistent with the separation of powers. They are also overlapped in a way that prevents each branch from doing whatever it wants without taking some notice of the others. Thus, the term *checks* is appropriate. But the Constitution's checks are in service of the separation of powers. Power is overlapped in order to maintain the separation of powers.[11] According to Madison, "if . . . [the three great departments of the government] are blended, it is in order to admit a partial qualification in order more effectually to guard against an entire consolidation." From this assessment of the Constitution's design plan, he inferred a constitutional principle:

> I think, therefore, when we review the several parts of this constitution, when it says that the legislative powers shall be vested in a Congress of the United

---

10. Ronald J. Oakerson is fond of describing the power of Congress vis-à-vis the executive as the power to say no. No one, as he says, can make Congress act.

11. See *The Federalist* Nos. 47–49 and 51, in which Madison argues that a pure separation is unsustainable, that extrinsic checks will not work to maintain the separation, that each department therefore must be given a mechanism of defending itself against the encroachments of other departments, and that doing this requires overlapping powers to a certain degree. His argument in these essays is still prescient, at least to this humble commentator.

States under certain exceptions, and the executive power vested in the president with certain exceptions, we must suppose they were intended to be kept separate in all cases in which they are not blended, and ought consequently to expound the constitution so as to blend them as little as possible.

The day before he made this statement, Madison argued that "so far as the constitution has separated the powers of these great departments, it would be improper to combine them together, and so far as it has left any particular department in the entire possession of the powers incident to that department, I conceive we ought not to qualify them farther than they are qualified by the constitution." Thus,

> The legislative powers are vested in congress, and are to be exercised by them uncontrolled by any department, except the constitution has qualified it otherwise. The constitution has qualified the legislative power by authorizing the president to object to any act it may pass, requiring, in this case two-thirds of both houses to concur in making a law; but still the absolute legislative power is vested in the congress with this qualification alone.

Madison then applied this line of reasoning to the executive:

> The Constitution affirms, that the executive power shall be vested in the president: Are there exceptions to this proposition? Yes there are. The constitution says that, in appointing to office, the senate shall be associated with the president, unless in the case of inferior officers, when the law shall otherwise direct. Have we a right to extend this exception? I believe not. If the constitution has invested all the executive power in the president, I venture to assert, that the legislature has no right to diminish or modify the executive authority.[12]

Thus, Madison moves from a basic insight about constitutional structure to constitutional principles. In what remains of this chapter I intend to flesh out just what Madison is up to and to show how we can get at the Constitution's normative presuppositions through just this kind of method.

---

12. *James Madison: Writings*, 460, 455–56 respectively.

Reasoning about Constitutional Structure

Inference to the Best Explanation, Stage 1:
Choosing among Alternative Explanations

In the last chapter I argued that it is helpful, in reasoning about the Constitution's normative assumptions, to disaggregate the discrete proposition
contained in the historical concepts of classical, modernist, and positivist. I
then proposed something of a conceptual reorganization—that is, any moral
theory can be understood as a set of normative propositions, where each
proposition in a normative theory is chosen from a subset of possible propositions. The possible propositions group around the various concepts of moral
theory such as the common good. In other words, every normative theory
takes a stand on the concept of the common good. Let us say, then that the
common good, inasmuch as different people mean different things by it, is a
conceptual category (or a normative category)—by this I mean that the term
common good can be used to refer to a number of logically possible realities,
including that reality in which the term has no actual reality corresponding to
it (i.e., that reality in which there is no common good).[13] In making its stand
on the concept of the common good (even when denying the existence of the
common good), the normative theory selects one proposition from among a
group of possible propositions (e.g., that the common good is nothing other
than peace or survival). In this book, I refer to sovereignty, the common good,
natural law, and natural rights as the concepts (or conceptual categories) of
normative theory. This list is not exhaustive, but it stands for the conceptual
categories that will be treated herein.[14] This mean that we can construct a list

13. What all meanings of the common good have in common is that there is some good common
to all human beings, however that good may be defined. Those who maintain that there is no common good are therefore committed to the proposition that there is no good, under any meaning of
good, that is shared in common by all human beings. One need not maintain that this version of the
common good, that there is no good common to all human beings, instantiates in some possible
world in order to maintain that it is merely a prima facie logical possibility. Perhaps maximal goodness itself is instantiated in all possible worlds, in which case it may follow that all humans share a
good in common in relationship to this maximal goodness. If this is the case, then we have good reason for ruling out the idea that there is no common good as being actually possible. But before such
an investigation is made, it remains an a priori logical possibility. Logical and metaphysical necessity, after all, are distinguishable.

14. Clearly some may take issue with my list or construction of "normative categories." For example, I am allowing the subject of virtue to be subsumed under the common good. Perhaps some
will think I should be giving the matter separate treatment. I think the matter of virtue and the common good to be so intimately connected that separating them would harm rather than help the ar-

of possible normative propositions for each conceptual category. Each proposition in this list attempts to state the truth of the matter concerning the concept under consideration. For instance, the idea that the common good is simply peace simply refers to the idea that the one good all humans desire or the one thing good for everyone is survival or peaceful existence. This is simply another way of stating the meaning of the disaggregation and conceptual reorganization at the end of the last chapter. But why is the disaggregation of the categories of intellectual history together with this conceptual reorganization helpful? Just what does it accomplish? Can any good come of this?

The benefit of the disaggregation of the intellectual historian's categories together with the conceptual reorganization proposed in chapter 1 is that it allows us to discuss the Constitution's moral meaning in a much more analytical way. Consider, for a moment, the concept of the common good. There is a list of propositions concerning the nature and/or existence of the common good, any one of which may be true. We can list these out. Any actual list may be incomplete and fail to exhaust all the possibilities. But it is theoretically possible to list them all. If the list is constructed correctly, each proposition will be irreducible to any of the others and the propositions will be mutually exclusive of each other. In chapter 1, I provided a list of three possible understandings of the common good: (a) there is no common good; (b) there is an objective common good—but it is nothing other than peace or survival (we can call this a limited common good); and (c) the common good is well-being—this includes the virtues and things thought to be objectively perfective of human nature. Clearly (b) and (c) are exclusive of (a), such that if (a) is true, then neither (b) nor (c) can be true, and such that if either (b) or (c) is true, then (a) is not. My claim is that all the variables here, (b) and (c) as well as (a), stand in such a relationship. Perhaps someone might suggest that (b) and (c) are not exclusive of each other. Our hypothetical objector maintains, of course, that (b) and (c) are not exclusive because well-being likely includes peace. But there is an important sense in which (b) and (c) are exclusive such that the truth of (b) entails the falsity of (c) and vice versa. After all, (b) posits

---

gument. Also, some might contest that sovereignty belongs to political rather than moral theory. Traditionally, however, matters of the common good and natural law have been treated side by side with sovereignty. See, e.g., Hobbes's *Leviathan*, Samuel Pufendorf's *On the Law of Nature and of Nations in Eight Books*, or even David Fordyce's *The Elements of Moral Philosophy*. I cite these modern examples rather than older works simply because most all admit that the separation of moral and political science would have been unthinkable to the ancients. These works illustrate that the early moderns were unwilling to make such a separation as well.

that the common good is nothing other than peace or survival. But (c) entails that the common good is more than just peace, even if peace is included. Thus, if (b) is true, (c) is not, and if (c) is true, (b) is not. This means, then, that among the list of possibilities, it is the case that (a) or (b) or (c) is true. I suggest that, so long as we have presented a list of alternatives that are truly exclusive of each other, then this sort of relationship always obtains among the possible propositions—that is, the truth of one of the alternatives precludes the truth of all the rest. The result is that when a normative theory commits to a proposition from a conceptual category, it picks a proposition to the exclusion of the other alternatives. Abstractly, suppose we have moral theory T that makes propositional commitments in conceptual categories X, Y, and Z and that *a, b,* and *c* are all the possibilities with respect to X.[15] If T is committed to *a*, then, by implication, it is committed to $\sim b$ (not *b*) and $\sim c$.[16] Conversely, if *b* or *c*, then not *a*.[17]

The relevance to reasoning about the Constitution's moral assumptions should be apparent. Suppose that the options within a normative category are truly exclusive of each other and that the list of options is exhaustive. In that situation the Constitution can presuppose only one of the possible propositions. To be more concrete, the Constitution cannot assume *a, b,* and *c* with respect to the common good. If the options in this list are mutually exclusive and the list is exhaustive, then, given the law of noncontradiction, only one can be presupposed. Assuming one to be true entails assuming the others to be false. In other words, the Constitution cannot presuppose both that there is no common good and that there is a common good identifiable with the classical notion of well-being (*eudaemonia*). This line of thinking can be applied to each normative category. So it is that, in that ideal world where we can

15. X, Y, and Z stand for hypothetical conceptual categories of any particular moral theory. This list is purely hypothetical. Clearly, one might propose that any such list is incomplete, although it seems to me that there is an ideal list that is in fact complete. That is, I rather doubt that there an infinite number of possible categories here.

16. $a \supset (\sim b \cdot \sim c)$.

17. Put another way: $a \vee b \vee c$ (*a* or *b* or *c*), which can be represented as $a \vee (b \vee c)$. Now according to commutativity, an axiom of replacement, $a \vee (b \vee c)$ is equivalent to $(b \vee c) \vee a$. If, for some reason, we are able to deduce $\sim a$, then we are left with $b \vee c$. If we can then deduce $\sim c$, we are left with *b*. We can say the same for any variable here. The idea is this, if we have listed all the possible normative assumptions, we can deduce which one is true by eliminating all the possibilities but one. As the eminent Aristotelian, Sherlock Holmes, used to say, when all other possibilities have been eliminated, that which remains, however improbable, must be true. This sort of reasoning, then, amounts to an application of the law of the excluded middle. For more on the terminology, rules of inference, and logical symbolism that I am following, see Patrick J. Hurley's *A Concise Introduction to Logic.*

list all the possibilities for each conceptual category, we can say that the Constitution has only one assumption in each. In theory we should be able to ascertain that assumption. Further, in such a scenario, if we eliminate all the possibilities but one, then we can infer that the possibility remaining is the correct one. But two related problems emerge at this point. First, it remains possible that we will not be able to construct such a list. Will our argument then lack all validity? Second, what if we cannot eliminate every possibility but one? For instance, what if two understandings of the common good remain consistent with the Constitution's particular institutional arrangement?

When it comes to listing all the alternatives for each of the conceptual categories, I find it quite possible that any list proffered will be incomplete. It is possible that no one has or will ever list all the alternatives for the possible meanings of the common good. It is also possible that various definitions in the history of thought over the last few millennia have failed to exhaust the possibilities, and, as a result, historical inquiry will fail to uncover such a list. Does this mean that this study cannot even get off the ground? My contention is that this possibility does not undermine the study right from the start. All this means is that the argument might not provide deductive certainty. The argument will not render a necessary conclusion. But then we accept arguments that lack deductive certainty all of the time without questioning their legitimacy. Most of our reasoning about ordinary life fails to possess deductive certainty. Indeed, one might suspect that nearly all conclusions of substance lack deductive certainty. But this does not imply that we cannot reason about matters of substance.[18]

As it happens, there is an argument form called inference to the best explanation that allows us to infer that "the best of the available explanations is the actual explanation."[19] I want to suggest that there are three senses of *best*. The first involves an application of the disjunctive syllogism being applied to a potential rather than exhaustive list of explanations. If we eliminate all but one of a group of potential explanations, the remaining explanation is the best be-

18. Recall the earlier invocation of Sherlock Holmes. All the explanations Holmes considers for a crime (or an otherwise suspicious scenario) presuppose a commonsensical notion of efficient causation. He never considers explanations that go along with that strange philosophical idea that goes by the name of occasionalism. That is, Holmes never produces a perfectly exhaustive list of explanations. He provides, instead, a reasonably exhaustive list. We need do nothing more when applying this way of reasoning to the Constitution's moral structure, though we should aim to be as exhaustive as we can be.

19. Peter Lipton, *Inference to the Best Explanation*, 60.

cause, compared to the others, it is possible where the others are not. An explanation is best in the second sense when, compared to competing explanations that may be good on a number of counts, it is the simplest and most consilient explanation. The third sense of best is that explanation that fits the best—that explanation to which the facts themselves point. For the rest of this section I elaborate on the first sense of best. The next two sections address the latter two meanings.

Consider for a moment a hypothetical list of positions about the common good that is indeed both mutually exclusive and exhaustive. We can call this set of possibilities concerning the common good G. G is a theoretical list that exists whether or not anyone in the real world, or even in some possible world, has ever drawn it up. Let us consider an actual list drawn up by some person in some possible world. Let us call this list G_1 and stipulate that G_1 includes mutually exclusive alternatives. Let us also stipulate that G_1 is not exhaustive. Clearly G_1 constitutes an attempt to approximate G. G_1 contains real alternatives; G_1's only failing is that it does not include all the possibilities. Still, it is possible to treat G_1 *as if* it were G. Our conclusion, in that case, will be of a conditional nature. Let's elaborate a bit. G_1 contains possible meanings *a, b,* and *c.* We want to know whether a particular constitution, C, assumes the truth of *a, b,* or *c.* Now say that we are able to rule out *b* and *c* on the grounds that these understandings of the common good are inconsistent with C's institutional structure because they contradict or entail something that contradicts something in the basic design of C or something entailed by that design. If G and G_1 were identical, then we would conclude that *a* is in fact presupposed by C. But they are not. Even so, if *b* and *c* can be ruled out, *a* can be a reasonable conclusion. We just state the conclusion with the following qualification: if G_1 stands for G, then *a* follows. The first part of the conditional assumes that G_1 is a reasonable *approximation* of G even though it is not exhaustive of the possibilities. In putting matters this way, one accepts that the list proffered in G_1 might be inadequate. One way to refute the argument is to reveal an alternative that has not been considered. One might also show that we can eliminate all the assumptions in G_1. Grant that we have C and that G_1 (with options *a, b,* and *c*) stands for a list of C's possible understandings of the common good and for various reasons we rule out *b* and *c.* So long as we are justified in letting G_1 stand for G (in instantiating G_1 as G), we are reasonably justified in saying that C presupposes *a.* We treat G_1 *as if* it were G and concede at the outset that our conclusion only follows with this "as if" proviso.

Inference to the Best Explanation, Stage 2:
Choosing among Competing Explanations

Even given the foregoing, a problem still threatens to undermine this study. What if we cannot deduce contradictions with all the options except one? That is, what if we find ourselves faced with more than one possible option that might in some sense fit with the Constitution's structure? The argument form known as inference to the best explanation helps us solve this problem.[20] To assert that the Constitution assumes some notion of the common good is to say that some understanding of the common good explains (at least in part) why we have this particular institutional arrangement. Where we have alternatives *a, b,* and *c,* these constitute a list of (partial) explanations for why we have this Constitution. If we cannot eliminate all options but one by deducing contradictions, the options that remain possible are competing explanations. Fortunately, inference to the best explanation allows us to select from among competing explanations.[21] As Gilbert Harman maintains,

> In making [an inference to the best explanation], one infers, from the fact that a certain hypothesis would explain the evidence, to the truth of that hypothesis. In general, there will be several hypotheses which might explain the evidence, so one must be able to reject all such alternative hypotheses before one is warranted in making the inference. Thus one infers, from the premise that a given hypothesis would provide a "better" explanation for the evidence than would any other hypothesis, to the conclusion that the given hypothesis is true.
>
> There is, of course, a problem about how one is to judge that one hypothesis is sufficiently better than another hypothesis. Presumably such a judg-

20. Although I do not provide an exhaustive overview of the literature on inference to the best explanation, I do draw on that literature where it is helpful for the task of this project. For a more thorough examination of this form of argument, see Gilbert Harman, "The Inference to the Best Explanation" and "Enumerative Induction as Inference to the Best Explanation"; Paul R. Thagard, "The Best Explanation: Criteria for Theory Choice"; and Lipton, *Inference to the Best Explanation.* Much of the early literature on this argument form (especially Harman's work) seeks to differentiate it from enumerative induction (or to argue that enumerative induction is a species of inference to the best explanation) and to distinguish the argument from Mill's method. Steven Rappaport, in "Inference to the Best Explanation: Is It Really Different from Mill's Methods?" provides an interesting critique of Lipton's attempt to distinguish inference to the best explanation from Mill's methods.

21. Harman argues that the best explanation is "the best" among "competing explanations and not the best of *alternative* explanations." It may be possible to infer more than one possible explanation. In this case, we are forced to ask what it means for one option to be better than another ("Enumerative Induction as Inference to the Best Explanation," 530).

ment will be based on considerations such as which hypothesis is simpler, which is more plausible, which explains more, which is less *ad hoc,* and so forth.[22]

Harman tells us that we are warranted in inferring that the best explanation is the true explanation (even if we do not infer this with anything like deductive certainty). He also hints at the grounds for considering an explanation to be good or better—though he never elaborates these grounds. Paul Thagard, however, does.

Among competing explanations, how do we know that one explanation is better than the others? Thagard advances two criteria relevant to this study: consilience and simplicity. According to Thagard,

> Consilience is intended to serve as a measure of how much a theory explains, so that we can use it to tell when one theory explains more of the evidence than another theory. Roughly, a theory is said to be consilient if it explains at least two classes of facts. Then one theory is more consilient than another if it explains more classes of facts than the other does. Intuitively, we show one theory to be more consilient than another by pointing to a class or classes of facts which it explains but which the other theory does not.[23]

Some qualifications are necessary. First, the facts in question belong to a broader, related class of facts (e.g., facts pertaining to physics). Second, the idea that one theory is more consilient than other theories competing to explain the same class of facts does not entail that the most consilient theory explains all of the facts explained by other theories (or by any one of the others).[24] Say we have theories T1 and T2 explaining some related facts in an area such as physics. So long as T1 explains more facts than T2, then T1 is more consilient than T2. This does not mean that T1 has to explain all the same facts as T2. Perhaps T1 fails to explain some facts that T2 explains quite well. Even so, if T1 explains more facts, then it is more consilient and, by Thagard's standards, a better explanation. Consider an apt example posed by Thagard:

22. Harman, "Inference to the Best Explanation," 89.
23. Thagard, "Best Explanation," 79.
24. Another qualification deserves mention. Thagard's method is not just a method of crass counting. He is quite aware that some facts in a class of facts are more important than others. Thus the most consilient theory is also one that explains the greatest number of the salient facts—and determining which facts are the most salient requires qualitative investigation. This amounts to a defense of qualitative inquiry in scientific investigation.

[Newtonian mechanics] afforded explanations of the motions of the planets and of their satellites, of the motions of comets, of the tides, and so on. But the general theory of relativity proved to be more consilient by explaining the perihelion of Mercury, the bending of light in a gravitational field, and the red shifts of spectral lines in an intense gravitational field. Quantum mechanics far exceeds any competitor in that it provides explanations of the spectral frequencies of certain atoms, of the phenomena of magnetism, of the solid state of matter, and of various other perplexing phenomena such as the photoelectric effect and the Compton effect.[25]

Thagard's second criterion for a theory to count as the best explanation is simplicity. T1 is a better explanation than T2, if T1 is simpler than T2. But Thagard does not use the term *simplicity* in the way we commonly do. Some, for example, might think of the classical notion of simplicity. The simplest object is completely undifferentiated. Following this line of thinking, between two theories, the simplest theory might be thought of as the one with the fewest premises or hypotheses. In contrast, for Thagard, T1 is simpler than T2 if T1 has fewer *auxiliary hypotheses* than T2. He argues, "The explanation of facts F by a theory T requires a set of given conditions C and also a set of auxiliary hypotheses A." Further, "An *auxiliary hypothesis* is a statement, not part of the original theory, which is assumed in order to help explain one element of F or a small fraction of the elements of F." We should note that auxiliary hypotheses are ad hoc and are not derived directly from the theory itself. They are assumptions added to the theory that are applied only very narrowly to one or a few facts. Indeed, auxiliary hypotheses are like assumptions that we must make to explain why a theory we take to be true on other grounds is not explained away by facts that do not quite seem to fit the theory or is not discredited by facts for which the theory's basic premises appear to provide no explanation. Consider the phenomenon of light. In 1690 Christiaan Huygens advanced the wave theory of light, which was later contested by Newton's particle theory. On Huygens's theory, light "consists of waves in an ether," and "light waves are propagated according to Huygens' principle that around each particle in the medium there is made a wave of which that particle is the center." Huygens explains the laws of refraction and reflection, along with other

25. Thagard, "Best Explanation," 81–82. Consilience is not the only reason Newtonian mechanics was discarded, for Newtonian mechanics contained a basic contradiction with the nature of physical reality. Newtonian theory posited an infinite universe. This entails a night sky as bright as the day sky, which is clearly not the fact. Newtonian theory is therefore problematic, in part, because it entails a contradiction with reality as we have it.

phenomena, by assuming that light waves are spherical. But this fails to address the irregular refraction of light in the Iceland crystal. To explain this, "Huygens supposes that some waves are spheroidal."[26] This assumption applies to only one class of facts—the refraction of light in the Iceland crystal. It is also clearly an addendum to the theory. Thus, this assumption is auxiliary to Huygens's wave theory of light. To be sure, most scientific theories make auxiliary assumptions of some sort. Thagard's suggestion is that where we have two scientific theories explaining the same phenomena, scientific investigators tend to accept as better the theory with the fewest auxiliary assumptions. Of course, it might be problematic if we took this in a strict, quantitative sense. To borrow from Thagard, "The matter is not neatly quantitative." After all, any set of auxiliary hypotheses "could be considered to have only one member, merely by replacing its elements by the conjunction of those elements." Further, given theories T1 and T2 seeking to explain a set of facts, F, and given a set of auxiliary assumptions for each theory AT1 and AT2, each explaining facts unexplained by the theory itself, we cannot simply compare the set of facts that AT1 and AT2 seek to explain, since there may be no facts in common.[27] In the end, "A qualitative comparison" must be made.

But how does all of this apply to constitutional thinking? Consider for a moment competing theories explaining why the framers put the Constitution together the way they did—an extended republic, separation of powers, checks and balances, the structure of the individual branches, etc. Suppose someone says that this structure is designed to maximize freedom by restraining the government and thereby to keep it from interfering in the private sphere. The freedom of people from the government or from abuse by the government is the primary value. Call this theory Tf.[28] But a second theorist

26. Ibid., 86.

27. The first problem means that, for any theory, the number of auxiliary hypotheses can be reduced to one, simply by a principle of conjunction. One might be tempted to resolve the matter by saying, "Now, look here, we can simply compare the facts or the number of facts that the auxiliary hypotheses in these competing theories seek to explain. The one with auxiliary hypotheses or an auxiliary hypothesis seeking to explain the fewest facts that do not quite fit the theory has got to be the one." Thagard would object to such thinking because that amounts to saying that T1 has auxiliary hypotheses for a, b, and c, whereas T2 has auxiliary hypotheses for a, b, c, and d. But the set of auxiliary hypotheses for each might not even contain any overlapping facts to be explained. These difficulties do not mean the notion of simplicity here advanced is worthless. This just means that some qualitative investigation is in order.

28. In Tf, I am using the term *freedom* to refer to freedom in a negative sense, as libertarians would employ it—freedom from governmental intrusion into one's life. I am aware that the founders would not have used words such as *freedom* and *liberty* in this sense. The Millian notion of the sphere of liberty exists in considerable tension with the framers' notion, which parallels the Lockean sphere of duty.

comes along and says that the Constitution is designed to maximize govern-mental power, to create a government of powers. The second theorist main-tains that the Constitution seeks to create a mighty state, capable of enforcing its will on the people. The goal of this mighty state is perhaps, as Hobbes sug-gests, the maintenance of peace. But this can only be done by creating a gov-ernment capable of exercising great control over individuals, so as to keep peo-ple from destroying each other. Call this theory Tp. The advocate of Tf fears the government and thinks the Constitution embodies that fear. In contrast, the advocate of Tp fears the people and thinks the government embodies that fear. But now a third theorist appears who is a little disturbed by the advocates of Tf and Tp. For, he maintains, the Constitution aims at justice. Put another way, the goal of the Constitution is prevent people from being deprived of their due. Let's call his theory Tj.

For the purpose of the argument, let us maintain that these theories all re-main possible explanations after an attempt to deduce some contradiction with each one from the constitutional structure. We have done our level best to eliminate alternative explanations and find that each of these fits in certain ways—for each explains certain facts about the Constitution. Say, for exam-ple, that Tf explains federalism, popularly elected officials, the bicameral leg-islature, and checks and balances more generally. Tp, however, explains why the Constitution reaches to individuals rather than just to states, why we have a single or unitary executive, and why the Constitution is in fact considerably stronger than the Articles of Confederation. Tj explains the inclusion of the Bill of Rights, the allowance of judicial review, and constitutional provisions that might be taken to encourage the election of leaders whose virtue is better than average, as well as checks and balances, federalism, popular elections, and the extended sphere. There may, of course, be some overlap. Perhaps Tj and Tf both explain checks and balances. However that may be, the theory that is the best explanation of the Constitution, on Thagard's argument, will be the one that explains the most facts concerning the Constitution's design and that has the fewest auxiliary hypotheses. Advocates of each theory will surely argue that my presentation here is incomplete. But let us ignore their plaintive cries and simply stipulate that I have provided a comprehensive list of what each theo-ry explains. In this case, Tj is the most consilient of the theories because Tj ex-plains more facts about the Constitution than does either Tf or Tp. Given this, we would take Tj to be a better explanation than either Tf or Tp.

As for simplicity, consider Tp in comparison with Tj. Tp, as I have present-ed it, fails to explain why we have checks and balances. It just isn't one of the facts Tp covers. Tp also fails to explain the federal aspects of the Constitution. Advocates of Tp, however, do not usually therefore despair; rather, they add auxiliary hypotheses to explain these facts. In this case, one auxiliary hypothesis is usually added to explain both checks and balances and the federal structure of the Constitution. On the face of it, these ideas are conceded to be in tension with the idea that the Constitution seeks mainly to create a government of powers. But including these things was necessary in order to get the Constitution ratified. These features of the Constitution are viewed as incentives for ratification. Clearly this explanation does not follow from Tp itself. Therefore, the hypothesis is auxiliary. In contrast, perhaps Tj has no need to recur to any auxiliary hypotheses in comparison to Tp. For instance, Tj might provide a valid explanation for why the Constitution calls for a significantly more powerful government than did the Articles of Confederation, and Tj might explain why the Constitution reaches to individuals rather than to states. The advocate of Tj can easily maintain, as a central part of his theory, that threats to justice come both from the people and from the government, that this means a government of appropriate strength, but with checks and balances, is necessary to restrain popular injustices, and that government under the Articles of Confederation was nowhere near the appropriate strength for dealing with such injustices. Thus a significantly stronger government was needed for the protection of popular rights. But the framers did not erect a government that was so strong as to allow the government to become an unmitigated tyranny. Thus, Tj arguably explains the Constitution's relation to power as well as Tp. One can explain the need for the central government to reach individuals in much the same way. Granting my characterization of these theories for the sake of argument, Tj is able to explain the facts contained in Tp without recourse to auxiliary hypotheses, whereas Tp needs at least one auxiliary hypothesis to explain some of the facts explained by Tj. This makes Tj simpler than Tp and therefore a better explanation. If Tj also employs fewer auxiliary hypotheses than Tf, in explaining the class of facts we call the Constitution, then Tj is the simplest theory and, by this criterion, the best explanation of the Constitution when compared to Tp and Tf.

Inference to the Best Explanation, Stage 3: Teleological Fitness

The application of disjunctive syllogism shows us why some options in various normative categories are bad options. Inference to the best explanation shows us why one explanation (or normative proposition), among competing explanations (or propositions), is in fact better than the other explanations (or propositions). Yet, after eliminating competing explanations and after seeing why one explanation is better vis-à-vis alternative explanations, we still want to see an explanation exhibiting a certain kind of fitness, which I call *teleological fitness*.[29] An explanation enjoys teleological fitness if it fits the facts—that is, if the facts point to it. The teleological element here points to purpose or proper function, so the explanation in view is a purpose or goal pointed to by the facts themselves. Clearly some people are quite skittish when it comes to talking about purpose. It is also equally clear that not all facts point to specific purposes very well. But in everyday life and even in scientific thinking, biology included, we find ourselves constantly saying that the facts under consideration point to a particular goal or purpose. Therefore, I propose setting skittishness aside and considering the possibility that facts of a certain sort can indeed point to goals and purposes, even normative goals and purposes. This being the case, it is legitimate to try to infer the Constitution's moral assumptions from its basic framework.

A brief word, I hope, will suffice to help us set aside our skittishness about teleological thinking. Clearly we do not ascribe functions to everything that exists. We tend to think of a rock lying in the woods as just a rock lying in the woods. Further, we have come to think that if we can explain where a thing comes from and what it is made of, then we have no need to recur to any other mode of explanation. Put more technically, we think that we can explain things simply in terms of efficient and material causes and therefore have no need to pay serious attention to final causes. This is not the achievement of Darwin but predates him by many years.[30] Social sciences have frequently approached human behavior the same way.[31] We hear talk of historical pro-

29. On teleological explanation more generally, see Albert Hofstadter, "Objective Teleology"; Larry Wright, *Teleological Explanations: An Etiological Analysis of Goals and Functions;* Andrew Woodfield, *Teleology;* Ernest Nagel, *Teleology Revisited and Other Essays in the Philosophy and History of Science,* esp. chap. 12; Etienne Gilson, *From Aristotle to Darwin and Back Again: A Journey in Final Causality, Species, and Evolution;* Ruth Garrett Millikan, *Language, Thought, and Other Biological Categories* and "In Defense of Proper Functions"; Mark Bedeau, "Where's the Good in Teleology"; Susan Sauve Meyer, "Aristotle, Teleology, and Reduction"; Ernst Mayr, "The Idea of Teleology"; Paul E. Griffiths, "Functional Analysis and Proper Functions"; Alvin Plantinga, *Warrant and Proper Function;* and Robert C. Koons, *Realism Regained: An Exact Theory of Causation, Teleology, and the Mind.*

30. Darwin's achievement, if it really was an achievement, was to show how to talk about biology without recourse to final causation. But in this he was simply extending a line of thinking that begins in Occam, receives some impetus in the Reformation, and is articulated in the thought of Hobbes, Pufendorf, and Descartes, among others.

31. The paradigmatic attempt to reduce the Constitution to efficient causation is Charles A. Beard's famous book, *An Economic Interpretation of the Constitution of the United States.* The work has proven

cesses and underlying economic motives and the dominance of self-interest. If we are honest, however, quite a lot of thinking along these lines simply begs the question. Much thinking simply assumes that things can be fully explained simply by elaborating what they are made of and where they came from. But why should this be the case? In fact, ancient teleological thinking arose because of perceived inadequacies in trying to explain things with recourse only to efficient and material causes.[32] And today there is much buzz about the inadequacies of the contemporary mechanistic paradigm, which endeavors to explain things without reference to final causes.[33]

Our language frequently betrays us.[34] We find it impossible to speak of many things without referring to their functions. This frequently shows up in thinking about biology. Fred Dretske wrote,

> We are accustomed to hearing about biological functions for various organs. The heart, the kidneys, and the pituitary gland, we are told, have functions—

---

to have serious historical flaws and has received powerful criticism. See in particular Forrest McDonald's *We the People: The Economic Origins of the Constitution.*

32. Reflecting on Aristotle's physics, R. J. Hankinson maintains,

> The search for form and finality in nature has often been ridiculed, from Bacon onward; but it needs to be stressed that Aristotle's conception of natural teleology is by no means a naïve and jejune one: on the contrary . . . he is drawn to it among other things by what he takes to be the evident and spectacular failure of the dominant purely mechanistic paradigm of his time, Democritean atomism, to provide anything like a remotely satisfying account of how structure and regularity can emerge from what is at bottom nothing more than a buzz of atoms in the void. ("Philosophy of Science," 138)

I suspect we are in something of the same place in our own day.

33. Many of the flaws of the mechanistic paradigm, especially as it pertains to theory of knowledge, were laid bare by the work of C. S. Lewis. See Lewis's now-famous essay entitled "The Cardinal Difficulty of Naturalism," in *Miracles: A Preliminary Study,* and Victor Reppert's contemporary defense of Lewis's argument in *C. S. Lewis's Dangerous Idea: In Defense of the Argument from Reason.* Alvin Plantinga, in *Warrant and Proper Function,* has advanced a powerful critique in this area. When it comes to causation, Etienne Gilson provides a highly critical assessment of Darwin and a powerful defense of Aristotle in *From Aristotle to Darwin and Back Again.* See also Koons, *Realism Regained.*

34. I find myself rather inclined to agree with Plantinga:

> the idea of proper function is one we all have; we all grasp it in at least a preliminary rough-and-ready way; we all constantly employ it. You go to the doctor; he tells you that your thyroid isn't functioning quite as it ought (its thyroxin output is low); he prescribes a synthetic thyroxin. If you develop cataracts, the lenses of your eyes become less transparent; they can't function properly and you can't see well. A loss in elasticity of the heart muscle can lead to left ventricular malfunction. If a bird's wing is broken, it typically won't function properly; the bird won't be able to fly until the wing is healed, and then only if it heals in such a way as not to inhibit proper function. Alcohol and drugs can interfere with the proper function of various cognitive capacities, so that you can't drive properly, can't do simple addition problems, display poor social judgment, get into a fist fight, and wind up in jail. (*Warrant and Proper Function,* 5)

things they are, in this sense, *supposed to do.* The fact that these organs are supposed to do these things, the fact they have their functions, is quite independent of what *we* think they are supposed to do. Biologists *discovered* these functions; they didn't invent or assign them. We cannot, by agreeing among ourselves, *change* the functions of these organs.[35]

This notion is not just of function, but of proper function. This is indicated by the words "supposed to." So it is that scientists and philosophers juxtapose this notion of function to the notion of malfunction. As eminent molecular biologist David Baltimore noted, "many instances of blood disorders, mental problems, and a host of other disabilities are traceable to a malfunctioning gene."[36] But something malfunctions when it fails to function properly, and so the whole notion of malfunction is parasitic upon the logically prior notion of proper function. So it is that there are many things of which we cannot even speak without invoking the idea of proper function. In fact, the whole practice of medicine is built on the notion of proper function. This betrays our belief about the teleological structure of much of reality. Does such belief make sense? Can we ascertain the proper function of a thing? If so, how might we go about this? Suppose we have a way to do this. How does this help us in ascertaining the Constitution's ultimate ends or purposes, in uncovering its basic moral commitments?

I would like to suggest that there is a connection between the proper function of a thing and the goal of a thing. Before exploring how this is the case, let's consider why it is. In order to distinguish between the function of a thing and its malfunction we must have some kind of criteria. Consider two refrigerators designed from the same schematics and made with the same basic parts and materials. Let's refer to these two refrigerators as A and B. Suppose that while A and B came off the same assembly line that, nevertheless, they seem to perform quite differently. A is cooling the food stored in it, but B is not. Refrigerator B is warming up the food. It is not cooking the food as, say, an oven would; nor is it keeping the food at room temperature. Instead, B is spoiling all the food stored in it. Now, suppose a repairman is called to fix refrigerator B. Upon opening the refrigerator and catching a whiff of the contents inside, he loudly proclaims that B is in poor repair. Just how does he know this? Let's add that the people who bought A call the same repairman to check their refrigerator. He opens refrigerator A, sees that it's cooling the food so as

35. Dretske, *Explaining Behavior*, 91.
36. Baltimore, "Limiting Science: A Biologist's Perspective," 336.

to preserve it. He proclaims refrigerator A to be in good working order. What was it about these refrigerators that allowed him to deduce that one was working properly and that the other wasn't? The repairman arrived at his judgment because the goal for both A and B was the preservation of perishable foods by means of keeping them cool, and B was failing to achieve this ultimate goal precisely because it was warming up its contents.

But how do we ascertain the goal of a thing such as a refrigerator? We might ascertain it from, say, reading schematics. But we don't need to read schematics to make this deduction; we know enough about the world to arrive at this conclusion. For instance, we understand that humans must consume food to live. Food is essential to the health of the body. We also know that people gather food in order to consume it, in order to live. Now, if that's why people gather food (whether by hunting and farming or by going to the grocery store), then it seems the reason people store food, after gathering it, must be in keeping with this goal of eventual consumption. A refrigerator that heats perishable foods, however, ruins such food for consumption. It renders the food useless. Of course, some people may consume spoiled perishables, but that consumption is likely to be damaging rather than helpful to the body. If one consumes such food, the goal of consumption is defeated. Therefore, B is proclaimed to be malfunctioning because it fails to achieve the ultimate goal of preserving perishable foods by the means of keeping them cool. Therefore, it is that the notion of function (or proper function) implies the notion of a goal. A thing, Q, is functioning properly if it is functioning in a way conducive to the realization of some goal aimed at by Q's design. Of course, a great deal more must be said about this, but the point here is that the distinction between proper function and malfunction implies the existence of a goal.[37] But say we have some thing, Q. How are we to decide upon Q's proper function or purpose or goal?[38] This has been a matter of discussion throughout the history of

---

37. Nagel, *Teleology Revisited*, 311–12, provides a formalization of this notion: "I want to make explicit in a semiformal manner what I think is a presupposition in the application of functional statements. A functional statement of the form: a function of item *I* in system *S* and environment *E* is *F*, presupposes (though it may not imply) that *S* is goal-directed to *some* goal *G*, to the realization or maintenance of which *F* contributes."

38. At this point some philosophers like to distinguish function from goal. I am willing to concede the distinction so long as the caveat is added that this distinction is not hard and fast. Those philosophers who make this distinction think of a thing's function as certain of that thing's effects. In this sense it is the function of blood vessels to direct the flow of blood. In contrast, the goal of a thing is said to be the outcome toward which that thing is directed. One such philosopher is Ernest Nagel: "One distinction that will be useful . . . is between 'goal ascriptions' and 'function ascriptions.' The former state some outcome or goal toward which certain activities of an organism or its parts are di-

philosophy. Without surveying that history, it remains helpful to consider some ideas articulated in times past.

Plato tells us, in *The Republic,* that we can figure out the purpose of a thing by figuring out that work which is unique to it—that work which the thing does better than anything else. Thus Socrates asks Thrasymachus whether or not there is some work proper to a horse. A horse's work, according to Socrates, is "that which one can do only with it, or best with it."[39] As Thrasymachus is a bit puzzled, Socrates poses another question: "Is there anything with which you could see other than eyes?"[40] Or, for that matter, is there anything with which one could hear other than ears. Thrasymachus concurs that indeed there is nothing else with which a person can hear other than the ear or with which one can see other than the eye. Therefore, Socrates asserts that seeing is the work of the eye and hearing is the work of the ear. But there is more to say. After all, sometimes more than one thing can accomplish the same task. For instance, "you could cut a slip from a vine with a dagger or a leather-cutter or many other things." And yet, "I suppose you could not do as fine a job with anything other than a pruning knife made for this purpose." A thing's purpose is more than simply what it can do or what it does—it is what it uniquely does or does better than anything else. In general, then, says Socrates, "the work of a thing is what it alone can do, or can do more finely than other things."[41]

But this is not the end of the story. Socrates tells us that "there is a virtue for each thing to which some work is assigned." The eyes, says Socrates, have unique work assigned to them, and they have a virtue. The virtue of a thing is that which helps it do its work well. "Could eyes ever do a fine job of their

---

rected. . . . On the other hand, function ascriptions state what are some of the effects of a given item or of its function ascription." Thus, one might say that the goal of a woodpecker's pecking is to find insect larvae, whereas the "function of the valves in the heart of a vertebrate is to give direction to the circulation of the blood" (*Teleology Revisited,* 277).

39. Plato *Republic* 352d–e.

40. Nagel suggests, given the distinction between goal and function ascriptions, that "seeing is customarily said to be a function of the eyes, rather than their goal" (*Teleology Revisited,* 277). I suspect he is wrong. Seeing is not something that occurs in the eye. Consider, for instance, the retina, which is basically a receptor plate receiving the reflection of light. The information received by the eye is interpreted by the brain. To be sure, seeing may not be the ultimate goal of the eye—we can inquire, for instance, into the purpose of sight—but it is surely a proximate goal. After all, one's eyes might be functioning exactly as they should without one actually seeing. Suppose a tumor has advanced to the part of the brain that has to do with sight. One might go blind or have faulty image production, even though the eyes are working completely as they should. If sight was a function of the eyes in Nagel's sense, this should not be the case.

41. Plato *Republic* 353a.

work," Socrates asks, "if they did not have their proper virtue but, instead of the virtue, vice?" So a thing, such as the eye, with some work proper to it, can do its work well or poorly. A thing's work is "done well" when it has the virtue proper to it and done "badly with vice."[42] The same, of course, is also true of ears. Eyes see poorly and ears hear badly when they are deprived of the virtue proper to them.

Therefore, Plato has a notion of proper function: the proper function of a thing, Q, is that work which only Q does or that which Q does better than anything else. But Plato's account also has a refinement. Q may do that task for which it is uniquely or best fit either well or poorly. It all depends on whether Q has its virtue. Thus, for any thing, Q, Q achieves its purpose, first, when it performs that task that only Q does or that Q does better than anything else and, second, when it possesses the virtue that enables it to do that task well. A knife's unique function is cutting and its virtue is sharpness. A knife cuts well when it is sharp. But there are things that cut better than a dull knife. In fact, perhaps a dull pruning knife will not even succeed in cutting a vine where a sharp dagger will. In that case, a pruning knife without its particular virtue cannot attain its goal. Thus Plato is clearly right to suggest that a thing must have its virtue (to some degree), in order to achieve its goal. The inference to a thing's purpose, however, focuses on the first condition—though the virtue of a thing has to be present for us to discern it.

Notice that Plato's rule for discerning the work appropriate to a thing, its purpose, has nothing to do with the intentions of a designer. To be sure, there are those who maintain that there is no designer for things like eyes and ears. Perhaps an esoteric reading of Plato shows that he agrees with such people. Be that as it may, he surely thinks that someone designed the pruning knife. Yet he applies his rule to the pruning knife without any reference to the knife's designer. We can figure out the work of the knife without asking the designer what he or she intended the knife to do. Most of us tend to agree with Plato here. We speak of the purposes of things such as hearts, eyes, and ears and pruning knives, word processor programs, lights, telephones, and parts of automobiles (pistons and cylinders) all without ever asking what the designer intended or what the designer said.[43] We think we can tell the purpose in these

---

42. Ibid. 353b–c.

43. That does not mean that the intentions of the designer may not be helpful in discerning the purpose of a thing. But more is needed for ascribing a function. The inference from intentions to purpose requires that the thing in question actually produces the intended outcome. Thus, Koons argues, "if I learn that a competent designer intended the artifact to crush olives, and it does in fact

cases by considering the design itself. Even if we disagree with Plato's particular rule, we tend to think that he is on to something here.

It is worth considering why we might disagree with Plato's rule. One way in which we tend to disagree is that we find the rule to be, so to speak, too steep. It is really a rule for detecting a thing's purpose if the thing in question has been optimally designed. But it doesn't account for less-than-optimal designs very well. Consider the case where a poorly constructed walking bridge spans a creek or a small river. The bridge exists so that people can cross the river. But a poorly constructed bridge might have this as its purpose and nevertheless present great danger to those who would use it. In fact, perhaps an old rope swing proves a more effective way to cross the flowing water. That the bridge is constructed poorly and that the old rope swing is better at helping people cross the river in no way means that the bridge does not have the goal of helping people to cross the river. Further, Plato's rule fails to account for the possibility (at least the logical possibility) that very different designs might perform the same task equally well. On the other hand, we tend to think that Plato's rule works in some sense. If indeed Q is the only thing that does work R or Q does work R better than anything else that might be used to do R, then we are inclined to think that R is the proper work of Q and that Q's goal or purpose is to do R. But, given the above, we think Plato's rule also lets a lot of things slip through the cracks. It fails to detect the purpose in many things that do in fact have a purpose. Plato's rule, in short, only detects a thing's purpose in cases where the design is as good as it can be.[44]

If Plato's rule for detecting the proper function of a thing is maximal, let us consider something less stringent. Let's call Plato's rule, rule A and the modified rule for detecting purpose rule B: If a thing, Q, does task R better than Q does any other task (say, tasks S, T, and U), then R is Q's primary purpose. This allows for the possibility that Q be put to different uses. Consider the human heart. We all refer to the heart's purpose as circulating blood throughout the body, thereby contributing to the overall health and well-being of the body. Suppose, however, that the heart not only does this, but also works extraordinarily well in a rugbylike game. Perhaps the material of which the heart is made and its particular shape make it ideal for kicking and throwing or shoot-

crush them, and in the way envisaged, then I have learned that crushing olives is one of its functions" (*Realism Regained*, 152).

44. Koons contends, "Imperfect functions can be discovered with as much objectivity and certainty as can optimally designed functions" (ibid.). This being the case we will need some rule other than Plato's to detect design in these instances.

ing and passing in this game. Perhaps the heart is the best kind of "ball" for this game. Must we then conclude that the heart's purpose isn't the pumping of blood or that its purpose is both the pumping of blood and being used as a ball for this particular game? That doesn't seem right. To be sure, while the heart might be best both for pumping blood and for playing this game, the heart nevertheless circulates blood throughout the body much better than it performs as a ball in the game. One might contend that such a judgment cannot be made; but we make similar judgments all the time. Consider a possible world in which the games of soccer and basketball both exist and in which a soccer ball not only is used for both games but is the best ball available for both. The soccer ball in such a world may be the best ball for both games and yet still be better suited for soccer than for basketball. Of course, anyone who has had only a soccer ball available when they wanted to play basketball and who has played both games at least a bit understands the truth of this claim. Basketballs are better for dribbling. But if you don't have one, a soccer ball will do. Thus, perhaps artifact Q achieves tasks R and V better than any other thing known to exist. Q's primary purpose will nevertheless be R. Rule B, then, seems to account for our intuition that just because something can be put to different uses, that does not mean that all the uses to which a thing can be put are identifiable as equal purposes of the thing. Use and purpose are distinguishable. This rule also has the advantage of allowing for suboptimal instances of design. With this rule, we can infer that the purpose of a badly designed bridge is to aid people in crossing the river so long as the bridge is better at that than it is at any other use to which the bridge might be put. Rule B also skirts another problem endemic to rule A. Rule A fails to allow for the possibility that very different designs might accomplish the same goal—perhaps equally well. Rule B allows that two different designs may well have the same goal—and allows for the fact that they might accomplish that goal equally well or that one might do a better job than the other. If Q is better at accomplishing R than Q is at accomplishing anything else and W is better at accomplishing R than W is at accomplishing anything else, then R can be assigned as proper function of Q and W. Yet rule B faces a rather significant difficulty. After all, don't some things have more than one function? The tongue, for example, works in speech, in the initial stages of digestion, and in the sense of taste. Plato's rule faces no problem here. The tongue may be unique in having any of these functions or at least may be better at any of these functions than anything else. In that case, Plato's rule leads to the conclusion that all these things are the proper function of the tongue. Just here rule B faces serious trouble, for so long as

Q does L, M, N, and R and does R better than it does L, M, and N, rule B only assigns R as the goal of Q. There doesn't seem to be any good reason to say that Q might have multiple functions or multiple goals, if we accept rule B.[45]

Clearly rule B is unworkable. But perhaps our example of the heart that both pumps blood and is employed in a rugbylike game can still be of help. Perhaps the reason we're likely to say that a heart is better at pumping blood and contributing to the overall health of the body than at serving as a ball in a game has to do with the fact that the heart's design is more at use in the former case than in the latter. The circulation of blood throughout the body makes use of many more aspects of the heart's structure or organizational pattern than does our rugbylike game in which the heart serves as a ball. The various parts of the heart's structure can be said to coordinate around the task of circulating blood throughout the body. But various aspects of the heart's structure do not coordinate around serving as a ball in a game. Indeed, most of the heart's structure is superfluous if its primary purpose is to serve as a ball in such a game. Here we begin to see a connection between a thing's design and a thing's purpose. A thing's purpose can be defined as what its overall design pattern aims at (at the effect it aims at achieving). To consider this more fully, it becomes appropriate to turn to Aristotle.

In keeping with what has been said of Plato's account, we might note that a thing's purpose is distinguishable from the thing itself—from its form or from its particular design. The distinction finds an antecedent in Plato's reasoning from what a thing is to what it is for—we can figure out what a pruning knife is for by analyzing what a pruning knife is. Of course, what a thing is for, in a certain sense (maybe in the highest sense), is part of what it is. But we can nevertheless distinguish the shape a thing takes or its pattern from its purpose—and we can reason from the former to the latter. It is this distinction, I would argue, that gives rise to Aristotle's distinction between formal and final cause. Aristotle, in his *Physics*, poses this question: how are we to describe the nature of a thing? Answering this question leads Aristotle to posit his famous four causes. That out of which a thing is made, its material, is part of its nature, as are the causes that bring the thing about or effect change in it, its efficient cause(s). But this does not exhaust the nature of a thing because we have

---

45. There is another significant problem with rule B. Whereas one might complain that rule A fails to ascribe functions where it should, rule B appears to ascribe functions where it should not. It seems we can say of any particular thing that there is some use to which it might be put and at which that thing is better than it is at anything else. In other words, rule B fails to distinguish things with design and in-built purpose from things with no in-built purpose.

not fully considered a thing's nature until we have also considered its form: "Another account is that 'nature' is the shape or form which is specified in the definition of a thing."[46] Finally, Aristotle indicates that a thing's nature has to do with the telos, or goal, of the thing in question—it is "that for the sake of which" a thing exists or is done. Thus, health is the cause of walking about (at least some of the time): "'Why is he walking about?' we say. 'To be healthy', and, having said that, we think we have assigned the cause."[47]

Therefore, we have a distinction between a thing's design or pattern and the reason for which a thing exists. Plato's rule implies a distinction made along such lines. And Plato gives us a rule for how to infer a thing's proper work from its design. But Plato refrains from providing any explicit argument for how a thing's work connects to its design. This is a connection, however, that we must understand if we are to be able to infer purpose from design. Given this, we might wonder if Aristotle's explicit distinction between kinds of causes provides us with any help here. If there is help to be had, this help might be found in exploring Aristotle's comments on the connection between formal and final cause.

As R. J. Hankinson reminds us, Aristotle divides the world into two kinds of things: "things that exist by nature, and those which exist for other reasons." Another way to talk about this distinction is to say that it is between natural and nonnatural things. According to Hankinson, "The paradigm case of things existing by nature are living things—plants, animals, and the heavenly bodies." The constituent elements of these things are also natural. In contrast, the paradigm case of a nonnatural thing is an artifact or something contrived, such as a bed or a house. Some characterize Aristotle's distinction between natural and nonnatural things as "causal": "natural objects are such as to contain within themselves their own principle (*arche*) of growth, movement and rest." "By contrast, artificial objects have no such internal principles—or rather, insofar as they do, they do not have them *qua* the thing that they are, but only derivatively, in virtue of the nature of the material from which they are made." So it is that natural objects pass from one form to another according to an internal principle governing their change, whereas nonnatural objects have their structure imposed upon them by some artificer. The creation of a bed requires the imposition of a form upon the materials of which the bed is composed. An acorn, however, grows into a particular tree according to a pattern that is

---

46. Aristotle *Physics* 194a. Another word for "shape" is *pattern*. Therefore, I would maintain that formal cause includes what Plantinga calls a "design plan" (*Warrant and Proper Function*, 21).

47. Aristotle *Physics* 194b–195a.

already contained in the seed. Hankinson contends, "Such things have a principle of growth and propagation innate to them, a principle which seeks, so far as is compatible with the material exigencies of the environment, to realize itself in an adult instance of the species to which it belongs (and also to propagate further instances of that species)."[48]

Thus, the growth of a natural thing is governed by an internal principle. And Aristotle refers to this internal principle of growth as the nature of the thing. He also says a thing's nature is exhibited in the shape a thing reaches at the end of the growth process: "We also speak of a thing's nature as being exhibited in the process of growth by which its nature is attained. . . . What grows *qua* growing grows from something into something. Into what then does it grow? Not into that from which it arose but into that to which it tends. The shape then is nature."[49] There is a connection here between formal and final causes, for if a thing grows, naturally, from A into B, then A tends to B. That is, B, the terminus of growth, is that at which A aims. The acorn's aim is to be an oak tree. Thus, the tree is the end or goal of the seed. How, then, can we tell that A aims at B? When it comes to natural things, part of the way we tell is from the fact that B is in fact the terminus of the growth process.

But, of course, not all acorns turn into oak trees. The end-state of some acorns is in some little boy's collection of nuts. Such acorns may never be planted and may never grow. Aristotle is surely aware of such situations. Acorns arrive at different end-states. This being the case, not every terminal state of an acorn can be considered to exhibit the acorn's nature in the Aristotelian sense. Indeed, perhaps most acorns fall to the ground and never grow into mature oak trees.[50] In that case, most acorns will fail to exhibit the nature

---

48. Hankinson, "Philosophy of Science," 120; cf. Aristotle *Physics* 192b8–9, 13–14; Aristotle *Metaphysics* 1015a13f, 1043b14 ff.

49. Aristotle *Physics* 193b.

50. To see why the failure of most acorns to become oak trees fails to count against the idea that the purpose of the acorn is to become an oak tree, consider Plantinga's discussion of the proper functioning of one's cognitive faculties:

> it is of first importance to see that this condition—that of one's cognitive equipment functioning *properly*—is not the same thing as one's cognitive equipment functioning *normally*, not, at any rate, if we take the term "normally" in a broadly statistical sense. Even if one of my systems functions in a way far from the statistical norm, it might still be functioning properly. (Alternatively, what we must see is that there is a distinction between a normative and statistical sense of "normal".) Carl Lewis is not defective with respect to jumping by virtue of the fact that he can jump much further than the average person. Perhaps most adult tomcats get into lots of fights and ordinarily move into late middle age with patches of fur torn out; it does not follow that an old tomcat with all of his fur suffers from some sort of tonsorial disorder. Perhaps most male cats get neutered; it does not

of the acorn in the Aristotelian sense. How then can we tell that the acorn exists for the sake of the tree? We know this because the oak tree is the state into which an acorn grows on its own. This is a development arrived at as a result of its own particular structure; it is what the acorn's own pattern produces. There is, to be sure, the matter of having the right sort of environment—a particular thing is not likely to achieve its goal unless it is in the right environment.[51] Soil and water are essential. But granted some basic natural conditions, acorn seeds grow into oak trees according to their own design.

Conversely, nonnatural things, such as artifacts, do not have an internal principle of growth. The form they receive, as Aristotle notes, is imposed from the outside. And things such as constitutions are contrived things, so their forms are also imposed from the outside. In such instances, the connection between formal and final cause is not exhibited in a process of growth or development.[52] Can we then learn anything from the connection of formal to final

---

follow that those that don't are incapable of proper function. If, by virtue of some nuclear disaster, we were nearly all left blind, it would not follow that the few sighted among us would have improperly functioning eyes. So your belief's being produced by your faculties working *normally* or in normal conditions—that is, the sorts of conditions that most frequently obtain—must be distinguished from their working properly. (*Warrant and Proper Function*, 9–10)

In general, the proper function of any particular thing x must be distinguished from most frequent use or working of x.

51. Plantinga shows that the notion of proper function presupposes, in a sense, the notion of right environment. He takes this up in connection with epistemology. Suppose we say that the goal or proper function of our cognitive faculties is the production of true beliefs. With this in mind, Plantinga poses an example:

You have just had your annual cognitive checkup at MIT; you pass with flying colors and are in splendid epistemic condition. Suddenly and without your knowledge you are transported to an environment wholly different from earth; you awake on a planet revolving around Alpha Centauri. There conditions are quite different; elephants we may suppose, are invisible to human beings, but emit a sort of radiation unknown on earth, a sort of radiation that causes human beings to form the belief that a trumpet is sounding nearby. An Alpha Centaurian elephant wanders by; you are subjected to the radiation, and form the belief that a trumpet is sounding nearby. There is nothing wrong with your cognitive faculties; they are working quite properly; still, this belief has little by way of warrant for you. (Ibid., 6–7)

The example shows that cognitive faculties designed to produce true beliefs may well function properly and yet fail to attain their goal—and the problem is clearly that the faculties are not functioning in the appropriate environment. So it is that it only makes sense to say that something that functions properly attains its goal if that thing is functioning in the environment in which it was designed to function.

52. Although one may consider a constitution as setting a polity on a particular trajectory, in which case one might posit a certain end-state or a certain state of development as the goal of a constitution. Of course, here we would have to follow the qualifications already mentioned. Not just any end-state of constitutional development could be characterized as the goal of a constitution. It is always

cause in natural things that will help us here? I believe that we can. First, in natural things, the final cause is the end-state of a process of growth. This means that the goal of a natural thing is the realization of an actual state (or outcome). A natural thing's goal has to do with the actualization of its end-state. But if artifacts can be said to have goals in an analogous way, then, seemingly, the goal of an artifact has to do with the realization of some actual state aimed at by the artifact's organization or pattern. The artifact's pattern aims at the end-state or outcome in the sense that its parts coordinate together to produce the outcome.

Take Aristotle's example of a bed. A bed does not exhibit a process of growth or development. But a bed is constructed according to a pattern that makes it conducive to being slept in. To be sure, a bed can be put to other uses. A bed with a sturdy frame, box springs, and a new mattress is great for bouncing on or diving onto (at least a few times—even well-constructed beds, after all, tend to weather badly if bounced on too often). But the different parts of a bed's design coordinate around having a person sleep in the bed. Two things seem to follow. First, while a bed can be put to uses other than sleeping (bouncing, diving, blocking doorways from unwanted intruders), the best use of the design is for sleeping. Second, if a bed's purpose or goal is to provide a person with rest by providing that person with a place to sleep, then the purpose is an actual state that can be realized. A bed achieves its purpose when the state of having someone sleep in it, thereby receiving rest, is achieved. Thus, even with artifacts, a thing's purpose can be understood as an outcome at which the thing's form, or structural design, aims. Before attempting to refine this, let me put this more succinctly. Given the foregoing, it seems that the purpose of a thing, a thing's telos, is that outcome that is realized as a result of the thing's design. A thing's purpose and its form are analytically distinguishable, and yet intimately related.

This definition, however, needs some refinement. Reconsider, for a moment, our discussion of rule B. We said that some things about the heart suggest that even if it is the best possible ball for a rugbylike game, it seems strange to argue that this is the proper function of the heart in the same way that contributing to the life of the body is the purpose of the heart. Why might one think that? Well, there are all sorts of structural features of the heart that are entirely superfluous in the rugbylike game but that work quite well in pro-

possible, for instance, that the constitution got placed in the wrong environment and led to an outcome not intended by its particular design.

moting the circulation of the blood. Put another way, the various parts of the heart coordinate around the pumping of blood, which when done leads to the health and life of the body. Here I want to pirate terminology used in various sciences and in philosophy of science for my own purposes. What I suggest here is a criterion of *specified complexity*. Consider some artifice, Q, with a number of parts. Q's goal can said to be R if R is an outcome that results, at least in part, from the cooperative activity of Q's coordinate parts.[53] In order to make a goal ascription on this criterion, Q must exhibit some kind of complexity as well as a kind of coordination. As indicated earlier, this does not entail statistical reliability in the production of the outcome in question, and, as with the acorns, the right sort of environment is presumed.

This criterion helps us deal with a particular problem that Alvin Plantinga points to in his treatment of the notion of proper function. Granted that the proper function of a thing has to do with some particular effect or outcome resulting from that thing's design plan, we cannot say that this is true of just any effect or outcome. Plantinga asks us to consider the unintended by-products of a given design. He poses the example of a refrigerator: "I design a refrigerator; one consequence of my design is that when a screwdriver touches a certain wire, the refrigerator will emit a loud angry squawk. I didn't *intend* for it to work this way; I have no interest in its doing that under those conditions and don't care whether it does so or not. Its working that way is no part of the design plan. . . . But of course its working that way is a consequence of how it is designed."[54] Now, let's modify his example. Let's make it so that instead of a squawk, when a certain wire is touched by a screwdriver, the refrigerator emits a perfect concert A—better than any instrument, better than even a tuning fork. Perhaps this makes our refrigerator the best thing in the world for tuning orchestras and pianos and such. Does this mean that this is *the* or even *a* purpose of the refrigerator? It does not, and for just the reasons Plantinga articulates. But more can be said here. If the refrigerator's design existed for the purpose of emitting a concert A, then quite a bit (which is to say, most all) of the refrigerator's design is superfluous. If the refrigerator's goal is to preserve food for consumption by keeping it cool, however, then we can explain all the various parts of the refrigerator's design, because they all coordinate around producing this outcome.

53. I am particularly influenced by Koons's important work *Realism Regained.* All that is required in ascribing a teleofunction, he argues, "is that there exist a number of separate factors whose existence can be economically explained by reference to their common effect" (152).

54. Plantinga, *Warrant and Proper Function,* 24.

To the foregoing, I want to add just a few qualifications by drawing on Ernest Nagel's famous essay entitled "Teleology Revisisted." Nagel develops what he calls the systems-property view of goal-directed behavior. He lays out two criteria of goal-directed processes: plasticity and persistence. He takes the criterion of plasticity to mean that the aim of goal-directed processes "can generally be reached by the system following alternate paths or starting from different initial positions." Persistence, on the other hand, has to do with "the continued maintenance of the system in its goal-directed behavior, by changes occurring in the system that compensate for any disturbances taking place (provided these are not great) either within or external to the system, disturbances which, were there no compensating changes elsewhere, would prevent the realization of the goal."[55] The first criterion, plasticity, requires some elaboration. Nagel holds that plasticity points to a certain independence between the goal of a process and the process itself. If we treat each of these as variables we can say that they exist in an orthogonal relationship to each other—"within certain limits the value of either variable at a given moment is compatible with any value of the other variable at the same moment."[56] To see this more concretely, consider the example of a constitutional process designed to produce laws in keeping with and that promote the common good. For the sake of the example, let's simply postulate that there is a common good, G, without stipulating its contents. Add to this some particular constitutional structure, C, which is designed to bring about the common good. The requirement that these variables be orthogonal means that the common good has an independence from the process that brings it about. We can analyze whether or not it has been realized without analyzing whether or not it was brought about by a certain process. Put another way, C may be sufficient for the realization of G, but it is not necessary for it. All of this suggests that the relationship in view here is contingent rather than necessary. In the sort of analysis I am doing, one way to preserve contingency in the relationship between the various normative propositions and the Constitution is to say what it means for each understanding to obtain prior to our discussion of the Constitution and to construct our list of possible presuppositions prior to our discussion of the Constitution itself. This is just what I will do.

To summarize, teleological explanation can be said to operate in the following way: we ascribe a goal to a thing, Q, when (1) the goal is understood to

---

55. Nagel, *Teleology Revisited*, 286. Interestingly enough, Nagel maintains, "These features can be regarded as identifying marks for ascertaining whether a process has a goal, and if so what it is" (286).
    56. Ibid., 287.

be an outcome resulting from Q's design; (2) Q exhibits coordinated complexity, and it is the coordinated operation of the various components of Q that give rise to the particular outcome; (3) the processes giving rise to the goal and the goal exist in an orthogonal relationship (such that we need not know anything about the process to know whether or not the goal has been realized); and (4) the processes giving rise to the goal work to maintain the goal or outcome despite external factors that may arise and that would otherwise preclude the realization of the goal. None of this involves an appeal to the intentions of the designer (though the attribution of a purpose may nevertheless entail the existence of a designer). Still, we need not say that designers' intentions have no relevance. Robert C. Koons argues that if the designer of Q says that R is the purpose of Q, we are justified in ascribing R as the purpose of Q, if Q does in fact lead to R, to the realization of the specified purpose or goal.[57]

By way of example, consider the Constitution in connection to justice. Let's say that a key part of justice is that people not be deprived of their natural rights. So long as we can stipulate those rights, we can analyze whether or not those rights are being realized, without considering any particular constitutional structure. On this account, justice and the Constitution would be in an orthogonal relationship to each other. Let's add to this that preventing tyranny (whether by the government, a majority, or some privileged minority) is essential to preventing the privation of rights (one might say that tyranny is the privation of rights and therefore unjust by definition). We further add that the Constitution is a complicated instrument with various parts. To ascribe justice (or perhaps the prevention of injustice) as a purpose of the Constitution, all we need add here is (1) that the various parts of the Constitution, working together, produce the outcome of justice (or the prevention of injustice) and (2) that it works to maintain justice (or to maintain the prevention of injustice), even when various factors arise, external to the Constitution, that would, apart from the Constitution's existence, lead to the prevention of justice. For instance, the Constitution must work to prevent government from tyrannizing, even if particularly heinous leaders are elected, and to prevent popular tyranny even if some powerful minority or majority with unjust demands emerges. We might also consider persistence in relation to the separation of powers. Say a goal of the Constitution is the separation of powers. We can posit this as a goal on Nagel's account only if the Constitution has structural features designed to preserve this separation even in the face of factors

---

57. Koons, *Realism Regained*, 152.

that would otherwise thwart the separation. The checks and balances built into the Constitution can be understood as just this. If the Constitution had no checks and balances, just a strict separation of powers, then there would be no mechanism to cope with attempts from some branch (say, the legislature) to aggrandize powers better suited to other branches. But consider the veto power of the president and judicial review. These are ways of thwarting attempted legislative aggrandizements. An unjust majority may form in the legislature and may desire to acquire more power. To gain more power, this majority may desire to obliterate the separation of powers. But the Constitution places tools in the hands of the other branches with which they can resist these advances, and then the Constitution arguably provides incentive for the officers in those branches to use these defensive tools. This meets the criterion of persistence required by Nagel for goal-ascription.

Conclusion

Given the foregoing journey, it is important to summarize our methodology. When it comes to the Constitution's moral assumption in some particular normative category, we begin by trying to deduce a contradiction between something in the Constitution's structure or entailed by that structure with as many of the assumptions in the category under consideration as possible. That is, given a list of possible truth statements concerning a category such as the common good, we attempt to eliminate as many of the options as we can by finding something in the Constitution that stands in contradiction with them. At the second stage, we try to figure out which moral assumption in a category is the most consilient and the most simple—which moral assumption explains or is consistent with the most constitutional features and which assumption requires the least auxiliary hypotheses in the course of providing an explanation. At the third stage, we advance to the teleological level of explanation. We treat the moral assumptions as goals or outcomes at which the Constitution aims. If, for example, the common good is an outcome resulting from the Constitution's basic design, then it can be considered a goal of the Constitution. We only make this inference, however, if the outcome is achieved as a result of different parts of the Constitution working together to produce it and if the outcome is something the Constitution works to produce even in the face of countervailing factors or circumstances. If a particular normative understanding, then, does not exist in contradiction with some fundamental aspect of the Constitution's structure, if it is the simplest and most consilient explanation of the Constitution's basic arrangement, and if it is an outcome produced as a result of the Constitution's design (as qualified above), then this moral assumption is not only the best fit, comparatively speaking, but also a good fit on its own terms. We are justified in inferring that the Constitution makes such a moral assumption.

— 3 —

The Constitution's Theory
of Sovereignty

HAVING SEEN THE need for and having developed a new approach to uncovering the Constitution's moral design, it is now incumbent upon us to apply the new approach to the normative categories discussed in the previous chapters. For reasons that will become apparent in chapter 4, sovereignty is the appropriate place to begin. Before unearthing just how the Constitution institutionalizes sovereignty, however, we must first give attention to the concept itself. In this chapter, I argue that we must not understand sovereignty as the exercise of certain governmental powers such as making laws and punishing transgressors. True sovereigns might delegate certain of their powers. Sovereignty must be understood as the right to determine what shall or shall not be law by giving consent to what will or to what has already gone into effect. I also argue that the Constitution, inasmuch as it presupposes the existence of a sovereign, may presuppose one of four understandings about the locus and extent of sovereignty: the sovereign is (1) wholly popular and constrained; (2) wholly popular and unconstrained; (3) not wholly popular (including not-at-all popular) and constrained; or (4) not wholly popular and unconstrained. I contend that if we apply the methodology elaborated in chapter 2, then the latter three options fall away, leaving us with the conclusion that the Constitution presumes the sovereign to be both popular and constrained.

Sovereignty Defined

Sovereignty is a slippery concept. It seems virtually impossible to define it in a way that is not normatively loaded. If, on the one hand, we say the sovereign is the one with the power to get others in a society to do whatever he wants, then the normative presuppositions tend to be positivistic or relativistic. If, on the other hand, we say the sovereign is the one with the right to command, and therefore to oblige, citizens however he sees fit for the preservation of the state, then the normative assumptions tend to be modern.[1] Finally, if we say the sovereign is the one whose commands are binding so long as they promote the common good and do not contravene the natural law (traditionally defined), then the normative assumptions are classical. Defining sovereignty in any of these ways will cause the ensuing chapters to beg the question.[2] For the normative theory of the Constitution can be elaborated simply by stipulating that there is a sovereign.[3] Take the case in which we stipulate that there is a sovereign and in which we've accepted the definition of sovereignty offered by the classical tradition. Having done so, we could then simply unpack the definition of sovereign. "Ah, the sovereign is the one whose commands oblige us to obey when those commands are in keeping with the common good and do not contravene the natural law. And the common good is nothing other than the realization of *eudaemonia* as described by Aristotle. And the only way to achieve this common good is by following natural laws

1. Given the way that I use the term *modern* in this work, Creon, from Sophocles' *Antigone,* must be considered an archmodern. According to Creon, "The man the city sets up in authority must be obeyed in small things and in just but also in their opposites" (720). The obligation to obedience, Creon implies, supersedes the obligations of justice. Why is the obligation to obedience so high that it overthrows even the demands of justice? Creon contends, "There is nothing worse than disobedience to authority. It destroys cities, it demolishes homes; it breaks and routs one's allies. Of successful lives the most of them are saved by discipline. So we must stand on the side of what is orderly" (730). All of this has a very Hobbesian ring.

2. There are three ways in which one might commit the logical fallacy of begging the question. The first is by leaving a key premise out of an argument "while conveying the impression that nothing more is needed to establish the conclusion." The second way is when the premise of an argument "merely restates in the conclusion in slightly different language." And the third is to reason in a circle. The reference to the fallacy above is to the second way of committing the fallacy (Hurley, *A Concise Introduction to Logic,* 158–59).

3. It is my belief that much writing on the Constitution does just this. I recall reading an article and a book that mentioned the tension in the Constitution between higher law principles and popular sovereignty. Both authors believed that such a tension existed simply because there was a popular sovereign, which they apparently took to presume the truth of positivistic normative theory or positivistic majoritarianism (See Robert G. McCloskey, *The American Supreme Court,* 6–8; Leslie Friedman Goldstein, "Popular Sovereignty, the Origins of Judicial Review, and the Revival of Unwritten Law").

described by Aquinas, laws known to us as he describes, via inclination." But then there would be no need to investigate the Constitution itself in order to ascertain its normative theory.

True though the above is, we must not let the insight push us into a different error. For the way in which a constitution institutionalizes sovereignty (say, for example, by seeking to institutionalize a constrained or an unconstrained sovereign) will have normative implications. That this is so does not mean the question has been begged. People sometimes mistakenly confuse logical implication with the fallacy of begging the question. I, however, will be seeking in the chapters that follow to show the normative implications of the Constitution's theory of sovereignty in a way that does not beg the question.

I propose stipulating a minimal definition of sovereignty, one to which adherents of various normative theories might all be willing to subscribe. This definition will leave open the locus of sovereignty (the question of who is sovereign: a monarch, a group of people, or all the people together); the question of whether the origin of sovereign power is popular or nonpopular (and if it is nonpopular, whether it is so by virtue of having been transferred from the community to a sovereign it establishes or by virtue of never having been popular to begin with); and the question of whether or not the sovereign's will is constrained.[4] However one defines sovereignty, it seems clear that it is logically possible for the sovereign to be popular, nonpopular, constrained, unconstrained, created by a transfer of popular right or not, and so on. Furthermore, the Constitution's answer to the foregoing questions can and should be inferred from its design. Thus our initial definition really ought not settle these matters. Bearing all this in mind, then, I offer the following definition of sovereignty: the sovereign is the one with the final say as to what shall or shall not be law and the one whose authority sanctions coercive enforcement of the law.[5]

Consider the definition I offer here in light of a different definition of sovereign power. One might be tempted to think that sovereign power resides in the one who creates laws, where the creative act in mind involves writing the laws, having an immediate say in whether or not the law goes into effect and a direct role in enforcement and application. These things are sometimes considered the parts of sovereign power or the functions of the sovereign. The observation that these are the parts of sovereign power is sometimes followed by

4. I deal with the question of the coherence of constrained sovereignty in the section entitled "Possible Conceptions of Sovereignty."

5. To borrow from J. Budziszewski, sovereignty is "where-the-buck-stops-ness."

the suggestion that these parts must be placed in the same hands (whether a king, a council, or the people as a whole). The idea is that the sovereign is the one who performs these functions and that the same person or body of persons must perform them all. We cannot lodge the legislative part of sovereignty in one set of hands and the executive or judicial parts in other hands. If the sovereign is truly sovereign, then he or they must exercise all the parts of sovereignty *so that* all these parts are exercised by the same, unified will. For unless the various parts are exercised by one will, each part will become empty and the attempt to exercise each function fruitless. If this line of thinking is correct, then to identify who the Constitution presumes to be sovereign we need only to find that person (or group) who performs these particular functions. I disagree with the assertion that the sovereign must perform directly the functions just described and with the suggestion that all the so-called parts of sovereignty must be placed in the same set of hands. But I want to consider why one might hold such a view by reflecting on the arguments of Samuel Pufendorf before advancing a criticism of this view.

For Pufendorf, the sovereign exists to bring about the attainment of the ends for which the state was created. Accordingly, doing what is necessary to realize those ends belongs to sovereign power. There are a number of ends and, correspondingly, a number of aspects (or parts) of sovereign power. Pufendorf therefore divides supreme sovereignty into a number of different components, all of which must be possessed by the same person or body of persons (whether an assembly of a few or the entire community). The sovereign's first role is to "indicate and prescribe what they [the members of the community] ought to do" and to do this with general rules that make clear to all "what things ought to be done or omitted." In addition to this, the sovereign has the responsibility of ensuring what the Constitution refers to as domestic tranquility—that is, the securing of peace and safety among the members of the community. This is done by creating a fear of the punishments that fall upon breakers of the law. The third part of sovereign power is judicial power: "It is the task of this judicial authority to hear and decide the disputes of citizens, to examine the deeds of individuals alleged to be contrary to the laws, and to assign a penalty appropriate to the laws." All of this effort to ensure domestic tranquility is for naught unless an adequate defense against external dangers is provided for. This also belongs to sovereign power, for this is one of the ends for which the state was created. Entailed here is the sovereign's power to declare war or peace. As a result, says Pufendorf, the sovereign has the role of raising an army to provide for the common defense. The sovereign cannot perform any of these functions unless he also has the power to raise the funds necessary for doing these things. Hence, the power of levying and collecting taxes is also annexed to sovereign power. Finally, it belongs to the sovereign to ensure as much agreement of opinion as possible among the people. This is to avoid the clash that invariably follows from each individual following his own opinion of good and evil.[6]

Pufendorf maintains that the parts of sovereign power must all be exercised directly by whoever is designated sovereign and that these roles cannot be separated or filled by different persons or groups of people. He argues,

> those who wish to maintain that, in one and the same state, the parts of sovereignty called potential belong in a fundamental sense to several distinct persons or councils, they must also admit that one to whom the same part of the sovereignty belongs must necessarily be furnished with the authority to compel the citizens to observe the things instituted by virtue of that part, and to defend that right of his if anyone should wish to attack or disturb it, even when the right of war belongs to someone else; and finally, that he can determine according to his own judgment and by his own right the time and manner in which that part of the sovereignty is to be exercised. For it is anything but sovereignty to have only the right to indicate to others what you wish them to do, and yet to lack the power also to compel those who are reluctant to observe what has been indicated.[7]

From these reflections, he concludes,

> the conjunction of all the parts of the supreme sovereignty is such that one part cannot be torn from the other without the regular form of the state being destroyed, resulting in an irregular body held together only by an infirm pact. For if the legislative authority belongs in the end to one part and the punitive power to another, fundamentally and independently to each, either

---

6. Pufendorf, *On the Law of Nature and of Nations*, bk. 7, chap. 4, secs. 2, 4, 5, 7, 8. According to Pufendorf,

> Now since all voluntary actions are initiated by and dependent on the will, but the will to do or not to do something depends on the opinion of the good or evil, reward or punishment, that everyone conceives will follow for himself from his deed or omission (and the actions of all are therefore ruled by each person's own opinion), there will surely be need for external means so that those opinions and judgments do as much as possible agree or at least so that their discrepancy does not disturb the state. Hence it is expedient that the state publicly profess, as it were, doctrines that agree with the end and function of states, and also that the minds of citizens be imbued with them from childhood.

7. Ibid., bk. 7, chap. 4, sec. 10.

the former will necessarily be without substance or the latter will minister to it. This is because passing laws which you are unable to put into effect is a hollow exercise, and to have the strength by which you may compel others, but only if another decides that it should be brought to bear, is characteristic of a minister or a bare executor. But if you also give the latter the privilege of making an informed judgment about the application of his own strength, you by the same act reduce the legislative authority to nothing. It is necessary, that both faculties depend on one and the same will.[8]

We might characterize Pufendorf's theory of sovereignty as follows. Individuals come together and create the state in order to achieve peace among themselves and protection from outsiders. But the creation of the state is pointless unless someone or some group is given the power to achieve these goals. Thus, there must be some entity that can express a will that puts into effect the means for achieving these ends, an entity to whose will all individual wills are subordinated. But unless there is only one such will, the goal will not be achieved or will not regularly be achieved due to the clashing of the various wills attempting to exercise sovereign power. The reason for having created the sovereign in the first place is, in such a case, nullified. And unless the sovereign has significant power to secure obedience to his one will, then the

---

8. Ibid., bk. 7, chap. 4, sec. 11. The same reasoning applies to the other parts of supreme sovereignty as enumerated by Pufendorf (bk. 7, chap. 5, sec. 7):

> [It] is obvious that the right of war and peace, and the right to impose taxes, cannot be separated from this right. For no one can rightfully compel citizens to take up arms, or to assume the expenses of war and peace, unless he can rightfully punish those who do not comply. It would be absurd, moreover, to assign the right of making treaties conducive to peace and war to someone other than the one who has the right to decide about war and peace. For in that case either the latter will be a pure minister or the former will depend on someone else's decision in readying the means useful for the exercise of his own right. Thus, if you wished to entrust a certain matter to someone yet did not at the same time give him the authority to constitute and hold accountable the ministers without whom it cannot be accomplished, you would in fact make him the ministers' equal. Therefore, the authority to constitute magistrates cannot be separated from the remaining parts of the supreme sovereignty.

Finally, Pufendorf maintains that the part of sovereign authority dealing with the examination of doctrines must be lodged in the same hands as all the other parts of sovereignty.

> For if someone has commanded the citizens to do something on pain of natural death and another persuades them that by doing it they will incur the punishment of eternal death, and each by his own separate and independent right, it not only follows that citizens can by right be punished even though they are innocent, but also that the civil state will be reduced to an irregular status where it has two heads. For no one can serve two masters, and he who we believe must be followed on fear of eternal punishment is no less a master than he who is obeyed on fear of temporal death.

mere existence of a unified sovereignty is pointless because that one will cannot have effect unless the sovereign can ensure that it will be followed.[9]

Given the nature of this study, it is important to ascertain what a popular
sovereign looks like within a Pufendorfian framework. Popular sovereignty, in
this framework, can only be established with some version of direct democracy. Thus, Pufendorf says, to have a democracy the people must establish "a
certain place and time . . . for assemblies where the pubic interest is to be de-
liberated and decided."[10] He knows, of course, that the people as a whole can-

---

9. Consider all of this in a slightly different light. Individuals come together for the ends just mentioned. These ends can only be achieved if the individuals are bound together in a sufficiently strong
manner. Now, per Pufendorf, there are two ways by which the wills of many men and groups can be
connected. These are pact and sovereignty. A pact is like a mutual promise without any coercive element. In this case, people pledge to each other to live in peace and to lend mutual support against
others who would harm some member of the pact. In contrast, sovereignty introduces coercive enforcement of rules governing social order. Because pacts lack any coercive element, they provide an
insufficiently strong bond for holding people together. For while one violates the natural law in breaking a pact, those "in whose interest it was that the pact be kept, have nothing with which to bring the
violator back into line besides violent war, in which he who did the injury predominates as often as
the one who received it." "It appears from this that pacts alone are not sufficiently strong bonds, at
least for keeping many persons collected into one moral body for a long time, especially since it is not
always the few and the weak who depart from a pact to the detriment of those more numerous and
strong, but also the many to the detriment of the few." In contrast, sovereignty provides a stronger
bond than a pact for holding a group of people together because "those who are held together by the
same sovereignty do not remain equal to the one in whom it resides. Rather, when one man or council has conferred on it the authority to issue prescriptions and to threaten those who neglect to obey
them with some evil punishment, there is incumbent on everyone a far greater necessity to obey than
if they were bound by a pact alone, by which the equality among allies and the right of each to decide about his own things according to his own judgment is not eliminated." What, then, is the bond
of sovereignty? It is the submission of individual wills to another single will charged with the protection and preservation of the community, to a will sufficiently strong to ensure domestic peace and
safety from outside threat by virtue of its ability to say what shall and shall not be done and by virtue
of its strength to ensure compliance with its decrees by punishing transgressors and by establishing
sufficiently strong punishments to induce the obedience, through fear, of those who would otherwise
transgress the rules of social order, and to a will able to wage war against external threats when they
arise (a will with the ability to declare war or peace, to raise and maintain an army and to levy taxes
for the purposes of supporting war efforts). For any of this to work, the sovereign cannot be the same
as a mere collection of individual wills. Even in a democracy, Pufendorf considers the citizens assembled together to be one moral person. The majority determines the precise direction of this will,
but each individual will has been submitted to the unified will of this moral person—a will that legislates, judges, and directs execution and does these things to secure peace among and protection for
those who have joined together in mutual society. After all, a will that does not extend to all the parts
of supreme sovereignty is too weak to serve as a bond for society, and a weak bond does not provide
the requisite incentive for individuals to behave in ways conducive to the society's preservation. If the
parts of sovereignty are in different hands and there is a clash of wills, then there is a question about
what will to obey. People may be directed in opposite ways by clashing sovereign wills. Or they may
conclude that there is no need to pay attention to any of it. All of the quotations in this note are from
Pufendorf, *On the Law of Nature and of Nations,* bk. 7, chap. 5, sec. 7.

10. Ibid.

not be constantly assembled and that it is inconvenient for the people to have to come together with great frequency. He therefore allows that the people may delegate a council to handle everyday affairs. Even so, the council can only take action with respect to those affairs. This council can look into important matters but cannot decide on such matters. All important matters must be referred directly to the citizens when they assemble together. All important legislative, executive, and judicial decisions must, in principle, be made by the people in assembly. Popular sovereignty, on Pufendorf's theory, is rather like ancient democracy.

To summarize Pufendorf's understanding, to legislate, to judge, to determine war and peace, to raise armies, to levy taxes, and to enforce the will decreed in legislation is what it means to be sovereign. The one who does these things is by definition the sovereign. You find the sovereign in any given political system by looking for the person (or the people) who performs these functions.

As I have said, I am inclined to think a bit differently about sovereignty. As I see it, the concept of sovereignty does not, by itself, tell you who actually possesses it—that is, it does not tell you that the person (or group of people) who legislates is in every instance sovereign—or dictate who must. Thus, while the sovereign may exercise all the parts of Pufendorf's supreme sovereignty, he (or they) doesn't have to do so. The parts of sovereignty can in fact be delegated and delegated in such a way that the sovereign has almost no hand in these activities. It follows that legislative, executive, and judicial functions might indeed be placed in different hands, for a sovereign might choose to delegate these different functions to other people or groups of people. But how can a sovereign delegate to others what many have deemed to be essential characteristics of sovereignty and still remain sovereign? The fact is that the exercise of these functions is not essential to sovereign power. It is sufficient for the sovereign to be able to weigh in on how these functions are performed, so long as the sovereign is possessed of a final determining power should he decide to exercise it—a power to override, for instance, the decision of the legislature as to what shall be law or of the executive as to what laws shall be given effect.

Let's approach the matter by considering a historical example. During the Roman Empire, emperors did quite a bit of governing by delegation. Many conquered lands were governed by Roman proconsuls who were given great discretion in overseeing the territories assigned to them.[11] The authority of

---

11. My understanding of Roman government is shaped by the great historian A. N. Sherwin-White's

such proconsuls extended to legislative and judicial as well as executive matters. Granting for a moment that Rome was rightly sovereign over her conquered territories and that the proconsuls exercised many or all of the parts of sovereign power over the territories assigned to them, it does not follow that the proconsuls were sovereign or even partly sovereign, at least not in any ultimate sense. Nor does it imply that the proconsuls possessed sovereignty because they exercised the parts of sovereign power and that the emperor (or, nominally, the Senate) did not possess sovereignty over those same territories on the grounds that he (or they) did not exercise the parts of sovereign power over those same territories. After all, whether the emperor called the proconsuls to account or not, it was his (and, nominally, the Senate's) prerogative to do so. Power was retained in Rome to relieve proconsuls of their duty and even to undo or countermand their actions. Imperial legislation also set boundaries for proconsul action. Thus, proconsuls were not sovereign because the final say about their actions did not rest with them. Yet they did exercise all the parts of sovereign power. It follows that exercising all the various parts of sovereignty is not a necessary condition for predicating sovereign power of some person or group of persons.[12]

Note carefully what this means. The definition I have offered as sufficient for sovereignty leaves open the question of whether those exercising the legislative, executive, and judicial functions are in fact sovereign. He, she, or they might be, but, then again, those exercising these functions may have been delegated these tasks by the sovereign. To determine if this is the case, we will have to see if the consent of some other person or persons is required for laws and for the application and enforcement of the laws to retain their effectiveness.

---

seminal study *Roman Society and Roman Law in the New Testament*. See especially "Lecture One: 'Coercitio', 'cognito', and 'imperium' in the first century A.D." Speaking of the Julio-Claudian period of Roman history, Sherwin-White wrote, "Unless the proconsul offended the wealthy magnates of his province, he was unlikely to be called to account at Rome for abuse of power when his proconsulship was over. He was under no compulsion to consult the Senate, which was his nominal director, and still less the Princeps, about the problems of his province. Having the *imperium*, the proconsul had the total power of administration, jurisdiction, defense—in so far as that arose—and the maintenance of public order" (2).

12. It is possible that someone will object that while exercising the various so-called parts of sovereignty is not essential to sovereignty, the capacity or ability to exercise them is essential. This is no real objection to my argument. For all I have said is that *the sovereign doesn't have to exercise them.* But let's set that aside. Our objector's point is not at all obviously true. For one could exercise final say as to how the parts of sovereignty are exercised without ever exercising the "parts of sovereign power." And this observation seems sufficient to conclude that possession of the capacity to exercise the "parts of sovereign power" is *not* essential for the possession of sovereign power.

In other words, to determine whether or not the hands into which legislative, executive, and judicial functions are placed are in fact those of the sovereign, we have to determine whether those hands do in fact have the final say when it comes to law or whether those with the power to make law and put it into effect depend on the consent of some higher authority for the laws they make to stay in effect. One way to do this is to see if there are institutional constraints that cause those officials performing legislative, executive, and judicial functions to seek the approval of some yet higher will, a will that has the power to say whether these governmental functions have been rightly exercised. A constitution, for instance, might turn the eyes of governmental officials constantly toward the people and cause them to constantly seek popular approval. Or, conversely, a constitution might seek to make those exercising legislative, executive, and judicial powers sovereign over the community by distancing government officials from the passing whims of the popular will.

In sum, whether or not sovereignty is absolute or constrained, popular or transferred cannot be determined by definition. Nor can we simply say that the sovereign is the person, or the group of people, who makes, applies, and enforces the laws and who secures the community from external threats. A proper definition of sovereignty leaves all these things open. Thus, to rearticulate that definition, the sovereign has the final say as to what shall or shall not be law and the authority to sanction coercive enforcement of the law.[13] When it comes to the Constitution, we will have to analyze the Constitution itself in order to determine who is sovereign and whether or not the sovereign exercises or delegates legislative, executive, and judicial functions. In analyzing the Constitution, we will, in part, be looking to see if those exercising legislative, executive, and judicial powers are constrained in some sense by the will of a higher authority. If those exercising these functions are constrained by some other human power, neither the legislature nor the executive nor the judiciary nor all these together can be called the supreme sovereign. Indeed, the sovereign will be the one who has delegated these powers and the one upon whose consent the highest governmental officials depend in order for their actions to have authority.

---

13. Another way to define sovereignty is to say that the sovereign is the one with final say as to the exercise of Pufendorf's parts of sovereign power, whether or not that one exercises that say so directly. I think this is covered by the first definition. But for those who read it differently, then this definition should suffice.

Possible Presuppositions of Sovereignty

If we are to determine the Constitution's theory of sovereignty using the method outlined in chapter 2, then we need a list of possible theories. The disaggregation and conceptual reorganization at the end of chapter 1 generated just such a list:

1. *Positivist:* The Constitution presupposes that the people retain an unconstrained sovereignty. They authorize officials and institutions to carry out their will, and they are free to command anything.

2. *Modernist:* The Constitution presupposes that the people transfer sovereignty from themselves to the authority they establish. That authority is then free to command however it sees fit. The sovereignty of the governing authority, not that of the people, is unconstrained.

3. *Classical:* The Constitution presupposes a sovereign constrained by the dictates of justice, whether this sovereign be popular, mixed, etc.

This list provides us with three distinct understandings of the origin, locus, and extent of sovereignty. Each of these positions reflects positional commitments along two different dimensions of sovereignty. The first measures the degree to which the sovereign is popular, the second the degree to which sovereignty is constrained. These dimensions can be dichotomized. Sovereignty is either wholly popular or not wholly popular and either constrained or unconstrained. Table 3.1 reflects these two dimensions. The vertical dimension measures whether or not sovereignty is popular and the horizontal dimension whether or not it is constrained:

Table 3.1

(a) Wholly Popular and Constrained	(c) Wholly Popular and Unconstrained
(b) Not Wholly Popular (or Nonpopular) and Constrained	(d) Not Wholly Popular (or Nonpopular) and Unconstrained

There are three things about this table that should be immediately noted. First, and most important, the Constitution can fit into one and only one cell, for the cells are mutually exclusive. But, second, the cells are not quite exhaustive. There is a prima facie possibility that the Constitution presupposes that there is no sovereign at all. I find this implausible for a number of reasons. Most significantly, it seems obvious that if a "political system" lacks a sovereign under the definition provided above, then, it is not really a political system at all. Rather, such a state of affairs seems to be a state of anarchy rather than a state of political society, at least in any meaningful sense of the phrase. In addition, I argue that the Constitution presupposes a sovereign *because* the people as a whole possess the kind of *final say* discussed in the previous section. And third, we should note how our initial possible presuppositions relate to this table. Positivist belongs in cell (c); the modernist in (d), except in the case of direct democracy in which case it belongs in (c); and classical belongs in (a) or (b), depending on whether the sovereign is the people, not the people, or mixed. A balance of orders system belongs in cell (b).

A brief word is necessary concerning a key modern assumption about sovereignty. Political theorists of a modernist bent, and many of those we would call social contract theorists (but who are properly called social compact theorists),[14] believe that the origin of all sovereignty is popular. However sovereignty may be institutionalized, whoever may be established as sovereign, the right of sovereign power originally belongs to individuals who come together and in a covenant or compact agree to lay their power aside and establish a sovereign sufficiently strong to secure domestic peace and to protect society against outsiders. In setting up the sovereign, each individual transfers his individual sovereignty first to the community and then to the sovereign established by the community.[15] Now say this sovereign set up by the people is a monarchy or an aristocracy. In such cases it seems that sovereignty is popular in origin but then no longer popular after the sovereign has been created. Perhaps it is even possible to create a constitutional government with elected officials and to transfer sovereignty to offices created in the writing of a constitution, offices then filled by election. Here again we would say that the original source of sovereignty is the people, but that the people are no longer sovereign, having surrendered that power to the person or council they have established. My contention is that sovereigns who receive power in such a transfer, because such sovereignty, at day's end, is not-at-all-popular, fall into the "Not Wholly Popular" row, *unless* the sovereign established is the will of the whole

---

14. See Donald Lutz, *Origins of American Constitutionalism*, 16–22, esp. 18.

15. Hobbes's *Leviathan* fits this pattern (with the amendment that for Hobbes the covenant is made among the members of the community, but individual sovereignty is transferred directly from the individual to the newly created sovereign), but so does Locke's *Two Treatises* as well as other works of political philosophy influenced by covenantal theology. See Lutz, *Origins of American Constitutionalism;* Charles S. McCoy and J. Wayne Baker, *Fountainhead of Federalism: Heinrich Bullinger and the Covenantal Tradition;* and Daniel J. Elazar's magisterial *The Covenant Tradition in Politics,* vols. 1–4.

community. In that case, while individuals may in fact transfer individual sovereignty to the will of the community as a whole, we might still accurately describe the sovereign as popular. But in those circumstances where the community as a whole does choose to establish a sovereign other than the community itself by transferring sovereign power, then sovereign power is really transferred away from the community. It makes no sense to say that the community is the real sovereign simply because the creation of the sovereign derives from a communal act. What something is and how it came to be are not the same thing.[16] Put another way, even if the origin of all sovereignty is popular, it does not follow that the people are sovereign now. Some maintain that the community could never relinquish sovereign power. Perhaps this is so; but if it can and if it does, then it has in fact transferred sovereignty away and is therefore, by implication, no longer sovereign. In this chapter, we want to know who the Constitution considers sovereign now—the governmental officials engaged in legislative, executive, and judicial activities, the states, or the people.

Another word of clarification is needed here. Some might object to the table containing a dimension measuring whether or not sovereignty is constrained. Sovereignty is sometimes said to be inherently absolute. A sovereign can be called absolute in two different senses. Sometimes when political theorists refer to the sovereign as absolute, they simply mean that the sovereign possesses final say. That is, there is no other human will over the will of the sovereign to which one can appeal. The sovereign is the final human authority, the highest rung of authority on the ladder of obligation when it comes to laws framed by men.[17] But absolute can also mean uncontrollable. Hobbes says,

> It is evident therefore that in every commonwealth there is some *one man* or
> *one assembly* [concilium] or *council* [curia], which has by right as much power over individual citizens as each man has over himself outside of the commonwealth, that is, *sovereign* or *absolute* power, which is to be limited only by the strength of the commonwealth and not by anything else. For if its pow-

16. To say that it is, is to commit the genetic fallacy. According to Peter A. Angeles, in *The Harper Collins Dictionary of Philosophy,* the genetic fallacy is "(a) arguing that the origin of something is identical with that from which it originates. Example: 'Consciousness originates in neural processes. Therefore, consciousness is (nothing but) neural processes.' (b) appraising or explaining something in terms of its origin, source, or beginnings. (c) arguing that something is to be rejected because its origins are known and/or are suspicious." (110)

17. Perhaps this is what Jean Bodin meant when he referred to the sovereign as "absolute" (*On Sovereignty,* bk. 1, chap. 8. This Cambridge edition excerpts from Bodin's *Republique*).

er is to be limited, it has to be by a greater power than the one restrained by limits. The restraining power therefore is either without limit, or is restrained in its turn by a greater power; and so it will come down at last to a power without other limit than that set by the strength of all the citizens together in its full extent. This is the so-called *sovereign power.*[18]

According to Hobbes, then, there can be no will over the sovereign's will, controlling him. For if there is such a will, then that will is sovereign. If that will is the will of the community, then, per Hobbes, the community never surrendered its sovereign power but retained it. For Hobbes, the sovereign's will is absolute in the sense that there is nothing over it to control it. It is therefore unconstrained. The sovereign is free to do as he pleases, though doing this might not be advisable. All absolute sovereigns, in the Hobbesian sense, belong in the unconstrained column of the table.

But I see no reason to believe that Hobbes is all right about this. Perhaps one can maintain with some theoretical plausibility that sovereignty should not be constrained. But one cannot claim that it cannot be solely on the grounds that it should not be. If it should not be constrained, it at least remains theoretically possible that sovereignty can be poorly institutionalized, perhaps by constraining it. And the constraining will need be none other than the sovereign's. Hobbes will, naturally, protest that this makes no sense: "No one can give anything to himself, because he is already assumed to have what he can give to himself. Nor can one be obligated to oneself; for since *the obligated and the obligating party* would be the same, and the obligating party may release the obligated, obligation to oneself would be meaningless, because he can release himself at his own discretion, and anyone who can do this is in fact free."[19] In other words, if the sovereign has constrained himself by his own will, then by his own will he can simply remove the constraint. He is only subject to the constraint in the sense that he desires to behave in a particular way. But should he decide to behave differently, there is no real obstacle in his way. Granting that Hobbes may have a point, I am unwilling to concede that the notion of real self-limitation is philosophically incoherent. Hobbes's argument turns on the premise that for any person (or sovereign) x who imposes any limitation, y, upon himself, then x is capable of removing y anytime x

18. Hobbes, *On the Citizen*, 88.
19. Ibid., 84. One can easily replace "obligation" with "self-limitation" in the preceding citation. Can't anyone who limits himself and who is not being limited by someone above him simply cast the limit aside? But this is to beg the question. The appropriate response is "possibly not."

pleases. But why should anyone accept this premise? There doesn't seem to be any reason, which is probably why Hobbes asserts rather than argues for it. Thus, beyond mere assertion, there doesn't seem any reason to maintain that the notion of self-limitation is incoherent. There does seem to be, however, good reason to accept the possibility of real self-limitation.[20] And so long as the notion of self-limitation makes sense, then the sovereign can in fact impose real limits upon himself. And I see no reason that he might not do this in ways that do not abdicate sovereign authority.[21]

Finding the Constitution's Theory of Sovereignty

The Field of Facts

In order to put to use the methodology developed in the first two chapters, we need to establish a field of facts for two reasons: First, we need to identify constitutional features if we are to deduce contradictions between the Constitution and various theories of sovereignty, the common good, natural law, and natural rights. Second, we need a field of facts that competing theories

20. On this matter, see Eleonore Stump's important article, "Augustine on Free Will," chap. 10, esp. 127–28. Let me present Stump's example. Consider the case of an agent who has two preferences in conflict with each other. She has a lower order preference, an appetite, to smoke, and a higher order preference (perhaps motivated by a concern for her well-being) to not smoke. Now suppose that in terms of motivating action the preference to smoke always carries the day and, other things equal, always will. But suppose our agent recognizes her desire not to smoke as the better preference and really wants to do what's best but is simply too weak to resist the temptation to smoke. Further, suppose someone has created a device that will remove the desire to smoke. Perhaps the device is a brain implant or some such thing that overrides the desire to smoke every time the desire arises. Suppose even further that accepting the implant is a once-and-for-all decision. Then receiving the device will indeed be a matter of self-limitation. And the agent will really be constrained by the choice. She is making a choice at moment T1 to restrain the field of choices for all future moments (T2, T3, T4 . . . Tn). Such a case does not seem implausible or philosophically incoherent. In fact, it seems like just the sort of choice free and responsible agents might make. But if that's the case, then the notion of self-limitation is indeed coherent, even when the limitation, once imposed, cannot be removed.

21. One might also consider the instance of divine sovereignty. Whether or not one believes in God, if he exists, then he is surely a sovereign for which there is no true parallel. If any sovereign is unconstrained, then surely God is. But Plantinga, the foremost philosopher of religion in the United States, has demonstrated that God faces limitations imposed by his nature (see *Does God Have a Nature?*). He also shows that if God chooses to create creatures with libertarian free will, then the sort of world God chooses to actualize is limited by the choices of those creatures. Thus it is logically possible that creatures possessed of libertarian agency go wrong in every possible world and that God cannot therefore create a world with creatures of libertarian agency in which they do not go wrong (see *The Nature of Necessity*, esp. chap. 9). All of this means that it is simply nonsense to insist that sovereignty, as a matter of definition, be unlimited, which is to say, unconstrained.

seek to explain in order to call one of them best. In this, and in the remaining chapters, we will use the following field of facts:

1. The popular components, whether direct or indirect, in selection of the president, members of the House and Senate, and members of the Court.

2. The nonpopular or, at least, indirect-popular features for selecting members of the court and electing presidents.

3. The constitutional separation of powers or functions into three branches with the preponderance of legislative power going to Congress, the bulk of executive power being vested in the president, and the majority of judicial power going to the Courts.

4. Constitutional checks in which powers are overlapped rather than being entirely separated.

5. Length of terms for elected and appointed offices, especially senators, the president, and justices.

6. The partly national, partly federal structure of the system as a whole.

7. The delegation of specific powers to the Congress, rather than a general grant, including Article 1, Section 8, detailing the delegation/enumeration of legislative powers.

8. Limitations on power, including restrictions on the power of the federal government (e.g., Article 1, Section 9 and the Bill of Rights), and restrictions on the power of the states (e.g., Article 1, Section 10, the supremacy clause, and the post–Civil War amendments).

9. The vast extent of territory covered by the union—the extended sphere —together with the large population and therefore large number of factions embraced within this sphere.

10. The proportionately small size of the legislature.

11. The election of representatives from single-member districts.

I anticipate two sorts of objectors. The first maintains that some important facts have been left out. I am not sure what those might be. But for the objector to succeed, he'll have to show how the relevant facts topple the conclusions I draw. The second argues that I have included facts that do not belong. For instance, the Constitution nowhere requires single-member districts.[22] But I consider the Constitution to be a pattern of institutional arrangements, and the fact that representatives are all elected to the Congress from single-mem-

22. See Christopher L. Eisgruber, *Constitutional Self-Government*, 15.

ber districts seems to be a part of the overall institutional structure. In fact, if the states decided to shift to some sort of proportional method in selecting representatives, turning the whole states into multimember districts, we might consider this an alteration of the Constitution's structure. Indeed, it would be much like amending the Constitution, though there need be no amendment process to effect this particular change. On the other hand, I do not think a change of this nature would undo the argument I advance herein.[23]

Inference to the Best Explanation, Stage 1: Eliminating Possible Propositions

In Table 3.1 we laid out four possibilities: the Constitution presupposes that the sovereign is (a) wholly popular and constrained; (b) not wholly popular (this includes the possibility that the Constitution is not-at-all popular) and constrained; (c) wholly popular and unconstrained; or (d) not wholly popular (possibly not-at-all popular) and unconstrained. My contention is that the Constitution presupposes a constrained sovereign and therefore belongs in cell (a) or (b). Thus, the goal here is the elimination of (c) and (d).[24]

If facts about the Constitution stand in opposition to the idea of unconstrained sovereignty, then we can eliminate both (c) and (d). To find out if this is true, we need to know who the Constitution might presuppose to be sovereign. First, and most obvious, are the people. The Constitution says that the people ordain and establish the Constitution. This proclamation isn't by itself sufficient to say the people are sovereign, but perhaps an examination of the Constitution's structure will reinforce this express declaration. Second, given Pufendorf's argument concerning the parts of supreme sovereignty, we might consider the officials of the national government to be sovereign. Pufendorf would tell us that it's a bad idea that the parts of sovereign power are placed in different sets of hands. But perhaps that just means that the Constitution does a bad job of institutionalizing sovereignty. Third, perhaps the Constitution establishes one of the branches of the government as truly sovereign. Maybe the legislature is truly sovereign. Perhaps it has a kind of final authority that the other branches do not have.[25] If this is the case, then the Consti-

---

23. This is the case with the change in the electors for senators from the state legislatures to the people in the respective states. I don't think this particular change alters any major conclusions drawn herein.

24. I must note that I do not believe the argument that follows stands in any tension with the description of the separation of functions advanced in chapter 2.

25. One might ask why the Constitution might presuppose this. Well, some might argue that the

tution presumes sovereignty to have been transferred from the people to the legislature. Or perhaps the Constitution favors the president or the Supreme Court over the other branches.[26] Fourth, political scientists have sometimes referred to the Constitution as creating a system of dual sovereignty[27]—in other words, the national government is sovereign within its sphere and the state governments are sovereign within their sphere. Fifth, it has been maintained at times in our history, namely, by Calhoun and by the South during the Civil War, that the national government is nothing other than a creature of the state governments.[28] According to this view, sovereignty originates with the state governments and is retained by them to such an extent that they are free not only to disregard the orders of the national government, to nullify its commands, but also to withdraw from the union so as to totally remove themselves from its influence. Sixth, the Constitution might presuppose a mixed sovereignty as occurs in balance of orders systems. In this case, the people as a whole would share final say with some other person or group—a monarch, an aristocracy, oligarchs, etc.

Before we set about the task of determining who the Constitution takes as sovereign, we should ask whether any of these potential sovereigns can be considered unconstrained. Let's consider the people last and begin with the national government as a whole. We want to know if there are any facts about the Constitution that stand in tension with considering the national government an unconstrained sovereign. In *The Federalist* No. 51, Madison famously observes, "In order to lay a due foundation for that separate and distinct ex-

---

legislature has a kind of end of the day, final say authority that we described as being indicative of sovereignty. This could be argued to show up in the impeachment power, in Congress's ability to shape the executive branch by creating or abolishing departments, by funding projects, by passing laws indicating what the executive branch shall do, by exercising congressional oversight via committees, and by the power to control the Supreme Court's appellate jurisdiction. Through these mechanisms some may contend that Congress can weigh in with a final say about what government can do, a final say not possessed by the other branches and that the other branches must always keep in mind.

26. Following the arguments offered by the antifederalist Brutus, we might contend that if the Constitution controls the various branches and if the Supreme Court says what the Constitution means, then the Supreme Court is the highest power in the system. Brutus wrote, "There is no power above them that can correct their errors or controul their decisions—The adjudications of this court are final and irreversible, for there is no court above them to which appeals can lie, either in error or on the merits" (see essay 15 in Murray Dry, ed., *The Anti-Federalist: An Abridgement by Murray Dry, of "The Complete Anti-Federalist,"* edited, with Commentary and Notes, by Herbert J. Storing, 184).

27. One prominent introductory text for American government says just this. See Morris P. Fiorina and Paul E. Peterson's *The New American Democracy,* 75. Forrest McDonald offers perhaps the best treatment on divided sovereignty in the U.S. from a historical perspective in *States' Rights and the Union: Imperium in Imperio, 1776–1876.*

28. See Harry V. Jaffa, *A New Birth of Freedom: Abraham Lincoln and the Coming of the Civil War,* chap. 7, esp. 403–6. See also McDonald, *States' Rights and the Union,* particularly chaps. 5 and 8.

ercise of the different powers of government, which to a certain extent, is admitted on all hands to be essential to the preservation of liberty, it is evident that each department should have a will of its own; and consequently should be so constituted, that the members of each should have as little agency as possible in the appointment of the others."[29] Madison maintains that Pufendorf's parts of supreme sovereignty should be operated by separate wills that may in fact collide. Conversely, Pufendorf thinks the supreme sovereignty is emptied where the parts of sovereignty are placed in different hands. Perhaps Pufendorf goes too far. But, at the very least, where these powers are placed in different hands, if those exercising those powers are indeed considered sovereign, the sovereign is certainly constrained and constrained for the very reasons that Pufendorf thinks the supreme sovereignty is emptied when the different parts are placed in different hands. For when legislative and executive powers are separated, the legislature is given the authority to decide what shall be done without possessing the actual authority to do it. This must be considered a great constraint indeed.

The Constitution does in fact place legislative, executive, and judicial powers into different hands. But this might not matter much if the will of officials in other branches can be bent to the will of one particular branch. That is, perhaps the Constitution's separation of powers is really nominal. Perhaps the overlapping of powers, done in the name of creating checks, really bends the executive to the will of the legislature. After all, Congress can impeach and remove the president from office. Or perhaps the will of Congress is really bent to the president's will. After all, he can veto their legislation. True, Congress can override a president's veto. But it requires a super-majority that is rather difficult to muster, especially in a legislature reflecting such diverse and wide-ranging interests as those embraced by the large extent of territory contained in the union. Therefore, most of the time Congress must consider whether or not the president will consent to its decision, before choosing either to pass or to not pass a law. Finally, perhaps the wills of the executive and of Congress are bent to the will of the Supreme Court—for the Court is said to have the power to determine which laws are constitutional and therefore valid. If the president simply enforces what Congress decides (or does mostly this) and Congress makes its decisions based on what the Court will consent to, then perhaps we should consider the Court sovereign.

It is rather implausible to maintain that some particular branch of the na-

29. *The Federalist* No. 51, 261.

tional government is the true and unconstrained sovereign. This could only be the case if the wills of the other branches were bent completely to the will of that one branch. But none of the branches are totally dominated by the others—none are like the Ringwraiths completely bent to Sauron's will to do his every bidding. Indeed, it is the case that the president who, in his actions, must consider the possibility of impeachment and removal. These may be very difficult, but they remain possible. Therefore, the president must act with an eye to Congress, and this possibility sets a boundary to his actions. Moreover, if Congress doesn't like various activities of the executive branch, it can always circumscribe those activities, by, for example, defunding various departments (and in some cases by abolishing them). The will of the executive, in most instances, is carried into effect by departments that depend upon the Congress for their funding. Congress can also create new laws charging these departments of the executive branch with new activities. In fact, Congress exercises oversight over various executive branches via its various committees. Thus we are forced to conclude that the chief executive's very subordinates must consider not only his will, but also the will of the legislature. It is implausible, then, to maintain that there is some constitutional tendency to turn the executive into an unconstrained sovereign. He is constrained by the legislature. But the legislature is likewise constrained by the executive. While the executive's veto may not be absolute, two-thirds majorities can be difficult to muster. The eyes of the legislature must therefore frequently be on the president. Congress must also keep its eyes on a Court that may declare acts of Congress unconstitutional or that may, in application, interpret the laws in ways unintended by Congress. To put it another way, the Supreme Court can make sure that the will of the Congress does not go into effect.[30] Just because the Supreme Court is said to decide the final meaning of the Constitution, however, we need not

---

30. Here we can contrast the constrained legislature effected by the U.S. Constitution with William Blackstone's description of the British Parliament as absolute and unconstrained. Consider James Wilson's summary of Blackstone's position:

> Sir William Blackstone says [the supreme power] resides in the omnipotence of the British Parliament, or in other words, corresponding with the practice of that country, it is whatever the British Parliament pleases to do: so that when that body was so base and treacherous to the rights of the people as to transfer the legislative authority to Henry the Eighth, his exercising that authority by proclamations and edicts could not strictly speaking be termed unconstitutional, for under the act of Parliament his will was made the law, and therefore his will became in that respect the constitution itself. (cited in Mark David Hall, *The Political and Legal Philosophy of James Wilson, 1742–1798*, 91–92)

Wilson himself had a hard time with Blackstone on both a descriptive and a normative level. He thought that Blackstone's political theory was too much like that of Thomas Hobbes.

take this to mean that the Court is sovereign or even the strongest branch. The Court cannot implement its own decisions. According to one story, on the heels of a Court decision that Andrew Jackson did not like, the colorful president observed, "John Marshall has made his decision. Now let him enforce it."[31] Beyond this, the Supreme Court hears most of its cases through its appellate jurisdiction rather than through original jurisdiction. But Congress has virtually complete control over the Court's appellate jurisdiction.[32] Indeed, it could abolish circuit courts and so restrict the Supreme Court's jurisdiction so that it heard virtually no cases. Congress has not done so but has instead tended to increase the Court's jurisdiction over time. Even so, this is a possibility that remains open. Beyond this, because the Court does not want to appear powerless and its decisions to appear meaningless and because it has neither the power of the purse nor the sword, it must constantly consider what the executive will be willing to enforce and whether the legislature will be willing to give teeth to its decisions by enacting laws that then require the enforcement of the Court's decision. One political scientist has demonstrated that even a significant decision such as *Brown v. Board of Education* failed to lead to any significant amount of desegregation until the legislature and executive decided to act many years later.[33] People sometimes cite as an example of the Court's great unassailability Roosevelt's failed attempt to pack the Court—"The switch in time saved nine." Of course, Roosevelt wouldn't have failed had Congress and the public been willing to go along. Further, the whole reason he wanted to pack the Court was to get it to go along with his policies. The switch in time got the Court to do that, though the second New Deal was arguably more restrained than the first. In the end the Court bent its will to the president's to save the number of justices on the Court. This seems to me a pyrrhic victory. And it shows that the power of the Court is greatly constrained by the political branches.[34] Indeed, the legislature's ability to control the size of the Court is a legislative check on the Court allowed by the Constitution, and in times past Congress has in fact adjusted the size of the Court. Congress changed the number of justices to eleven to allow Abraham Lincoln

31. While the story is probably not true, Jackson's actions in response to Marshall's decision in *Worcester v. Georgia* and in a subsequent appeal embody the spirit behind the story.

32. See U.S. Constitution, art. 3, sec. 2. Congress has in fact chosen to restrict the Supreme Court's appellate jurisdiction at times. In ex parte *McCardle* Congress removed a case from the Court's jurisdiction after the Court had heard the case but before it had rendered its decision. The Court complied.

33. See Gerald N. Rosenberg, *The Hollow Hope: Can Courts Bring about Social Change?* chap. 2.

34. We might note that Court decisions can be and in fact have been overturned by constitutional amendment on more than one occasion.

to choose "Union men." When Andrew Johnson became president, Congress reduced the number to seven so that Johnson couldn't make any nominations. After Johnson left office, the number was raised back to nine. Some day a president may yet again convince the legislature to go along with a plan to pack the Court. If that happens, the Court will be able to do nothing to resist. From the foregoing, we infer that *if* the national government is in fact sovereign, *then* it is a constrained one.[35] We also infer that *if*, implausible though it seems, someone were to call one branch the real sovereign, *then* it would have to immediately concede that that branch (even if it's the legislature) is a greatly constrained sovereign at best.

Consider a possible objection to the idea that the national government is internally constrained by checks that entail each of the branches being constrained as well. On the face of it, it does seem that the national government is internally constrained by the separation of powers together with checks by which each branch can protect itself from the intrusions of the others. And it seems that the national government is constrained by virtue of having only delegated powers and by virtue of federalism—that is, by virtue of having been delegated the authority to legislate only in certain areas. But perhaps these constraints are only apparent. Antifederalists such as Brutus believed that the various branches of the national government would not likely interfere with each other overmuch.[36] After all, he thought those branches had an incentive to cooperate with each other. Like Madison, he agreed that men love power and that those with power like to keep from losing the power. He also thought, like Madison, that those with power are inclined to want more.[37] Perhaps Madison thought that the branches of the national government would be continually locked in combat with one another, each trying to gain power at the expense of the other branches, each branch exercising the checks given to it to keep from losing power. But, says Brutus, there is another way for the branches to gain power. The judiciary need not steal it from the legislature, nor the legislature from the judiciary; rather, the branches of the national government can work together to steal power from the states. This shared incen-

---

35. So you've shown it's constrained, someone might say. What of it? Haven't you merely shown that there are just procedural constraints? My contention is that procedural constraints entail prior substantive constraints. But that matter is for chapter 4. I wish only to show in this chapter that the Constitution establishes a constrained sovereignty of some sort or other. And this fact alone sets the Constitution at odds with modern notions of sovereignty.

36. I owe the interpretation of Brutus that frames the objection in this paragraph to J. Budziszewski.

37. This is the assumption behind Madison's argument that each branch needs a way to protect itself from the others.

tive might create a unified will in the national government even though the functions of government are placed in different hands. Should the national government decide to increase its power by taking it from the states, the Constitution provides the national government with the means to do so through the supremacy and necessary and proper clauses. Any law passed by Congress, pursuant to the Constitution, nullifies any conflicting state law. Brutus points out that Congress can pass any law it wants and say that it is pursuant to the Constitution—for it might deem anything at all necessary and proper for carrying out constitutionally delegated and enumerated ends. The necessary and proper clause allows Congress to pass any law it wants, and the supremacy clause means any state laws that conflict with federal laws are set aside. Thus Congress can effectively set aside any state laws (including provisions in state constitutions) that it wants to by simply passing laws of its own.[38] As we look over our political history, we can see that the national government has indeed been able to amass power over the states. This has happened by and large via the mechanism of the commerce clause. Congress has used the commerce clause to pass legislation that many might think constitute exercises of the police powers, which are traditionally said to be reserved to the states. Congress and the Court have maintained that Congress can legislate about anything touching interstate commerce. And it happens that nearly everything touches interstate commerce.[39] As one law professor whose lectures I remember used to say, an analysis of our political history seems to suggest that the power to regulate interstate commerce is in fact all power.[40]

The argument of Brutus is powerful and not without merit. Nevertheless, I do not think the Constitution makes the national government an absolute sovereign. Consider a hypothetical world in which the national government, arranged according to the Constitution, had in fact amassed all the powers that had once belonged to the states. Brutus's nightmare had come to pass (perhaps we'll call it the "Nightmare on Pennsylvania Avenue"). Could we then declare the national government an unconstrained sovereign? I think not. For then the incentive for the various branches to cooperate will have been removed.[41] Without that incentive, the unity of will, will no longer be present.

---

38. See essay 1 by Brutus in Dry, ed., *The Anti-Federalist*, esp. 112.

39. A fact of which nearly every student of constitutional law is well aware. Consider in this relation the Supreme Court's decision in *Darby v. United States*.

40. The law professor in question is Lino Graglia.

41. Why is that incentive removed? To answer this we must consider a prior question. What was the incentive in the first place? It was to amass more power. That is, it was an incentive appealing to the branches of the government to set aside their desire to take power from one another and to work

In that case the legislature's decisions are again constrained by the executive's decision to enforce them and the Court's decision to consider them constitutional; and, for reasons already given, the executive must keep an eye on the legislature, as must the Court keep in mind the willingness of the legislature and the executive to give teeth to its decisions. Further, even in Brutus's "Nightmare on Pennsylvania Avenue," a popular check or constraint remains in place. In particular, congressional officials must consider whether or not the people will decide to reelect them; and even though the president has never been appointed directly by the people, the electoral college system, together with congressional checks on executive action, has meant that the executive has always in some sense been constrained by the popular will. Finally, consider again our political history. It is not the case that the national government has always reflected a unified will fixed on amassing power from the state governments. Despite the broad range of so-called commerce clause legislation, the states still retain a great deal of independence. Furthermore, the national government certainly does not have a history of unabated interbranch cooperation. Perhaps the branches have cooperated a great deal of the time, but there has always been conflict between them. And there is certainly conflict today.[42]

Is it possible that the Constitution takes state governments to be unconstrained sovereigns and the national government merely to be the creation of the states? This seems doubtful. For even if the Constitution takes state governments to be sovereign (and it seems not even to do this), the creation of a national government with real governing powers places a serious constraint on the sovereignty of the states. If the states were truly sovereign, then the national government would be constrained by their collective will. But the Constitution establishes a national government that is in no way subservient to the will of the states. Indeed, the Constitution seems to create, by design, a national government that has some distance from the states. This becomes evident when considering the Articles of Confederation.

---

together to increase the overall power of the national government by stealing that power from the states and from individuals. But once that power had been amassed the reason that gave rise to the cooperation has vanished for their shared interest has vanished as well. In our hypothetical world, all the power to be had is divided or shared between the branches of the federal government. If the members of the respective branches want to amass more power, they'll have to take it from one another, and they'll have to protect the power already possessed from attempted seizures by other branches. So every move to amass more power by one branch will lead to a blocking action by the branch on the defensive. And these power grabs and blocks do indeed present us with constraints on the actions of the national government.

42. See Louis Fisher, *Constitutional Conflicts between Congress and the Presidency;* see also Charles O. Jones, *The Presidency in a Separated System.*

Under the Articles, the national government truly was a creature of the states and could not operate outside of their will. Officials of the federal government were appointed by the state governments. The federal legislature was unicameral and arranged so that each state had one vote. Legislation required a vote of a majority of the states to pass—some matters needed unanimous consent. Nor could the legislature levy taxes or raise an army in the usual sense, for while the federal legislature could pass laws "binding on the members of the Union," the federal government depended on the states to put that legislation in effect. This meant that the states decided for themselves whether or not to obey, the federal government having no mechanism to coerce the individuals in the states to obey its commands. The federal legislature legislated only "for the states in their corporate or collective capacities." With no mechanism to enforce its will on the states, federal laws amounted to mere requests that the states send financial aid or more soldiers for the war effort.[43] Under this arrangement, therefore, the states were the true sovereign, for decisions of the federal legislature had no effect unless the state governments consented to them. If those governments did not consent, they could simply disregard the federal legislature—as many state governments in fact did when it came to paying for the war. Put another way, the states had the ability to prevent federal law from going into effect; they could therefore nullify it, which means, practically speaking, they were possessed of the *final say.*[44]

Government under the Constitution is a different matter. First, with the advent of the Constitution, the national government has the power to put federal laws into effect without the consent of the state governments. In the eyes of the Constitution's defenders, the national government's ability to reach individual citizens through its laws was the key to creating a government whose

43. This is Hamilton's argument in *The Federalist* No. 15, 70. To reproduce the relevant passage in full:

> The great and radical vice in the construction of the existing Confederation is the principle of legislation for the states in their corporate or collective capacities and as contradistinguished from the individuals of whom they consist. Though this principle does not run through all the powers delegated to the Union; yet it pervades and governs those, on which the efficacy of the rest depends. Except as to the rule of apportionment, the United States have an indefinite discretion to make requisitions for men and money; but they have no authority to raise either by regulations extending to the individual citizens of America. The consequence of this is, that though in theory their resolutions concerning those objects are laws, constitutionally binding on the members of he Union, yet in practice they are mere recommendations, which the States observe or disregard at their option.

44. This is not to say that the states had any sort of legal right to behave as they did under the Articles of Confederation.

will could not be thwarted by states choosing to ignore its decrees. Second, under the Articles, state governments were represented in the national government, whereas under the original Constitution, the state governments' primary role was to appoint senators (though they initially appointed electors as well). But the long terms of senators ensured their independence from the will of those same legislatures, for state legislators served comparatively short terms, and the turnover rate in state legislatures was rather high.[45] Furthermore, the state legislatures did not possess the power to recall the senators they had appointed.[46] All this served to distance particular senators from the will of the legislatures that appointed them. Indeed, those same senators, individually, came to have great power vis-à-vis their respective state legislatures. So much so that the push to have senators selected by popular election rather than by state legislatures was a movement that came out of those same legislatures, so the legislators in them could remove themselves from under the thumb of the senators they had appointed.[47] But, setting all this aside, even if the Senate was completely subject to the will of the state legislatures, this would not suffice to make the states' power supreme in the present order. For the states in their collective capacities have little power over the branches of the federal government. As well, the state governments are greatly constrained by the national government. The delegation of certain powers to the national government and constitutional provisions preventing the state governments

45. In *The Philosophy of the American Constitution: A Reinterpretation of the Intentions of the Founding Fathers,* Paul Eidelberg wrote,

> If a Senator's term of office were shorter than, or even concurrent with, the term of those who elected him, it might then be inferred that the Senate was meant to represent, primarily, the interests of the several states. For the effect of this would be to increase the influence which members of the state legislatures could exert over their appointees; or the general tendency would be to make the Senate subservient to local interests. However, at the time of the Federal Convention, all save one of the states had annual elections for the first (or only) branch of their legislatures—the exception being South Carolina which had biennial elections. And as concerned those states having a second branch, the average term was approximately two-and-a-half years, the longest being Maryland's, which had a five-year term. (49)

46. Eidelberg addresses the inability of state legislatures to recall the very senators they appointed in his discussion of the Virginia Plan. The Constitutional Convention followed the Virginia Plan in providing long terms for senators and in refusing to make senators subject to recall by the legislatures that appointed them, thus diminishing the influence of those very legislatures. He contends, "So in view of the much longer term of office intended for the Senate, it is evident that the members of the state legislatures would not be in a very favorable position to influence their senatorial appointees—indeed, this influence might even be reversed" (ibid., 48–50).

47. In the last few sentences I'm drawing upon material in a work by Ronald J. Oakerson that remains in manuscript form.

from making certain sorts of laws (e.g., coining money, power to regulate interstate commerce, etc.) together with the supremacy clause, which sets aside state laws in conflict with the Constitution or laws made pursuant to the Constitution, place serious constraints upon the states.[48]

Very few today take seriously the idea that the state governments are sovereign and that the national government is simply their creation. But some do say that the states have a share in sovereign power. They think the Constitution creates a system of dual sovereignty.[49] I disagree with this theory, but let us suppose for a moment that it is true. If so, each person is subject to two sovereign governments. I don't see how such a division of sovereignty could be anything but constraining. Perhaps some will say that the state governments have absolute sovereignty within their own sphere. But we must note that the Constitution greatly circumscribes the spheres of state governments and many of the most important matters are placed in the hands of the national government.[50] Beyond this, the republican guarantee clause implies that the national government has a right to prevent state governments from operating in an entirely arbitrary manner. The states, given this clause, cannot set up monarchical systems of government within their territory. Thus, if the Constitution in fact accepts the system of dual sovereignty, I cannot see how it could possibly presuppose that the respective sovereigns are unconstrained.

But the idea that the Constitution sets up a dual sovereignty was certainly *not* one believed by the Constitution's framers or by its opponents.[51] Both of these camps thought that the Constitution was premised on the sovereignty of the "people" of the United States.[52] While the Constitution's framers saw this as a virtue of the new system, it simply irked the Constitution's opponents. Patrick Henry said, "What right had they to say, *We, the people?* Who authorized them to speak the language of *We, the People,* instead of *We, the States?*"[53] Henry recognized that the Constitution itself suggests that its authority is de-

---

48. The constraints upon the state governments, under the Constitution, are made express in the proscriptions upon the states found in article 1, section 10; the *republican guarantee* clause of article 4, section 3; the *supremacy clause* of article 6; and, eventually, the Thirteenth, Fourteenth, and Fifteenth Amendments.

49. Fiorina and Peterson, *New American Democracy,* 75.

50. Here I refer to a number of the powers delegated to Congress in article 1, section 8, and proscribed to the states in article 1, section 10.

51. I don't mean to say that this is the constitutional presupposition just because they thought so. But I do think that their assessment of the matter is correct.

52. The belief of neither group is sufficient to make this so. In the section on teleological fitness, I will show how the Constitution promotes popular sovereignty by giving the people the final say.

53. Cited in Walter Berns, *Taking the Constitution Seriously,* 66.

rived from the sovereignty of the people rather than from the sovereignty of the states. According to Mark David Hall, James Wilson "contended that every institution of the government described by Constitution is based on the people."[54] Wilson maintained that even the

> executive and judicial powers are now drawn from the same source, are now animated by the same principles, are now directed to the same ends, with the legislative authority: they who execute, and they who administer the laws, are as much the servants, and therefore as much the friends of the people, as they who make them. The character, and interest, and glory of the two former are as intimately and as necessarily connected with the happiness and prosperity of the people, as the character, and interest, and glory of the latter are.[55]

When Wilson confronted the criticism that the Constitution reduced state sovereignty, he replied that the people, not the states, are sovereign.[56]

What if Henry and Wilson are correct about who the Constitution takes to be sovereign? Does that mean that the Constitution also takes the people to be absolute and unconstrained in their sovereignty? It's hard to see how it could. In *The Federalist*'s famed fifty-first essay, Madison observes, "In framing a government which is to be administered by men over men, the great difficulty lies in this: You must first enable the government to controul the governed; and in the next place oblige it to controul itself."[57] In Madison's view, the purpose of government is to control (or constrain) *both* those who govern *and* those who are governed. The national government creates, administers, and enforces laws written for the governance of the people. These laws are given teeth by the power of the national government to enforce its laws directly upon individuals. That is, the national government can coerce obedience by creating and implementing severe penalties for the violation of its laws. If the people are indeed sovereign, the foregoing observations surely mean that they are a greatly constrained sovereign. Beyond this, the very structure of the Constitution means that the people cannot get what they want, right when they want it. Moreover, various elements of constitutional design place the government at some remove from the people. The six-year terms of senators and the four-year term of the president, for instance, place these branches beyond the reach

---

54. Hall, *Political and Legal Philosophy of James Wilson*, 117.
55. Ibid.
56. Ibid., 154.
57. *The Federalist* No. 51, 262.

of immediate public opinion. These branches, by virtue of their long terms, are able to resist popular will. Furthermore, the multiple veto points contained in the Constitution, such as the requirement that two branches of the legislature concur on a bill before it becomes a law and the executive veto, serve as mechanisms that delay decision making. A consequence of institutionalizing delayed decision making is that the people cannot get whatever they want, right when they want it.[58] But if the people are an absolute and unconstrained sovereign, then the *will* of the people should be absolute. The people should be able to get what they want, *when* they want it, and they should be able to decide however they please. Moreover, when it comes to getting what they want, some things will only be demanded in the heat of passion.[59] Some desires cannot be sustained over long periods of time across a great number of people.[60] Thus, delaying decision making prevents the people from attaining certain desires. And this entails that if the people are sovereign, then they are a constrained sovereign.

Just here I think a certain objection emerges. Doesn't the final say of the people extend to amending just about anything out of or into the Constitution? Doesn't this mean, finally, that if the people are sovereign, then they are an unconstrained sovereign? This objection deserves some attention, because,

58. Alexander Hamilton provides a defense of multiple veto points and delayed decision making in the legislative process in *The Federalist* No. 70: "In the legislature, promptitude of decision is oftener an evil than a benefit. The differences of opinion, and the jarrings of parties in that department of the government, though they may sometimes obstruct salutary plans, yet often promote deliberation and circumspection; and serve to check excesses in the majority" (358). In *The Federalist* No. 73, defending the executive veto because it helps protect the community against the passage of bad laws, Hamilton wrote,

> The oftener a measure is brought under examination, the greater the diversity in the situations of those who are to examine it, the less must be the danger of those errors which flow from want of due deliberation, or of those missteps which proceed from the contagion of some common passion or interest. It is far less probable, that culpable views of any kind should infect all the parts of the government, at the same moment and in relation to the same object, than that they should by turns govern and mislead every one of them. (273)

59. This is entailed by Madison's defense of long terms for senators in *The Federalist* No. 63, 320. He wants a body of elected officials that can resist popular will that is stimulated by some irregular passion until reason and justice regain ascendancy in the public mind and the cool, deliberate sense of the community governs once again. This implies that if you hold out long enough, passion will wane. It is strong, but not long lasting.

60. This seems to be the heart of *The Federalist* No. 10's solution to the problem of faction: "Extend the sphere, and you take in a greater variety of parties and interests; you make it less probable that a majority of the whole will have a common motive to invade the rights of other citizens; or if such a common motive exits, it will be more difficult for all who feel it to discover their own strength, and to act in unison with each other" (48).

at the end of the day, the people, as a result of the amendment process, are possessed of a considerable final say. Nevertheless, the objection can be met. First, there is one thing that is virtually (though not absolutely) unamendable. No state can be deprived of equal representation in the Senate *without* that state's consent. Second, the amendment process contains rules that must be followed in order for an amendment to be valid. Amendments are proposed either by a two-thirds majority in each branch of Congress or by a convention called for by two-thirds of the state legislatures (though amendments have never been proposed by the latter route). Proposed amendments must then be ratified by three-fourths of the states, either by their legislatures or by conventions meeting therein. Because of these rules, the amendment process, like the ordinary legislative process, favors long-term majorities over immediate majorities and broad majorities over narrow ones. As a consequence of the three-fourths state ratification requirement, the majority in support of it must be nationally distributed, which is to say that it must be broad. Such majorities are rare and take time, usually considerable time, to build. As a result, the U.S. Constitution is rarely amended. The fact that nationally distributed majorities take time to build means that the amendment process favors long-term majorities over immediate popular majorities. Moreover, as a result of distinct ratification and proposal stages, the amendment process is multitiered. Thus amendments must be "passed" at two stages. Consequently, the amendment process can be said to include multiple veto points. And, as we've already seen, multiple veto points indicate a favoring of long-term over immediate majorities. Third, suppose the Constitution was radically amended such that an entirely different frame of government was put into place. In this instance, I would be inclined to think that the Constitution had been replaced rather than amended. But we would be wrong to infer unconstrained popular sovereignty from the ability of a people to replace their constitution. To say this is to prove too much. It is akin to saying that a people who lived under a hereditary monarchy for centuries but who rose up in revolution and replaced that monarchy with a republic were actually an *unconstrained* popular sovereign all along. This seems absurd. An argument that can prove this has gone wrong somewhere. For the purposes of our inquiry, we are interested in who is sovereign and the extent of that sovereign's power under this Constitution.

I conclude that the Constitution rejects unconstrained sovereignty. The very notion stands in contradiction with its institutional design. This means that from Table 3.1 we can eliminate cells (c) and (d), wholly popular and unconstrained and not wholly popular and unconstrained. Consequently, we are left with either (a) or (b), wholly popular and constrained or not wholly popular and constrained.

But no sooner do we reach this conclusion than an objector jumps up and maintains that there are facts about the Constitution in tension with (a), the notion that the sovereign is wholly popular and constrained. Our objector suggests, however, that it is surely difficult to square popular sovereignty with the virtual inability of the people, as a result of Article 5, to amend the constitutional provision concerning the equal representation of states in the Senate. We must note that the equal representation of states in the Senate is not unamendable; it is only that no state can be deprived of equal representation *without its consent*. Of course, that consent may, in practice, prove impossible to get. Suppose that it does. Can the people be sovereign even if they have placed themselves under what amounts to an absolute limitation? I see no problem here. There is a difference between the self-limitation of the sovereign and the alienation of sovereignty. Just because a sovereign has placed a permanent or absolute limitation upon himself, it does not follow that he has transferred final say to another party and, consequently, it does not follow that he has alienated sovereignty. I have argued that there is no reason to think sovereignty incompatible with the notion of real self-limitation. I would add that I see no reason that a sovereign might not place himself under an absolute or permanent self-limitation and do so in a way that does not place the sovereign under the power of another and therefore in a way that does not abdicate sovereignty. This brings us to a second objection concerning (a). Our objector wonders whether federalism doesn't contradict (a). Our objector might have two reasons for thinking this. First, he might take federalism to suggest state sovereignty. Second, he might think of federalism as instantiating mixed sovereignty, thereby producing a contradiction of the Constitution with (a). I refuted the first reason earlier when I argued against the plausibility of state sovereignty in our constitutional system.[61] But what about federalism and mixed sovereignty? Well, we must ask our objector why he thinks that federalism institutionalizes mixed sovereignty. He will likely tell us that in our federal system sovereignty is mixed between the states and the people as both are repre-

---

61. Even if the national government were a creature of the states, it would not follow that the states are sovereign, *for* it would not follow that the states possess final say. If the people of the states possess sovereignty vis-à-vis their state governments, then the state governments would have at most a proximate authority in relation to the national government. The people as a whole would be sovereign. It would simply be the people as incorporated in and represented by their state governments rather than the people incorporated nationally.

sented in the national government. If this is what our objector says, then he betrays a misunderstanding of popular sovereignty. When I speak of a popular sovereign, in describing (a), I do not mean to describe the people as an "undifferentiated mass" but rather as a "highly structured composite."[62] As I see it, Madison was right. Popular sovereignty requires only that all governmental authority traces back either directly or indirectly to the people. And even when the states had a greater foothold in the national government, the power of the state governments traced back to the people in those states. In our compound republic, it is accurate to say that governmental authority traces back to the will of the whole people, aggregated nationally, *and* to the will of the whole people as aggregated in states.[63] Such an arrangement is a form of popular sovereignty, for all governmental authority traces back to the will of the whole people, though that will is aggregated in two different ways. Our objector has not only misunderstood popular sovereignty as it relates to federalism. He has also misunderstood mixed sovereignty. For mixed sovereignty is not a mixture of the people incorporated in different ways (i.e., incorporated nationally and incorporated in states), but rather a giving of final say to the will of the people in conjunction with a will independent of the community. The Constitution nowhere does this. I will elaborate upon this matter later. For now it suffices to say that (a) is not precluded as a constitutional presupposition by federalism or the Article 5 provision concerning state representation in the Senate.

Inference to the Best Explanation, Stage 2: Consilience and Simplicity

In this stage of the argument concerning the Constitution's theory of sovereignty, we are looking for the most consilient and the simplest theory.[64] In

---

62. I owe the phraseology to J. Budziszewski.

63. Put another way, governmental authority in our system traces back to the will of the whole people incorporated nationally and to the will of the whole people incorporated in states.

64. As discussed in chapter 2, the most consilient theory will be the one that explains the most classes of facts about the Constitution. The simplest theory will be the one that requires the fewest ad hoc hypotheses to explain particular facts not covered by the theory. And finally, as when applied in science and in the philosophy of science, consilience and simplicity is not a strictly quantitative measure. It may be more important for a theory of sovereignty to explain certain facts about the Constitution than it is for it to explain other facts about it. It would be damning for a theory of sovereignty if it explained all facts but the separation of functions. Theories that cover the separation of functions and all the other major facts would rightly claim to be better theories even though they require more ad hoc hypotheses than theories that fail to explain the separation of functions.

the last section, I argued that the Constitution stands in contradiction to the notion of an unconstrained sovereign, thereby eliminating options (c) and (d) and leaving only options (a) or (b). But, for the sake of argument, I want to reintroduce (c) and (d) as possible constitutional theories of sovereignty to see how they fare against (a) or (b) in terms of consilience and simplicity.

Let's consider (d), not wholly popular and unconstrained, again. At the out-set, (d) presents us with an unconstrained and not-at-all popular or an un-constrained and partly popular sovereign. In either case, (d) appears to explain all the nonpopular features of the Constitution. Thus, (d) explains all the facts concerned with distancing the national government from the people—the long terms of the president and of senators and the appointment of judges for life or good behavior.[65] Some might suggest that (d) explains nonpopular fea-tures of the Constitution more generally, features such as judicial review or the veto power of the president. After all, these powers allow the federal govern-ment to resist the branch of the government closest to the people. But a cer-tain problem emerges here. Even if (d) explains such features *inasmuch* as they are nonpopular, it fails to explain them *inasmuch* as they constrain either the federal government as a whole or a branch of the government (namely, Con-gress) that in turn constrains the holders of these powers. As well, (d) explains the indirect method of selecting senators under the original Constitution, the election of the president via the electoral college, and the appointment of judges by the president with the consent of the Senate *inasmuch* (but only *inas-much*) as these features make the national government independent of popu-lar pressure.[66] These particular constitutional features make it difficult for the people to direct the government to do whatever they see fit. But if all govern-ment officials are merely delegates of the people, then the people should be able to do just this.

Option (d) also explains facts in the Constitution that seem to make the na-tional government an absolute sovereign (e.g., the supremacy clause). Even so, (d) comes up short on a number of points. It fails to explain the separation of powers, checks, federalism, and Article 1, Section 8 (or the fact that the Con-

65. I think representation might be included here, where representation stands in contrast to di-rect democracy. With representation the possibility emerges that the will of the legislature and the will of the people can diverge. This is one reason Hamilton gives for judicial review in *The Federalist* No. 78. So (*d*) can explain a legislature that represents the people while being distinct from it. What it cannot explain is the direct popular election of representatives and incentives, as in biennial elec-tions, that make the House sensitive to popular will.

66. What (*d*) explains is the result of the indirect method of selection—insulation of officials from popular pressure. It does not explain the fact that the people are doing the choosing.

stitution creates a government of delegated powers).[67] And it certainly does not explain the restraints on the power of government contained in Article I, Section 9 or in the Bill of Rights. That is, (d) has no way of making sense of any of the constraints on the government (and therefore not of the veto power or judicial review inasmuch as these constrain the government as a whole or some part of it). Explaining these requires auxiliary hypotheses that complicate (d). Walter Berns says that the main thing about the Constitution is that it creates a government of powers. Here the observation generating the insight is that the Constitution creates a considerably more powerful national government than did the Articles. Berns seems to think that the constraining features of the Constitution are ways of making modern power palatable to Americans.[68] In other words, to get the Constitution ratified, the framers included elements that would constrain national power. But this is more or less an attempt to explain away facts about the Constitution that do not fit with the idea that it creates an absolute sovereign. Therefore, auxiliary hypotheses will be necessary to explain every the constraining feature of the Constitution just mentioned.

I should also mention that the idea of an unconstrained, partly popular sovereign seems incoherent. If the people are only partly sovereign, then some will independent of the community has a partial share in sovereignty. This means that the sovereignty is mixed. But mixed, and therefore shared, sovereignty seems inherently constraining. Thus (d) is only coherently instantiated where the unconstrained sovereign is not-at-all popular. The only plausible candidate for a nonpopular sovereign without constraint (and this is a stretch) is the federal government. In that case, (d) fails to explain all the Constitution's popular features (e.g., the direct election of senators). It especially fails to explain the direct election of representatives elected for short terms thereby ensuring the impact of popular will upon House action together with Congress's great power (which Congress may be driven to use by popular pressure) to check or restrict the actions of the executive and even of the Court.[69] But even

67. It fails to explain federalism, because federalism, along with a limited delegation of powers, implies that there is some power the national government does not possess, power that is reserved to the people and to the states. And this is inconsistent with absolute, unconstrained sovereignty.

68. Berns, "Judicial Review," 77.

69. I mean to emphasize the direct election of representatives together with the idea that political power is vested in Congress in such a way that the other branches must act with at least an eye on Congress. In particular, much of what the executive does depends on the sorts of laws that are passed (thus contemporary executives are constantly lobbying Congress to see some law or other put into effect). Put another way, not much governmental action is going to occur unless Congress con-

worse for (d), it cannot explain the indirect, popular role in the selection of the executive and of the Senate under the Constitution before the Seventeenth Amendment *inasmuch* as the people have some say in determining who shall govern.[70] To explain the Constitution's popular ties some auxiliary hypothesis will be necessary. It will likely be one that says these elements were necessary for ratification. Or perhaps it will be said that governmental offices have to be filled some way or other and that this was simply the way chosen to carry out this task. These are not explanations generated by (d), but ad hoc explanations for why (d) is not done away with by these particular facts.[71]

Option (c), the suggestion that the Constitution takes the sovereign to be wholly popular and unconstrained, explains the popular features of the Constitution—the direct election of representatives, requiring the House's consent (by requiring its participation) for significant governmental action to take place, the direct election of senators in the present day, the popularization of electoral college, and the role of the people (though indirect) in the appointment of the president, of senators under the original Constitution, and of judges (particularly the requirement of the Senate's consent in the appointment of judges). Clearly, however, the apparently nonpopular features of the Constitution pose problems for (c). These features seem to be explained by (d). The reason for thinking that the nonpopular features are explained by (d)

---

sents. And the consent of Congress requires the concurrence of both houses. This means that the other branches must keep an eye on the House and consider what the House will consent to. But the House is tied rather closely to the people (so closely that representatives are said to be constantly campaigning). So it is that the eyes of the other branches are turned toward the people. This is not to say they always follow and never thwart popular will. I only maintain that popular consent, via the direct election of the representatives at first and then of senators serves to make the consent of the people essential to governmental action. The eyes of presidents are also turned toward the opinion of the people by the way in which the electoral college system now works. But I am arguing that popular consent set the bounds to governmental action before the popular election of senators and before the popularization of the electoral college and that it did so by virtue of the Constitution's design.

70. After all, the people chose the legislatures that chose the senators, a scheme arguably protected in the Constitution under the republican guarantee clause.

71. If one wanted to posit the state governments as an unconstrained, nonpopular sovereign, then (*d*) fails to explain all the popular features of the state governments, the republican guarantee clause in the Constitution, all the features in the Constitution that seem to constrain the states and popular features of the Constitution, such as direct election of the House, that are in no way connected to the state governments. If one wanted to identify the Supreme Court as such a sovereign, then (*d*) fails to explain selection of Court members by a president indirectly elected by the people with the consent of a Senate initially of indirect popular origins and now of direct popular origins. But the big thing left unexplained is all the features constraining upon the Court (e.g., Congress's power of impeachment of judges and control of the Court's appellate jurisdiction), not the least is its lack of sword or purse, thereby leaving the determination about the execution of its judgments altogether in other hands.

is that these features seem to prevent government according to popular will. But there are really two possible explanations here. These features mean either that the people are not altogether sovereign or that they are a constrained sovereign. To make sense of the nonpopular features, we must deny one of the terms in (c)—either wholly popular or unconstrained. It follows that (c) requires auxiliary hypotheses to explain these features. The main problem with (c) is that it cannot explain any of the features that keep the people from getting what they want when they want it. An unconstrained popular sovereign, after all, is, by definition, possessed of the ability do as he pleases when he pleases. Therefore, all constitutional features that delay decision making (e.g., bicameralism and the executive veto) stand at odds with (c). Put another way, (c) cannot explain constitutional checks *inasmuch* as those checks prevent immediate realization of popular will, something the delay mechanisms in the Constitution in fact do. Nor can (c) explain the separation of powers. The Constitution separates power so as to give each branch a will of its own. But if the people are absolutely sovereign, then shouldn't the will of the other branches be bent to the popular branch? The defender of unconstrained popular sovereignty has an adequate response. We should not always suppose that the representatives of the people will be good representatives. Close to the people though they are, they may well betray their trust.[72] Suppose we grant this.

---

72. In *The Federalist* No. 78, Hamilton premises the need for an independent judiciary, partly on the basis that the legislature may betray their trust and prove unfaithful to the Constitution and thereby to the people. He maintains that judicial independence, in a republic, provides a salutary barrier "to the encroachments of the representative body" (393). In response to the possibility of legislative infidelity, Hamilton lays down a basic principle:

> There is no position which depends on clearer principles, than that every act of a delegated authority, contrary to the tenor of the commission under which it is exercised, is void. No legislative act therefore contrary to the Constitution can be valid. To deny this would be to affirm, that the deputy is greater than his principal; that the servant is above his master; that the representatives of the people are superior to the people themselves; that men acting by virtue of powers may do not only what their powers do not authorize, but what they forbid. (395)

In other words, the representatives of the people may betray the people by passing laws going beyond or contrary to their delegated authority. Such acts are unconstitutional and therefore void. But the mere fact that they are unconstitutional does not keep such laws from going into effect. To prevent this, some sort of barrier is needed. An independent judiciary serves as just such a barrier, for an independent judiciary is able to prevent representatives of the people from substituting their own will for the will of their constituents. They can do this because they stand as intermediaries between the people and the legislature. They can therefore refuse to apply unconstitutional laws. And their independence from the legislature means they will not feel constrained to apply unconstitutional laws. The courts are therefore designed to keep the legislature "within the limits assigned to their authority" by the Constitution (395). See also Ackerman, *We the People,* chap. 7, esp. 191–95.

If the people's sovereign will is unconstrained, then the government should be structured so that the other branches are wholly determined by the popular will. The other branches should therefore be tied as closely to the people as the House is. But the framers did not endeavor to make the other branches directly dependent on the people. Perhaps (c) can explain why the other branches are independent of the will of the House, but it cannot then also explain why these branches are simultaneously placed at a distance from the popular will. The thesis that these branches are designed to, at times, resist popular will is the only thesis that adequately explains this design feature. Finally, (c) fails to explain the popular sovereign's delegation of legislative, executive, and judicial functions. It seems likely that an unconstrained popular sovereign would have to retain these functions, because in delegating these functions, the popular sovereign makes it possible for the government to control the people. This self-limitation can surely be lifted, but until it is, it seems that the people have placed a real constraint upon themselves, one that raises real obstacles to the popular will getting whatever it wants whenever it wants it. Like (d), (c) fails to cover many facts and seems to require many auxiliary hypotheses.

This brings us to the consideration of cell (b). Some will be inclined to dismiss (b) simply because it posits a constrained sovereign that is not wholly popular. Clearly (b) is quickly dismissed if it posits that the sovereign is not-at-all popular. But (b) also covers mixed sovereignty, an idea that has its share of adherents. Paul Eidelberg refers to the Constitution as effecting a mixed regime.[73] He argues that the Constitution employs nonpopular features to remedy the defects of popular government. According to Eidelberg, it is ridiculous to label as democratic solutions to the problems inherent in democratic form.[74] They must be something else—in our case, namely, oligarchic or aristocratic. The Constitution seeks to temper the deficiencies of the will of the many by the wisdom of the will of the few (where the few wise are thought to be found among the wealthy, for it is the wealthy who have had the best chance to acquire the requisite education for wise governance). For Eidelberg,

---

73. Eidelberg, *Philosophy of the American Constitution*. Eidelberg's work is a response to Martin Diamond, in particular his "Democracy and *The Federalist:* A Reconsideration of the Framers' Intent," which first appeared in *The American Political Science Review* in 1959 and is reprinted in *As Far as Republican Principles Will Admit: Essays by Martin Diamond*.

74. In contrast, Diamond recognizes the framers' concern with the defects and diseases incident to popular government but says that "if what the founders considered to be defects *are* genuine defects, and if the remedies, without violating the principles of popular government, *are* genuine remedies, then it would be unreasonable to call the founders anti- or quasi-democrats" ("Democracy and *The Federalist*," in *As Far as Republican Principles Will Admit*, 22).

the Constitution indeed seeks to create a constrained sovereign. This is the very purpose of mixed sovereignty. Therefore, because (b) posits a constrained sovereign, it explains many of the features that (c) and (d) cannot. It explains the separation of powers together with checks to maintain that separation; the delegation of powers in Article 1, Section 8; federalism; and the direct election of the House. To be sure, where the sovereign in view is not-at-all popular, then (b) fails to explain all the popular features of the Constitution. But where a mixed sovereignty is in view, then (b) can explain some of the Constitution's popular features. Likewise, because the sovereignty is mixed, it can explain apparently nonpopular features of the Constitution, such as the long terms of senators and their originally indirect appointment; the electoral college method of electing the president (though perhaps not its present functioning); the long terms of presidents; and the tenure of judges together with the method by which they are appointed. Option (b) can also provide one of the reasons for the vast extent of territory covered by the Union together with the proportionally small Congress. According to Madison, these features increase the probability that the better sort, the wise and virtuous, will be elected to office.[75] This sounds suspiciously like giving the few a share in sovereignty. For scholars such as Eidelberg, this means that the Constitution is not wholly popular.

Notably, option (b) clearly fares much better than (c) and (d), particularly where the sovereignty in view is mixed. It explains a far greater number of significant facts about the Constitution, making it more consilient than any of the other options. And because it also requires fewer auxiliary hypotheses (only because it covers so many of the significant facts), it is a much simpler option. This being the case, (b) seems a better explanation than (c) or (d). The primary problem with (b) is that it fails to explain why *all* political offices are appointed either directly by the people or by officials who are also elected by

---

75. According to Madison,

> In the first place it is to be remarked that however small the Republic may be, the Representatives must be raised to a certain number, in order to guard against the cabals of a few; and that however large it may be, they must be limited to a certain number, in order to guard against the confusion of the multitude. Hence the number of Representatives in the two cases, not being in proportion to that of the Constituents, and being proportionately greatest in the small Republic, it follows, that if the proportion of fit characters, be not less, in the large than in the small Republic, the former will present a greater option, and consequently a greater probability of a fit choice. (*The Federalist* No. 10, 47)

Lance Banning makes some interesting comments on this issue in *The Sacred Fire of Liberty: James Madison and the Founding of the Federal Republic,* chap. 7.

the people.[76] Even the Supreme Court, which seems quite remote from the people, traces back to the people both because the president who nominates the justices is indirectly appointed by the people and because the senators who confirm them are appointed by the people, at first indirectly and then later directly. Furthermore, (b) does not explain constitutional features that make the more nonpopular branches such as the Court dependent on the more popular branches (e.g., the House's power to impeach and the Senate's power to remove justices from the bench and the inability of the Court to enforce its own decisions) for its decisions to have effect. Moreover, Congress possesses considerable power to regulate the Court's jurisdiction. Indeed, Congress has virtually total control over the Supreme Court's appellate jurisdiction, the jurisdiction through which it hears most of its cases and therefore through which it exercises most of its power. Even more, the Court's power derives from a constitution amendable by the people. Justices have the power they have and continue to be selected the way that they are *because* the people have not amended the Constitution to change these things. Option (b) fails to explain why this is so. Indeed, in order for (b) to fit with the Constitution, it seems to require the erection of a will altogether independent of the people that has a share in governing the community and whose existence is not dependent upon the people's discretion. No such will exists. No offices are filled by heredity or established for life without qualification. All officials serve for a constitutionally limited period or can have their position revoked for bad behavior by branches dependent upon the people (or by the people through amendment). Auxiliary hypotheses will certainly be required to explain the absence of a will totally independent of the community in the Constitution; the origin of all appointments in popular power, whether directly or indirectly exercised; and the fact that all officials serve only for a limited term or good behavior (i.e., that none serve for life). But the foregoing observations suggest that (b) is in even

76. Consider, in this connection, Madison's words in *The Federalist* No. 39:

> we may define a republic to be, or at least may bestow that name on, a government which derives all its powers directly or indirectly from the great body of the people; and is administered by persons holding their offices during pleasure, for a limited period, or during good behavior. It is *essential* to such a government, that it be derived from the great body of the society, not from an inconsiderable proportion, or a favored class of it. . . . It is *sufficient* for such a government, that the persons administering it be appointed either directly or indirectly, by the people; and that they hold their appointments by either of the tenures just specified. (190)

According to Madison, the Constitution erects a government of this description. He proceeds in the essay to show how all offices derive directly or indirectly from the people and to show that all officials enjoy their tenure only so long as the people consent to it.

deeper trouble. If mixed sovereignty is defined as giving final say as to law to the community as a whole and to a will independent of the community, then mixed sovereignty entails the existence of a will independent of the community (i.e., a will not subject to the power or authority of the community). But, as we have noted, no such will exists. This amounts to a denial of the consequent in conditional statement. Per *modus tollens,* we must also deny the antecedent—namely, that sovereignty is mixed. And this amounts to a denial of (b).

This leaves us with (a)—a wholly popular and constrained sovereign. Option (a) has much to commend it including Publius's contention that Constitution sets up an unmixed regime.[77] Because (a) posits a constrained, popular sovereign, it rather clearly explains all the popular features of the Constitution as well as the features that keep the people from getting whatever they want, whenever they want it. Option (a) also explains all the features constraining the government, for such features represent an attempt to keep the government within prescribed bounds—bounds that are prescribed by the people in the very act of ordaining a constitution. Of course, we should note that checks on the legislature exist both because the legislature may not always represent the will of the people and because the popular will, which may in fact be driving the legislature, sometimes needs to be constrained. The notion of constrained popular sovereignty helps us get at why a popular sovereign might delegate legislative, executive, and judicial functions. These are delegated so that the government might in fact control the people. But, as Publius argues, all governmental power traces back to the people, in order to turn the eyes of governing officials to the long-term will of the people. The fact that all appointments and elections trace back to the people means that all appointments in some sense derive from their consent. Even under the pre–Seventeenth Amendment arrangement for electing senators, state legislators were not likely to risk getting tossed from office for electing to the Senate those opposed by the people. If it turned out that the majority of the people in their state came to strongly dislike someone they had appointed, state legislators would not likely reappoint that person. Perhaps they would be turned from office and a new group of legislators would have come to power. Even so, these replacements would not retain in office a person strongly opposed by the people. Thus, if the popular will in the state was sufficiently strong and long-

---

77. In *The Federalist* No. 14, Madison concedes that Europe has the merit of discovering the principle of representation. America, however, "can claim the merit of making the discovery the basis of unmixed and extensive government" (63).

lasting, then it could indeed make a significant impact. And this possibility would have been something that all state legislators and all those elected to the Senate would have had to keep in mind. Changing the selection method of senators to direct popular sovereignty makes the Senate even more dependent on popular will than it had previously been. To be sure, the long terms of senators (and the provision effecting the partial reelection of the Senate every two years) allow the Senate to resist immediate popular will. But popular selection of the Senate certainly means that it cannot resist sufficiently strong, long-term popular will. Moreover, the Senate has a role in the appointment of key executive officials and of Supreme Court justices. To the degree that senators must keep their eye on the will of their constituents, to that degree will the popular will impact the executive and judicial appointments to which the Senate is willing to consent. Option (a) also readily explains federalism as embodied in the Constitution. A popular sovereign might very well want to delegate power to two distinct levels of government, charging each level with different tasks. Moreover, federalism allows the will of the people as incorporated in the states to check the will of the people as incorporated nationally and the will of the people incorporated nationally to check the will of the people as incorporated in the states.

Although more can be said here, for the moment, let me advance a briefer argument. It seems that (a) covers the same range of facts as (b). For all the constitutional features that (b) calls nonpopular can in fact be explained as constraints on popular sovereignty—so long as all these features represent some tie to the people (e.g., to the people via direct or indirect appointment to office). That tie may simply be the people giving consent to who is in office and/or to who stays in office by having either a direct role or an indirect role in their appointment. That role may be realized by giving the branches closest to the people—the House and the Senate—great power to restrict the activities of the branches farthest from them—the executive and the judiciary.[78] As I have argued, Congress does have such power, even if it seems to have largely abdicated it over the last century.[79] The branches that the people have the least agency in appointing officials are subject the greatest degree of control by the branches closest to the people. The point is that (a) explains all the facts

78. In speaking of the president as farther from the people than the House or the Senate, I mean to say that this is formally the case. In contemporary practice, the president is strongly attached to the people.

79. On congressional abdication of power, see Jeffrey K. Tulis, "Panel II: The Appointment Power: Constitutional Abdication: The Senate, the President, and Appointments to the Supreme Court."

that (b) does without recourse to auxiliary hypotheses. No auxiliary hypotheses are necessary to explain why those establishing a constrained popular sovereign might place some branches at some remove from the people, while leaving some tie in place. No auxiliary hypothesis is necessary to show why, with constrained popular sovereignty, you might sometimes want government officials to be capable of resisting immediate popular will. That's the whole point of constrained popular sovereignty—to ensure that immediate popular will is sometimes resisted. Option (a) can also explain facts for which (b) requires auxiliary hypotheses. For example, (a) requires no auxiliary hypothesis to explain the fact that all branches are rooted in the people in some way, directly or indirectly, or to explain that fact that the tenure of all public officials is limited in time or limited to good behavior. Furthermore, (a) readily explains why there is no will in the government independent of the society as a whole. This leads me to the conclusion that (a) is, of the four options, the most consilient and the simplest. And from this I infer that (a) is indeed the best account of the Constitution's theory of sovereignty.

Inference to the Best Explanation, Stage 3:
Teleological Fitness

I wish only to make three additional points here. First, it is my belief that if we look not only at how the Constitution functions today, but also at how it has functioned historically, it becomes apparent that the Constitution's tendency is to promote popular sovereignty, because its tendency is to turn officials to consideration of popular opinion (perhaps too much so).[80] This is particularly true today. Representatives are said to be constantly campaigning. Senators, particularly since the advent of the direct election of the Senate, must keep their eyes on public opinion. Indeed, if they desire to see their legislation pass, they must get the House to go along. They are not likely to succeed in this without some sort of public support. The current operation of the electoral college works to turn the eyes of the president to the people, and not just to seek majority support, but the support of a national majority. Likewise, if the president wants to see his legislative recommendations to Congress succeed, he has to take public opinion into account. And we observe today that members of both houses of Congress and the president are constantly making ap-

---

80. Consider these words of James Madison: "Public opinion sets bounds to every government, and is the real sovereign in every free one" (*James Madison: Writings,* 500). This quote first appeared in an essay entitled "Public Opinion," which was published in the *National Gazette,* December 19, 1791.

peals to the people and lobbying the people. This is a result of constitutional design. No legislation goes forward without Congress, and Congress will not act without the people. No judgments of the Court will be effective without a legislature and a president willing to give the Court's decisions teeth.[81] And if the people are hostile to a decision, then neither the Congress nor the president will act to put a decision made by the Court into effect.[82]

My second point is simple. At the beginning of this essay, I said that sovereignty amounts to a consenting to what shall or shall not be law (and by implication to what shall and shall not be enforced). This consent need not be exercised before a law goes into effect but can be exercised after a law has been made and put into effect. We can see the requirement for popular consent in the Constitution's design in the fact that not much effective governing can be done unless laws are made. The president and Supreme Court have little to work with if Congress decides not to act. But there are no laws without the consent of the branch closest to the people. Beyond that, Congress can greatly circumscribe the activities of the Court and the executive should it choose to do so; tacit consent is given by Congress not choosing to do so. And Congress would surely move to take such action if it felt popular pressure. When the people choose not to pressure Congress in this way, they tacitly consent to the laws that are passed. Furthermore, in our system the people are possessed of the right to amend the Constitution, giving them a *final say* of the strongest sort.

My third and final point is that while the Constitution's design effects a popular sovereign, the popular sovereignty that results is not unconstrained. For the Constitution does tend to constrain the people. It does this by effecting a government over a large territory in which majority formation is possible but difficult. And it does this by forcing majorities to be large enough to capture both houses of Congress and long-lasting enough to capture the approval of the Senate and the president (and perhaps long-standing enough to override the president's veto). The people are sovereign. But the Constitution makes passing laws and putting them into effect a long process. The difficulty of majority formation and the necessity for the majorities to be long-last-

<hr>

81. See Rosenberg, *Hollow Hope,* 336–43.

82. There is much talk about the so-called countermajoritarian difficulty—the Supreme Court, because of the tenure of the justices and the way in which they are appointed seems not to fit with popular sovereignty. Interestingly, for all the talk about the difficulty, the current data on public opinion and Court decisions show that while Court decisions lag behind public opinion a bit, the overwhelming tendency is for Court decisions to follow public opinion, though there are clearly important exceptions.

ing constrains the sorts of majority that will form. Finally, if the people are sovereign, they are clearly constrained by the creation of a government that passes laws enacted upon individuals and enforced by a government with a certain degree of distance from popular will. The passage of such laws is an outcome of our constitutional design. Thus, constrained popular sovereignty is the proposition that exhibits teleological fitness with the Constitution.

Conclusion

Given the foregoing discussion, I conclude that the Constitution presupposes a wholly popular and constrained sovereign. Key constitutional features contradict the notion of an unconstrained sovereign—whether popular or not. I reject the idea that the sovereign is not wholly popular and constrained on the grounds that this also leaves much of the Constitution unexplained. Such an idea fails to explain the facts that all appointments have a popular origin, whether direct or indirect; that all officials serve either a limited term or for good behavior, making the continued service of all officials a matter of the people's discretion; that the people can amend the Constitution to increase their oversight over the less popular branches; and, consequently, that the Constitution nowhere erects a will totally independent of the people. Finally, I argue that the various parts of the Constitution's design do in fact cooperate to effect a constrained popular sovereign. All this together, then, suggests that the Constitution takes the sovereign to be the people, but not in any absolute or uncontrollable sense. The people are constrained.[83]

---

83. Even if our Constitution created a system of mixed sovereignty, my conclusions in what follows still hold. For the will of even a mixed sovereign, under our system, is constrained in a way that favors long-term preferences and desires over immediate ones. This means that even if the Constitution establishes a system of mixed sovereignty, some exercises of sovereign will are favored over others. This is the only premise I need for the argument that follows.

— 4 —

The Constitution and
the Common Good

IN THE LAST CHAPTER we concluded that the Constitution presupposes a constrained popular sovereign. But one might reply, "So what? So the sovereign is constrained. All you've managed to show is that the sovereign is procedurally constrained. Even conventionalists of a procedural bent admit this." These procedural constraints, however, have implications that can be summarized as follows: the Constitution constrains the popular sovereign in such a way as to favor certain kinds of preferences (long-term and broad) over others (short-term and narrow) thereby distinguishing some exercises of the popular will from others. But preferences (or desires) cannot be distinguished on the basis of preference, and will cannot be distinguished on the basis of will. To deem some preferences or exercises of the will as good in contrast to others requires recourse to a standard external to preference and will. Convention cannot serve as such a standard because it is merely a construct of preference or will. In this chapter, therefore, I will argue that the Constitution presupposes a real common good, transcendent of human willing and normative for human behavior. I maintain that this common good is both thick and teleological (rather than deontic or thin and teleological). The good in view has to do with reason's governance of the self and of the political community as a whole, and the Constitution's very design aims at the realization of this goal. Someone might object that I'm actually showing what the Constitution ought to presuppose rather than what it actually does presuppose. But what the Constitution can presuppose is constrained by the real world, which includes the laws of logic.[1]

The Nature of the Common Good

Possible Presuppositions

At the end of chapter 1, we concluded that there are three possible theories about the nature of the common good:

1. *Positivist:* The Constitution presumes that there is no objective common good toward which all laws must aim. All obligation derives from the command of the sovereign—in this case, the will of the people.

2. *Modernist:* The Constitution's conception of the good is preservation or peace—a peace attained by bracketing the questions that bring about violent dispute, such as questions about religion or goods and evils other than the good of peace.

3. *Classical:* The Constitution presupposes the existence of an objective common good, which includes more than mere peace or preservation. It conceives a "thicker" common good that includes all of the dimensions of human well-being and rightly ordered relationships.

For each of these understandings there is some scholar who argues that it constitutes the Constitution's theory of the common good,[2] and together these theories seem to cover the options presented in the literature on the philosophical underpinnings of the Constitution. Logically speaking, the Constitution might presuppose any of these three understandings to be true. Furthermore, these options are exclusive of each other. But they are not sufficiently exhaustive. For our application of disjunctive syllogism to work, we need a fuller list of possible options. Consider, therefore, Diagram 4.1, which presents

---

1. My methodology is, as J. Budziszewski notes, like the old rules of statutory construction in which laws are construed so as to make sense. I am in effect arguing that the Constitution makes sense in that it presupposes what it logically entails.

2. Bruce Ackerman, Walter Berns, and Morton White, respectively.

Diagram 4.1

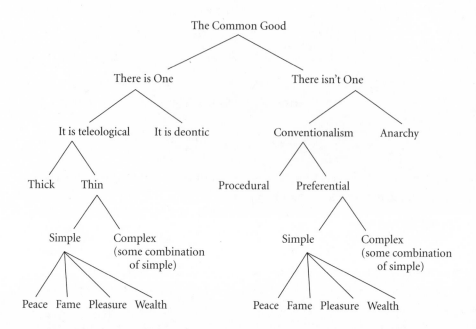

us with many more distinctions and therefore more possible propositions about the reality of the common good.

It should be fairly obvious, right at the outset, that these options are quite exclusive of each other and that there is at least something of an exhaustiveness in the list. We should also note that these possibilities concern the ontological status of the good without telling us anything about how we come to know the good (which will be discussed in chapter 5).

As Diagram 4.1 shows, when it comes to the common good, either there is one or there isn't. These options are designed to get at the realism/antirealism distinction. Thus, affirming the common good means affirming a good that is normative for human beings and independent of or uncreated by human willing. Denying the common good's existence means denying that there is any good independent of human willing. On this option, either there is no moral realm at all and no goodness per se, or to the extent that we can speak of a good or a common good, that good is a creation of human willing. Given its etymological derivation, I use *anarchy* to denote the view that there is no real good for human nature—either independent of or created by human willing.

In contrast, conventionalism is premised on a denial of real goodness, but it suggests that human beings create a moral realm by exercising their wills—that is, exercises of will determine whether some actions are viewed as good and therefore to be done and others as bad and therefore to be avoided. There is no goodness as such and thus no common good in any deep sense, but there are norms, actions, and institutions that people (or some people) have decided shall be called good and considered binding. Conventionalists can be divided into two camps. The first camp is of a teleological bent. These conventionalists define *good*, with Hobbes, as the object of desire—whether that be peace, pleasure, profit, or fame. What is called good here has the nature of an end or goal. But, as I will show later in this chapter, and in chapter 5, something cannot be considered obligatory simply by virtue of being desired. Therefore, preferentialists add human will to the equation.[3] Survival is a good because it is desired. But preferentialists (as conventionalists) speak as though it only acquires normative status via convention, which is collective willing. Preferentialists can be distinguished from proceduralists, who are of a more deontic bent. For proceduralists, some exercise of human willing establishes some basic norm or law or institution as normative. What is created is basically a standard to which human willing must conform or some process from which a law must emerge to be considered binding. Proceduralists don't think that norms or procedures can be evaluated in terms of the outcomes they produce, for outcomes and ends as such are morally indifferent. When it comes to the good, there is only a human decision to consider some rule or set of rules as good.

On the other side of a great, deep river are those who affirm a real common good, normative for human beings and governments and independent of human willing. The common good is a rule and measure of human willing. Among these realists there are both those of a deontic and those of a teleological bent. Those of a deontic bent think of the good in terms of objectively good rules to which the will should conform. The goodness is in the rule and in conforming to it, rather than in the realization of some end at which the will might aim. In contrast, others of a teleological bent conceive of a real common good in terms of an end to be attained. And this end is objectively good, and therefore obligatory, independent of human willing. Among those who think of a real common good in teleological terms, some think of it as thin and some think of it as thick. Those who think of it as thin tend to iden-

---

3. I am using the term *preferentialists* to cover the same territory as Walker's "teleological conventionalism." I think *preferentialist* a more appropriate label for the concept (Walker, *Moral Foundations of Constitutional Thought*, 31–34).

tify the good with objects of desire like peace, pleasure, or fame as real good. Such goods are teleological because they are goals to be attained and because the attainment of such goods is fulfilling of desire. Such goods are thin because, among other reasons, they are minimally substantial (i.e., almost any act might turn out to be conducive to the procurement of such goods depending on the circumstances). In contrast, thick teleologists conceive of the common good in more Aristotelian or Thomistic terms.[4] The common good has the nature of an end to be attained. Human nature "aims" at the good in the sense that this good completes human nature. Human well-being depends on the attainment of this good. Because well-being is not determined by desire, this good is regulative of desire. On this view, the common good includes things like classical virtues and particular goods like friendship.

Thus the structure of the argument is this: either there is a real common good or there isn't. If there isn't, then either humans construct a common good (conventionalism) or they do not (anarchy). If humans do construct the common good, then either they determine to call good something that everyone wants, the object (or objects) of some common desire (preferentialism or teleological conventionalism)—say, survival or the maximization of pleasure—or they simply decide to elevate some norm or pattern of behavior or institution to normative status (proceduralism or deontic conventionalism). In contrast to all these options, if there is a real common good that is independent of human artifice, then either that common good is purely deontic—purely a matter of some rule or rules normative for all and to which everyone's will must conform—or that good is teleological. If that good is teleological, it is either thick or thin. If it is teleological and thin, then something that everyone desires is really good, such as peace, pleasure, profit, or fame, or some combination of these. If it is so in the thick sense, then the good is completing of human nature, whether desired or not. The list is sufficiently exhaustive to suggest that if the Constitution stands in tension with all of the options save one, then it is reasonable to infer that the remaining presupposition is the correct one. Likewise, there is sufficient exclusivity in the list to tell us that if the Constitution presupposes one of these options, then it cannot presuppose any of the others. An important qualification must be made here, for surely a thick teleological theory of the common good will also include elements from the thin theory, such as peace and pleasure. But there is clearly an exclusivity in

---

4. Although it bears mentioning that Plato and St. Augustine subscribe to a substantively thick realism that is also teleological.

our list, for the thin theory does not include the thick theory, and the thick theory entails an understanding of ends or goals not entailed by or included in the thin theory.

There Is No Common Good

To assert that there is no common good is to say that there is no good that all humans hold in common, no good that can only be realized in human partnership. To deny that the common good exists is to deny that there is a good for everyone. But it is also to deny more. For underlying this denial is the dark idea that there is no real good at all. There is no good for human nature, and there is no goodness as such. It would be too generous to call this actuating premise moral skepticism, for it is really moral nihilism. It is a dogma rather than a doubt.[5] This means that there is no standard normative for human willing or normative for exercises of power. Thus, there is no standard over and above human law that can serve as a measure for human laws, no standard we can invoke to claim that some allegedly unjust law is not binding.

There are, as it happens, two versions of moral nihilism. The first denies moral postulates any real standing because it denies such standing to everything. Such a position sounds quite postmodern and contemporary. But it is a position as old as Protagoras. Protagoras allegedly said, "man is the measure of all things, of those that are that they are, of those that they are not that they are not."[6] Such a statement is principally metaphysical and about any reality

5. According to Walker, in his *Moral Foundations of Constitutional Thought,*

> The term *skepticism* in its classic sense meant simply a posture of doubt for the sake of sturdy inquiry. This classic skepticism recognized that if doubt is heuristic, it is necessarily provisional in character. But heuristic doubt is not the posture of the conventionalist thinkers who dominate contemporary constitutional theory. Typically, their "skepticism," as skepticism, is either spurious or incoherent; it is not an attitude of doubt but of certainty. Those thinkers are not doubting the ultimate soundness of some proposed moral standards, nor are they wondering whether the good is an independent reality that we can know or glimpse. Rather, they have come to the settled conclusion that there is no reality, or that it is unavailable to our minds, or that it must in all instances be treated as if it were. In other words, the ostensible "doubt" of such a "skeptic" is really the certainty of the nihilist (whether ontological or epistemological). (27)

6. Cited in Frederick Copleston, *A History of Philosophy: Volume 1: Greece and Rome: From the Pre-Socratics to Plotinus,* 87. There has been some debate about the meaning of this phrase. Some have maintained that "by 'man' Protagoras does not mean the individual man, but man in the specific sense. If this were so, then the meaning of the dictum would not be that 'what appears to you to be true is true for you, and what appears to me to be true is true for me,' but rather that the community or group or the whole human species is the criterion and standard of truth." I, however, side with Copleston in accepting Plato's understanding that the dictum is highly individualistic.

whatsoever. The idea underlying this interpretation is that all reality is relative to individual perception. As Graham Walker notes, "Plato presents Protagoras's doctrine as pertaining in the first instance to perception of physical nature, making the natural realities around us wholly dependent on human perception and construal, thus making ontology strictly contingent on human epistemology."[7] Such a position is strange and self-referentially incoherent.[8] But suppose we grant it. If in fact all reality is up to individual perception and if moral postulates, beliefs, or, dare one say, truths are not grounded in reality, then they too are a matter of individual perception. Any moral statements are the mere creation of the human mind because all factual statements are so created.

As I mentioned, the coherency problems with Protagorean antirealism are quite deep. Therefore, most moral nihilists subscribe to a second version of moral nihilism. Advocates of this alternative acknowledge only physical reality, rejecting morality any reality of its own. Granted this, one might infer that moral statements have no meaning at all on the grounds that they refer to nothing. Or one might infer that moral statements really do refer to something. But the something referred to is feeling, speech in the injunctive mode, the conventions of some group, or instrumental reason.[9] Whatever the case

7. Walker, *Moral Foundations of Constitutional Thought*, 35.

8. Something is self-referentially incoherent when in order to argue for a conclusion x we must incorporate a premise (or assume as true a premise) that is or entails not x. In this particular instance the conclusion to be defended is that all reality depends upon or is relative to perception. Walker rightly notes that this makes metaphysics depend upon epistemology. Reality is, so to speak, in the eye of the beholder. But that very statement is a statement about reality itself that tacitly claims independence from the eye of the beholder. It is an attempt to say something about reality as such. Furthermore, if it is true, then not all of reality is in the eye of the beholder. Any argument for the truth of the position that reality is in the beholder's eye, then, must assume some reality independent of the beholder for the conclusion to make any sense. And so the position collapses into self-referential incoherency. But even if it did not, it would not get us very far. For if reality is in the eye of the beholder, then the reality that "reality is in the eye of the beholder" is itself in the eye of the beholder. It is just one perception that some people happen to have and can freely be discarded or ignored by those who do not share it. If some perceive reality as independent of the beholder's eye, then reality is as they perceive it and those who believe reality is wholly in the beholder's eye have nothing to say to convince them otherwise. Put another way, if reality is in the eye of the beholder, then realists cannot be said to perceive reality wrongly.

9. I have in mind what Jean Hampton calls, in her *The Authority of Reason*, "moral antiobjectivism." The actuating premise here is the belief that the "commitments of science preclude acceptance of objectivist moral theory—and so much the worse for moral theory." According to Hampton's more precise formulation, moral antiobjectivism "is the view that there are no irreducibly moral facts (facts that cannot be reduced to natural facts recognized by science) insofar as such irreducibly moral facts are not, and could not be, admissible by scientific criteria." There are a number of forms of moral antiobjectivism:

> moral nihilists and skeptics (who deny or doubt that there is any such domain as the moral, such as Quine), moral noncognitivists (who deny that there are irreducibly moral facts but

may be, insofar as these physicalists grant a moral realm, they think so-called moral facts are reducible to other nonmoral facts such as emotion or emphatic speech. The point is that there is no realm of the moral as such, because the physical is all there is and the moral as such is not physical. This view is not unproblematic. Among other problems (all of which will be discussed in chapter 7), there is little by way of argument for materialism. Materialistic belief seems to result more from faith than from evidence. But I leave that for later.

Anarchy

Those who deny the existence of the common good maintain that what people call "morality" is relative either to individuals (as in subjectivism) or to groups of people (as in cultural relativism). Relativists of the individualist sort, if they are fully consistent, are anarchists.[10] They are anarchists for just the reasons described by Arthur Allen Leff in his seminal article "Unspeakable Ethics; Unnatural Law." Suppose that there is no standard of right and wrong outside of the individual. Suppose also that some person or group of persons attempt to come up with a standard that will be normative for some other person or group of persons or even everyone. Leff poses the following question: how will the standard withstand the "the grand sez who?" What rational appeal can be made by those imposing the standard to those questioning it? According to Leff, there is no rational appeal that can be made, and it is hard to see why he is wrong. Supposing there is no goodness as such, then every statement someone else makes about what I should do is really just a statement about what they would like me to do. And in that case, what of it? When I reply with "sez who?" unless they can reply with "sez me!" and then force me to obey, they can offer no reason that I should comply with their demands. All that is left is appeal to strength. Yet clearly those who would impose obedience cannot coerce

---

explain morality as constituted by expressivistic assertions, such as Gibbard or Hare), and theorists who believe that "moral judgments can be analyzed into or reduced to factual statements of the sort clearly compatible with the scientific worldview" (Brink 1989). This latter group includes moral relativists such as Bernard Williams, who argue that morality is defined by different sets of social conventions in different societies. It also includes those who put forward what I call "Hobbesian" contractarian moral theories such as Gauthier (1986) and Mackie (1977), who inspired by Hobbes (1651), attempt to reduce moral facts to facts of (instrumental) reason. (2–3)

I should note that I am following Walker in using moral nihilism more broadly than does Hampton.

10. I am arguing that individualistic relativism, or moral anarchy, entails political anarchy. I am emphatically *not* arguing that political anarchy entails moral relativism.

all the obedience they need. We are left with nothing other than the clash of wills, for each individual is, according to Leff, a "godlet."[11]

I suppose someone might object that an appeal could be made to mutual self-interest. But such an objection misses the point in a rather crucial respect. If there is no objective good, then the person telling me that x is in my self-interest cannot on account of that tell me that I should do x. He might conditionally tell me that *if* I would like to act according to self-interest or in accordance with our mutual interest, *then* I should do x. But that conditional has absolutely no normative import. Perhaps I don't want to follow my self-interest. Or perhaps he and I interpret my self-interest (or our alleged mutual self-interest) differently. Or perhaps our interests are in conflict. Or perhaps I have different interests that conflict with each other and still have to decide which interest to pursue. Even on a basic matter of shared self-interest, such as mere survival, it is clear that not all people share this interest to the same degree and some seem to value it hardly at all. Self-interest and mutual interest, then, have no normative import. Thus, there being no objective good, we are still left with the decisions of each individual. And here, as Leff points out, the prospects are not at all appetizing.[12]

Conventionalism

Most, however, who deny the existence of the common good are not consistent enough to be anarchists; rather, they are conventionalists of some stripe or other. Conventionalism is the idea that there is no good with a reality independent of human beings. Any "good" is a matter of human artifice. Human beings, either as individuals or in groups, create a "conventional good" that is taken to be normative for their behavior. As Walker argues, "Conventionalists insist that the good cannot, in the final analysis, be treated as anything more than a contingent human artifact—whether of personal, social, or

11. See Leff, "Unspeakable Ethics; Unnatural Law," 1230–36.

12. Leff asserts, "All I can say is this: it looks as if we are all we have. Given what we know about ourselves and each other, this is an extraordinarily unappetizing prospect; looking around the world, it appears that if all men are brothers, the ruling model is Cain and Abel. Neither reason, nor love, nor even terror, seems to have worked to make us 'good,' and worse than that, there is no reason why anything should. Only if ethics were something unspeakable by us, could law be unnatural, and therefore unchallengeable. As things now stand, everything is up for grabs" (1249). He concludes with a poem: "Nevertheless: / Napalming babies is bad. / Starving the poor is wicked. / Buying and selling each other is depraved. / Those who stood up to and died resisting Hitler, Stalin, Amin and / Pol Pot—and General Custer too—have earned salvation. / Those who acquiesced deserve to be damned. / There is in the world such a thing as evil. / [All together now:] Sez who? / God help us."

historical manufacture.”[13] Yet conventionalists of all stripes share a commitment to moral nihilism in the sense that they reject a standard independent of and normative for human willing. Consequently, there is no standard over humans that tells them how to construct the good. Rather, the good is open to any particular content whatsoever. It's all a matter of human decision. As Walker rightly notes, “There is a symbiosis between conventionalism and nihilism. Nihilism is the actuating premise of conventionalism. . . . More simply, conventionalists are conventionalists *because* they are nihilists. After all, if one thought real goodness were available, why would one claim that *only* artifacts are available? In the absence of the real, only the man-made remains.”[14] Because of this, conventionalists must maintain that human conventions are not open to outside criticism. Thus, for example, one culture has no normative ground for criticizing the conventions of another culture. Likewise, a culture being criticized has no normative ground for complaining about it.

Therefore, it follows that for the conventionalist there are no meaningful constraints upon human willing. Even so, conventionalists frequently speak *as if* human willing really is capable of constructing some sort of common good that somehow has real normative status. Thus, the norms of particular cultures, though they are said to be mere conventions, are taken to have real binding power for the members of that culture. But because it takes more than *mere* willing or habit or exercises of power to create obligation, if those norms are really conventional and if they really do oblige, then we must assume that a real good was brought into being by human determination (in particular, the determination to have certain norms). I suppose someone might wonder why it takes more than mere willing or habit or exercises of power to create obligation. I hope the following proves sufficient. To say that I am obliged to do x, means that I ought to do x. It does not mean that I am under some sort of physical or causal necessity. Rather, it means that it is right and good to do x and wrong to fail to do it. But this oughtness cannot be found in mere willing for one cannot discriminate among exercises of will on the basis of will. If we have no standard that is normative for human willing, then any exercise of the

---

13. Walker, *Moral Foundations of Constitutional Thought,* 25. Notice that Walker thinks the term *conventionalism* might be applied very individualistically. This is because the conventional good is constructed. Therefore, one might construct it at the individual or group level. Individual-level conventionalism is still to be distinguished from anarchy. For consistent anarchists recognize that there is no discriminating between various exercises of the will across individuals or within a single individual. If consistent, the individual-level anarchist does not take himself to be creating his own good. Rather, he takes each exercise of his own will to constitute a denial of any good at all.

14. Ibid.

will is as good as any other. True, some exercises may be stronger than others—perhaps you are holding a gun and asking for my wallet—but strength of will is morally indifferent. From a normative standpoint, when presented with strength of will, one can simply say, "who cares?" and let it go at that. To say that one exercise of will is good and another bad, one needs recourse to a standard outside of the will. The same applies to habit and exercises of power.

We might speak, therefore, of constructivist conventionalism and take this to mean that some sort of real good can be constructed. The problems with such a view are intractable, and the view inevitably collapses into nihilistic conventionalism. What human will can create, it can also destroy. Likewise, on such a view, human willing could bring into being two competing common goods—two contradictory common goods, binding upon the same group of people, and obliging them in contradictory ways. How could one decide between such competing common goods? But even more damning is a basic metaphysical problem. If there is no goodness to begin with, just what about human willing could bring it into being ex nihilo? And how could we tell that it had been brought into being so as to discriminate between exercises of will that construct or enforce a conventionally created common good and those that do not? In the end it looks as if the only basis of discrimination, on such a view, is that some exercises of will are *called* good and others are not. But this calling is just another exercise of will that is not in itself good. And just who is doing the calling anyway? It certainly isn't an entire society. Rather, the calling is being done by people with power. Thus it looks as if conventionalism, while it appears to construct a real good, simply chooses, arbitrarily, to name some exercises of will good and to refrain from so naming other exercises of human will. And apart from some real standard of goodness, this naming has no normative power (no *potestas*). What I have called constructivist conventionalism, then, cannot avoid metaphysical collapse into nihilistic conventionalism. I therefore see little point in distinguishing the two.

Preferential Conventionalism

Conventionalism takes at least two forms: preferential conventionalism and procedural conventionalism. Preferential conventionalism ties to many traditional interpretations of Hobbes and Bentham.[15] In preferential convention-

---

15. Preferential conventialism is essentially the same as Walker's teleological conventionalism. Walker maintains that Hobbes and Bentham

are teleological thinkers because they justify their ethics by reference to a governing end. For Bentham's utilitarianism, the end is pleasure. For Hobbes, the governing end is peace,

alism, the constructed good (or goods) has the nature of an end. For in preferential conventionalism, the good is defined, as with Hobbes, as the object of desire.[16] Such a good could be peace (survival), pleasure, profit (wealth), or fame, or anything else like this. The good here (say, for instance, that it is peace) is an end or goal for the reason that attaining it leads to the fulfillment of desire or the realization of some preference. For example, if Joe survives, then his desire is realized. But such a good does not have anything like moral status simply by virtue of being the object of desire. Something must be added to preference or the end in view to give it normative status. And this added something is simply an exercise of the human will to the effect that some particular preference or desire, say, pleasure or survival, shall be given normative status. This can play out in a couple of ways. Human willing might accord normative status to some overriding preference or desire such as survival or it might accord normative status to more than one preference at the same time. Perhaps, then, the conventional good is a complex composed of peace and pleasure or wealth and fame or any other combination of these. Perhaps human willing decides to accord normative status to maximizing the realization of preferences. There is, of course, a problem with conceiving of the common good as complex, teleological, and conventional. For any of these ends might come

---

or in the final analysis, survival. They are conventionalists because whatever *normativity* their theories have is simply posited or stipulated, not given in the nature of reality. This is because pleasure and survival, while not themselves simply matters of convention, are not in themselves compelling on a moral basis. For example, the observation that people seem generally to pursue pleasure and avoid pain does not make for the prescription that they ought to. History and ordinary experience show that the pursuit of individual or group gratification can produce blameworthy or even reprehensible behavior.

"Similarly," he adds,

the observation that many—even most—people in fact consider self-preservation the highest good does not make for the prescription that they ought to. Indeed, history is full of stories of moral heroes who—to the acclaim of their fellows—spurned self-preservation for the sake of a higher good. Nor is it easy to invest "survival" with an ultimate moral authority by pitching it at the level of a social community or the human race instead of at the level of the individual. For the desirability of the preservation of the race is not simply self-evident. Nor is it universally agreed upon; we have certainly heard existentialist misgivings on the subject, not to mention those inclined to suicide or terrorism or both.

Walker concludes, "Utilitarian and Hobbesian moral theory represent, then, a kind of teleological conventionalism. For the principles they select are not mere artifacts of convention, but the normativity attributed to them is" (ibid., 30–34).

16. Hobbes, *Leviathan*, 6, 7, 24. According to Hobbes, "But whatsoever is the object of any mans appetite or Desire; that is it, which he for his part calleth *Good*: And the object of his Hate, and Aversion, *Evill*; and of his Contempt, *Vile* and *Inconsiderable*. For these words of Good, Evill, and Contemptible, are ever used with relation to the person that useth them: There being nothing simply and absolutely so; nor any common Rule of Good and Evill, to be taken from the nature of the objects themselves" (28–29). On Hobbes's understanding of the good, see especially Jean Hampton's seminal work, *Hobbes and the Social Contract Tradition*, esp. 27–57.

into competition with each other. What then? Well, given conventionalism, human willing can choose to ignore such competition, arrange the goods hierarchically, or solve the matter on a case-by-case basis. Such a hierarchical arrangement, however, entails that the common good is not really complex. The good for which the others are sacrificed is the true good in such a case.

But even if the complex version of teleological conventionalism could be made to work, there is a deeper problem here. For on conventionalist normative assumptions any exercise of the will must at the most basic level be as good as any other exercise (whether by an individual or by a group). Thus, whatever object of desire is given normative status by some exercise of human willing can also lose that status by a different exercise of human willing. The moment that a desire for some object becomes greater, there is no reason to think the common good won't change. In short, there is no real limiting factor in preferentialist conventionalism. Consequently, preferentialist conventionalism leaves human will unrestrained. For whatever is deemed normative by virtue of being preferred at one moment may and likely will be dethroned the moment a stronger preference arises.

Procedural Conventionalism

According to procedural conventionalism, if some basic facts are accorded normative status, then those facts are not particular ends, goals, or objects of desire, but rather the norms, laws, and institutions (in however primitive a state) by which some group of people (or even an individual) chooses to govern themselves.[17] The norms, laws, and institutions may lead to *any* particular outcome. That is not of consequence. Rather, some ways of shaping rules or some institutional processes are identified as good apart from the outcomes to which they might lead.[18] Frequently, these patterns or institutions receive such goodness as they are taken to have from some fundamental norm that is accorded final authority independent of outcomes resulting from following the norm or from the operation of the institutions in question. There is no ap-

17. Procedural conventionalism covers the same ground as Walker's deontic conventionalism (*Moral Foundations of Constitutional Thought*, 34–40). Procedural conventionalism can be considered deontic because the norm(s) or institutional processes in question provide a standard to which human will is to conform, however things turn out or however much a person finds himself otherwise inclined. In other words, the conformity of human willing to some particular rule is the fundamental thing.

18. I mention this as a logical possibility rather than as a serious metaphysical possibility. Philosophically speaking, the idea seems positively incoherent.

peal beyond the norm.[19] Whatever the fundamental norm is, it is established as such by human will. It has normative status because humans have decided that it will have normative status. This fundamental rule could be the consensus of the community developed over time. It could even be something like representative democracy.[20] Or it might be the Constitution itself.[21]

It simply must be pointed out here that there are serious questions as to whether procedural conventionalism constitutes a viable category. I present it in this chapter because it is a prima facie logical possibility and because some scholars do in fact interpret the Constitution in this way. But so long as we are talking about conventionalism, then the procedures or patterns of human behavior or the norms that people accept all derive their normative status (their ability to obligate) simply by human willing. But then for any particular convention we can ask why it was chosen. And here it's not clear how the procedural conventionalist can answer without appealing to preference of desire. He is certainly left *without* the ability to say that the convention was chosen *because* it was good. That would seem to leave three options: it was chosen arbitrarily or because it was itself the object of desire (which seems to make little sense) or because it was the means to attain some desired good or goods. The latter two options return us to some form of preferential conventionalism. The first option seems an unlikely candidate. But if you were to ask a conventionalist why some norm or institution was chosen he might reply that it just was and that's that. There was no reason and no correspondence with desire or preference. Arbitrary selection of a fundamental norm beyond which there is no appeal may not seem wise or good or desirable. But however foolish arbitrarily selecting some norm or institution or patterns of behavior as good might be, it's possible to maintain that some person or group of people

19. According to Koons, this very position is faced with "a vicious regress that threatens the coherency of the project." See his critique of this position in *Realism Regained,* 275–76. I present his critique in my treatment of positivism in chapter 5.

20. Consider Ely's position in *Democracy and Distrust,* 5, 87. According to Ely, although we have always accepted representative democracy, there is no moral basis for this acceptance. He does not say we have representative democracy for the sake of realizing some good or desire. We simply accept it and that's that. It's a matter of convention. Human will has set up for the fundamental norms certain procedures that are taken as the most fundamental fact about how we govern ourselves. See also Walker, *Moral Foundations of Constitutional Thought,* 34.

21. Some constitutional theorists speak as if the Constitution belongs to the natural law tradition simply because it preserved a distinction between higher law and ordinary law, even though they view the Constitution itself as taking on the role of higher law, replacing traditional natural law. But this is conventionalism and antirealism with a vengeance. It is procedural conventionalism rather than preferentialist conventionalism, and perhaps that's why many are so easily confused. For many conceive of natural law as more about rules than ends, in more deontic than teleological terms.

has done just that. Even so, if some people have done just that, we must still point out that one arbitrary exercise of the will is no more good than any other exercise of the will. In which case there is no true limiting factor in procedural conventionalism. If people at any point want to replace the fundamental norm or change their mind about what patterns of behavior are to be called good or want to change their basic institutions, there is nothing in procedural conventionalism to suggest that they cannot or should not. Everything that human will can make can be unmade by a different exercise of the will.

Thus all conventionalism reduces to the idea that the people should get whatever they want, whenever they want it—or, more aptly, whatever they will, whenever they will it.[22] This is because all forms of conventionalism presuppose, like (moral) anarchism, the truth of moral nihilism. In that case, conventionalism is neither better nor worse than anarchism. To even make such an evaluation we need access to a real moral standard, which, on the assumption of moral nihilism, doesn't exist.

There Is a Common Good

Before considering different conceptions of what a real common good might look like, it is important to give some consideration to what those conceptions might have in common. In other words, we should try to see if there is any basic form that different candidates for the common good are competing to fill. I think we can say something to the matter, even if we can't say too much without begging the question. We think of the common good, first and foremost, as the good that everyone seeks.[23] But we also tend to think of it as more than this. After all, the idea behind the common good is that there is some good or some thing, x, that is good for everyone or to the mutual advantage of all and that the *mere* fact that it is sought is not the reason for either of these (i.e., survival might be seen as being to everyone's advantage even though some people eschew it).[24] We also usually think of the common good

22. Oliver Wendell Holmes held such a view, suggesting that "if my fellow citizens want to go to Hell I will help them. It's my job" (cited in Sandel, *Democracy's Discontent*, 44).

23. See Aristotle *Nichomachean Ethics* 1094a.

24. One way to distinguish thin commonality from thick commonality is by noting that a thin common good is good for everyone individually (one might say, good for each person as a subject), whereas a thick good is common in this sense and in the sense of partnership—that is, cooperation brings the good about, and once the good is brought about, one person's enjoyment of the good does not detract from another's. In other words, a thick common good possesses jointness of supply; therefore, a thick good is more than a thin one, but it is not less, and hence these different conceptions have some common ground.

as something that can only be realized by cooperation, and so we think of it as entailing an ongoing partnership of some sort (though this need not mean partnership in a deep sense). That is, there is a mutual and reciprocal aspect to the common good. Furthermore, to the extent that there is a common good, it is taken to be normative for human law and lawmakers in the sense that human law is supposed to aim at it. If the good is survival, then human legislators are to aim at procuring this good for their citizens. Finally, entailed by the last point is the idea that if we are affirming a real common good, if we are claiming that the common good has real ontological status, then we are claiming that its existence is not dependent on human willing. But we are also affirming a standard for human nature that is not only independent of but also normative for human behavior.

Deontic Realism

If the Constitution presupposes a real common good, then this good might be deontic. To apprehend whether the Constitution presupposes such a good (and, indeed, whether this is even possible), we must first know what it looks like. The *locus classicus* of deontic ethics, Immanuel Kant, helps bring the idea into focus (though some think his exposition as opaque as can be). Kant opens his *Grounding for the Metaphysics of Morals* with the famous remark, "There is no possibility of thinking of anything at all in the world, or out of it, which can be regarded as good without qualification, except a *good will*."[25] But just what is a good will, anyway? According to Kant, a good will has nothing to do with outcomes, consequences, qualities, character, and the like.[26] And here he lists things such as courage and moderation that belong to the classical canon of virtues. Moreover, he detaches goodness from well-being and happiness.[27]

---

25. Kant, *Grounding for the Metaphysics of Morals; with, On a Supposed Right to Lie because of Philanthropic Concerns*, 7.

26. Kant clearly means to reject Aristotle's teleological ethics. But he is also rejecting consequentialism. And it seems as if in presenting his argument, he conflates teleological and consequentialist ethics. But one could perhaps frame a kind of teleological ethic in a consequentialist way. In Hobbes and Bentham, the good has the nature of an end. And their systems seem to be rather consequentialist as well. But teleological and consequentialist ethics are not identical. There is nothing like complete semantic overlap here.

27. "Intelligence, wit, judgment, and whatever talents one might want to name are doubtless in many respects good and desirable, as are qualities of temperament as courage, resolution, perseverance. But they can also become extremely bad and harmful if the will, which is to make use of these gifts of nature and which in its special constitution is called character, is not good. The same holds with gifts of fortune; power, riches, honor, even health, and that complete well-being and contentment with one's condition which is called happiness make for pride and often hereby even arrogance,

From this it follows that we cannot think of the common good as completing or fulfilling of human nature or as that for which humans exist. Kant has ruled out the idea that goodness is an object to be obtained. For him, goodness can only be thought of in absolute and unqualified terms. What then is goodness or a good will? A good will is one that conforms to and is motivated by duty. This is because the moral worth of an action is completely determined by its conformity to duty, where conformity involves not only the act but also the motivation. Furthermore, according to Kant, "An action done from duty has its moral worth, not in the purpose that is to be attained by it, but in the maxim according which the action is realized. The moral worth depends, therefore, not on the realization of the object of the action, but merely on the principle of volition according to which, without regard to any objects of the faculty of desire, the action has been done."[28] To this he adds, "Duty is the necessity of an action done out of respect for the law,"[29] and he argues,

> only the law itself can be an object of respect and hence can be a command. Now an action done from duty must altogether exclude the influence of inclination and therewith every object of the will. Hence there is nothing left

---

unless there is a good will to correct their influence on the mind and herewith also to rectify the whole principle of action and make it universally conformable to its end.

"Some qualities are even conducive to this good will itself and can facilitate its work. Nevertheless, they have no intrinsic unconditional worth; but they always presuppose, rather, a good will, which restricts the high esteem in which they are otherwise rightly held, and does not permit them to be regarded as absolutely good. Moderation in emotions and passions, self-control, and calm deliberation are not only good in many respects but even seem to constitute part of the intrinsic worth of a person. But they are far from being rightly called good without qualification (however unconditionally they were commended by the ancients). For without the principles of a good will, they can become extremely bad; the coolness of a villain makes him not only much more dangerous but also immediately more abominable in our eyes than he would have been regarded by us without it.

"A good will is good not because of what it effects or accomplishes, nor because of its fitness to attain some proposed end; it is good only through willing, i.e., it is good in itself. When it is considered in itself, then it is to be esteemed very much higher than anything which it might ever bring about merely in order to favor some inclination, or even the sum total of all inclinations. Even if, by some especially unfortunate fate or by the niggardly provision of stepmotherly nature, this will should be wholly lacking in the power to accomplish its purpose; if with the greatest effort it should achieve nothing, and only the good will should remain (not, to be sure, as a mere wish but as the summoning of all the means in our power), yet would it, like a jewel, still shine by its own light as something which has its full value in itself. Its usefulness or fruitlessness can neither augment nor diminish this value" (Kant, *Grounding for the Metaphysics of Morals*, 7–8).

28. Ibid., 12. This is Kant's second proposition of morality. He never explicitly states the first proposition. But the first proposition of morality is rather clearly something like the idea that an action must be done from duty (must be motivated by duty alone) in order to have any kind of moral value (12n12).

29. Ibid., 13. This is Kant's third proposition of morality.

which can determine the will except objectively the law and subjectively pure respect for this practical law, i.e., the will can be subjectively determined by the maxim that I should follow such a law even if all my inclinations are thereby thwarted.[30]

Therefore, actions receive what goodness they have from conformity to a rule that is good in itself. Likewise, the will is good if it conforms to the rule for the sake of the rule, rather than for the sake of anything else. Here Kant has a rule in mind—the categorical imperative, which tells us to "Act only according to that maxim whereby you can at the time will that it should become a universal law."[31] And, of course, not everything can be so willed without self-contradiction. Kant reminds us that one cannot will as a universal law and without self-contradiction that everyone should borrow money, pledging to return it, but with no intent to keep the promise.[32] Finally, we must note that this one categorical imperative admits of other formulations such as that we must treat every person as an end in himself and never as a means.[33] Walker aptly summarizes the Kantian position:

> Kant's moral thought is similarly realist, but not teleological. That is, Kant regards the good as a reality whose existence and structure are not a function of human artifice. He regards it as a reality discoverable *in* the innately given structures of human reason and volition. A "good will," which Kant calls the only unequivocally good thing in the world, is good in terms of the structure of its willing rather than the excellence of its objects. In other words, he is interested neither in the ontological status of the good nor in its content, but instead in its right form. As such, Kant offers not so much an alternative kind of metaphysical thinking (versus that from the classics) as a substitute for metaphysical thinking altogether. From this perspective, the right struc-

---

30. Ibid.

31. Ibid., 30.

32. Ibid., 31.

33. Ibid., 36. "Act in such a way that you treat humanity, whether in your own person or in the person of another, always at the same time as an end and never simply as a means." Of course this version of the categorical imperative seems to be formulated on the following basis: "Now I say that man, and in general every rational being, exists as an end in himself and not merely as a means to be arbitrarily used by this or that will. He must in all his actions, whether directed to himself or to other rational beings, always be regarded at the same time as an end" (34). Just before he formulates this idea of the imperative Kant says, "rational nature exists as end in itself" (36). None of this seems to fit very easily with the three propositions of morality or with the idea that goodness does not have the nature of an end or object. But perhaps this points to an impossibility in working out a purely deontic system.

ture of the will is the source of moral imperatives and the basis of law and the social contract.[34]

From this summary we see that while this understanding of the good is realist, it is also supposed to be unsubstantial. The good isn't an object to be obtained and doesn't have specific content. Rather, the good is a norm to which human will must conform, however things turn out. Calling a view of the common good (rather than the good itself) deontic means that the rules in view apply universally, to all individuals. Perhaps there is an additional common element—perhaps it is impossible for every person to conform his will to the norm without the cooperation of others.

This view is not at all unproblematic for at least three reasons. First, it is in fact impossible to craft a rule or a set of rules indifferent to ends and outcomes, for all rules aim at the attainment of some state of affairs. Even proscriptions aim at attaining a state of affairs in which the proscribed actions are not done. Second, no will aims simply at being universal. And it is not easy to see how any will could, for when the will breaks forth into action, it always aims at the attainment or realization of some good that is external to the will. We don't will more will; rather, we will the attainment of some goal or the realization of some state of affairs (unless we act arbitrarily). We aim, at the very least, to make some possible world actual. This suggests that no will can function as Kant describes. Third, we cannot, by recourse to the will, determine whether any particular exercises of the will are good or bad. For considering the will alone, we have only this exercise of the will and that exercise of it. All this shows that normativity cannot be contained in the will itself. It must therefore be some thing or object external to it. To see this, consider this question: why should any person universalize his will? We cannot reply by saying that if he does not universalize it, then he cannot will consistently or without self-contradiction. First, willing consistently and without contradiction is an aim or goal. Moreover, the rule aims to produce a certain kind of person (or a person with a certain kind of existence)—a rationally consistent one. Second, perhaps the person in question doesn't care about the pitfalls of self-contradiction and of having an inconsistent or incoherent will. If such a state is bad, we can only know it by recourse to some standard outside the will itself. To posit that any will is good, therefore, requires positing a real goodness outside of the will.[35]

---

34. Walker, *Moral Foundations of Constitutional Thought*, 29.

35. Some, such as David Richards, seem to think that Rawls's theory of justice is the best attempt to make a go of Kantian thinking—for Rawls is supposed to have provided an ethic free of the prob-

And that means saying that there is something external to the will, at which the will must aim in order to be good. This in turn reintroduces all the teleological baggage Kant hoped to avoid.

Thin Teleological Realism

There are two sorts of teleological realism—a thicker and a thinner sort. In both, the good is real and obliging and has the nature of an end. In other words, in both versions the good is an object or state that individuals aim at attaining. The aiming might be done through human desires or preferences or through the design or pattern of human nature as a whole. In both cases, it is the fact that in both cases the good is good that gives rise to obligation of human beings to pursue it.

In the case of thin teleological realism, the possible candidates for the real good are peace (or survival), pleasure, fame, and wealth.[36] These goods are called teleological because their attainment is the goal or aim of human desire. Because of this, people sometimes confuse thin teleological realism with preferential conventionalism. After all, the objects of human desire play a crucial role in both. But in preferential conventionalism, while the good is defined as the object of desire, the normative status of such an object is wholly a matter of human determination. In contrast, in thin teleological realism, the normative status of the object of desire does not derive from some act of human determination. The normative status derives from the fact that the object in view really is good. Perhaps some exercise of the divine will made it so or perhaps the object possesses some kind of intrinsic merit.[37] After all, most realists say that peace or survival really is good, though it may not be a good of the highest order.

But why are the sorts of theories I am discussing here thin? The thinness of

---

lems attendant with utilitarianism, positivism, and natural law theories and to have helped to supply normativity without metaphysics (see Walker, *Moral Foundations of Constitutional Thought*, 41). But Rawls doesn't quite provide such a theory. He himself admits that his principles of justice depend upon a thin theory of good (*A Theory of Justice*, 347–96). And this thin good seems to be teleological. Rawls mentions that there is wide agreement along the lines of the account of the good that he has given, though with a great deal of variation. And he cites Aristotle and Aquinas right along with many others (350–51, 351n2). But it is clear that the thin theory of the good is much too thin. The failure of the thin theory is telling for the whole neo-Kantian project. See T. K. Seung's *Intuition and Construction: The Foundation of Normative Theory*.

36. I don't expect that this list is exhaustive. But neither do I think it must be for the argument of the chapter to succeed.

37. One way to read Hobbes is as a realist of just this sort.

such theories derives from the fact that they are minimally substantial. Suppose, for instance, that peace or survival is the common good. Well, most any action at some point or other (save suicide) might be compatible with survival. Saying that the goal to attain is self-preservation doesn't tell us much else. Things taken to be wrong in an unqualified sense, such as murder or adultery, may, for a thin teleological realist, become good if they turn out to be conducive to survival. And the other options—pleasure, wealth, and fame—are even less substantial. Saying that the good to be pursued is pleasure tells us virtually nothing about what actions to perform. For pleasure is a rather subjective thing and anything at all might bring pleasure. Saying the good is the most pleasure for the most people only makes matters worse, precisely because people take pleasure in many different things. Some people derive great pleasure from helping others, while others derive considerable pleasure from committing serial murders.[38] The same goes for profit and wealth. Therefore, these theories of the good are thin because they are minimally substantial. These goods are also thin because they are satisfactions of human desire,[39] which is limitless. The real good in view is that certain desires be satisfied. But the satisfaction of desire is something that can be increased indefinitely. That makes the goods in view limitless and indefinite.[40] These goods can still be regulative of human desire and of human behavior. Other desires can be evaluated in terms of whether or not they promote or hinder the satisfaction of the desire for survival or pleasure or wealth. Human actions can be evaluated in terms of whether they increase or diminish the satisfaction of these desires. Thus, in principle, human desire and action can go astray in terms of these goods. But these goods are only minimally regulative. Because they admit of limitless increase, the good is the maximization of satisfaction of these desires, ad infinitum. But almost any action might be calculated to maximally increase the satisfaction of these desires individually or all together. The thick theory is more strongly regulative of human desire and action because the good in view is more determinate (even if not completely determinate). Put another way, well-being, on the thick theory, is a qualitative measure (though it admits of

---

38. On this matter, see Robert K. Bressler, Ann W. Burgess, and John E. Douglas, *Sexual Homicide: Patterns and Motives*, 53. The authors point out that some serial murders feel exhilaration as a result of having committed murder (though, to be sure, there are those who are horrified by their actions).

39. At least, that is how they are experienced or momentarily "possessed."

40. If someone disagrees with my characterization of thin goods as the satisfaction of certain desires, one can still maintain that these goods are thin for the reason that they are quantitative and can be added to indefinitely. It follows that these goods limit human behavior only minimally because almost any (though not every) action might be ordained to the maximization of one of these goods or of all of them together.

degrees of approximation) rather than a purely quantitative measure (as the goods are on the thin theory). There is another sense in which these goods are sometimes said to be thin. They have a thin sense of commonality. These goods are good for each individual and therefore for all individuals rather than goods perfective of human association and partnership. The commonality here is subjective. And it is entirely possible that an individual's pursuit of such a good can come at the expense of others.

Thin teleological theories divide into two kinds: simple and complex. In the simple version, the common good is peace or pleasure or wealth or fame (or some other object of desire). It is only one of these. To be sure, peace might be conducive to pleasure, for the most part, but if the good is pleasure and peace is not conducive to it, then peace ought to be tossed aside. In such a scenario it is not inviolable. But it is also possible to conceive of the common good as thin and complex. Desires vary across people and even within a single individual. Therefore, perhaps the common good is a complex of peace and pleasure or fame and wealth, as in complex preferentialism. There is no reason to think that adding up thin goods yields a thick common good. Such a common good remains thin both because the goods, though real, are still the object of desire and because they are not construed in such a way as to be regulative of desire.

There are of course problems with the complex version. For instance, what happens when two objects of desire, say, peace and pleasure, come into competition. Perhaps a number of people take pleasure from an occasional murder spree, and perhaps these murder sprees undermine social peace. In such cases if we simply privilege one good over the other on its own terms (e.g., by saying that peace is more desired or by saying that allowing murder sprees threatens peace), then it's clear that we are still advancing a simple theory. If we let the tension stand, then the common good is riddled with contradiction. It seems that if both peace and pleasure are part of the common good and if these may come into conflict, then to resolve such conflict we must appeal to some standard outside these goods. What might such a standard be? One might suggest that the standard is what is best for human nature. But then one has begun to journey away from thin to thick teleology.

Thick Teleological Realism

"Substantive moral realism" operates within the larger context of realism proper. That is, a substantive moral realist is committed to a realist ontology, where "A realist ontology essentially vindicates the common human perception that nature, in both its physical and moral dimensions, really does exist. Its existence and its fundamental structure are not merely ascribed by convention."[41] Realist ontology has gotten a hard time in the academy for a while, of course, but it is currently making a comeback.[42] In such an ontology, human nature has real status. We are not free to remake it in whatever image we desire. Put another way, the reality of human nature is given rather than constructed. The good, in such a view, is that which is completing of human nature or productive of human well-being. And because human nature is given rather than constructed, because it is fixed rather than ever changing, what is good for human nature, what is consistent with or productive of the well-being of that nature, is also fixed.

This description of substantive moral realism needs some filling out. What is it, after all, to say that something is good for a person in the sense that it is completing of human nature? When substantive moral realists refer to human well-being, they have in mind something like Aristotle's concept of *eudaemonia*—"the state of living a perfectly good life."[43] But what is a good life? In the Aristotelian account, "The primary use of good would be in specifying what is *good for* this or that organism, and something would be good for an organism just in case it is or leads to the fulfillment of the organism's teleofunctions."[44] The good of an organism lies in the performance of its function, and the function of a thing is the work proper to it—that work a thing does and that explains why we have such a thing to begin with.[45] More aptly, the good or goal of an organism is that outcome that is aimed at by its very design. Thus the good of the human organism lies in the proper functioning of the design of human nature. That is, the goal of human nature is that outcome that results from operation of human nature, when it is functioning rightly in an appropriate environment.[46]

41. Walker, *Moral Foundations of Constitutional Thought*, 47.

42. For example, in works such as Koons's *Realism Regained*, which shows not only the plausibility of realist ontology but also the superiority of realism to other metaphysics.

43. Which is not to say such thinkers believe Aristotle got it exactly right. Eminent Aristotelian St. Thomas Aquinas thought that the Aristotelian account required modification in light of Christian revelation. Moreover, properly construed, I think Plato, along with his concept of human excellence, should be listed among the substantively thick, teleological realists.

44. Koons, *Realism Regained*, 260, 269–70.

45. See J. Budziszewski, *What We Can't Not Know*, 110, as well as *Written on the Heart: The Case for Natural Law*, 22–23.

46. How we ascertain the function of a thing was discussed in chapter 2 and need not be rehashed here. It suffices to point out that something like the methodology discussed in chapter 2 could be applied to ascertain the human function and therefore the human good. We need only note that for the thick theory, the human person is designed to function in a particular way (or in particular ways).

For advocates of the thick theory, human well-being is composed first and foremost of a rightly ordered soul—a soul in which reason governs the appetites through the passions (or the spirited part).[47] This is true because the human function, or work, is to live according to reason.[48] The governance of reason here, however, is not merely instrumental. Instrumental reason tells us how to get from x to z, *if* we want to get from x to z. There is no moral imperative in the operation of such reason, only prudential recommendations. Classical reason, however, apprehends goodness as such.[49] Even more, it apprehends the in-built purposes of things and therefore the purposes or functions of human life. Thus, reason apprehends that living according to reason is the work of the human being and then apprehends those virtues that help the per-

---

47. See Plato *Republic,* bk. 9. For a contemporary presentation of this line of thinking, see C. S. Lewis's *Abolition of Man,* originally presented as the Riddell Memorial Lectures at the University of Durham. Lewis wrote, "As the king governs by his executive, so Reason in man must rule the mere appetites by means of the 'spirited element.' The head rules the belly through the chest—the seat, as Alanus tells us, of Magnanimity, of emotions organized by trained habit into stable sentiments" (34). For the relevance of this way of thinking for the framers, see Daniel Walker Howe's seminal article, "The Political Psychology of *The Federalist.*" I commend this last piece not because it helps us understand the framers' intent, but because it is a superb exposition of this theory of human motivation.

48. Says Aristotle,

> The proper function of man, then, consists in an activity of the soul in conformity with a rational principle or, at least, not without it. In speaking of the proper function of a given individual we mean that it is the same as the man who sets high standards for himself: the proper function of the harpist is the same as the function of the harpist who has high standards for himself. The same applies to any and every group of individuals: full attainment of excellence must be added to the mere function. In other words, the function of the harpist is to play the harp; the function of the harpist who has high standards is to play it well. On these assumptions, if we take the proper function of man to be a certain kind of life, and if this kind of life is an activity of the soul and consists in actions performed in conjunction with the rational element, and if a man of high standards is he who performs these actions well and properly, and if the function is well performed when it is performed in accordance with the excellence appropriate to it; we reach the conclusion that the good of man is an activity of the soul in conformity with excellence or virtue, and if there are several virtues, in conformity with the best and most complete. (*Nichomachean Ethics* 1098a10)

49. Plato famously observes, "in the knowable the last thing to be seen, and that with considerable effort, is the *idea* of the good; but once seen, it must be concluded that this is in fact the cause of all that is right and fair in everything—in the visible it gave birth to light and its sovereign; in the intelligible, itself sovereign, it provided truth and intelligence—and that man who is going to act prudently in private or in public must see it" (*Republic* 517b–d). Aristotle distinguishes between voice, "which is possessed by other animals and also used by them to express pain or pleasure," and speech, which "serves to indicate what is useful and what is harmful, and so also what is just and what is unjust. For the real difference between man and other animals is that humans alone have perception (*aisthēsis*) of good and evil, just and unjust, etc. It is the sharing of a common view in *these* matters that makes a household and a state" (*The Politics* 1253a7–1253a18).

son to do just this. Living well, in accordance with reason, involves virtues such as courage, friendliness, generosity, and prudence. It also involves moderation and self-control and living in partnership with other human beings. These virtues are not only instrumentally good but good in themselves. In other words, friendship isn't just a means to the good life. It is also a constituent of human well-being. If reason is to govern the soul and if reason apprehends these things as really good, then it is clear that life according to reason is not open to any possibility whatsoever. On such a view, there will be actions that can never be conducive to human well-being that are therefore absolutely proscribed. Aristotle thought adultery was one such action.[50] On the Thomistic account of this view, giving false testimony against one's neighbor, taking innocent human life, and adultery are things that are always wrong and can never be right. The performance of such acts is always inconsistent with human well-being.

The Constitution and the Common Good

Inference to the Best Explanation, Stage 1: Eliminating Alternative Explanations

The Constitution is inconsistent with (moral) anarchism for two reasons: it is inconsistent with the policy or institutional inference the (moral) anarchist makes from moral nihilism *and* with the moral nihilism of the anarchist that underlies that policy recommendation. First, (moral) anarchists believe there is no real good common to all. They infer that no government is legitimate. But the Constitution attempts to erect a government. There is, therefore, a rather obvious contradiction between the Constitution and anarchy. I argued earlier in this chapter that *if* moral anarchy (individualistic relativism) is true, *then* political anarchy follows. Of course, political anarchy is incompatible with any plan of government, so "no plan of government" is entailed by political anarchism. The Constitution, however, is a plan of government; therefore, the Constitution rejects political anarchism. Thus, the Constitution entails a rejection of the consequent in the conditional. Consequently, in accordance with *modus tollens,* we must also reject the antecedent, which is moral anarchy or individualistic relativism. Second, the Constitution is at

50. See Aristotle *Nichomachean Ethics* 1107a11.

variance with the view of moral reality that animates the policy stance of the anarchist. On the anarchist's view, there simply is no basis (i.e., no intelligible ground) for political or legal obligation. This is entailed by radical moral nihilism. But the Constitution presupposes many obligations such as the obligation of officials to follow the procedures laid out in the Constitution's text and the obligation of citizens to follow rightly adopted laws.[51] To be sure, one might refer to these as legal, rather than moral, obligations. But there can be no legal obligation without prior moral obligation. I might be bound to do some action x according to the law. But this leaves open the matter of why I should obey any human law. The sort of oughtness that tells me that I should obey human laws (generally speaking) or at least follow ones that are well made (according to reason, promotive of the common good, etc.) can only come from outside of human law, from the moral realm proper.[52] And this is just the realm that the (moral) anarchist (and the antirealist more generally) claims does not exist. Therefore, the mere fact of the Constitution's existence does not fit with the anarchist's moral nihilism. It should be immediately clear that the Constitution fails to fit with any denial of a real common good—the conventionalist's as much as the anarchist's—for the same reason. To rule by law rather than simply by force presupposes a belief in the existence of some obligation to act in accordance with the laws. But this legal obligation acquires its binding power from goodness per se.[53] Of course, many will think this move too easy, though those who say this sort of thing never say why. Nevertheless, I will endeavor to discount conventionalism on grounds that discount conventionalism as such.

51. As Walker notes, "prescription implies a morally compelling standard empowering prescription" (*Moral Foundations of Constitutional Thought*, 10).

52. In other words,

all constitutions and written laws are human creations. Either it is possible for human beings to frame these laws inappropriately or not. If not, then the law itself is devoid of obligation. For if there no such thing as a good or bad law because there is no such thing as good or bad, then there is no such thing as good or bad behavior with respect to the law. One could not do wrong in failing to follow the law, and therefore one could not be said to behave inappropriately towards others in failing to adhere to a law or constitution. That is, one could not be said to behave unjustly, either towards a ruler or one's fellow citizens or anyone at all. In short, if there is no standard outside of the law telling us that we must obey good laws and render people their due, then it makes little sense to say that we are obligated to render people their due according to some law. For whatever that law is, it has no claim on our obedience. In such a situation law lacks any normative force (*potestas*). (Paul R. DeHart, "The Dangerous Life: Natural Justice and the Rightful Subversion of the State," 389)

53. I do not mean to say here that goodness is a sufficient condition for obligation. I think it is, at least, a necessary condition.

If anarchy doesn't fit well with the Constitution, neither does preferentialist conventionalism. This is due to problems internal to preferentialist conventionalism. As I have argued, on this version of conventionalism some object of desire (or multiple objects of desire) acquires normative status by some act of human willing. But what underlies such a decision? It can only be, as Hobbes suspects, that the object desired is in fact desired more intensely than anything else. If we use the phrase *common good* to refer to such an object, then we mean that everyone desires this object the most. But what everyone desires the most might change. Perhaps everyone yearned for peace the most, but now they desire pleasure even more than peace (and perhaps in a way that is at odds with peace). Should this happen, the common good will change, for on the preferentialist view the common good is determined by the strongest common desire.[54] Furthermore, because desires vary across people, it seems unlikely that we will find one thing that everyone desires the most. That means we will have to retreat to a weaker standard—that which most people desire the most. Just here a difficulty emerges, for we cannot make such distinctions on the basis of desire alone (making the standard incoherent). Distinguishing among desires requires a standard external to desire. Moreover, because strength of desire can vary within individuals, what most people most desire is likewise subject to change. And if strength of preference in this way determines whether or not a good is elevated to normative status, then the common good is once again subject to change. Regimes created with such a view of the common good will therefore be designed to ensure that the strongest desire, whatever it happens to be, is realized. Such regimes will be designed to do this rather than to help citizens attain one particular possible object of desire, such as peace. From this it follows that if the Constitution is in fact preferentialist, then it will not seek to differentiate between preferences. It will be designed to give sway to the most intense, most common desire at any given time.

The Constitution is frequently thought of as a preference-aggregating machine. But this is a rather simplistic view. The Constitution is actually rather resistant to desire. The strongest desires, in the framers' view, do not persist over time.[55] And the Constitution is a rather effective machine at delaying decision making.[56] To put my point another way, preferentialism does not distinguish among desires (except perhaps on the basis of intensity). In contrast,

---

54. By strongest desire here, I mean the most intense desire at the time.

55. See Madison, *The Federalist* No. 63, 320. I do not mean to invoke *The Federalist* as a way of invoking original intent but only as an example of the psychology of motivation being discussed.

56. Recall Hamilton's arguments in *The Federalist* No. 70, 358, and *The Federalist* No. 71, 363.

the Constitution does distinguish among desires. It favors, by virtue of an extended republic and multiple veto points in the policy process, preferences that are both widely shared and long-lasting. Because we cannot distinguish between long-term and short-term preferences on the basis of preference, this constitutional preference indicates either an arbitrary favoring of some preferences over others, in which case the Constitution is unintelligible, or a recourse to a standard outside of preference that points us to preferences that tend to be good.[57] But beyond this, favoring widely shared, long-term, or enduring desires and preferences arguably demonstrates a qualitative decision to favor preferences and desires for some things over others.[58] After all, only certain kinds of desires or desires for certain things are both widely shared and long-lasting.[59] Madison thought the desire for justice was one such desire. He also thought that narrow, selfish, and unjust demands were intense and short-lived. For instance, the desire for immediate gain at whatever cost is not the sort of desire that persists in everyone as the strongest desire for long stretches of time. If the foregoing is correct, then the Constitution deems some desires good and others bad (or at least deems some desires better than others) and therefore deems some outcomes (or end-states) good (or better than others). But this distinction cannot be made on the basis of preference or desire. The Constitution must therefore presuppose some standard of goodness and therefore of what is good for all in common, which is both independent of and normative for desire. And this means that the common good and the strongest desire cannot be identical. In terms of deducing a contradiction, one could say that all the delay mechanisms in the Constitution stand at odds with a preferentialist understanding of the common good, for these mechanisms are what favor long-term, widely shared desires. In sum, the Constitution favors some preferences (widely shared, long-lasting, and less intense) over others (very intense and short-lived). And this favoring cannot be explained with recourse to preference, for preference cannot tell us what preferences to favor. If we had only preference, then the strongest, most intense preference would always be

57. An arbitrary decision is one made without recourse to reason or some motivation. One may plausibly suggest that no such decision is possible. But that's another matter.

58. Moreover, as I've often remarked, it is impossible to make any distinction, in any kind of normative sense, on the basis of preference alone. Strength of preference and how long a preference lasts over time are morally indifferent if we consider only preference. If we decide to favor long-lasting but less intense preferences over immediate, more intense preferences, we either do so arbitrarily or with reference to some standard outside of and normative for our preferences and desires.

59. In other words, different outcomes or goods correspond to widely shared, long-lasting desires that correspond to short-term, narrow desires. This means a preference for long-lasting desires is tantamount to a preference for the goods corresponding to those desires.

favored. This decision is either made arbitrarily or with reference to some standard outside of human preferences and desires and normative for them. Either way, the determination cannot be made by recourse to preferences or desires; therefore, preferentialism fails as a plausible candidate for the Constitution's theory of the common good.

At just this point, an objector waiting in the wings pounces, Thrasymachus-like, upon the argument. The Constitution's favoring of long-term preferences reveals nothing other than a real or deeper or higher-order preference for long-term over immediate preferences. Our objector suggests that these long-term preferences correspond to some "suitably idealized set of preferences" possessed by a "well-informed, rational, dispassionate, mentally healthy" individual whose "first-order desires [are] in perfect harmony with his higher-order desires." Our objector also maintains that this idealized set of preferences is what people mean by "good."[60] But this argument fails on two grounds. The first ground is a problem endemic to the very nature of defining *good* in this way. There is no way to distinguish between ideal and nonideal preferences based upon preference alone. We require recourse to a real standard of goodness outside of preference even to make this distinction. Consequently, the Constitution's institutionalized distinction of (by virtue of its favoring of) long-term from immediate preferences can only be explained by recourse to a standard external to preferences.

There is a second, much deeper problem with our objector's argument. What does it mean to say that the Constitution betrays a *higher-order* preference for long-term desires over immediate ones? If the hierarchy in question is not normative, leaving us with preference alone, then all we have are competing preferences of varying strength. There is no reason in preference alone for distinguishing among these preferences except on the basis of strength, which has no normative import whatsoever. Strength of preference seems to mean, *ceteris paribus,* "more likely to impel toward action." But a constitution that institutionalizes delayed decision making, thereby actively resisting immediate preferences, necessarily presupposes that, all other things being equal, immediate preference (or desire) would govern human action. The Constitution, by virtue of its design, resists the stronger preference in favor of the weaker one. And if distinguishing among preferences, generally speaking, requires

60. Thanks are owed to Robert Koons for bringing this objection to my attention and to pointing out the response to it already latent in my prior argument. Quotation marks refer to his correspondence, used by permission.

recourse to an external standard, then the same applies to the particular instance of the Constitution's making of that distinction. Moreover, the fact that
the Constitution favors weaker preferences over stronger ones means that the
distinction is not made on the basis of strength of preference.[61]

If preferentialism fails, what about proceduralism? Proceduralism faces a
difficulty quite similar to that faced by preferentialism. Just as we can find no
reason to favor some preferences over others (say, strong over weak) on the basis of preference, we also cannot distinguish between acts of will on the basis
of will alone. Whatever some act of will can establish, can be undone by another act of will. If proceduralism presents us with the correct theory of the
common good, then the common good is established by some act of human
will that makes some norm or rule binding upon all. In other words, proceduralism is the idea that some act of the human will becomes, by the act of
willing, normative for other acts of the will. But then shouldn't we view every
action that fails to conform to the norm as an effort to unmake the old norm?
What if everyone engages in such a rebellion? Haven't they changed the common good? But universal agreement about a norm is a high and lofty dream
not likely to occur in the actual world. Thus the norm established here will
have to be by something like majority will. And it seems that the majority
might at any time want to change the governing norm. Because we can't distinguish among acts of the will on the basis of will alone a regime presupposing the truth of procedural conventionalism will have to be designed so as to
allow for the common good and the governing norms and institutions to be
undone and remade with relative ease. But the Constitution does not allow for
this. In fact, it makes its own alteration via amendment quite difficult. Further,
constitutional features such as the presidential veto or the allowance for judicial review mean that near unanimity of popular will can nevertheless result
in a failure to procure a desired or popularly willed outcome. It seems clear
then that the Constitution's delay mechanisms and multiple veto points discriminate among various exercises of the popular will, favoring some over others. Because such a discrimination cannot be made on the basis of will alone,
it follows that the Constitution is not purely procedural. We might further
mention Madison's suggestion that having a large republic rather than a small

---

61. We can frame the argument against preferentialism in another way. It is rather clear that the
Constitution does not take peace, pleasure, wealth, or fame to be the common good in any unqualified sense. I want to save this argument, however, for our consideration of thin teleological realism.
If we can refute these options there, then we will have refuted them here as well. And that will provide us with a further argument against preferential conventionalism.

one makes it less likely that majorities will be factitious.[62] If Madison is right, then the Constitution rather clearly distinguishes factitious exercises of the popular will from other exercises of it. But because such a distinction is meaningless if we are considering the will alone (popular or otherwise), it seems the Constitution, in making this distinction, must presuppose a nonproceduralist view of the common good.

Thus antirealism is at odds with the Constitution's basic design. But what about realism? We saw earlier that the very attempt to rule by law, an attempt clearly embodied in the Constitution, seems to presuppose realism, inasmuch as the notion of the rule of law requires some notion or other of legal obligation. But what kind of realism might be presupposed? The first candidate is deontic realism. But the problem here is analogous to the problems with conventionalism, for a constitution that seeks to embody such a view would seek only to conform the wills of officials and citizens to certain norms of willing and would not discriminate in favor of some outcomes and against others. Say, for example, we believe that there is a norm about fair procedures through which a law must pass to be just. The deontic realist maintains that the goal is only for lawmakers to conform their wills to the process. Whatever sort of law emerges is just or right so long as the correct procedures are followed. Thus the norm here is outcome-indifferent and also considered really good (perhaps because it embodies a yet deeper norm of fairness). If the Constitution embodies such a norm, it too must be indifferent to the outcomes produced by the operation of the institutional design. But there are provisions throughout the Constitution, particularly in Article I, Section 9 and in the Bill of Rights, that do in fact regulate outcomes by preventing Congress from enacting certain measures.[63] Moreover, the Ninth Amendment suggests that there are rights, not specified in the text, that are in fact protected by the Constitution. This in turn means that certain outcomes, even if they are not specifically named, are proscribed on the ground that such outcomes violate rights retained by the people. To be sure, the Ninth Amendment doesn't tell us which outcomes are unacceptable. But we need not know which outcomes are good and which ones are bad to know that the Ninth Amendment means some outcomes are precluded. And this is sufficient to generate the conclusion that the Constitution is not deontic realist, for it is not outcome-indifferent (of course,

---

62. *The Federalist* No. 10.

63. Of course there are limits placed on outcomes beyond those stipulated in the Bill of Rights. This is pointed out in *The Federalist* No. 84, which argues against adding a Bill of Rights to the Constitution partly on the grounds that the Constitution is itself already a Bill of Rights.

this conclusion holds, given my argument above, even if the Ninth Amendment were not part of the Constitution). Furthermore, the Constitution is arguably not outcome-indifferent for the reasons discussed above when considering preferentialism and proceduralism. It favors long-lasting, widely shared preferences and interests over narrow, short-lived, and intense ones. These different kinds of interests arguably correspond to different kinds of objects. Therefore, the Constitution favors the sorts of outcomes and objects that correspond to long-lasting, widely shared preferences.

Some might object to my argument on the grounds that "protecting individual rights should count as a deontic constraint" rather than as an "outcome" and that the Constitution's favoring of long-lasting preferences over immediate ones can be understood as "a mechanism designed to protect the rights-based deontic constraints that shelter minorities."[64] I think the criticism can be met. Suppose we view rights, with Robert Nozick, as side constraints upon action.[65] Then we might see the Constitution as incorporating the Bill of Rights and even the Fourteenth Amendment either as further specifications to the procedural rules for the passage of legislation or as rules supervening on the rules for making laws. But we must note just what sorts of rules these would be. The First Amendment says, "Congress shall make no law respecting an establishment of religion, or prohibiting the free exercise thereof; or abridging the freedom of speech, of the press; or the right of the people peaceably to assemble, and to petition the Government for a redress of grievances." Rules such as these are not outcome-indifferent *because* they take certain outcomes off the table. They expressly preclude certain legislative outcomes and, as a consequence, aim for the passage of laws not precluded. Therefore, if we see individual rights, protected under the Bill of Rights, as deontic constraints, then we cannot view them as purely deontic, because they favor some outcomes by precluding others.[66] Furthermore, this line of reasoning applies to the second objection. If the constitutional preference for "long-lived preferences over short-lived ones" is actually "a mechanism designed to protect the rights-based deontic constraints that shelter minorities," then the Constitution works so as to protect side constraints that once again take certain actions off the table, thereby favoring outcomes in which those

---

64. Robert Koons brought these objections to my attention. I borrow his wording in framing them.
65. See Nozick, *Anarchy, State and Utopia*, chap. 3.
66. I might note that I am not persuaded that the Bill of Rights is solely about protecting individual rights. It seems to me that rights, such as free speech, are protected *in order* to ensure an open public realm *in order* to allow for public accountability *in order* to prevent governmental tyranny.

actions not precluded obtain. To put all this another way, rights, understood as deontic constraints, are not purely deontic.

The inability of the Constitution to presuppose deontic realism results from one of the fundamental problems with Kantian thought discussed earlier in the chapter. No set of moral rules is ever truly outcome-indifferent. Every rule there might be aims at some outcome, some particular action, or the obtaining of some particular state of affairs. This makes all rules teleological to some degree. Take Kant's own reasoning behind the categorical imperative. We are to universalize *in order* to avoid willing a self-contradiction. But this rule has a goal—the rationally consistent human being. Kant calls a will that aims at this state of being a good will. But, of course, we cannot distinguish between a good will and a bad will on the basis of will alone. To say that a good will is a rationally consistent one is to concede that there is an objectively good state of being (being rationally consistent in our actions) external to the will that the will must aim to achieve in order to be called good. If Kantian thought fails for the reason that no rules, at day's end, can be outcome-indifferent and thus must be in some sense teleological, it follows that rules governing the lawmaking process (like rights, deontically construed) cannot be outcome-indifferent and therefore also must be teleological.

Finally, we come to teleological realism. If the rejection of the other options is sound, it is reasonable to infer that the Constitution presupposes the common good to be real, to be external to the will, and to have the nature of an end. But the Constitution might presuppose the truth of either thick or thin teleological realism. The only way to determine whether or not there are contradictions with thin teleological realism is to consider the options presented as possible candidates. Pleasure is the easiest option to eliminate, because it is derived from the attainment of some desired good. There are, however, all sorts of pleasures. There are pleasures corresponding to the fulfillment of long-term desires and pleasures corresponding to the fulfillment of short-term desires. If the Constitution favors some pleasures over others (the pleasure corresponding to the fulfillment of enduring desires), then it cannot be on the basis of pleasure itself. If the Constitution presupposes the good is real and distinguishes among pleasures, then it must assume that the good is a standard independent of pleasure that tells us which pleasures are good and to be pursued and which are not. I would suggest, then, that the decision-delay mechanisms in the Constitution and the large extent of territory (making majority formation a long process) are design features at odds with the notion that pleasure is the sole good at which the Constitution aims. Pleasure may be part of the good, but there is also a standard outside of pleasure that the Constitution accepts as true.

What about wealth? I suggest that the Constitution's creation of an extended republic is in fact very much at odds with the idea that wealth is the real good. Not as an appeal to original intent, but to see why this might be the case, let's consider Madison's argument in *The Federalist* No. 10. Madison points out that "the most common and durable source of factions, has been the various and unequal distribution of property." The distribution of property is unequal because people have "different and unequal faculties of acquiring property." Because people have different abilities, they acquire different amounts and kinds of property. To all of this Madison adds, "The protection of these faculties is the chief object of government."[67] The Constitution accomplishes this via the initial allowance of this diversity together with majority governance over an extended republic. Once the diversity has been allowed, if we have a system of majority rule, then the diversity can only be eliminated or mitigated by majority decision.[68] The extended sphere, however, makes majority formation difficult and makes it difficult for particular, rather than broadly shared, interests to succeed in getting policy to go their way. But the interest of those with little property to acquire lots more property through political mechanisms rather than through their own faculties is arguably too narrow to command the requisite support. Further, federalism, the delegation of powers, and mechanisms that delay decision making (multiple veto points) all tend to favor less regulation rather than more, including regulation of the economic sphere. If Madison is right, economic liberty and inequality are tied together. Therefore, if liberty is a presupposition of the Constitution's design (say, an implication of the extended sphere), then the Constitution also presupposes the acceptability of economic inequality. And this stands in contradiction to the notion that the common good is wealth. For if the common good is wealth, then the goal is for all to be wealthy.

But, someone might object, perhaps the goal is the aggregate wealth of society rather than the wealth of each individual. I am inclined to think that our objector misunderstands the sort of commonality attendant to a thin common good. A thin good is said to be common in the sense that it is good for each individual, considered only as an individual, and therefore for all individuals together. In terms of wealth alone, how can we say that the aggregate

---

67. *The Federalist* No. 10, 44.

68. In fact, my point would hold even if we had a mixed regime, so long as the majority had some real share in sovereignty, in exercising final say.

wealth is good for each individual?[69] Furthermore, a thin good is most definitely not a good completing of human partnership or association. Describing the common good as the wealth of society rather than of individuals, however, is to suggest that it is such a good. I am doubtful that wealth is legitimately described in such terms. In what sense is the wealth of society as a whole completing of human association? It seems at best an aid to or tool for human association to put to use. Indeed, if we ask how wealth is good for society as a whole, we are not likely to answer that it makes human association complete or that it is the final good aimed at by human association, but rather that it aids human association in attaining other higher-order goods. But if we so answer, then wealth is not the common good. For, as this answer indicates, wealth is only good insofar as it is ordered to the attainment of some higher good. It is only good in reference to something else. To be sure, a preferentialist might rightly note that a person can, in theory, desire money more than he desires anything else, making wealth a satisfaction of desire. But it is hard to see how wealth can be an aim in any other sense. In short, it is difficult to discern how the realist can hold wealth to be a real good. For, as suggested, wealth is a means to an end and therefore lacks the nature of a final or real aim of human action. It seems logically impossible to posit wealth as anything like a *real* final goal. But if this is the case, then the Constitution cannot presuppose that wealth is the real good that its design plan aims to attain. It could only ever aim at accumulating wealth *in order* to use it for the furtherance of other higher ends.

So much for wealth. What of fame? Again, if fame is the great good of the political system, it must not presuppose that such a good is common or universal. The larger the republic, the smaller the likelihood that any one person will command the requisite attention; the larger the republic, the smaller the proportion of the population that is actually noteworthy. Thus the very fact that the Constitution effects an extended sphere mitigates against the idea that fame could be the common good. Of course, it is contrary to the nature of fame for it to be a common good to begin with. The nature of fame is that some can have it *only if* others do not. If fame is a good, then it is neither universal nor common in any deep sense.

This brings us to the last of the thin options on the diagram, peace. Surely peace is a goal of the Constitution. The Constitution's preamble says that it is

---

69. If one replies that increasing the aggregate wealth is good for each individual *because* it raises the probability that each individual's wealth will be increased, then it isn't aggregate wealth that is good in view, but rather the increased wealth of each individual. In that case, we return to the argument of the previous paragraph.

ordained by the people to secure the domestic tranquility. Therefore, shouldn't any conception of what the Constitution takes to be good include peace? But this need not mean, as modernists seem to think, that the Constitution's understanding of the common good is restricted to peace. There are features of the Constitution, after all, not explained by the goal of peace. That, however, is a matter for the next section in this chapter. Here we need only point to some inconsistencies in the Constitution with the notion that peace is the common good or that highest end to which all others must bow. First, peace is usually understood in the Hobbesian sense of survival. But the Constitution does not endeavor to maximize everyone's survival; rather, it allows not only for domestic defense, but also for Congress to declare war. There is no textual or institutional restriction requiring Congress to do this only when the nation's very survival is jeopardized. This allowance seems at odds with survival being the high good. Second, the Fifth and Fourteenth Amendments to the Constitution allow for a citizen's life to be taken so long as it is done by due process of law. It is clear in terms of mere survival that we need not take the life of those who seem to threaten the preservation of others. We can simply incarcerate such people. These constitutional features point to a distinguishing of instances in which preservation is to be pursued from instances in which it can be sacrificed. This implies that mere preservation is sometimes not in keeping with the common good but is sometimes suspended in order to uphold a higher principle. Clearly, some will object that the good in view is the preservation of the community. But such an objection fails to comprehend the way in which survival is said to be a common good in terms of thin teleology. The commonality here is simply that this is good for everyone individually. It is the same for everyone. But if it is both the common and the high good, then we are bound to preserve everyone's individual life as much as possible, which is quite different from preserving a community. The objector is really positing the community as good and assuming that individuals exist, to some extent, for the sake of community. Such an assumption, however, doesn't belong to thin but rather to thick teleology.

We finally find ourselves with the option of thick teleology. I suggest that it is reasonable to infer that the Constitution assumes the truth of thick teleological realism. We have, after all, presented a reasonably exhaustive list of possible understandings of the common good. It is likely the case that any other understandings of the common good are really just some version of the options we have listed. Further, the options on Diagram 4.1 are exclusive of each other. So, let a stand for thick teleological realism and b stand for the set of all the other options on the diagram. For each option in the set of *b* we have deduced a contradiction from the Constitution's basic design with that option. The institutional structure created by the Constitution does not assume the truth of anything in *b*. From the above it is reasonable to say either *a* or *b*. And I have just provided good reason for saying not *b*. According to the rule of inference concerning disjunctive syllogisms, we are therefore constrained to infer the following: therefore *a*.

Inference to the Best Explanation, Stage 2: Consilience and Simplicity

For the sake of brevity, I am only going to say a word or two about consilience and simplicity. We have already seen that conventionalism cannot provide a rational basis for distinguishing among preferences. The same is true when it comes to exercises of the human will. This means that conventionalism fits best with a constitutional structure that doesn't distinguish among them—one that is indifferent to various acts of popular will and that doesn't favor some preferences over others. In other words, conventionalism itself cannot explain any of the features of the Constitution that favor abiding preferences over the more immediate sort. Nor can it explain constitutional features that resist the popular will. Conventionalism leaves unexplained such constitutional features as the combination of representation with an extended sphere (in other words, large electoral districts), bicameralism, and the presidential veto.[70] Even worse, conventionalism provides no rational explanation for any of the Constitution's features that promote popular sovereignty and majoritarianism. As conventionalism provides no ground for preferring some exercises of will to others, it follows that conventionalism provides no ground for preferring the will of the majority to that of the minority or the will of the people to a will independent of the community. Thus, conventionalism cannot explain any of the Constitution's electoral features. Nor can it explain any features that seem to make other branches of the government considerably dependent on the Congress. Nor can it explain the power of the

---

70. Ackerman construes judicial review in conventionalist terms, pointing out that the courts are supposed to protect the decisions of the majority against a legislature that has betrayed its trust. While this is certainly true, it is impossible to explain judicial review in conventionalist terms alone. But even if judicial review could be so explained, it would not count much against my argument. For there are other majority-constraining features that cannot be so explained.

people to amend the Constitution. Conventionalism stands at odds with all these features, and for all these features, conventionalism requires auxiliary hypotheses to show how the Constitution can have these features while simultaneously supposing conventionalism to be true. The number of features left unexplained by conventionalism, and even at odds with it, are indeed many. And if any form of realism explains just one feature more of the Constitution, then realism will, according to inference to the best explanation, constitute a better answer to our question—what is the Constitution's theory of the common good?

Does deontic realism fare better here? The problem is that with deontic realism we are supposed to have good norms that are indifferent to outcomes. If it is true that certain objects or goods correspond to long-term, widely shared desires while other objects or goods correspond to short-term and narrower or more immediate interests and if it is true that the Constitution distinguishes between these different desires, favoring the former over the latter, then it follows that the Constitution is not indifferent to outcomes. And it is not indifferent by virtue of the features that favor long-term, widely shared desires over short-term, narrow desires. Deontic realism therefore leaves unexplained almost all the same features that conventionalism leaves unexplained. And this means that deontic realism will also require a good many auxiliary hypotheses. I imagine that a neo-Kantian might want to object that Kantian moral theory need not be thought of as entirely indifferent to outcomes (which is another way of saying "ends" where "ends" include states of affairs). But insomuch as the neo-Kantian does this, to that extent he has departed from deontology and is headed toward teleology. Likewise, to the extent that the rules informing the Constitution's design favor some outcomes over others, to that extent the Constitution can be said to aim at substantive goals or outcomes. And to that extent the Constitution cannot be considered in deontic terms.

Thin teleological realism also leaves much to be desired in terms of the explanation provided. Here, clearly, pleasure and fame leave much of the Constitution unexplained. If the good is wealth, then the extended sphere, for reasons already given, is left unexplained. But then no one seriously thinks of wealth, by itself, as the common good presupposed by the Constitution. If peace is the only good, then the Constitution should be morally indifferent to anything other than peace. In other words, there should be no basic rights that cannot be sacrificed in order to obtain the good of preservation. The Bill of Rights and the delegation of powers constitute substantive limitations on governmental power that are not easily explained if the common good is nothing other than continued existence. Finally, peace as the sole good has a hard time explaining federalism. Federalism can, and did, lead to a brutally violent civil war.

Of course, a complex thin theory of the common good explains much more than any of the options proposed so far. One might think, upon a structural examination, that the Constitution only makes sense in terms of the sort of substantive ends mentioned in its preamble. The preamble states that the Constitution is ordained to "insure domestic tranquility, provide for the common defense," and to "promote the general welfare." Surely part of the general welfare includes some measure of prosperity. Given this we might say that the common good is substantive but composed mainly of peace, pleasure, and economic well-being.[71] But let us keep in mind that a thick teleological theory incorporates peace, pleasure, and economic well-being (which isn't to say wealth per se). Furthermore, peace, pleasure, and economic well-being, on thin realism, present real goods. But these goods are also objects of desire. We realize their goodness because they are desired so intensely on the thin theories. But none of the thin theories can explain elements in the Constitution that differentiate among desires by favoring some over others. Every feature of the Constitution that does this (e.g., separation of functions, veto points, and the extended sphere) will require an auxiliary hypothesis from advocates of any sort of thin theory—whether simple or complex. As should be obvious, thin teleological realism leaves key features of the Constitution unexplained.

Thick teleological realism, however, explains the very features these other theories cannot. For on thick realism, not everything a person wants is good for him; therefore, a constitution must be designed to distinguish between desires that are in keeping with the person's good and those that are not. And this provides the best explanation for why we would favor long-term, widely shared preferences over short-term, narrow ones. Further, as I will explain shortly, the features of the Constitution that delay decision making, thereby favoring long-term preferences, and features that force those preferences to have a broad basis in order to be efficacious favor the governance of reason over the passions. On a thick theory of the good, reason is designed to rule the passions and appetites. Thick realism therefore explains features of the Constitution that promote the rule of reason over passions. Finally, thick realism

---

71. Sotirios Barber maintains that "the American Constitution makes sense (and originally made sense) only in light of general substantive ends like national security, freedom of conscience, domestic tranquility, and the people's economic well being" (*Welfare and the Constitution,* 1). Barber seems to be advocating a complex, thin teleological theory.

can explain features of the Constitution that don't promote the survival of every individual. Such features allow, for instance, the sacrifice of life for the sake of preserving the community, because community is a good for which humans were made. Further, for the thick realist, mere survival is not always in keeping with the good of the individual. Thick realists, or at least some in this camp, recognize that sacrifice is a part of human well-being.

From the foregoing we see that thick teleological realism explains constrained popular sovereignty inasmuch as it explains constraints. Can it also explain why the constrained sovereign is popular? Well, at the very least, thick teleological realism has no more difficulty explaining why the sovereign is popular than any of the other theories. Moral anarchy and all forms of conventionalism enthrone human will above all else. But, as we've seen, one cannot differentiate among exercises of will on the basis of will alone. That means that moral anarchy and conventionalism provide no basis for favoring the rule of a monarch over the rule of a tyrant or the rule of the people over the rule of a monarch, a tyrant, or an aristocracy. Perhaps we can go further. It is possible to hold (1) that the common good is real, thick, and teleological and (2) that popular sovereignty or majoritarianism (appropriately constrained, to be sure) is the best way to ensure that governmental policy promotes the common good.[72] If the conjunction of these two ideas obtains, then thick teleological realism explains why the sovereign is popular.

Inference to the Best Explanation, Stage 3: Teleological Fitness

At this stage of the argument I want to show that we can mount an argument that the Constitution does indeed aim at an objective and thick common good. One component of this common good is the rule of reason in individuals and in the political community more generally. Just as the individual should be governed by his reason, so the political community as a whole should be governed by reasonable laws. I suggest that the Constitution aims at the rule of reason in the political community and that this ties to the Constitution's preference for just laws. It is possible to see how the Constitution does this by focusing on the argument Madison mounts in *The Federalist* No. 51.[73]

72. Donald Lutz observes, "Nevertheless, the commitment to the common good continued to have its effect on the design of political institutions. Perhaps the most obvious was the use of majority rule . . . [C]olonial Americans saw majority rule as the only reasonable way to determine the common good" (*Origins of American Constitutionalism,* 29).

73. I am not considering Madison as an instance of original intent, here, but as providing the best account of the Constitution's design.

In that essay, Madison argues that there can be no liberty where there is no justice. He therefore sets out to show how constitutional features such as the extended sphere promote justice and the common good.[74]

We can preserve free government, says Madison, by encouraging the formation of just majorities while discouraging the formation of unjust majorities. Extending the sphere of a republic (so long as the republic is not overextended) does just this. In *The Federalist* No. 51, Madison wrote, "In the extended republic of the United States, and among the great variety of interests, parties and sects which it embraces, a coalition of a majority of the whole society could seldom take place on any other principles than those of justice and the general good."[75] The extended sphere, therefore, exists to shape the way in which majority coalitions form and to favor the development of just over unjust majorities.

Of course, one might well wonder why extending the sphere will favor just over unjust majorities. Even if we prevent unjust majorities from ruling, what reason is there to think that majorities will therefore form along just lines? We must note here that the human inclination toward injustice is not absolute. In *The Federalist* No. 71, Hamilton states, "the people commonly intend the Public Good." There exists, then, some human inclination toward the common good. Madison, in *The Federalist* No. 63, maintains that the Senate exists to serve as a check upon popular demand for some unwise measure "until reason, justice and truth, can regain their authority over the public mind."[76] Suppose Madison and Hamilton are right (and I think they are). Entailed here is that reason, justice, and truth can and do sometimes exercise authority over the public mind. But this is only possible if there is some human inclination toward justice. Positing the existence of such an inclination does not contradict the idea that humans tend to be unjust. Rather, the picture of human nature in *The Federalist* is one in which humans have inclinations toward justice and the public good and yet nevertheless tend to behave unjustly. This occurs because the human proclivity toward injustice tends to override the human inclination toward justice.[77] Reason, justice, and virtue exercise a weak authority over the person. The motives leading to injustice are much stronger.[78]

---

74. In what follows I will take Madison to understand the rule of reason and justice to mean virtually the same thing.

75. *The Federalist* No. 51, 265.

76. Ibid., No. 71, 363, and No. 63, 320, respectively.

77. "Why has government been instituted at all? Because the passions of men will not conform to the dictates of reason and justice" (Ibid., No. 15, 72).

78. "Has it not . . . invariably been found that momentary passions and immediate interests have

This is the tragedy of human nature. Reason (and justice) should direct human action; interest and passion should be directed by reason and should exercise a weaker authority over human action than does reason.[79] But human nature, in its current state, is disordered. The passions and short-term, narrow interests are the strongest motives of human action. Reason and justice are the weakest. Yet, though they are the weakest of motives, they nevertheless exist and can therefore be brought to bear on the making of law in a properly constructed regime.[80]

The human inclination toward justice is brought to bear upon the making and enforcement of law by the construction of a constitution that makes it difficult for the passions and interests to hold sway.[81] Passion is a passing thing. Unjust factions animated by passion do not endure for long. If the lawmaking process is a slow one in which laws are repeatedly brought under reexamination, passionately driven factions will likely dissipate before their demands can be met. As for factions animated by some unjust interest, one must keep in mind the narrowness of their interest. It will be difficult to find majorities sharing the same narrow interest in a large republic. Even if the improbable occurs, it seems unlikely that such a group will be able to organize itself for action. People motivated by unjust interests tend to be suspicious of others. The larger the republic, however, the more people required for a majority. But this means that there are more people of whom each person in the group will be suspicious. And the more suspicious one is of these others, the less likely one is to work with them. Unjust interest undoes itself. Thus, the extended sphere uses self-interest to weaken self-interest, leaving the human inclination toward justice (toward reason) free to operate. This inclination can now be brought to bear on law and on the enforcement of law, so long as the republic is not too big for a public consensus to develop on matters of policy. This being the case, it is possible to have both justice and free government, to have justice and rule by the sense of the community.

Notice from what has been said how various elements of the Constitution coordinate around the goal of justice between individuals, something essential to preserving the good of community. The extended sphere favors justice

---

a more active and imperious controul over human conduct than general or remote considerations of policy, utility or justice" (Ibid., No. 6, 24).

79. "[I]t is the reason of the public alone that ought to controul and regulate the government," wrote Madison. "The passions ought to be controuled and regulated by the government" (Ibid., No. 49, 258).

80. In this paragraph I have drawn on Howe, "Political Psychology of *The Federalist.*"

81. What follows is an elaboration of Madison's tenth essay in *The Federalist.*

by supporting long-term, widely shared interests. The parts of the Constitution that delay decision making also do this as well. In particular, parts of the Constitution that delay decision making require that preferences for some policies persist over time in order to overcome the long process. One might add that the different electoral bases of the various branches cooperate with the extended sphere (and the encompassing of many factions) to ensure that the preferences driving policy formation are indeed widely shared.

If *The Federalist's* political psychology is even somewhat close to the political psychology assumed by the Constitution, then the Constitution should be understood as an institutional structure that takes the governance of the political community by reason for its goal. The Constitution blocks passions and appetites that would overthrow the rule of reason, thereby freeing reason to do its proper work, to provide direction in human affairs. This means that the Constitution assumes a teleological understanding of the common good and assumes that the common good is more than an object of desire. The foregoing also means that the Constitution distinguishes between good and bad desires based on a normative understanding of human nature. The governance of the self and of the political community by reason is what is good for human persons, and not every preference, desire, or act of willing is consistent with reason's rule in these arenas. Thus, the rule of reason in the self and the community provides a measure for evaluating preferences, desires, and acts of will (popular or otherwise) that is other than preferences, desires, and acts of will. Thus, if the Constitution structurally facilitates and presupposes the rule of reason, then we have rendered coherent its favoring of some preferences, desires, and acts of will over others by providing a basis outside of these for favoring some over others.

Conclusion

We have seen that the Constitution presupposes a common good that is real, teleological, and thick. The Constitution assumes a substantive common good that involves people in community, being governed by reason. None of the other candidates for the Constitution's conception of the common good fits well with the Constitution. They stand in tension with some key features of the Constitution and/or fail to explain many fundamental features of the Constitution's design. A substantial realist accounting of the common good, however, explains why the Constitution favors long-term, widely shared desires over immediate, intense desires. Further, it explains why the Constitution favors some exercises of popular will over others. Additionally, we have seen how the Constitution might be understood to aim at (or at least to endeavor to produce) the rule of reason in the political community. This suggests the Constitution's proper function is not only to favor some desires, and therefore some outcomes, over others, but to promote the rule of reason through these outcomes. When the Constitution is functioning as it should, the political community is constituted as it should be—reason rules the passions.

— 5 —

The Constitution's Theory
of Natural Law

S O   F A R   W E ' V E   S E E N that the Constitution presupposes a
constrained popular sovereign as well as a real and thick teleological common good. If we stopped our investigation just there, however, we would remain far from giving a full elaboration of the Constitution's normative framework. For, in that case, we would have failed to address the Constitution's
understanding of the relation of moral to legal obligation as well as the Constitution's understanding of our obligation to pursue the common good. To
get at these matters we must turn our attention to the Constitution's take on
natural law. In this chapter I will argue that the Constitution presupposes a
view of natural law in which the requirements of that law are known through
noninstrumental, or substantive, reason. I also will suggest that the content of
natural law is determined by the common good. If this is the case, then the
Constitution will view natural law as a prescription to pursue the understanding of common good argued for in chapter 4. Given the last chapter, then,
the content of the natural law, presumed by the Constitution is real, teleological, and thick—it is essentially Thomistic or Aristotelian.

The Nature of Natural Law

In the conclusion of chapter 1, we noted three understandings of natural law that the Constitution might take to be true:

1. *Positivist:* The Constitution presupposes that there is no common stock of knowledge about moral absolutes that derive from the purposes of human nature and that are ascertainable by reason. Rather, the Constitution presupposes that there is wide divergence on moral beliefs, that a moral consensus cannot be the basis of our governance, and that we must be governed by the will of the majority.

2. *Modernist:* The Constitution presupposes that there is a stock of moral knowledge—of natural laws—available to all via instrumental reason. These "natural laws" are merely counsels of prudence—rules that people must follow if they are to avoid living in the "state of nature," that state in which everyone has a right to everything. These "laws" commend the seeking of peace and the doing of what is necessary for the realization of peace.

3. *Classical:* The Constitution presupposes that there is a common stock of moral knowledge—natural laws—known in their most basic requirements to all, or nearly all, that are binding upon human beings and implicit in their nature or design. Further, humans have some natural inclination to obey them. No human enactment contrary to them has any validity.

Clearly these understandings do not exhaust the realm of possibilities. To ascertain the Constitution's conception of natural law, we will need to consider some of the alternative notions and nuances within these understandings not yet fully developed in these summaries.

Just here an interesting problem emerges, for the theories above make positional commitments along a number of dimensions. First, there is the ontological dimension that can be gotten at by asking just what sort of thing the natural law is. In connection to this inquiry is the related matter of the relation of the natural law to the common good. Second, there is the epistemological dimension that has to do with whether any moral requirements are known, and if any are known, how they are known (by noninstrumental reason, instrumental reason, or sentiment) and to what extent they are known (to some, to many, or to all).

I want to tackle the second dimension first by making use of Diagram 5.1, which poses the question, Is there a natural law?

Diagram 5.1

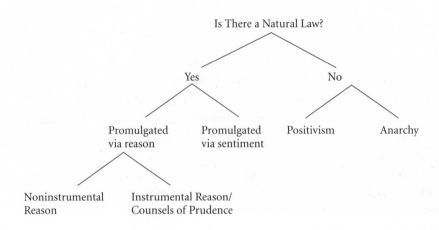

Is There a Natural Law?

Yes   No

Promulgated   Promulgated   Positivism   Anarchy
via reason   via sentiment

Noninstrumental   Instrumental Reason/
Reason   Counsels of Prudence

The Constitution presupposes either that there is or that there isn't a natural law. If *there is no natural law,* then one of two alternatives obtains. Either individuals are free to do whatever they want, in which case there is *anarchy,* or people recognize some sovereign entity whose right to rule means nothing other than its superior strength, in which case *positivism* obtains.[1] If there is no natural law and either anarchy or positivism obtains, it simply follows that the natural law is not known because it is not. In this case, there is no body of moral requirements imposing obligations upon people. Therefore, from a moral standpoint, individuals and groups are free to act however they please. If, on the other hand, the Constitution presupposes that *there is a natural law,* then it presupposes that there is a law normative for human behavior that is not reducible to rules constructed by human beings. But how might such a law be known? Inasmuch as the law is *natural,* the Constitution must take it to be promulgated, in some sense or other, via human nature.[2] Such promulgation

1. Some might object that I am blurring the distinction between Austinian and Hartian positivism. I will deal with this distinction later in this chapter. But for the time being, I would only suggest that there are features of Hartian positivism that reduce it, in the end, to either the Austinian theory, to the sort of procedural conventionalism addressed in chapter 4, or to a Hobbesian type theory that I will address in this chapter.

2. As A. P. Martinich, in *The Two Gods of Leviathan: Thomas Hobbes on Religion and Politics,* points out, even Hobbes believes that natural laws (a) must be promulgated and (b) are promulgated through human nature (namely, to human reason). The second element of Hobbes's definition of natural law, as Martinich maintains, is promulgation. According to Hobbes, only "commands that are

can be made by *sentiment,* by *reason,* or by *both.* While there is an analytical distinction between something delivered to us by sentiment and something delivered by reason, the fact that something is delivered to us by reason does not exclude the a priori logical possibility that it is also delivered by sentiment.[3] Still, we can preserve a degree of mutual exclusion in our diagram by construing the alternatives to read that the natural law is promulgated to us *primarily* through sentiment or *primarily* through reason. Suppose the Constitution presupposes that the moral law is promulgated *primarily* by *reason.* In that case, either *instrumental reason* (or *counsels of prudence*) or *noninstrumental (substantive) reason* apprehends the natural law. The deliverances of *instrumental reason* have the form of conditional propositions that present hypothetical imperatives: If you want x, then do y. To refer to such a conditional as a law of human nature is to say that if a person or group desires some thing *x,* then given human nature and the conditions under which humans live, he (or they) *must* do *y* in order to obtain it.[4] *Noninstrumental (substantive) reason,* in contrast, lays hold of some human aim or good as good or worthy of attainment in its own right rather than for the sake of something else.[5] In short, noninstrumental (substantive) reason apprehends goals or ends, whereas instrumental reason ascertains the means only to some end dictated by human desire or preference and where the end is considered as a goal to be attained simply because it is desired or preferred and for no other reason. If the natural law is knowable in any of these ways, then it might be known to *all,* to *most,* to *few,* or to *none.*

What Is Meant by Natural Law

To know whether the Constitution, in presupposition, affirms or denies the existence of natural law, we must determine what such an affirmation or denial

---

promulgated can be laws" and "the only way all humans can receive such promulgations is through deducing them by reason" (114, 123).

3. I believe that John Witherspoon and James Wilson, for instance, held sentiment *and* reason to be pointers to the same law of human nature.

4. To the degree that oughtness exists in such a conception, the oughtness must be construed as a function of necessity. That is, if we hear "one ought to do *y* in order to attain *x*" and we ask why one "ought" to do *y,* the only conceivable response seems to be "Because doing *y* is necessary to obtaining *x.*"

5. The distinction and the terminology I am employing here comes from Jean Hampton's *Authority of Reason,* chaps. 4 and 5. In chapter 5, Hampton maintains that "any conception of instrumental rationality must involve at least *some* components of a conception of the good" (167).

would mean. For this, we need to understand what it means for there to be a law of human nature of any sort. In this section, therefore, I will lay out some minimal common ground between alternative conceptions of the natural law.

At a minimum, affirming the existence of a law of nature involves affirming two distinct things: (1) that there is a standard for behavior that is independent of and therefore not reducible to human will; and (2) that this standard for human behavior has something to do with human nature—that is, something in human nature points to the natural law's requirements. These two conditions are necessary and perhaps together sufficient such that if a theory *t* meets (1) and (2) that that theory can be labeled as a theory of natural law. As Al Martinich notes, we must distinguish a moral theory from a good or correct one.[6] Likewise, we must distinguish a theory of natural law from one that is good or correct. And surely the conditions a theory must meet to count as a theory of natural law are not as stringent as the conditions it must satisfy to count as a good one.

In the sense I've just described, Aquinas, Occam, and Hobbes offer theories of natural law, even if one, some, or all of their theories fail to be good ones. Certain sentimentalist (though not emotivist) moral theories can also be considered theories of natural law. Each theory of natural law, *t,* can be understood as an attempt to explain certain *moral* facts.[7] Among the relevant facts is a certain content of morality or, more aptly, a set of moral requirements, *r.* Thus, Aquinas, Occam, and Hobbes offer moral theories designed to explain a basic content or a basic set of moral requirements—and in each of their theories, the content of morality is quite nearly the same.[8] That is, if we identify a set of Thomistic moral requirements, r(a), Occamist moral requirements,

6. Martinich argues, "we need to distinguish between a theory of morality and a correct theory of morality, just as we need to distinguish between a theory of science and a correct theory of science. Ptlolemy's theory is incorrect but it is a theory nonetheless" (*Two Gods of Leviathan,* 73).

7. It is likely that contemporary social scientists are leery of the idea of *moral facts,* due to an a priori and frequently knee-jerk acceptance of the so-called fact-value dichotomy. This old pillar of positivistic social science has proved impossible to sustain philosophically, and I find no good reason to hold to it or to turns of phrase derived from the alleged distinction. See Arkes, *First Things,* esp. chap. 6, and John R. Searle, *Speech Acts.* In addition to their arguments, I would add that part of the problem with the dichotomy (though not the only problem) is that "fact" is given a positivistic construal. What counts as a fact is subject to the principle of verifiability. But, of course, the self-referential incoherency of the principle of verifiability, which led to the fall of logical positivism, entails the falseness of this understanding of "fact."

8. I will elaborate Aquinas's theory a bit more later in this chapter. For now, I only want to note the basic requirements: good is to be done and evil avoided. Among the goods of human life are preservation of human life, sexual intercourse, the education of offspring, living in society, living according to reason, and knowing the truth about God (*Summa,* I–II, q. 94, art. 3). Concerning reason he maintains, "good morals are those which are in accord with reason" and that the moral precepts of

r(o), and Hobbesian ones, r(h), we see immediately that r(a), r(o), and r(h) are quite similar. The differences between them are sufficiently minimal to

---

the old law (namely, the Decalogue) belong to the law of nature. Some of the Decalogue's prohibitions belong to the natural law absolutely, such as "Honor thy father and mother," "Thou shalt not steal," and "Thou shalt not commit adultery." Finally, of the "first precepts of the Old Law," "Thou shalt love the Lord thy God" and "Thou shalt love thy neighbor as thyself," principles affirmed by Jesus in the Gospel of Matthew, he maintains, "Those two principles are the general principles of the natural law" (I–II, q. 100, arts. 1 and 3). Aquinas holds that the content of the natural law is known to human reason. The first, common principles, he says are not only self-evident in themselves, but recognized by all men. Then there are certain norms, derived from the common principles, but known to most all, and, finally, there are derivations from common principles known only to the wise (I–II, q. 94, art. 4; I–II, q. 100, arts. 1 and 3). Compare Aquinas's understanding of the law of nature with Occam's. All references will be taken from *A Dialogue*, in which Occam maintains that "natural law is a natural commandment" (pt. 3, tract 2, bk. 1, chap. 10, 261). He concurs with Aquinas as to the content of natural law. Like Aquinas, he believes that natural law contains absolute prohibitions such as "Do not commit adultery," "Do not lie," and "Do not bear false witness." Occam even agrees with Aquinas that there are self-evident principles of natural law. Thus, he says that there are three kinds (or categories) of natural laws. The first are "self-evident principles, or follow or are taken from such self-evident principles of morals . . . about such natural laws no one can err or even doubt." Ignorance of self-evident principles, however, is possible, "because it is possible not to think and never to have thought of them." Even so, "such natural laws occur [to us] immediately when we are obliged to do or omit something in accordance with them, unless we will proceed to act, or to omit such act, without any deliberation and rule of reason" (chap. 15, 273). Such ignorance, then, is inexcusable because it results from culpable negligence. As for the second kind of natural law, Occam says that there exist other natural laws "that are drawn plainly and without great consideration from the first principles of the law" (chap. 15, 274). These principles are inferred from the first principles without great consideration. As for the third category, some natural laws are inferred from the first natural laws only by a few experts who have studied them thoroughly. Indeed, these experts even sometimes disagree. The apparent similarities do not stop here. Occam also speaks of the relationship of natural law to reason. He says (later), "that is called natural law which is in conformity with natural reason that in no case fails" (bk. 3, chap. 6, 286).

There are also similarities between Aquinas and Occam and Thomas Hobbes. Hobbes defines natural law (*lex naturalis*) as "a precept or general rule, found out by reason, by which a man is forbidden to do that, which is destructive of his life, or that taketh away the means of preserving it; and to omit that, by which he thinketh it may be best preserved" (*Leviathan*, 79). For Aquinas (and Grotius), the content of the natural law is, as Martinich points out, the common good. Martinich argues that this is the same for Hobbes. Hobbes defines the common good solely in terms of self-preservation. Even so, Hobbes says that all the means to this good are good as well:

> [A]ll men agree on this, that peace is good, and therefore also the way, or means of peace, which, as I have shewed before, are *justice, gratitude, modesty, equity, mercy,* and the rest of the laws of nature, are good: that is to say *moral virtues;* and their contrary *vices,* evil. Now the science of virtue and vice, is moral philosophy; and therefore the true doctrine of the laws of nature, is the true moral philosophy. But the writers of moral philosophy, though they acknowledge the same virtues and vices; yet not seeing wherein consisted their goodness; nor that they come to be praised, as the means of peaceable, sociable, and comfortable living, place them in a mediocrity of passions. (cited in *Two Gods of Leviathan,* 117)

Hobbes further says in *Leviathan* that the second law of nature, "that a man be willing, when others are so too, as far-forth, as for peace, and defence of himself shall think it necessary, to lay down this right to all things; and be contented with so much liberty against others, as he would allow other men against himself," is identical to the law of the Gospel that "whatsoever you require that others should

warrant giving them a common designation, *r*. The theories Aquinas, Occam, and Hobbes offer to explain *r*, however, are sufficiently different to warrant separate designations—t(a), t(o), and t(h), respectively.[9] While t(a), t(o), and t(h) differ from each other in significant ways, they can all be described as theories of natural law because they seek to explain a common set of moral requirements, *r*, and to show that *r* is apprehended in some sense by or through human nature. For Aquinas and Hobbes, human nature is *aimed* at *r*— whether via natural inclination, such that human nature is only completed, fulfilled, or perfected by adhering to *r*, or by showing that human self-interest is realized only through following *r* rather than through alternative behaviors. For all three, this content of morality is promulgated via human nature and apprehended by reason.[10] Sentimentalists, of course, are not so likely to agree with Aquinas, Occam, and Hobbes that morality is apprehended via reason.[11] But they have historically identified a similar content of morality in addition to affirming that the design of human nature, via sentiment, points human persons toward this content.[12]

The foregoing leads to this question: What specifies the content of natural

---

do to you, that do ye to them" (*Leviathan*, 80–81). Indeed, says Martinich, "Hobbes is not trying to overthrow or replace the old morality with a new morality. His laws of nature are statements of conventional morality: make peace; do unto others as you would have them do unto you; keep your covenants; be gracious, be accommodating; pardon trespasses. . . . Hobbes is trying to provide a new foundation or theory for the content of the old morality, a theory that is consistent with orthodox Christianity" (*Two Gods of Leviathan,* 119). Neither John Stewart Mill nor Immanuel Kant thought they were offering something new concerning the content of morality. Rather, they thought the difference was in the theoretical underpinnings they were giving to a fairly traditional content. Consider in this connection C. S. Lewis's comments that "Kant did not differ remarkably from other men on the content of ethics" and that "The number of actions about whose ethical quality a Stoic, an Aristotelian, a Thomist, and a Utilitarian would agree is, after all very large. The very act of studying diverse ethical theories, as theories, exaggerates the practical differences between them" ("On Ethics," 45). Lewis does not think that the moral requirements of all these systems are precisely the same but that the points where they differ are exceptions rather than the main tendency.

9. Aquinas sees the origin of obligation in goodness per say or in goodness plus some act of divine will, whereas Occam and Hobbes ground obligation solely in the divine will or divine power. Aquinas's theory of goodness, at least for humans, is thickly teleological; Occam's and Hobbes's are nominalistic. Aquinas also speaks of natural inclinations, but Hobbes only of self-interest.

10. See note 8 above comparing their various theories of natural law.

11. I have deliberately abstained from using the term *emotivist* in this context. *Sentimentalist,* as I employ the term, refers to someone who affirms an objective, natural standard that is known via emotion rather than via reason. Some read Francis Hutcheson as a sentimentalist and a realist. However tenable such a combination is metaphysically, it is certainly an a priori possibility at the outset. Emotivists per se fall under the denial of natural law on Diagram 5.1.

12. I return, again, to Francis Hutcheson but also to other spokespersons for the moral sense or moral sentiment camp. Hutcheson did not disagree with Aquinas or Hobbes about the basic content of morality but rather, in his basic ideas about how morality is apprehended. Even the old utilitarian John Stuart Mill wasn't interested in identifying a new content of morality but rather in provid-

law? Abstractly, the natural law is the set of moral requirements designated *r*. The content of the natural law is all of the specific requirements contained within *r*. But what is it that specifies these requirements? On Occam's theory, the divine command by itself, with no reference to anything else, is what specifies human moral obligation.[13] The divine will writes these commands upon human reason.[14] Some of these commands are self-evident, first principles of all moral reasoning.[15] While God, in his absolute power (*potentia absoluta*), could have commanded anything, Occam thinks that in God's ordered or ordering power (*potentia ordinata*), he has actually commanded just the sorts of things that other natural law theorists describe in terms of human good.[16] God, in his absolute power, could have made obligatory, by commanding them, acts that redound to human misery. But in his ordered power, God has not done this; rather, he has commanded through right reason acts that redound to human felicity. God might have promulgated his will through something other than reason, but God has commanded natural laws through right reason that "in no case fails."[17] From this it follows that the person seeking to obey the natural law is governed by the first principles of right reason. Therefore, while the content of natural law is specified ultimately by divine command, it is specified proximately by self-evident (and absolute) principles of right reason and other principles derived from the first principles that promote human felicity and the common welfare.

In virtually all other kinds of natural law thinking, it is some sort of good

---

ing a utilitarian explanation of the same basic content that Aquinas, Occam, and Hobbes all tried to explain with their own theories.

13. According to Rommen, "For Occam the natural moral law is positive law, divine will. . . . God's will could also have willed and decreed the precise opposite, which would then possess the same binding force as that which is now valid—which indeed, has validity only as long as God's absolute will so determines." Therefore, "Moral goodness consists in mere external agreement with God's absolute will, which, subject only to His arbitrary decree, can always change. To such an extent were God's omnipotence and free will extolled that much subtle speculation was devoted to the question of whether God can, through His absolute power, will hatred of Himself; a question which Occam and many of his disciples answered in the affirmative" (*The Natural Law*, 52–53).

14. See Occam, *Dialogue*, bk. 3, chap. 6, 286.

15. See note 8 above and Occam, *Dialogue*, chap. 15, 273.

16. Martinich says something of interest concerning Hobbes view of God's commands and human happiness: "To say that God's commands must be different from human self-interest is to slander him. If God, having made humans imposed harsh laws on them, he would not be a gracious and merciful God. His laws are intended to make humans flourish, not suffer. God's yoke is gentle; his burden is light. His laws are designed to help humans achieve happiness, and happiness is in every person's self-interest. If God's laws conflicted with human self-interest, then they would conflict with human good" (*Two Gods of Leviathan*, 119).

17. Occam, *Dialogue*, bk. 3, chap. 6, 286.

(whether an intrinsic good or simply an object of desire), common to all, that specifies the content of the natural law.[18] I do not here mean to identify the common good and the natural law: they are analytically distinct concepts. But if we specify some thing or act, z, that it is for the common good, then we have not yet specified that it is to be done. From the fact that z is good, it does not follow that one is bound to pursue it. The natural law, however, is prescriptive, telling us that we are obliged to pursue good and avoid evil. We might say, then, that the natural law adds *prescription* to the common good and, concomitantly, that the common good gives content to the prescription of natural law.[19] Thus, if the natural law requires that some action, x, be done, then x is to be done because it promotes the common good. If the natural law prohibits some action y, then y is prohibited because it runs contrary to or in some way violates the common good. Therefore, the natural law is a set of requirements, r, where each requirement *specifies* some action that promotes the common good *together with* the *prescription* that it is to be done or, conversely, specifies some action that detracts from the common good together with the prescription that the action is to be avoided.

Given the foregoing, the range of possibilities for the content of natural law in conjunction with the ways in which it might be known can be diagrammed, as it is in Diagram 5.2. Given the argument in chapter 4 concerning the com-

18. Martinich wrote, "The content of law, according to St. Thomas, is the common good; according to Grotius, it concerns moral baseness or necessity (that is, goodness)" (*Two Gods of Leviathan*, 116). Inasmuch as natural law is *law*, then the content of natural law is specified by the common good. According to Martinich, Hobbes also fits this description: "What Hobbes thinks he sees is that long-term self-interest is the common good, the content of morality" (117).

19. I maintain, in basic outline, the position articulated by Francisco Suarez, which I take to be an elaboration of Aquinas's position (especially given his definition of law in general). Suarez rejects the idea that intrinsic goodness is sufficient for natural law and divine will unnecessary as well as the position that divine will is the sole ground of natural law and determinative of good and evil by the act of willing. According to Knud Haakonssen, Suarez rejects the intellectualist thesis, taken by itself, for the following reasons: "First, there is a difference between a proposition and a law. Furthermore, a judgment about moral values is a judgment of facts, moral facts, and is not itself a guide to action; in order to have any relevance to action, as a law has, something must be added to judgment." This missing something is *prescription*. In contrast to both the intellectualist and the voluntarist thesis, "Suarez's own notion of natural law combines elements from both the extremes that he presents and rejects. . . . The heart of the matter is that natural law is both indicative of what is in itself good and evil, and preceptive in the sense that it creates an obligation in people to do the good and avoid the evil. The natural law thus reflects the two inseparable sides of God's nature, namely his rational judgment of good and evil and his will prescribing the appropriate behavior" (Haakonssen, *Natural Law and Moral Philosophy*, 20 and 22, respectively). In the words of Suarez, "the subject matter of natural law consists in the good which is essentially righteous or necessary to righteousness, and the evil which is opposed to that good, in the one as something to be prescribed, in the other as something to be forbidden." He also says, "this law prescribes that which is in harmony with rational nature as such, and prohibits the contrary" (*De legibus*, bk. 2, chap. 7, 208).

Diagram 5.2

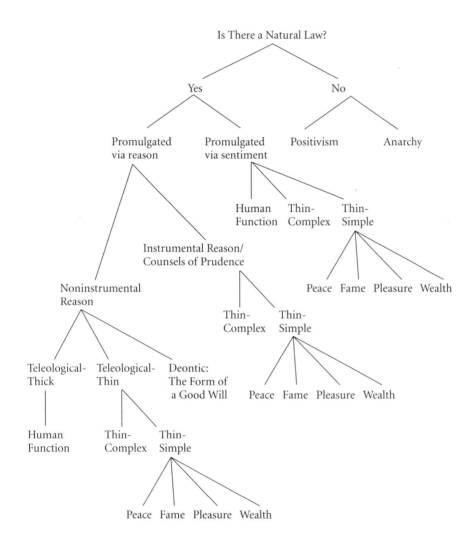

mon good, a number of options in the diagram fall away immediately. It would seem that we come to know a real, thick, and teleological good either through sentiment (or moral sense) or through noninstrumental (substantive) reason. Even so, in what follows, I will treat each way of knowing the requirements of the natural law (or the possibility that they are not known because they do not exist) as a possible option, needing argument to eliminate.

There Is No Natural Law

Now that we have some idea of what it means to affirm the existence of a law of nature, independent of the particular theory explaining that law, we can, as a result, understand what, at a minimum, it means to deny that there is any sort of natural law. To deny the existence of any sort of law of nature, one must disavow either of our two conditions or both. Thus, one can deny the existence of a natural law by maintaining that there is no standard of morality independent of human willing ($\sim$(1)) and/or by maintaining that if there is such a standard, it regulates conduct with no reference to human nature ($\sim$(2)). That it is, while affirming the existence of some standard regulating human conduct, one can nevertheless deny that it is in any sense natural to human beings (that is, (1) but $\sim$(2)). Such a denial can be made by stating that human nature in no way points to a moral standard (whether via reason or sentiment) and/or by stating that even if such a standard exists, following the moral requirements of the standard in no way leads to the completion or perfection of human nature. Perhaps the idea of a moral standard, normative for human conduct and completely independent of human nature, is hard to imagine. But advocates of nominalistic/voluntaristic renderings of divine command theory could plausibly suggest that divine positive law is normative for human conduct, that it is the only thing normative for human conduct, that this positive law runs contrary to both human reason and human sentiment, and that divine positive law is in no way concerned with legislating that which "perfects" human nature. Of course, for the standard to be a *standard* for human *behavior*, then it seems necessary that it be promulgated. If it is in no sense promulgated through or laid hold of by human nature (say, through the proper functioning of certain cognitive faculties), then supernatural, divine revelation seems to be the only possible means.

Anarchy

In chapter 4 we used the term *anarchy* to denote moral anarchy, a denial that any moral principles exist to govern human behavior. I noted that *moral* anarchy, or subjectivism, implies *political* anarchy. I don't want to suggest, however, that the entailment runs the other way. Political anarchy does not entail antirealism. One might be a realist and believe that all coercion is fundamentally unjust.[20] But, again, consistent antirealism, or moral anarchy, does seem to entail political anarchy, because for the moral anarchist, laws can never possess binding power (*potestas*). If there is no moral realm, then there is only force (only will, or *potentia*). And force (or intensity of strength), as such, creates no moral obligation.[21]

The foregoing requires some elaboration. Some scholars say that moral and legal obligation are two unrelated things.[22] I am deeply skeptical of this claim. First, in both cases we are specifying a kind of *obligation*, and it would be very strange indeed if *moral* and *legal* obligation had no common referent whatsoever. Moreover, while moral and legal obligation may, perhaps, be distinguished, this in no way entails that they aren't essentially related such that moral obligation grounds legal obligation. I maintain that they are distinct, but in such a way that one is ontologically grounded in the other. Second, we distinguish between commands that are binding laws and those that are not. Suppose Gollum says to Frodo, "Give me the ring. It's mine, my precious." He has clearly given a command. But no one supposes that Frodo is bound to do what Gollum says just because Gollum has spoken to him in the injunctive mode. But just what differentiates *mere* commands from law? Suppose we say that what makes the difference here is whether the command is arbitrary or whether it conforms to certain procedural rules about how law should be made. Suppose we call the procedural rules a legal system and say that laws are commands (or potential commands) that go through a process outlined by

20. See Stephen Nathanson, *Should We Consent To Be Governed: A Short Introduction to Political Philosophy*, chap. 4. It is arguable, to draw upon Nathanson's argument, that at least some political anarchists subscribe to their particular beliefs because they subscribe to the objective goodness of liberty, where liberty is construed as individual autonomy, and the objective wrongness of coercion. My argument is perfectly compatible with this observation because I am not contending that political anarchy entails moral anarchy or individualistic relativism.

21. As Arkes, explicating Jean Jacques Rousseau, notes, "moral conclusions can be entailed only by moral propositions. They cannot be drawn from such distinctly nonmoral attributes as brute physical strength. . . . In more exacting language, we would say that mere physical power cannot be the source of moral warrants. With Rousseau, we would say that power cannot be the source of its own justification" (*First Things*, 33). See also Rousseau, *The Social Contract*, bk. 1, chap. 3, 52–53.

22. When this distinction is made, those making it seem to mean, by legal obligation, that a law, valid under a certain legal system, because it comports with the requirements of the system, imposes a prescription upon those citizens incorporated under that legal system. That is, legal obligation means that a law is validly prescriptive according to a legal system. But, as I will ask, why call such legally valid laws binding? If the legal system as a whole is merely imposed by human will or force, then its "laws" are nothing other than impositions of force. And impositions of force are not obligatory, though they may be psychologically or physically compelling. If we define true law as more than this, we have made significant strides toward the natural law camp.

the system and that conform to certain side constraints contained in the system (say, a Bill of Rights). Aren't such laws valid and binding under the system in question? This suggestion falls apart the moment we ask a prior question: from where do the procedural rules or legal systems get the power to impose binding enactments? If the procedural rules or the legal system are *only* established by convention or by human commands (written or unwritten, general or specific), then they are *only* exercises of force. If we have no recourse to an external standard for evaluating exercises of will (including conventions and laws), then the only criterion for measurement is quantity of will (i.e., the amount of strength). But strength alone does not possess normative force (or binding power). It follows that if some acts of will are in fact binding, then the source of that binding power must come from somewhere outside of human willing. Human laws, legal systems, constitutions, and conventions are creations of human will. By implication, *unless* the laws, procedural rules, or legal system are grounded in something *more than* human willing, then they cannot bind. If some of these impose obligations, then the source of that obligation must be external to them. To put it another way, our obligation to obey human law must come from the conformity of human law to a standard external to human law. If no such standard exists, then no law is binding. If one wants to affirm such a standard, but call it legal obligation *rather* than moral obligation, then one seems to make a distinction without difference. Such a person seems to want to employ the same ideas as the natural lawyer without the word *moral* attached. That is strange indeed.

All of this suggests, rather strongly, that moral obligation is antecedent to and a necessary condition of legal obligation.[23] Thus, if there is no moral obligation, then there is no obligation to obey validly made law(s) under any legal system.[24] In which case everyone is free to do as they please. Mussolini

23. Or, at least, that the source of obligation is external to, transcendent of, and normative for human will and therefore for human law, whatever name we give it.

24. In this connection, witness the words of John Locke:

If the law of nature is not binding on men, neither can any human positive law bind them, since the laws of the civil magistrate derive all their force from the binding power of this law. . . . [I]f you would abolish the law of nature, you overturn at one blow all government among men, [all] authority, rank and society. Nor must we obey a king out of fear, because he is more powerful and can compel us. For this would be to establish the power of tyrants, thieves, and pirates; but [we must] out of conscience, because he obtains his rule over us by right, that is, at the command of the law of nature, that we obey a king, princes, and a legislator, or whatever name you would give a superior. Thus, the obligation of civil law depends on the law of nature, nor are we compelled so much to show obedience to a magistrate by virtue of his power as we are bound by the law of nature. (*Questions Concerning the Law of Nature*, 214–15).

understood the implications of moral antirealism or relativism. In 1921 he wrote,

> In Germany relativism is an exceedingly daring and subversive theoretical construction (perhaps Germany's philosophical revenge which may herald the military revenge). In Italy, relativism is simply a fact. . . . Everything I have said and done in these last years is relativism by intuition. . . . If relativism signifies contempt for fixed categories and men who claim to be the bearers of an objective, immortal truth . . . then there is nothing more relativistic than Fascist attitudes and activity. . . . From the fact that all ideologies are of equal value, that all ideologies are mere fictions, the modern relativist infers that everybody has the right to create for himself his own ideology and to attempt to enforce it with all the energy of which he is capable.[25]

Positivism

As used here, *positivism* refers first to the affirmation that *positive* law is all there is. This entails a denial of natural law.[26] Because the affirmation that positive law is all there is entails the denial of natural law, the view is sometimes called normative positivism.[27] Normative positivism, therefore, denies that there is any moral law common to all people. It therefore accepts moral nihilism as the truth of the matter. All of this, however, leaves open the question of just what counts as law. Here there are two ways of describing the nature of law: Austinian (or law-as-command) positivism and Hartian (or law-as-rules) positivism.

In the Austinian version of positivism, law is the command of the sovereign, where the command signifies the sovereign's desire that some act is to be done and where some sanction is attached to the command. According to this

---

25. Cited in Henry B. Veatch, *Rational Man: A Modern Interpretation of Aristotelian Ethics,* 20.

26. We might, with qualification, run the entailment the other way. Positivism might be defined as a denial of natural law, entailing that if there is law, then it is only positive law.

27. Normative positivism must be distinguished from methodological positivism (though we readily perceive something of a historical connection between these two doctrines). According to the latter view, morality and law are two distinct fields of study, and the student of law studies only the latter with no consideration of the former. Thus, as Rommen notes, "we must distinguish two forms of positivism: first, positivism as a consequence of an empiricist narrowing of reality, as a method; secondly, positivism as a philosophy of life, as a conception of the meaning of the universe and of man's place in it, as a Weltanshauung. The crudest expression of this second form of positivism has been materialism, whether in its metaphysical (Feuerbach, Buechner, Haeckel) or historico-economic dress (Marx). Moreover, the second form of positivism has played by far the more important role" (*The Natural Law,* 110).

theory, the sovereign inspires regular or habitual obedience out of a majority of the people in a particular society, on the condition that the person designated sovereign is not in the habit of obeying another person or group.[28] Anthony Lisska is entirely correct to characterize this sort of positivism as not going far beyond "What pleases the prince has the force of law."[29] And, as Lisska points out, positivism had not developed much beyond this point by the time of the Nuremberg trials.[30]

Of course, there are positivists, such as H. L. A. Hart, who reject the Austinian theory as a complete failure.[31] According to Hart, the Austinian theory fails in two crucial respects—it does not explain "the continuity of the authority to make law possessed by a succession of different legislators, and the persistence of laws long after their maker and those who rendered him habitual obedience have perished."[32] Hart asks his readers to consider the example of a monarch, Rex I, who dies and is succeeded by Rex II. What happens when Rex I dies? Austin's theory seems to require maintaining that all law has died with Rex I. For since Rex I is no longer here to be habitually obeyed, he cannot be considered sovereign. But if he is not sovereign, then his commands no

---

28. Austin wrote,

> The essential difference of a positive law (or the difference that severs it from a law which is not a positive law) may be settled thus. Every positive law, or every law simply and strictly so called, is set by a sovereign person, or a sovereign body of persons, to a member or members of the independent political society wherein that person or body is sovereign or supreme. Or (changing the expression) it is set by a monarch, or a sovereign number, to a person or persons in a state of subjection to its author. Even though it sprung directly from another fountain or source [e.g., custom or morality], it is positive law, or a law strictly so called, by the institution of that present sovereign in the character of political superior. . . . The superiority that is styled sovereignty, and the independent political society which sovereignty implies, is distinguished from other superiority, and from other society, by the following marks or characters: 1. The bulk of the given society are in a habit of obedience or submission to a determinate and common superior: let that common superior be a certain individual person, or a certain body or aggregate of individual persons. 2. That certain individual, or that certain body of individuals, is not in a habit of obedience to a determinate human superior. . . . If a determinate human superior, not in a habit of obedience to a like superior, receives habitual obedience from the bulk of a given society, that determinate superior is sovereign in that society, and the society (including the superior) is a society political and independent. (cited in Jeffrie G. Murphy and Jules L. Coleman, *Philosophy of Law: An Introduction to Jurisprudence,* 23)

29. Lisska, *Aquinas's Theory of Natural Law: An Analytic Reconstruction,* 8. Lisska takes the quote from Justinian's Code. Some may think he misunderstands the code. But this quote by itself seems to capture the essence of classical positivism.

30. To be sure, Kelsen attempted to patch the Austinian theory in some places.

31. In what follows I will use not only Hart's work, but also Murphy and Coleman's presentation of Hart's theory in *Philosophy of Law,* as their presentation is frequently more systematic.

32. Ibid., 24.

longer possess the status of law. Well, can't Rex II simply reissue the commands of Rex I? Hart says no. Rex II has not been in charge long enough for a majority of the people to obey him as a matter of habit. But that means he is not sovereign. And if he is not sovereign, then his commands cannot be considered law. From this it follows that, if Austin's theory is true, the society over which Rex I ruled as sovereign finds itself without a sovereign and without any law upon Rex's death, at least until Rex II is habitually obeyed. Until that time, no law can be made.[33] This conclusion seems absurd because it makes every period of transition between sovereigns a revolutionary time. Yet we observe orderly and lawful transitions of sovereign power all the time. According to Hart, "it is characteristic of a legal system, even in an absolute monarchy, to secure the uninterrupted continuity of law-making power by rules which bridge the transition from one lawgiver to another."[34] But can't Austin avoid Hart's criticism by referring to the office of the sovereign rather than the person of the sovereign? In their discussion of Hart, Murphy and Coleman show why Austin's theory cannot be salvaged in this way:

> At this point of course someone might say that we are being unfair to Austin. Surely the habitual obedience is given, not to a person, but an *office*. This may well be true, but then the question becomes: will Austin's theory allow him to define the concept of an office in a satisfactory way? It seems not. Typically (in those societies that even have an Austinian sovereign), the office of sovereign will be defined in terms of certain legal *rules*. Such rules will typically state the criteria for sovereignty and will provide procedures for legal or rightful succession—e.g., "The sovereign is the oldest living male member of the Dingbat Clan." Such a rule provides authoritative guidance in recognizing the current sovereign and in replacing him in an authoritative way when he dies. But can Austin's theory make room for such a rule? Surely not. For Austin, all laws are commands of the sovereign, but this rule or law, since it defines who shall count as the sovereign, is presupposed by sovereignty and thus cannot be generated by it. Thus, such concepts as "office," "legal right of succession," and "legally legitimate succession" are all without a home in Austin's theory, and he cannot account for continuity of law and legal authority, one of the (thankfully) most salient features of stable legal systems.[35]

Murphy and Coleman help us get at how Austin, according to Hart, misunderstands the nature of law. Austin's theory leaves out the idea of rules. But

33. Hart, *The Concept of Law*, 53.
34. Ibid., 54.
35. Murphy and Coleman, *Philosophy of Law*, 24.

rules are fundamental to law. So fundamental, in fact, that Hart defines law as "a union of primary and secondary rules."[36] Primary rules address individuals within a social group, telling them the appropriate behavior for certain circumstances. Because of this, primary rules can be said to impose obligations upon individuals.[37] They impose obligations upon individuals in the sense that they provide standards for justifying or criticizing behavior. Thus, primary rules include things such as "Thou shall not steal," "Don't drive faster than fifty-five miles per hour," "A follower of religion X must marry another follower of religion X," "There shall be no work on the seventh day of the week," etc. Even though primary rules provide standards for behavior, they do not, by themselves, a legal system make. Hart gets at this by imagining a prelegal society governed only by primary rules of obligation. What sorts of problems emerge? First, one might be uncertain about the rules in two ways: one might be unsure that an act is proscribed by a rule or one might be uncertain about what to do when different rules a society accepts come into conflict. "Since the primary rules are just a collection or aggregate of separate rules, they do not form a system; there is no authoritative way to distinguish 'really is one of our rules' from 'is claimed, perhaps falsely, to be one of our rules' and no authoritative way to answer the question of priority among conflicting rules."[38] Second is the problem of "the static character of the rules." Rules are adopted to address a particular set of circumstances. But circumstances change. In a prelegal society, there is no means "of deliberately adapting the rules to changing circumstances, either by eliminating old rules or introducing new ones."[39] In order to do this we need rules of a different sort than the primary rules of obligation. Third, Hart points to the problem of inefficiency in a prelegal society. This issue emerges when there is agreement over what a rule requires but disagreement over whether or not someone has followed it or when there is a recognized rule that has been violated by some party. In either case, there is no means of resolving the problem in a prelegal society. For Hart, this points to the need for secondary rules, or rules about rules. These secondary rules "specify the ways in which the primary rules may be conclusively ascertained, introduced, eliminated, varied, and the fact of their violation conclusively determined." There are three types of secondary rules: rules of recognition, rules of change, and rules of adjudication. A rule of recogni-

---

36. Hart, *The Concept of Law,* 79.
37. I do not mean to endorse this understanding of obligation. I am simply presenting Hart's view.
38. Murphy and Coleman, *Philosophy of Law,* 29.
39. Hart, *The Concept of Law,* 92–93.

tion specifies "some feature or features possession of which by a suggested rule is taken as conclusive affirmative indication that it is a rule of the group to be supported by the social pressure it exerts."[40] "Rules of change will establish authoritative mechanisms (e.g., legislatures) for enactment and repeal of rules and will overcome the static character of a system of primary rules. Rules of adjudication will establish mechanisms (e.g., courts) to overcome the problem of inefficiency present when controversy over primary rules exists." Given all this, Hart's secondary rules can be construed as "rules that create powers and authorities (to validate rules, create rules, and adjudicate controversies about rules)" and "not as rules that impose obligations." We should note that on this theory, rules belong to the same system to the degree that they can be traced to the same rule or rules of recognition. Furthermore, "Some rule R exists as a rule in a legal system S if its pedigree can be traced to the rule or rules of recognition defining legality for S."[41] So, whether or not something counts as a law for a particular society is, on Hart's theory, a function of whether or not this rule was produced in conformity with other rules that define legality for a society. And this is quite different, at least on the face of it, from defining law as the command of the sovereign.

Some may find the Hartian approach helpful in considering the Constitution. After all, the Constitution seems to give us a system of rules for the making of valid laws rather than anything like an Austinian sovereign. Furthermore, if one tried to identify an Austinian sovereign, it might be hard to say just who it was. But does the Hartian theory provide us with a truly distinct alternative from Austin, Hobbes, or even the procedural conventionalism of the last chapter? This is much harder to say. After all, for Hart, *only* primary rules impose obligations while *only* secondary rules determine which primary rules are valid and therefore obligating. In other words, obligation is generated when rules are ratified, made, changed, and adjudicated by a legal system. But just what makes the legal system or the rule(s) of recognition valid such that they can produce obligating rules or laws? It seems strange to suggest that secondary rules that have no obligating power by themselves can generate (by endorsing or making them) primary rules that do in fact oblige.[42] Furthermore, what is it that determines the validity of the legal system as a whole or of the rule(s) of recognition? There seem to be only two options:

---

40. Hart, cited in Murphy and Coleman, *Philosophy of Law,* 30.

41. Ibid., 31–32.

42. It seems as if, in this instance, obligation is being created ex nihilo. I am tempted to quote King Lear at this point: "Nothing will come of nothing. Speak again."

these are underwritten by the natural law or are established by force, by decree of the sovereign or strongest party. Hart thinks, of course, that the existence of the rule(s) of recognition that establish validity for a legal system is a matter for empirical observation. Thus he says,

> The statement that a [primary] rule exists . . . [is] an internal statement applying an accepted but unstated rule of recognition and meaning (roughly) no more than "valid given the system's criteria of validity". In this respect, however, as in others a rule of recognition is unlike other rules of the system. The assertion that it exists can only be an external statement of fact. For whereas a subordinate rule of a system may be valid and in that sense "exist" even if it is generally disregarded, the rule of recognition exists only as a complex, but normally concordant, practice of the courts, officials, and private persons in identifying the law by reference to certain criteria. Its existence is a matter of fact.[43]

What gives the legal system its own validity, then, is simply the fact that government officials, the courts, and citizens observe the rule(s) of recognition. In other words, the decisions of the will of most people in a society to observe some of the rule(s) of recognition determine the existence of a legal system for that society. Hart's view therefore seems to entail that the legal system is established by an act of force of the society (or of a majority)—which in turn makes the society sovereign.

Perhaps someone will want to say that the legal system could simply be the product of a society's conventional norms. Hart cannot adopt this position without arguing in a circle, for he has already said that the legal system, with its rule(s) of recognition, is what determines which societal norms are valid and binding. But even if this were not the case, still, the norms of the society would be *either* underwritten by natural law *or* purely conventional, in which case, however habitual, it would be the will of most of the people in the society that established the norms. If the latter obtains, the norms underwriting the legal system are nothing but acts of force. As such, they lack binding (obligating) power.

Important as Hart's critique of Austin is, it misses a crucial point. We can get at it by asking a simple question: is normative positivism the truth of the matter or not? If normative positivism is the truth of the matter and if we can identify a sovereign for a given society, then that sovereign is free to command

---

43. Hart, cited in Murphy and Coleman, *Philosophy of Law*, 32.

as he pleases. If that sovereign is the people, then the people are absolutely free to command as they please. A positivistic constitution, to be consistent, must not distinguish among exercises of the sovereign's will by favoring some over others. But perhaps a sovereign under a legal system is unidentifiable, and yet we can identify a legal system. In that case, Hart's position reduces to some species of procedural conventionalism. But procedural conventionalism, at least tacitly, treats the will of the major part of the community as sovereign in constructing a view of the good or, more aptly, in constructing a process for the establishment of community norms.[44] Hart as good as admits this in the quoted passage above. Procedural conventionalism, however, shares the same moral assumptions as normative positivism.

A constitution that accepts Hart's view should be indifferent to the sorts of primary rules that emerge from the legal system. That is, a Hartian constitution should *not* favor some rules over others. But rules about rules do this by establishing some primary rules and abolishing others (or by changing them).

At this point, we must acknowledge that positivism faces a coherency problem. In *Realism Regained,* Robert Koons argues that the whole positivistic project presents us with "a vicious regress that threatens the coherency of the project." He demonstrates this by considering the legal positivism of Hans Kelsen:

> Kelsen recognizes that not every pattern of behavior, and not even every pattern that is coercively enforced, counts as a legally valid rule. There must be meta-rules, norms of legal validity or recognition, that bestow legal validity upon the law. So, for example, in Britain the principal norm of recognition consists of the principle that a law is whatever has been passed by Parliament. In the United States a Statute is recognized as a federal law when it has been passed by both houses of Congress and signed by the President, or passed by a supermajority in both houses overriding a Presidential veto, so long as the statute has not been declared unconstitutional by the federal courts. These norms are, Kelsen recognizes, themselves rules of law. Their validity must be grounded in some yet deeper norm. Ultimately, we reach what Kelsen called the *Grundnorm* of the legal system, a rule whose validity is somehow given independently of the other norms. . . . In the analysis of the *Grundnorm* Kelsen faced a dilemma. Is the *Grundnorm* itself a valid rule of law, or a raw exercise of power? Qua raw exercise of power, the *Grundnorm* has no legal validity, and so cannot convey any such validity to any other rule. The very

---

44. After all, constitutions and laws don't simply exist by fiat. They are created by acts of human will.

distinction between the validity of rules in the system and the invalidity of patterns outside it comes crashing down. However, qua legal rule, the *Grundnorm* must derive its legal validity from some outside source. By hypothesis, the social practices in play provide no more fundamental basis than that provided by the *Grundnorm*. Hence, there must be some principle of natural law that bestows upon the *Grundnorm* whatever validity it has.[45]

It doesn't take much to see how this yanks the rug right out from under Hart's apparently steady feet. In order for Hart's rule(s) of recognition to bestow legal validity, they must first have it to pass on. This legal validity cannot be grounded in community norm or patterns of behavior or the fact that the community tends to recognize certain rules of recognition. For these, if they themselves do not possess the power to obligate cannot then pass it on to the legal system. Thus, Hart's theory explains what it means to have a legal system at the expense of any system possessing legal validity, *unless* he is willing to abandon positivism for natural law. Perhaps he does this. After all, he says a lot about natural necessities. Drawing on what he calls the "core of good sense" in natural law thinking, Hart maintains that human nature is subject to certain contingencies that the law must respect and that create the need for human beings in society to adopt a legal system of some sort. At this point, however, his theory begins to resemble a version of the Hobbesian instrumentalist theory of natural law.

Natural Law Promulgated via Sentiment

If, in contrast to (political) anarchism and Austinian and Hartian positivism, the Constitution presupposes that there is moral knowledge to be had, then it might take this moral knowledge to be promulgated by sentiment or by reason. But just what does it mean to say that natural law is promulgated via sentiment? Clearly the early moral-sense thinkers, such as Francis Hutcheson and Jean Jacques Burlamaqui, wanted to say that human beings possess a faculty that apprehends moral truth and that this faculty is distinct from reason.[46] Their reasons for wanting to do so were good, although, as I will show,

---

45. Koons, *Realism Regained*, 275–76.
46. Hutcheson argues,

> We are not to imagine, that this *moral sense*, more than the other senses, supposes, any *innate ideas, knowledge*, or *practical proposition*: We mean by it only *a determination of our minds to receive amiable or disagreeable ideas of actions, when they occur to our observation*,

they frequently mischaracterized what many now refer to as the rationalist or intellectualist school of morality. Moral-sense theorists believed that all people have some degree of moral knowledge. But they pointed out that not everyone has equal reasoning abilities. They argued that God would have been a terrible bungler had he left morals to human reasoning, as this would have left stranded those with lesser cognitive faculties or those without the time to engage in the activity of reasoning.[47] So God gave to everyone a nonrational faculty that apprehends basic moral truths immediately.[48] Thus, the moral sense

---

antecedent to any opinions of advantage or loss to redound to ourselves from them; even as we are pleas'd with a *regular form,* or an *harmonious composition,* without having any knowledge of *mathematics,* or seeing any *advantage* in that form, or composition, different from the immediate pleasure.

Speaking of moral instinct, or moral sense, Burlamaqui contends, "Moral instinct I call that natural bent or inclination, which prompts us to approve of certain things as good and commendable, and to condemn others as bad and blameable, independent of reflection. Or if any one has a mind to distinguish this instinct by the name of moral sense, as Mr. Hutchinson has done, I shall then say, that it is a faculty of the mind, which instantly discerns, in certain cases, moral good and evil, by a kind of sensation and taste, independent of reflection." Both Hutcheson and Burlamaqui are quoted in White, *Philosophy of the American Revolution,* 102, 108.

47. Thomas Jefferson wrote to Peter Carr,

Moral philosophy. I think it lost time to attend lectures in this branch. He who made us would have been a pitiful bungler if he had made the rules of our conduct a matter of science. For one man of science, there are thousands who are not. What would have become of them? Man was destined for society. His morality therefore was to be formed to this object. He was endowed with a sense of right and wrong merely relative to this. This sense is as much a part of his nature as the sense of hearing, seeing, feeling; it is the true foundation of morality . . . This sense is submitted to reason; but it is a small stock which is required for this: even less one than what we call Common sense.

In a dialogue between the head and the heart, contained in a letter to Mrs. Cosway, a married woman with whom Jefferson was smitten, he has the heart say, "Morals were too essential to the happiness of man, to be risked on the uncertain combinations of the head. She [nature] laid their foundation, therefore, in sentiment, not in science. That [sentiment] she gave to all, as necessary to all; this [science] to a few only, as sufficing with a few" (Jefferson quoted in White, *Philosophy of the Revolution,* 118, 119).

I must note that Jefferson's moral theory is open to interpretation at this point. This is certainly not all he says on the matter. Some are convinced that he continued to subscribe to the primacy of reason in laying hold of moral truth. White himself interprets Jefferson this way (see ibid., esp. 119–27). See also Daniel Walker Howe, *The Making of the American Self: Jonathan Edwards to Abraham Lincoln,* where, referring to the famed dialogue sent to Mrs. Cosway, he says, "the fact that Jefferson attributed daring sentiments to the *Heart* in a romantic dialogue does not mean he actually endorsed them, only that he was titillating himself and his correspondence with them. Eventually, Jefferson followed the prudential dictates of *Head* and allowed his relationship with Mrs. Cosway to wind down" (71). Howe provides compelling evidence that Jefferson subscribed to the notion of faculty psychology (see 66–77), which was discussed in chapter 4.

48. According to Hutcheson, "Some actions have to Men an immediate Goodness" and the "Moral sense" is what perceives this (cited in Charles Taylor, *Sources of the Self: The Making of Modern Identity,* 260).

simply sees that murder is wrong and that one is bound not to murder others.[49] As everyone possesses a moral sense, there is therefore something of a shared access to the morally good life.[50]

But this brings up an interesting question. What does it mean to *sense* that murder is wrong? It seems this is *either* an act of understanding and therefore an insight arrived at by cognitive faculties *or* an emotional aversion to the act of murder. To concede that the wrongness of murder is an act of understanding and thus an insight attained by cognitive faculties amounts to admitting that it is reason that apprehends the truth of the statement "murder is wrong."[51] Yet is this to do any more than to rename the practical reason of classical thinkers? Classical moral theory, particularly as represented by Thomas Aquinas, maintained that the practical reason of every person apprehends some properly basic moral truths, moral truths that constitute something like the first premises or basic axioms of moral reasoning (e.g., love thy neighbor). These premises are underivable by reason, but they are held in the reason as the first principles of all moral reasoning.[52] Aquinas also added that there are secondary moral principles, derivable from first principles, that are nevertheless inferred by nearly everyone almost immediately (e.g., thou shalt not murder).[53] Arriving at the truth of immediate principles requires no lengthy rea-

49. In this connection, White points out that what the moral sense knows immediately are *propositions* (*Philosophy of the American Revolution*, 103).

50. In his letter to Carr, Jefferson even says, "State a moral case to a ploughman and a professor. The former will decide it as well, often better than the latter, because he has not been led astray by artificial rules" (ibid., 118).

51. According to White, Hutcheson "often speaks of the moral sense as *discerning* things." Thus, "Hutcheson's allegedly noncognitive moral sensing allegedly entitles us to assert moral propositions that we can claim to *know*." Hutcheson later seems to deny the sufficiency of the moral sense, without the judgment of reason, to provide moral knowledge. White argues, "In his early writings this claim to knowledge seems to be established immediately by the sensing, but later . . . Hutcheson acknowledged the need for some kind of correction of the moral sensations by reason before we could claim to have moral knowledge about an action" (ibid., 103). On Hutcheson's understanding of the moral sense, see also Haakonssen, *Natural Law and Moral Philosophy,* 65–85; Taylor, *Sources of the Self,* 259–65; and Alasdair MacIntyre, *Whose Justice? Which Rationality?* 260–80.

52. According to Aquinas, "the precepts of natural law are to the practical reason, what the first principles of demonstrations are to the speculative reason" (*Summa*, I–II, q. 94, art. 2). This entails that the first principles are indemonstrable.

53. Aquinas makes the following statements in *Summa:* "Now all men know the truth to a certain extent, at least as to the common principles of the natural law: and as to others, they partake of the knowledge of truth, some more, some less" (I–II, q. 93, art. 2); "the precepts of natural law are to the practical reason, what the first principles of demonstrations are to the speculative reason" (I–II, q. 94, art. 2). (This entails that the first principles are indemonstrable); "Consequently we must say that the natural law, as to general principles, is the same for all, both as to rectitude and as to knowledge. But as to certain matters of detail, which are conclusions, as it were, of those general principles, it is the same for all in the majority of cases, both as to rectitude and as to knowledge; and yet in some

soning process. These are accessible to all people and accessed by nearly every-one. The fear of the sentimentalists about so-called rationalist natural law the-ory—namely, that such theory makes moral truth inaccessible to many peo-ple—was unfounded in this regard. In sum, if the moral sense that these theorists discussed delivers *immediately to the understanding* basic principles of morality, then there seems to be a distinction without difference between moral sense and the first principles of practical reason. Moral-sense theorists are simply calling basic elements of the practical reason (i.e., the insight into first, indemonstrable moral principles and faculty of the practical reason that infers the immediate principles) by a different name.

Moral-sense theory, however, also came to be referred to as the theory of moral *sentiments*.[54] Thus, many moral-sense theorists seem to say that it is our sentiments or emotions (our hearts) rather than our cognitive faculties (our heads) that direct us in the true path of morality. Adherents of the moral sen-timents school of thought, as I have pointed out, need not be characterized as emotivists (who believe that all ethical statements are expressions of subjec-tive feelings). Some sentimentalists are; but others are committed realists.[55] Realists of a sentimentalist bent maintain that our emotions are better indi-cators of moral truths than our heads. But these sentimentalists clearly believe that the moral requirements revealed by human emotion are real require-ments pointing to real obligations binding upon humans and transcendent of human willing. In other words, emotions point to a standard normative for human behavior that human beings did not create.

---

few cases it may fail, both as to rectitude, by reason of certain obstacles . . . , and as to knowledge, since in some the reason is perverted by passion, or evil habit, or an evil disposition of nature; thus formerly, theft, although it is expressly contrary to the natural law, was not considered wrong among the Germans, as Julius Caesar relates (*De Bello Gallico* vi)" (I–II, q. 94, art. 4); "For there are certain things which the natural reason of every man, of its own accord and at once, judges to be done or not to be done: e.g., *Honor thy father and thy mother*, and, *Thou shalt not kill, Thou shalt not steal*: and these belong to the law of nature absolutely.—And there are certain things which, after a more care-ful consideration wise men deem obligatory. Such belong to the law of nature, yet so that they need to be inculcated, the wiser teaching the less wise: e.g., *Rise up before the hoary head, and honor the per-son of the aged man*, and the like.—And there are some things, to judge of which, human reason needs Divine instruction, whereby we are taught about the things of God: e.g., *Thou shalt not make to thy-self a graven thing, nor the likeness of anything; Thou shalt not take the name of the Lord thy God in vain*" (I–II, q. 100, art. 1). Now the principles just enumerated are from the Decalogue, which Aquinas describes as derivations from two general first principles, namely, that we should love God and neigh-bor. "Those two principles the first general principles of natural law, and are self-evident to human reason, either through nature or through faith. Wherefore all the precepts of the decalogue are re-ferred to these, as conclusions to general principles" (I–II, q. 100, art. 3).

54. À la Adam Smith. See Smith's *The Theory of Moral Sentiments*.

55. Hutcheson seems to present us with a clear instance of a sentimentalist who was also a realist and therefore not an emotivist in the common meaning of the term.

The idea that emotions (or sentiments) are the surest indicator of moral truth poses a difficulty. Do all our emotions point to the standard? That seems a stretch. For the emotions of an individual may conflict (hence the phrase *bittersweet*) and an individual's emotional responses may change with time. Moral sentimentalists do not usually despair because of this. Rather, they argue that some emotions are morally significant and reflective of a real moral standard whereas others are not. Sometimes benevolence is identified as the fundamental *moral* sentiment indicative of how humans ought to act. More generally, moral sentimentalists could say that the deepest, most abiding emotions are the true ones—most representative of what we really feel—and therefore the ones that correctly tell us what we ought to do. All of this is highly problematic. Emotions, or sentiments, as such, are entirely noncognitive. Thus, if we consider only emotion, then James can only tell that he feels x or y and that he feels x more strongly than y, and thus is directed in his actions by x. Emotions don't by themselves tell us that some are deeper and truer than others or that some are moral and others not. We cannot distinguish emotions on the basis of emotion alone other than in terms of strength, where strength is measured by likeliness to determine action. In order to distinguish some emotions from others qualitatively, we require access to a standard external to emotions. Such a standard is a necessary guide for behavior. After all, our emotions are in conflict and change. We therefore need to know which ones to allow to govern our actions. We need to know which ones to encourage and which ones to constrain. Such knowledge (of which emotions we *ought* to allow to govern our actions) must be delivered to us by something other than mere emotion. As reason is generally conceived of as our faculty of knowing, it seems reason is the best candidate.

This does not preclude the possibility that reason and emotion work in tandem to point human beings toward moral truth. Many American revolutionaries and framers as well as many Enlightenment philosophers thought just this.[56] Generally, however, either reason or sentiment was given the primary role in delivering moral knowledge to individuals. But suppose someone suggests that reason and sentiment work together in delivering moral knowledge *and* that neither of these plays a more fundamental role than the other. At a minimum, it's difficult to see how this could be the case. Given that any person's sentiments or emotions may be in conflict at any given moment of time

56. See White, *Philosophy of the American Revolution;* Hall, *Political and Legal Philosophy of James Wilson;* and John Witherspoon, "Lectures on Moral Philosophy."

or that they may vary over time, individuals need guidance as to which emotions to follow, as to which emotions are *moral*. As we have seen, that standard is not intrinsic to emotion or sentiment. Knowledge of which sentiments are moral and which are not must come, as I have argued, from outside of emotions. In this case, because we're positing that reason and sentiment work in tandem, reason must have the regulative role. But this means that reason has primacy in perceiving moral truth and in directing action. In fact, the very need for reason and sentiment to work in tandem in directing the individual toward moral truth seems to suggest the supervenience of reason.[57]

Instrumental Reason

Jean Hampton aptly summarizes the distinction between instrumental and noninstrumental reason: "Many philosophers and social scientists argue that the only acceptable theory of the nature of practical reason is what is called the 'instrumental' theory, which says, roughly, that reason's only practical role is working out and recommending action that best achieves the end of the agent. Such theorists dismiss the idea that reason could ever play a noninstrumental role by dictating or determining ends themselves."[58] Instrumental reason presents us with conditionals or hypothetical imperatives. J. L. Mackie describes these hypothetical imperatives in this way: "'If you want X, do Y' (or 'You ought to Y') will be a hypothetical imperative if it is based on the supposed fact that Y is, in the circumstances, the only (or the best) available means to X, that is, on a causal relation between Y and X. The reason for doing Y lies in its causal connection with the desired end, X; the oughtness is contingent upon the desire."[59] Oughtness in a hypothetical imperative may be contingent upon desire, but it is determined *both* by desire *and* by the necessity of using certain means (or refraining from certain means) in order to obtain the object of desire. These hypothetical imperatives have a lawlike causal structure that might be thought to mimic the causal laws of the natural order. For a physical phenomenon to occur, say, rain falling on the plains in Spain, a certain set of conditions must obtain. But when those conditions all obtain, then the rain *must* fall on those poetic Spanish plains. Thus, when a physical event X occurs, the occurrence of X has been necessitated because a set of condi-

---

57. Which, as White notes (in note 51 above), seems to be a conclusion reached by Hutcheson himself.

58. Hampton, *Authority of Reason*, 125.

59. Mackie, cited in ibid., 127.

tions, Y, together sufficient for the occurrence of X, have obtained. When Y obtains, X follows. Likewise, says Mackie, if we have a hypothetical imperative such that we ought to do Y, then this means that (1) doing Y is the only way to obtain some object of desire X and that (2) doing Y will necessarily bring it about that X obtains.

According to the standard interpretation of his work, Thomas Hobbes tries to explain natural law in just this way. Hobbes famously conceives people in a state of nature, a state in which there is no sovereign authority to restrain human behavior and no right or wrong, justice or injustice, normative for human behavior.[60] Humans there possess the right of nature, the ability or liberty to do anything and everything that they think is conducive to their own survival.[61] In this state of absolute freedom, people have infinite or unlimited desires and the desire for power (if need be, over others) to obtain the objects of desire while living in a world of limited goods.[62] Hobbes describes these people as being moved by desire after desire and the desire for power upon power in order to obtain the objects of desire.[63] These power-hungry people are further described as equal in two key respects: strength and prudence. No person is so strong that he cannot be killed (nor, in the end, is any person so

60. "To this war of every man against every man, this also is consequent: that nothing can be unjust. The notions of right and wrong, justice and injustice, have there no place. Where there is no common power, there is no law; where no law, no injustice. Force and fraud are in war the two cardinal virtues" (Hobbes, *Leviathan*, 78).

61. Says Hobbes, "The Right of Nature, which writers commonly call *jus naturale*, is the liberty each man hath to use his own power, as he will himself, for the preservation of his own nature, that is to say, of his own life, and consequently of doing anything which, in is own judgment and reason, he shall conceive to be the aptest means thereunto." Further, he argues that because, in the state of nature, "the condition of man . . . is a condition of war of everyone against everyone (in which case everyone is governed by his own reason and there is nothing he can make use of that may not be a help unto him preserving his life against his enemies), it followeth that in such a condition every man has a right to everything, even to one another's body" (ibid., 79–80).

62. Concerning the first part of the sentence, Hobbes says that "felicity of this life consisteth not in the repose of a mind satisfied." Rather, "Felicity is a continual progress of the desire, from one object to another, the attaining of the former being still but the way to the latter. The cause whereof is that the object of man's desire is not to enjoy once only, and for one instant of time, but to assure forever the way of his future desire" (ibid., 57). The second part of the sentence I infer from Hobbes's statement that from equality of strength and prudence "ariseth equality of hope in the attaining of our ends. And therefore, if any two men desire the same thing, which nevertheless they cannot both enjoy, they become enemies; and in the way to their end, which is principally their own conservation, and sometimes their delectation only, endeavour to destroy or subdue one another" (75), together with his insistence that the state of nature is necessarily a state of hostility between individuals.

63. "So that in the first place, put for a general inclination of all mankind, a perpetual and restless desire of power after power, that ceaseth only death," the reason of which is that a man "cannot assure the power and means to live well which he hath present, without the acquisition of more" (ibid., 58).

weak that he cannot kill—either by himself or with the aid of others). Further, says Hobbes, equal time bestows equal experience, and equal experience leads to equal prudence. This is not to say that all people are equally good at things like mathematics so long as they live long enough. Rather, Hobbes seems to think that all people are equally good at figuring out how to obtain the objects of desire. Thus, this equality of strength and prudence produces in people equal hope in obtaining the objects of desire. The world of limited goods, inhabited by people with unlimited desires and with equal hope of obtaining their desires, places each person in a hostile stance toward others, a hostility that leads to violence. Some people desire glory, others are simply competitive, and others simply want to survive. All of these motives lead people to "invade" others. Because no person is safe from invasion by others, others trying to eliminate competition or to take someone else's goods, the rational strategy becomes the preemptive strike. In the end, the state of nature cannot but be a state of war, a war of each against all.[64]

The state of nature can be avoided, Hobbes tells us, *if and only if* certain natural laws are followed.[65] That is, Hobbes has a list of conditions that must obtain or, put another way, actions that must be done, if the state of nature is to be avoided. These conditions are both necessary and sufficient such that (1) people must act in the way he recommends if the state of nature is to be avoided, and (2) if they do so act, then, as a causal result, the state of nature will be avoided. Thus, Hobbes's laws of nature are arguably analogous to the laws of physics. They are, in fact, commonly construed as hypothetical imperatives and therefore as counsels of prudence. They are also thought to generate a kind of "oughtness" *for everyone* just because, on Hobbes's view, everyone wants more than anything else to survive and as a result wants, or should want, to avoid the state of nature. These laws are well known: "every man ought to endeavor peace, as far as he has hope of obtaining it, and when he cannot obtain it, that he may seek and use all the advantages of war" and "that a man be willing, when others are so too, as far-forth as for peace and defense of him-

---

64. "And from this diffidence of one another, there is no way for any man to secure himself so reasonable as anticipation, that is, by force or wiles to master the persons of all men he can, so long till he see no other power great enough to endanger him." In fact, "if others (that otherwise would be glad to be at ease within modest bounds) should not by invasion increase their power, they would not be able, long time, by standing only on their defence, to subsist" (ibid., 75; see also 74–76, more generally for Hobbes's argument concerning equality and motives for invasion in the state of nature).

65. "The passions that incline men to peace are fear of death, desire of such things as are necessary to commodious living, and hope by their industry to obtain them. And reason suggesteth convenient articles of peace, upon which men may be drawn to agreement. These articles are they which otherwise are called the Laws of Nature" (ibid., 78).

self he shall think it necessary, to lay down this right to all things, and be contented with so much liberty against other men, as would allow other men against himself."[66] This second law of nature, Hobbes maintains, is the same as the Golden Rule laid down by Jesus in the Gospels.[67] Hobbes, of course, adds other laws of nature (e.g., "That all men perform their covenants made") that point us to the creation of a commonwealth by covenant (or social contract in contemporary parlance) in which each person surrenders the right of nature. But this surrender is accomplished by an act of transfer in which each person transfers the right of nature to an absolute sovereign.[68] *If and only if* these things are done will the state of nature be avoided.

Noninstrumental Reason

In contrast to instrumental reason, "noninstrumental theorists present reason not as a tool designed solely either to achieve or to discover the ends of our actions, but as something that, in addition to its instrumental functioning, quite literally, defines the ends of action."[69] In this vein, consider Robert George's defense of Germain Grisez, John Finnis, and Joseph Boyle's theory of natural law against criticisms offered by Jeffrey Goldworthy. Goldworthy holds the noncognitivist view of human action and explicates that view by analogizing human behavior to a guided missile. On his view, "desire determines the target and supplies the propulsion, while reason locates the target and guides action towards it."[70] In contrast, "Grisez, Finnis, Boyle and other natural law theorists affirm . . . that people can have, and be aware of noninstrumental reasons for action. What distinguishes rationally motivated actions is precisely that people perform them for non-instrumental reasons." Furthermore, "Someone who acts for a non-instrumental reason acts ultimately not on the basis of a brute desire, as non-cognitivists believe people always inevitably act, but, rather, because of his intelligent grasp of the intelligible point of performing the action. Such a person does not merely want, or want to do, something; he wants it or wants to do it, *for a (non-instrumental) reason*."[71] Put another way, a person motivated by a noninstrumental reason is seeking to do some act or to attain some goal that is done at least in part be-

---

66. Ibid., 79–80.
67. Ibid., 80–81.
68. Ibid., 81–118.
69. Hampton, *Authority of Reason*, 232.
70. Goldworthy, cited in Robert P. George, *In Defense of Natural Law*, 18.
71. Ibid.

cause the act is good or the goal is worth attaining in and of itself. Thus, for instance, one might aim at the attainment of knowledge or friendship simply because these things are good. On the instrumental theory, these things are means to fulfill some desire and are viewed as desirable because they are desired. For the noninstrumental theorists, in contrast, these things may be desired because they are desirable for their own sake.

All noninstrumental natural law theorists share some commonalities. They hold that the goods desirable for their own sake are goods perfective of human nature and that this knowledge as well as the prescription that such goods are to be pursued are apprehended by human reason.[72] For all noninstrumental theorists, first moral principles are apprehended immediately, without reflection.[73] Beyond this consensus, however, lie a variety of noninstrumental (or substantive) natural law theories.[74] Because Thomas Aquinas represents

---

72. Sometimes the "new natural law theory" of Grisez, Finnis, and Boyle is said *not* to be grounded in human nature. Grisez and company's principal defender, Robert George, maintains that such criticism misunderstands their theory:

> It would be tedious, but not difficult, to show that neither Grisez nor any of his principal followers has ever denied that basic human goods and moral norms have grounding in human nature. Nor have they ever alleged that theoretical knowledge . . . is irrelevant to practical reasoning and morality. . . . Indeed, Grisez and his followers affirm that basic goods and moral norms *are* what they are because human nature *is* what it is. Finnis, for example, . . . *endorses* the proposition that "were man's nature different, so would be his duties." ("Natural Law and Human Nature," 33)

Finnis himself asserts that if we consider ontology (in contrast to epistemology), "the goodness of all human goods (and thus the appropriateness, the *convenientia*, of all responsibilities) is derived from (i.e., depends upon) the nature which, by their goodness, those goods perfect. For those goods are the *rationes* of practical norms or 'oughts'—would not perfect that nature were it other than it is" (35).

73. According to Joseph Boyle, "central to the natural law account of its tradition dependence and independence is the claim that the basic principles of natural law are universally accessible, and, apparently, universally known" ("Natural Law and the Ethics of Tradition," 18). He acknowledges that some will think this claim implausible, but he thinks Aquinas and his followers have a response:

> Thus, part of the natural law response to the charge that it requires people to have knowledge that they evidently do not have is that knowledge of basic moral principles possessed by everyone need not be articulate, philosophically elaborated knowledge. Principles can be present and operative within knowledge without being explicitly formulated. Basic moral principles can therefore be operative within a person's moral thinking, as the grounds of norms he or she regards as true, even if they are not explicitly articulated, and they can be teased away from these norms sufficiently to allow for serious moral criticism. Those who deny their philosophical elaboration may do so because they do not understand that elaboration or its context. It is also possible that the denials of the elaborations of these principles are merely verbal, and possible also that they are based on an unwillingness of people to accept some of the implications of the philosophical formulations. (25)

74. Thus, the natural law theory initiated by Grisez, elaborated by Finnis and Boyle, and defended

the *locus classicus* of noninstrumental natural law theory, I will focus my attention on him.

Aquinas begins his consideration of the natural law's precepts with a famous analogy: "the precepts of the natural law are to the practical reason what the first principles of demonstrations are to the speculative reason, because both are self-evident principles." Aquinas is here concerned with things that are self-evident in themselves. A proposition is self-evident in itself "if the predicate is contained in the notion of the subject." Even so, Aquinas agrees with Boethius that "certain axioms or propositions are universally self-evident to all" because their "terms are known to all" (e.g., every whole is greater than its part). When it comes to moral knowledge, good "is the first thing that falls under the apprehension of the practical reason," just as being is the first notion to be apprehended by speculative reason. Further, good is "directed to action, since every agent acts for an end under the aspect of good." From this Thomas concludes that the first principle of practical reason is founded on the notion of good, understanding the good as that which all things seek. Thus, "this is the first precept of law, that good is to be done and pursued, and evil is to be avoided."[75] This first precept is known to all. The common principles that are self-evident and known to all, however, extend beyond this.

According to Aquinas, "All other precepts of natural law are based upon the first precept, so that whatever the practical reason naturally apprehends as man's good (or evil) belongs to the precepts of natural law as something to be done or avoided." Further, "Since good has the nature of an end, and evil the nature of a contrary, hence it is that all those things to which man has a natural inclination are naturally apprehended by reason as being good and, consequently, as being objects of pursuit, and their contraries as evil and objects of avoidance." Thus, the natural law, via consideration of the objects to which the natural inclinations point, tells us that we ought to pursue three sorts of goods, "according to the order of natural inclinations," where "inclination" means not "desire" or "preference" but rather the aim or goal (i.e., the disposition) of the design plan of human nature (i.e., human essence).[76] Human na-

---

by George differs from the classical theory elaborated by Aquinas and his contemporary defenders. St. Augustine's Platonically grounded natural law theory is both classical and noninstrumental, yet it arguably differs from the Thomistic theory in certain respects as well.

75. All quotations take from Aquinas, *Summa*, I–II, q. 94, art. 2.

76. To understand what Aquinas means by "natural inclinations," we must first understand the idea of dispositional essences. Lisska wrote in *Aquinas's Theory of Natural Law*,

What then is an essence for Aquinas? It is a "supreme set of dispositional properties." Using terminology gained from Aristotle, Aquinas argues that a temporal essence is made up

ture is a complex composed of three parts. Each of the three parts has corresponding inclinations aimed at the attainment of some object. First, humans have the nature of a substance or of an existing thing.[77] Human beings are therefore inclined to that which completes existence, namely, to self-preservation—"every substance seeks the preservation of its own being." Therefore, "by reason of this inclination, whatever is a means of preserving human life and of warding off its obstacles belongs to natural law." Second, humans are possessed of an animal nature and have inclinations toward things pertaining to that nature. Thus, to the natural law belong those things "'which nature has taught all animals,' such as sexual intercourse, education of offspring, and so forth." Third, humans have a rational nature, with inclinations to the goods

---

of matter and form. A form is what specifically differentiates one kind of a thing from another kind of a thing. This is Aquinas's concept of a "substantial form." The properties which make up a substantial form, which in turn specify the content of an essence are dispositional in character. They are not static. . . . The model of a tulip bulb developing during the spring is closer to Aquinas's concept of an essence than the definition of a triangle. (97)

Essence is therefore developmental in nature, so Aquinas's theory of essences is teleological. "Teleology" means "Nature acts for an end." For both Aristotle and Aquinas, "the end or 'telos' is the point at which the dispositional properties in the primary substance reach their development or perfection. . . . In Aquinian terminology, the potency or disposition has reached a state of actualization." None of this means that there is "a conscious direction on the part of the properties themselves" (99). What then is human essence? Lisska summarizes Aquinas's definition of the human being as a being "composed essentially of a set of dispositional properties divided into three sets"—substantial, animal, and rational (100). What then is human good? Human good is an instance of *good* more generally. In the *Summa,* Aquinas defines good as an end (I–II, q. 94, art. 2). Thus, according to Lisska, "the completion of a developmental process—the natural termination point—is a good" (102). Human good, therefore, is the natural termination point of human dispositional traits. In the end, human good pertains to human function. The good is realized when a person is functioning well, and one is functioning well when one reaches the "developmental potential of one's essential properties" (103). Lisska concludes that the elements of natural law arise in accordance with our particular dispositions (101). Therefore, "When the essence of a human person is determined, then this becomes the normative ground for what human beings are to be and to become. It is the foundation for *eudaemonia,* which is the functioning well of the essential properties common to the individual in a specific natural kind" (105). Immoral action becomes wrong because it hinders this "natural developmental process." An act is wrong when it "prevents the completion—the self-actualization, as it were—of the dispositional properties which determine the content of human nature" (104). What Lisska calls the elements of natural law are best understood as specifications of the natural law's requirements. They specify those requirements because they tell us what things are in fact good for human persons (and, concomitantly, what sorts of things are not). But these things only become obligatory given the first precept that indicates that good is to be pursued or preserved and evil avoided. This best explains why Aquinas thinks all the other precepts of the natural law flow from this one: "All other precepts of the natural law are based on upon this [that good is to be done and evil avoided], so that whatever the practical reason naturally apprehends as man's good (or evil) belongs to the precepts of the natural law as something to be done or avoided" (*Summa,* I–II, q. 94, art. 2). By this I think he means that they are *logically* dependent upon it for their prescriptiveness.

77. Lisska translates substance as "living thing" (*Aquinas's Theory of Natural Law,* 101).

corresponding to the fulfillment of that nature. Accordingly, "man has a natural inclination to know the truth about God and to live in society; and in this
respect whatever pertains to this inclination belongs to the natural law, for instance, to shun ignorance, to avoid offending those among whom one has to
live, and other such things regarding the above inclination."[78]

The Constitution and the Natural Law

Inference to the Best Explanation, Stage 1:
Eliminating Alternative Explanations

As I suggested in the discussion of Diagram 5.1, there are only two possibilities logically consistent with the position that moral truth is not known because it does not exist to be known: anarchy or positivism. *Moral* anarchy (the
idea that morality is relative to individuals) was rejected in the last chapter for
rather obvious reasons. *Political* anarchy (the view that no political regime
possesses the right to coerce obedience) didn't fare much better. Both deny
that law legitimately prescribes, thereby obligating individuals to obey. But the
Constitution is prescriptive and, as a function of its design, produces prescriptions for individuals. Thus, because the Constitution is prescriptive, and
therefore presupposes that the prescriptiveness of law is valid, and because anarchy rejects the validity of legal prescription, the Constitution and anarchy
stand in irreconcilable tension. But this is rather obvious, so we won't let it de-
tain us further.

What about positivism? We noted that normative positivism instantiates in
two forms—the classical, command-based positivism of Austin and the contemporary rules-based theory of Hart. As for the former, to embrace it is to
embrace the idea that the sovereign is absolutely free to command whatsoever he will and that whatsoever the sovereign commands possesses the force of
law. When the Constitution is described in positivistic terms, the sovereign indicated is usually the people, whose will is said, following Locke, to be determined by the majority.[79] Thus, when the Constitution is described in positivistic terms, it is characterized as a mechanism for translating the will of the

---

78. All references to Aquinas in this paragraph are from the *Summa*, I–II, q. 94, art. 2

79. According to Locke, "For when any number of Men have, by the consent of every individual,
made a *Community*, they have thereby made that *Community* one Body, with a Power to Act as one
Body, which is only by the will and determination of the *majority*" (*Two Treatises*, 331).

majority into law. Furthermore, as a corollary to the general premise of normative positivism that there is no transcendent moral law binding upon individuals generally and on the sovereign in particular, the will of the majority must be said to be unconstrained. The majority is free to command however it pleases. Entailed here is the idea that there is no rational justification for constraining the will of the majority in any way. For if there is no natural law or transcendent moral code, then all exercises of the sovereign will, in this case the will of the majority, are equally valid. To put it another way, there is no basis in positivism for distinguishing among different exercises of majority will.[80] Consequently, a positivistic Constitution ought to be equally compelled by or indifferent to all exercises of majority will. Austinian positivism falls to the ground very quickly, then, given the argument of chapter 3. According to chapter 3, all the realistic candidates for the sovereign under the Constitution are greatly constrained. Under the Constitution, given the constraining mechanisms, the sovereign is not free to command however he or they please. Even if one were to concede (though I do not) that all the constraints are procedural, even so they constrain the sovereign by forcing his or their will to conform to the procedure. Furthermore, the Constitution favors long-term majority will (or preference or desire) over immediate popular will. But this is just the sort of distinguishing among exercises of will that makes no sense in terms of normative positivism. Consequently, I think we must reject normative positivism as a possible constitutional presupposition.

Hartian rules-based positivism fares little better than traditional positivism. On the one hand, if Hartian positivism accepts normative positivism together with the possibility of a real sovereign and it turns out that some party is sovereign under the Constitution, then there is no normative basis of any sort for constraining the will of that sovereign. Normative positivism per se is inconsistent with constrained sovereignty because constraints of any sort distinguish exercises of will. But the Constitution establishes a popular sovereign whose exercises of will are greatly constrained. On the other hand, if the Hartian rules-based theory denies that there is any sovereign, in favor of the idea that laws are determined by fundamental rules of recognition (or of validity),

---

80. Certain features of the Constitution that seem at odds with majoritarian rule (the design of the Supreme Court and judicial review) are considered to pose a "countermajoritarian dilemma." Scholars then endeavor to show how such apparently countermajoritarian features are actually consistent with majority rule. Of course these difficult features in the Constitution that seem inconsistent with majority rule really do pose a problem for what we might call normative majoritarian positivists. They pose not only a dilemma for normative positivists, but a contradiction to their understanding of the Constitution's philosophical foundation.

then two contradictions with the Constitution emerge. First, the Constitution presupposes that there is a very real, albeit constrained, sovereign—the people. The sovereign is the one with the final say as to what shall be law, and the tendency of the Constitution is to give the people just this sort of say. In short, under our Constitution, it is not simply secondary rules that determine legal validity. The will of the people performs some function in determining legal validity, especially given the amendment procedures outlined in the Constitution. Second, in this case Hartian positivism begins to resemble procedural conventionalism. But we saw, in the last chapter, that the Constitution's design is inconsistent with procedural conventionalism. The only way to salvage Hartian positivism, so that the Constitution can be described in Hartian terms, is to reject the problematic premise above—but the problematic premise is the foundational premise of normative positivism and procedural conventionalism, namely, that there is no real good transcendent of human willing that is also normative for human willing. In short, for the Hartian theory to fit the Constitution, it must become realist and grounded in the natural law. But this is to make Hartian theory un-Hartian indeed.

Given our discussion here of Austinian and Hartian positivism, it would seem that the Constitution rejects positivism. But there is a form of positivism we've yet to consider in this section. Someone could maintain that there is a standard normative for human willing and transcendent of it that is nevertheless not natural to human beings. This troublesome someone might say that the standard is positive law contained only in supernatural divine revelation. It is surely difficult, however, to see how the Constitution could take this to be the case. A constitution that takes this to be the case should somehow incorporate that sacred revelation into the lawmaking process as a standard to which the laws must conform, and this is something that our Constitution does not do.

If the Constitution is inconsistent with anarchy and positivism, then it seemingly rejects the idea that there is no natural law. As a result, the Constitution must presuppose the validity of some view or other of natural law and of how such a law is known. The remaining options are sentimentalism, instrumental reason, and noninstrumental reason. Each of these views takes it to be the case that some standard, in some sense normative to human conduct, is promulgated to human beings via some aspect of human nature (i.e., either through human emotions or through human reason).

Suppose the Constitution assumes that human sentiments or emotions are the best indicator of the common good and of real moral requirements binding every individual and every society. How would it manifest this assumption? Arguably, the Constitution would be designed so that the strong passion of the moment determines policy decisions. The Constitution would favor a system in which popular will is determined by popular emotion. Just here a conflict emerges. The delay mechanisms in the Constitution are resistant to governance by passion. They prevent *immediate* emotion from holding sway. Only motives that last over the long term can successfully influence what becomes law. Thus, the Constitution does not presuppose the normativity of human sentiments.

"Not so fast," someone objects. "Sentimentalists aren't committed to the normativity of every human sentiment. Sentimentalists want *moral* sentiments or emotions to govern human law and human behavior. You've only shown that the Constitution doesn't allow the governance of every breeze of passion. But the *moral* sentiments are the deep-seated enduring sentiments rather than the passion of the moment." These objections can be met. Recall that we *cannot* distinguish, qualitatively, among emotions on the basis of emotion. If we want to consider any sentiment or emotion vis-à-vis others, we can consider only strength (or felt-ness). But we can only measure the strength of various emotions in terms of their influence on our actions. And the only real test here is whether or not an emotion is sufficiently strong to determine action. The Constitution's decision-delay mechanisms, however, favor the influence of long-term over immediate emotion or sentiment, thereby distinguishing the two. This distinction is not made on the basis of strength of emotion. If the Constitution institutionally resists governance of the popular will by *immediate* emotion, then it presupposes that, *ceteris paribus,* immediate emotion determines human will. This entails that, *ceteris paribus,* immediate emotion is stronger than long-term emotion. If long-term emotions naturally governed human will and if the governance by these emotions was desirable, then the decision-delay mechanisms in the Constitution would be entirely unnecessary. The only logical explanation of their place in the Constitution is that the Constitution presupposes that immediate emotions are the strongest and that government by these emotions is to be resisted. If the Constitution distinguishes (by favoring) some emotions or sentiments (long-term) from others (short-term), especially if the favoring has nothing to do with strength of emotion, and if such a distinction cannot be based on sentiment or emotion (as it cannot be for the reasons already given), then the distinction (and favoring) must be (if the distinction is rational) founded on the conformity of certain sentiments (or emotions) to a standard external to emotion. Moreover, the Constitution can't presuppose that this standard is known by emotion. As I have argued, emotion alone only tells us that some emotions are stronger than others. Knowledge of strength of emotion cannot include the idea that weaker, long-term emotions are to be favored and more immediate ones resisted. This bit of *moral* knowledge must come from outside emotion or sentiment. But a bit of knowledge such as this is of a standard external to emotion and sentiment, and it is to this standard that emotion and sentiment must conform in order to be *moral*. This, in turn, implies that moral knowledge comes from outside sentiment and emotion. In sum, the Constitution's favoring of weaker, long-term emotions over immediate stronger ones seems to presuppose the externality of moral knowledge to the sentiments.

Instrumental reason also falls to the ground and for just the same reasons that preferential conventionalism was rejected in chapter 4. If natural law is a matter of instrumental reason, then, as we saw, it is human desire that determines the good to be pursued. Natural law, on this view, is simply a matter of the means to an end. Oughtness is generated by the "causal" necessity of using certain means to obtain a desired end. A constitution reflective of this conception, in the name of consistency, ought to be designed to reflect the supremacy of human desire. And if human desire determines the good, thereby determining the aim of natural law, then the Constitution must be indifferent among human desires except insofar as it reflects the strongest desire. But the Constitution does not treat all desire as equally valid. Rather, it favors long-term, widely shared desires over short-term and narrow ones. But distinguishing between desires in this way requires recourse to some standard outside of desire. Furthermore, there is simply no reason to suppose that long-term, widely shared desires are the strongest. Rather, the reason the Constitution is resistant to immediate desire and favors long-term desire over immediate desire is because, all other things equal, immediate desire tends to be stronger and more determinate of human action. Therefore, the Constitution seems to favor weaker desires over stronger desires. And all of this is deeply inconsistent with the supremacy of desire. But the supremacy of desire is an essential plank of the theory of instrumental reason. Thus, the instrumental-reason account of natural law falls to the ground as well.

This leaves noninstrumental reason on the table. Given the argument of chapter 4 concerning the Constitution's theory of the common good, the following is entailed: the Constitution presupposes a noninstrumental account of natural law in which a real, teleological, thick common good is promulgated to human beings through reason and made obligatory for them. But why do I say that the Constitution presupposes that the common good promulgated to human beings is also obligatory for them? The Constitution is prescriptive and produces prescriptive laws. Its underlying assumption must therefore be consistent with prescriptive validity. Prescription presupposes obligation and norms that rightly impose obligation. But mere goodness is not yet obligatory. Rather, there must be a further norm that says that good is to be done (and, conversely, that evil is to be avoided). If the Constitution doesn't presuppose a norm of natural law underwriting its own prescriptions, then it is merely an act of force (even if the force is the will of society exhibited in the choice to honor certain conventional norms). But acts of force do not impose obligation. Thus, if the Constitution doesn't presuppose a natural law that imposes obligations upon human persons, then it presupposes both that it is and that it is not binding, obligatory, and prescriptive. And that would be rather absurd. So, to be consistent, the Constitution must presuppose norms of obligation transcendent of human willing.

But an objector might pose this considerable challenge: What about the provisions of the Constitution dealing with slavery? How can a constitution that presupposes a real common good, as described in the last chapter, and natural law, as described in this chapter, have contained provisions that protected the institution of slavery, a practice obviously contrary to preserving the noninstrumental, intelligible good that is every human person? The objection, of course, is raised because of three key constitutional provisions—the three-fifths clause for apportioning representation in the House (Article 1, Section 2); the importation clause (Article 1, Section 9); and the so-called fugitive-slave clause (Article 4, Section 2). The most obvious response is that the Thirteenth Amendment obviates this objection by banning slavery and involuntary servitude, thereby overturning these provisions. But suppose our objector wants to know how the natural law interpretation fares absent the post–Civil War amendments. What sort of answer can we give?

Before proceeding, we must note that many in the academy today will puzzle over this objection. After all, many hold the strange idea that moral realism and, in particular, natural law support and even underwrite the idea of slavery. Perhaps they have read Aristotle's discussion of the "slave by nature" and also somewhere heard Aristotle referred to as "the father of natural law." In chapter 7 I will show why the suggestion that moral realism and natural law underwrite slavery is actually false. For now, it suffices to underscore a few points that will receive some elaboration later. First, moral nihilism in any of its variants (subjectivism, relativism, conventionalism, normative positivism, etc.) makes it impossible to claim, in any meaningful sense, that slavery is wrong. The normative positivist, for instance, has no ground from which to proclaim slavery wrong because he has already denied the very possibility of anything being wrong at all. Second, moral realism (and natural law as well, I think) are necessary conditions for condemning slavery and for holding any person or society culpable or blameworthy for practicing it. In light of these points, we see immediately that our objector has presented a real difficulty. So the question is, Do the three constitutional provisions just mentioned present a contradiction with the idea of natural law?

Despite the severity of the foregoing criticism, a number of points can be raised in defense of the natural law interpretation of the Constitution. First, natural law is certainly incompatible with a constitution that commands that wrong be done. Given the great wrong of slavery, natural law would certainly be incompatible with a constitution that commanded the holding of slaves. But the Constitution never contained any such requirement; rather, it allowed an existing wrong to continue. Natural law is compatible with the allowance of wrongful acts when such allowance is, on balance, for the common good. These problematic provisions could be so construed as allowing slavery in order to secure the ratification of the Constitution by slave states, thereby establishing a Union, something essential for the elimination of slavery in North America. Second, the first two provisions mentioned at least admit of anti-slavery interpretations. Let's take them in order. The infamous three-fifths compromise can be understood as weakening the power of proslavery forces in the national government. As Earl M. Maltz argues, "The Convention determined that each state's representation in the House would be determined by its population. If slaves were to be considered persons, then the representation . . . would be increased; if property, then that representation . . . would be correspondingly reduced." However,

> Treating slaves as persons for this purpose did not promise to improve their status in the slave states. Slaves could not vote; therefore, counting them fully in the basis of representation would serve only to enhance the political power that the slave states (and thus the slaveholders) would have in the national government. Such an increase in power could only work to the detriment of the slaves themselves by tilting federal policy toward the pro-slavery position.[81]

81. Maltz, "Slavery, Federalism, and the Structure of the Constitution," 469.

In other words, the Constitution would have been considerably more proslavery if, for the purposes of apportioning representation, slaves had been counted as full persons. Therefore, the three-fifths compromise admits of an antislavery interpretation. If slavery is contrary to natural law and the three-fifths provision admits of an antislavery interpretation, then I fail to see how this provision contradicts a natural law interpretation of the Constitution.

But what about the importation clause of Article 1, Section 9? This clause too admits of an antislavery interpretation. The clause prevents Congress from banning the importation of slaves (without ever using the word) *until* 1808, though it allows the levying of a tax (up to ten dollars per person) on the importation of persons (i.e., slaves) "as any of the states now existing shall think proper to admit." The clause tacitly concedes that, without this provision, Congress would have had the power to ban the importation of slaves. Moreover, by implication, it acknowledges Congress's power to eliminate the importation of slaves from 1808 forward and to burden, by taxes, the importation of slaves until that point. And, it seems to me, the grant of such power is best understood (or at least plausibly understood) as a step toward the eventual elimination not only of the slave trade but also of slavery itself. Madison seems to have held such an interpretation of the clause:

> It ought to be a considered as a great point gained in favor of humanity, that a period of twenty years may terminate for ever within these States, a traffic which has so long and so loudly upbraided the barbarism of modern policy; that within that period it will receive a considerable discouragement from the federal Government, and may be totally abolished by a concurrence of the few States which continue the unnatural traffic, in the prohibitory example which has been given by so great a majority of the Union.[82]

If the clause admits of an antislavery interpretation, then there is no direct or formal contradiction between the Constitution and natural law.

This brings us to the third provision mentioned by our objector—the so-called fugitive-slave clause. According to the clause, "No person held to service or labour in one state, under the laws thereof, escaping into another, shall, in consequence of any law or regulation therein, be discharged from such service or labour, but shall be delivered up on claim of the party to whom such service or labour may be due." As Maltz observes, this clause clearly requires "even

---

82. *The Federalist* No. 42, 213.

free states to recognize the claim of an owner who could demonstrate that a person was a runaway from his service."[83] Granting the antithesis of natural law rightly understood to slavery, the fugitive-slave clause appears to produce a real tension with the Constitution. And this holds even if the clause fails to underwrite the fugitive-slave acts adopted by Congress in 1793 and 1850 (after all, the clause nowhere empowers Congress to provide federal enforcement for the provision).[84]

What can be said at this point? First, we have seen that all moral theories competing with the natural law interpretation also stand in some contradiction to the Constitution. Second, the natural law interpretation is contradicted only by this clause. More important, no part of the Constitution's institutional framework stands in contradiction to the natural law interpretation. In contrast, competing moral explanations of the Constitution are contradicted by structural features of the Constitution and, as a result, by a greater number of clauses. Consequently, the natural law interpretation stands in the least tension with the Constitution. Third, the slavery provisions taken together can be understood as allowing slavery, in order to secure ratification of the Constitution by slave states, while providing constitutional means to work for its eventual elimination. Fourth, the Thirteenth Amendment (especially in conjunction with the Fourteenth and Fifteenth Amendments) alleviates the tension of natural law with the Constitution by overturning the slavery provisions of the original Constitution. This point is of some importance. What I'm suggesting is that before the adoption of these post–Civil War amendments the natural law interpretation I'm advancing was the interpretation with the least against it. After the adoption of the post–Civil War amendments, nothing stands in its way. If you will, the Thirteenth Amendment (as well as the Fourteenth and Fifteenth Amendments) make the Constitution fully consistent with traditional natural law theory.[85]

---

83. Maltz, "Slavery, Federalism, and the Structure of the Constitution," 471. Although we can readily observe a certain ambiguity in the clause, "As Lincoln noted, the Constitution was silent as to who it was who had the obligation to 'deliver up' the slave" (Arkes, *Beyond the Constitution*, 42).

84. See Barber, *On What the Constitution Means*, 199–201.

85. According to Barber, "slavery was never really constitutional on any theory that would preserve the coherence of the Constitution as law. Slavery was there, but as a mistake, not as a part of a coherent whole" (ibid., 201).

Inference to the Best Explanation, Stage 2:
Consilience and Simplicity

In terms of consilience and simplicity, anarchy clearly fares the worst. It cannot explain the existence of a constitution, much less any of its institutional features. It therefore lacks consilience and requires a plethora of ad hoc hypotheses. We can therefore set it to the side and move on.

Positivism fares better here. If the Constitution establishes a popular sovereign and if we hold, with Locke, that the will of said sovereign is determined by the majority, then positivism explains the Constitution's majoritarian features. That is, positivism can explain the extraordinary control the popular sovereign possesses over the government. But normative positivism, because it shares the moral nihilism that animates conventionalism, cannot explain *any* of the Constitution's constraining features. There is no basis in normative positivism for distinguishing among exercises of the sovereign's will. But the constraining features of the Constitution inevitably do just this, favoring long-term, widely shared preferences over short-term, narrow ones. Given this, positivism will require auxiliary hypotheses to explain the Constitution's constraining features.

Two objectors pipe up at this point. The first objector, his fingers stroking his long, gray beard, says in wavering voice that the constraints are purely procedural. The sovereign can will anything he wants. He just has to will it in a certain way. The second objector, a gentleman younger than our first and who has the look of a Yale law professor, maintains that the Constitution's constraining mechanisms all operate on the government so as to protect an absolute popular sovereign from governmental usurpation of sovereign power. Let's take them in order. As for our older objector, it looks as if he has missed the point. What normative positivism cannot explain are *constraints* upon the sovereign per se. And procedural constraints are, indeed, constraints. If normative positivism cannot explain constraints, then it cannot explain purely procedural ones either. But why can't the normative positivist be for procedural constraints upon the sovereign will? Well, he can be in favor of them if he wants, but not on any ground provided by normative positivism. Normative positivism, at least in its classical form, accepts that law is nothing other than the command of the sovereign and that the sovereign's will is obliged by nothing external to it. Consequently, the sovereign is free to command however he pleases. But to say that the sovereign can command whatever he wants but that he *must* do it in a certain way is to presuppose an obligation to will in a particular way, whether he pleases or not. If there is no necessity for the sovereign to will in a certain way, then there is no real constraint here, procedural or otherwise. Put another way, normative positivism entails that all exercises of the sovereign's will are equally valid. But procedural constraints upon sovereign willing presuppose that only exercises conforming to the relevant procedure possess validity. Therefore, so long as the sovereign is really constrained, our procedural positivist has a problem. But just here our younger, sprier positivist mounts his attack against us. The Constitution's constraints aren't placed upon the popular sovereign at all. They're placed upon the sovereign's delegate or trustee—the government. Our young positivist, however, has not saved the day for positivism. For the Constitution rather clearly constrains both the government and the people, as I argued in chapter 3. Laws passed upon individuals and backed with coercive sanction are constraining indeed. Further, if the people want to exercise their final say, then they must conform their actions to certain procedures—to elections or to the amendment procedure. Finally, against both objectors stands the argument, presented in chapters 3 and 4, that the Constitution's procedural constraints favor certain outcomes over others. This means that they are not purely procedural.

Hart proves of no help in saving positivists from these difficulties. The problem that creates these difficulties is the assumption of normative positivism. If Hart accepts normative positivism, then the problems discussed follow. If he rejects normative positivism, then he embraces some form of natural law theory or realism, normative for human willing, including those acts of will by which law is made. But if that's the case, then he's the strangest sort of positivist.

The sentimentalist is in the same boat as the positivist. The sentimentalist can explain constitutional features that promote rule by the majority and that attach the government to the popular will, such as popular elections and the short terms of representatives. But because the sentimentalist cannot distinguish sentiments on the basis of sentiment, sentimentalism provides no logical grounds for saying which sentiments should govern action—immediate or long-term. Given this, the theory provides no reason for resisting certain emotions and favoring others. It follows that the theory fails to offer an explanation of the constitutional mechanisms that resist immediate passion. Perhaps the sentimentalist will be able to construct auxiliary hypotheses to show why his theory is not contradicted by the constitutional mechanisms that delay decision making thereby favoring weaker, abiding emotions over immediate ones. But the sentimentalist will need one for each decision-delay mechanism in the Constitution—that is, one for every structural feature that causes the passage of law to be slow and that causes the process to resist immediate popular will (which is most influenced by the most intense emotion of the moment) and for every place where a legislature driven by popular will can nevertheless be told "no" by the other branches. This means sentimentalism cannot explain, in and of itself, bicameralism, the qualified executive veto, the allowance of judicial review, the longer terms of presidents and senators, and the appointment of judges for good behavior.

Instrumental reason runs aground upon the same meddlesome rocks that posed obstacles for positivism and sentimentalism. Like these prior explanations, it can explain majoritarian features of the Constitution. It seems to account for the fact that the Constitution creates a strong national government endowed with powers to ensure domestic tranquility and to protect against external threats. Like these prior explanations, it can explain constitutional mechanisms that make the government responsive to the popular sovereign. But also like them, it fails to explain the Constitution's constraining features. If the Constitution takes the instrumentalist theory to be true, then it should allow the strongest popular desire to determine governmental action. But the Constitution has many mechanisms resistant to immediate popular desires that would, but for the delay mechanisms, determine governmental action. Therefore, the instrumentalist theory founders upon bicameralism, the executive veto, the allowance of judicial review, long terms for senators and presidents, and the appointment of judges for good behavior as well, for these mechanisms make it difficult for immediate desire or emotion to hold sway. If the instrumental theorist thinks that the Constitution nevertheless embodies a commitment to his theory, he will have to come up with auxiliary hypotheses to explain all these features.

This leaves us with a noninstrumental or substantive account of natural law as a possible constitutional presupposition. This theory explains constraints upon the sovereign, as it assumes that all law is to conform to natural law. Likewise, it explains the constitutional features resistant to passion because it tells us that the natural law is known through reason and assumes that the human self is properly governed when reason reigns over passions and appetites. It also accounts for constraints upon desire because it assumes a standard that is regulative of human desire as well. According to instrumental theorists, desire sets the goal. In contrast, noninstrumental theorists hold that desire should only animate action when the desire is first rightly aimed. Finally, the noninstrumental account of natural law is at least consistent with all the majoritarian features of the Constitution. Oddly enough, many seem to believe that classical natural law is hierarchical and that it is somehow at odds with popular sovereignty. This is almost always asserted rather than argued. We can counter the objection with a question: why is classical natural law theory said to be hierarchical and therefore inconsistent with democracy? Someone might answer that natural law is at odds with the equality of ideas. After all, it suggests that some propositions about moral reality are true and others false. But equality of ideas and equality of persons are different things. It's possible to have ontological equality among persons together with an ontological hierarchy among ideas. In fact, equality among persons entails hierarchy among ideas. For if all persons are equal, then the affirmation and denial of equality among persons are not on equal footing—one is true and the other false. Moreover, only some version of noninstrumentalist natural law can safeguard popular sovereignty as an inference from human equality. If moral nihilism, the underlying premise for moral anarchism, conventionalism, and positivism, is correct, then there are no moral precepts binding upon anyone (much less everyone). In that case, tolerance and intolerance, freedom and tyranny, equality among persons and the most brutal slavery are all equally indifferent. Moral nihilism eliminates the possibility of calling any of these good or bad. For the moral nihilist, no *morally compelling reasons* can be given for preferring one type of regime over another. In contrast, it is at least possible for the natural lawyer to affirm that the institutionalization of political equality is obligatory because it is good. Or the noninstrumental natural lawyer might maintain that there are no human traits or dispositions that find a developmental terminus in being ruled or in ruling. This means that political subjection cannot be based on nature and must, therefore, be based upon consent. At the very least, classical natural law theory presupposes an equality among human persons not envisaged by moral nihilism. All persons share a degree of moral knowledge and all fall under certain moral obligations. Arguably, classical natural law is actually a far more democratic doctrine than conventionalism (witness Plato's presentation of Thrasymachus and Pindar on this count).

Given the foregoing discussion, we are once again presented with the challenge of the three slavery clauses. Slavery is inegalitarian in the highest degree, and, as I have argued, natural law is the only doctrine adequate to underwrite democracy and popular sovereignty. Please note that I have argued that democracy and popular sovereignty entail natural law and not that natural law entails democracy. Natural law may serve as a necessary condition for democratic arrangements and yet remain compatible with other regime types. Of course, it seems popular sovereignty or consent is necessary, according to natural law, if people are in fact equal (something Aristotle himself recognized).[86] The immediate response to the challenge from slavery to the natural law interpretation is, as I mentioned before, the Thirteenth Amendment's removal of the slavery clauses. But, absent the Thirteenth Amendment, natural law theory can offer some explanation of the first two clauses. Those clauses do not command slavery but allow for it, while depriving proslavery forces of the amount of representation they might have had in the federal government *and* while providing Congress with the power to eliminate the importation of slaves after 1808. Arguably, natural law does not require the immediate instantiation of full democracy (and, concomitantly, the immediate elimination of slavery) but allows for the removal over time of the injustice of slavery. To be sure, the natural law interpretation requires an ad hoc hypothesis to explain the fugitive slave clause. Given our earlier discussion, the hypothesis might be this: to end slavery, Union was necessary; to form the Union, providing for the protection of slavery *for the time being* was necessary. In other words, this clause could be understood as necessary to get slave states to join a Union that looked and even planned for the eventual elimination of slavery. But even if ad hoc hypotheses are necessary for this and even for the other two slavery clauses, the natural law interpretation doesn't require as many of them as the other competing theories do. And it offers a better ad hoc hypothesis to explain these provisions than do other theories.

Inference to the Best Explanation, Stage 3: Teleological Fitness

Does noninstrumental natural law possess teleological fitness? Well, for it to fit with the Constitution, the Constitution has to favor the rule of reason in individuals and in the policy process. And multiple features of the Constitution will have to do this. Furthermore, noninstrumental natural law theory maintains that everyone knows the basics of this moral law and that everyone or nearly everyone knows the most immediate inferences from the basics. That is, it presupposes a kind of equality in moral knowledge. Finally, for noninstrumental natural law to fit with the Constitution, the Constitution must presuppose the idea in theory concerning the relation of natural to human law.

Concerning the first matter, I argue, with Madison and Hamilton, that the Constitution's constraining features work to favor the rule of reason in indi-

---

86. On Aristotle and consent, see Jean Hampton, *Political Philosophy,* 28–34.

viduals and in public policy. Consider Madison's argument in *The Federalist* No. 63, in which he defends long terms for senators and the distance this places between them and the people on the grounds that

> such an institution may be sometimes necessary, as a defense to the people against their own temporary errors and delusions. As the cool and deliberate sense of the community ought in all governments, and actually will in all free governments ultimately prevail over the views of its rulers; so there are particular moments in public affairs, when the people stimulated by some irregular passion, or some illicit advantage, or misled by the artful misrepresentations of interested men, may call for measures which they themselves will afterwards be the most ready to lament and condemn. In these critical moments, how salutary will be the interference of some temperate and respectable body of citizens, in order to check the misguided career, and to suspend the blow meditated by the people against themselves, until reason, justice and truth, can regain their authority over the public mind.

Hamilton defends the veto power of the president in much the same way in *The Federalist* No. 71:

> The republican principle demands, that the deliberate sense of the community should govern the conduct of those to whom they entrust the management of their affairs; but it does not require an unqualified complaisance to every sudden breese of passion, or to every transient impulse which the people may receive from the arts of men, who flatter their prejudices to betray their interests. It is a just observation, that the people commonly intend the public good. This often applies to their very errors. But their good sense would despise the adulator, who should pretend that they always reason right about the means of promoting it. They know from experience, that they sometimes err; and the wonder is, that they seldom err as they do; beset as they continually are by the wiles of parasites and sycophants, by the snares of the ambitious, the avaricious, the desperate; by the artifices of men who possess their confidence more than they deserve it, and of those who seek to possess, rather than to deserve it. When occasions present themselves in which the interests of the people are at variance with their inclinations, it is the duty of the persons whom they have appointed to be the guardians of those interests, to withstand the temporary delusion, in order to give them time and opportunity for more cool and sedate reflection.

According to Madison and Hamilton, the Constitution has mechanisms resistant to immediate passion and desire. These same mechanisms, by resisting immediate passion and desire, are said to favor the governance of reason and the conformity of legislation to justice and the common good. But is this a good explanation of the Constitution? If the Constitution resists government by immediate popular passion, it must do this for some reason. If we look at decision-delay mechanisms in the Constitution, we see that they are not just delay mechanisms. They are also decision-reconsideration mechanisms.[87] Bicameralism is a delay mechanism and a possible veto point, by virtue of the fact that all legislation must be considered by two houses of the legislature. Furthermore, an executive negative on legislation, qualified by the possibility of override by a supermajority, suggests that reconsideration, rather than mere negation, is in view. All of this seems designed to encourage deliberate or reflective decision making. And reflective decision making is the purview of reason rather than of sentiment or desire. Thus one might argue that the Constitution's decision-delay mechanisms are also designed to encourage deliberative policy and therefore the governance of reason.

Concerning the second matter, the extent of moral knowledge, I would argue that the Constitution's establishment of popular sovereignty fits with the commitment of classical natural law to widespread moral knowledge. Consider the Constitution's possible assumptions concerning the extent of moral knowledge. The Constitution might presuppose that nobody knows the moral requirements of natural law (this is ruled out by the foregoing argument), that only a few know them, that most people know them, or that everyone knows them. I would argue that the Constitution seems to presuppose, at a minimum, that most people know the requirements of the natural law, for we have seen that the Constitution aims a real common good through the governance of a constrained popular sovereign. If the Constitution aims at a real common good through the governance of the majority, the best explanation of this is that it assumes that most people have some knowledge of this common good and some knowledge that they ought to pursue it. Put another way, the assumption of a real common good that humans are bound to pursue, together with the establishment of popular sovereignty as the means of pursuing it, seems to entail (or assume) universal or near-universal knowledge of the common good, of how it is best pursued (at least at the most basic level), and of the requirement to pursue it.

The third matter, the relation of natural law to human law, is not at all easy

---

87. As Hamilton says, "The oftener a measure is brought under examination, the greater the diversity in the situations of those who are to examine it, the less must be the danger of those errors which flow from want of due deliberation, or of those missteps which proceed from the contagion of some common passion or interest" (*The Federalist* No. 73, 373).

to address. But perhaps we might deal with it this way. Any prescription supposes that an obligation is being imposed. This prescription is either an act of force or a mere declaration of will, in which case it doesn't really have any binding power, or it gets what binding power it has from a standard external to human prescription. It seems to follow that decrees or commands that run contrary to that standard fail to receive and pass on what binding power might be derivable from that standard. If we call this standard the natural law or a real common good, then we are saying that laws that do not derive from the natural law and the common good fail to carry with them the obligating power of the natural law. As such, they are not obligatory. The Constitution is prescriptive and produces prescriptive laws. Therefore it must presuppose the preconditions of prescription. And we have just suggested that this entails presupposing that laws that don't comport with natural law have no binding power. Furthermore, if the Constitution presupposes a noninstrumental account of natural law, then it would be odd if it didn't presuppose that this natural law is to be followed. If it presupposes this standard for normative willing, it would also seem, as a matter of consistency, to favor the priority of obedience to this standard over any merely human act.

Conclusion

In this chapter I argued that the Constitution presupposes that the requirements of the natural law are known through noninstrumental reason. Anarchy stands in obvious tension with the Constitution. Positivism, sentimentalism, and instrumentalism all founder on the notion of constitutional constraints that limit the sovereign's will and that prevent it from being determined by the strongest desires and emotions. This leaves only noninstrumental reason as a possible constitutional presupposition. I also contended that noninstrumental reason explains more constitutional features and requires fewer auxiliary hypotheses than the other candidates considered, primarily because classical natural law theory provides a ready explanation for constitutional features that constrain the sovereign's will, where other possible presuppositions do not. Finally, I suggested that a noninstrumental account of natural law fits with the Constitution in that the Constitution promotes the rule of reason over desire and sentiment, presumes, at a minimum, widespread moral knowledge, and seems to fit with the classical natural law account of the relationship between natural law and human law.

— 6 —

The Constitution's Theory
of Natural Rights

W HAT IS THE Constitution's theory of natural rights, especially as it pertains to the relationship of natural rights to natural law?
I argue that the Constitution presupposes that natural law precedes natural
rights and grants to natural rights what obliging force they have. This stands
in stark contrast to the widely held notion that natural rights generate natural duty or somehow precede natural law.

Possible Presuppositions

In chapter 3 we saw that the Constitution might presuppose three things
about the foundation or ground of natural rights:

1. *Positivist:* The Constitution presupposes that there are no natural rights.
The only rights of citizens are those established by the Constitution itself.
Thus, the positive law of the Constitution is the source of all rights.

2. *Modernist:* The Constitution presupposes that there are natural rights,
that natural rights are prior to natural duties, and that natural laws derive from
natural rights.

Diagram 6.1

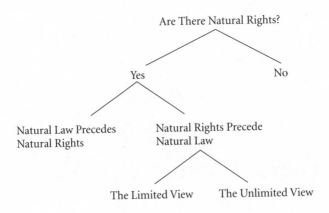

3. *Classical:* The Constitution presupposes that there are natural rights, but that natural duties are prior to natural rights and that natural rights are derive from natural laws.

Clearly there are more conceptions of rights than just these three. But given our limited purpose in this chapter, there is no need to survey all the possible conceptions. I am primarily concerned with the relationship of natural rights to natural law or natural duty, and I contend that the Constitution can only presuppose one of the options presented in Diagram 6.1.

According to our diagram, either there are natural rights or there are not. If *there are not,* there may still be legal rights. On this view, if there are rights, they are entirely conventional or positive. Of course, on positivistic assumptions one can also conceive of a political system in which no one has any rights at all.[1] If, on the other hand, *there are* natural rights, such rights may precede natural law and even create natural duties or they may derive from a prior natural law. If natural rights are prior to natural law, we are presented with two options: the *limited view* or the *unlimited view.* According to the unlimited view, natural rights are those possessed by humans in a Hobbesian state of nature. Every person has a right (i.e., sheer liberty) to everything and to do any-

---

1. Positivistic moral assumptions leave no ground in reason for preferring a regime under which citizens enjoy rights and one in which they do not. For normative positivism is committed to moral nihilism/skepticism, a view that must, given what it is, be equally indifferent to either system. Neither one is better or worse than the other in any meaningful sense.

thing in order to secure his own survival. On such a view, no right possessed by person x can impose any obligation upon person y. On this view, the establishment of the state entails a surrender of the right of nature. Hobbes, of course, thought every right, except the right to defend oneself when one's life is endangered by another, had to be laid down and then transferred to an absolute sovereign, if the state of nature is to be avoided. Others have objected to this idea, suggesting instead that the state is established to protect inalienable natural rights (sometimes said to be self-evident), but without indicating that natural rights derive from natural law or prior natural duties. On such a view, the natural rights of x impose behavioral limitations and/or make positive claims upon y, thereby limiting y's behavior vis-à-vis x. If, however, there are natural rights and these derive from natural law (or natural duties or obligations), then natural rights are ontologically grounded in natural law and receive what *potestas* (moral or obligating power) they have from natural law.[2] Accordingly, natural rights can be construed as protections of natural duties. I must note here that there is a prima facie possibility that there are both basic natural rights that impose obligations and natural rights that derive from natural duties. I will have something to say about why this is not an actual possibility later in the chapter.

What Is a Natural Right?

Before considering the Constitution's possible presuppositions of natural rights, we must first have a general sense of what natural rights are. This is essential to affirming or denying that some conception or other (or that no conception) of natural rights is a constitutional presupposition. But defining natural rights is the most difficult of tasks. In order to understand what a natural right is, we must understand both of these terms and their relation. But one of the terms, in particular, presents no end of difficulty. Consider the assessment of G. E. M. Anscombe, in this matter: "The notion of a right is very fundamental and philosophically very intractable. It seems absurd to introduce it as an unexplained primitive. But how to explain it? No one has succeeded in this."[3]

---

2. Here I mean to distinguish moral power or ability, *potestas*, from mere physical ability, *potentia*, to do a thing. One may be physically able to do that which one has no moral power or authority to do. One may have the *potentia* to do a thing while lacking the *potestas* to do it. On this, see White's *Philosophy of the American Revolution*, 186–95.

3. See Anscombe's "On the Source of the Authority of the State," 138.

Given the difficulty of explaining what a right is, let's begin our consideration with the modifier, *natural*. When we speak of natural rights, we mean rights that are somehow or other connected to or grounded in nature. The nature in question is, of course, *human* nature. And here we refer not to the efficient or material causes of the human being, to speak Aristotle's language, but to the formal and final causes of the person. It seems to me that formal and final causes are intimately related, such that the form of a thing is ordered to the purpose (or final cause) of the thing. The form of the acorn is ordered to the growth and development of the oak tree. But let's set this consideration aside for the moment. To say that certain rights are grounded in human nature is to say that human beings possess these rights by virtue of their humanness. These rights, whatever sorts of things rights may be, result from the sort of thing that a human is or the sort of thing a human exists to do (or both).[4] Given this, it is clear that not all rights can be considered natural. Some rights, at least, are created by human law and are therefore positive rather than natural—they result from acts of human will rather than from human essence. The right of an unemployed person to receive a certain allotment of money every week so long as he is looking for employment is a legal, rather than a natural, right, though it may in some way be grounded in natural right upon final consideration. Thus, natural rights result from human essence rather than from acts of human will. If we say John has a natural right, we mean that he is in possession of some thing called a right, the possession of which results from the fact that John possesses a human nature.

But what sort of thing is a *right*? About this there is much dispute. Sometimes people speak of positive and negative rights or, what amounts to the same thing, of active and passive rights. According to Richard Tuck, "To have a passive right is to have a right to be given or allowed something by someone else, while to have an active right is to have the right to do something oneself." Tuck points out that this distinction is not as clear as it might be given the presence of "at least one common theory about rights the implication of which is that all rights have at any rate a 'passive' component. This theory is that all rights entail and are entailed by duties on other people to secure the posses-

4. Just what features of human nature give rise to natural rights is a matter of dispute among those who affirm the existence of natural rights. For some the relevant feature is that human beings are made in the *imago dei* and therefore valuable in their own right, and then there are those who ground natural rights in human duties, tasks, or purposes that are woven into the fabric of human design. For others the relevant feature has to do with the human drive for self preservation; yet others ground natural rights in freedom and autonomy; and for some the relevant feature is that humans are self-owners.

sor of the right that which he has a right to." To make things more concrete, my active "right to walk about the street correlates necessarily with a duty imposed on other people to allow me to do so, and thus to have a right to walk about the street is simply to have a right to be allowed to walk about when I want to do so. Any active right can thus be re-phrased as a passive right of this kind." Tuck thinks such a view problematic indeed:

> The notorious problem with this theory . . . is that it appears . . . to render the language of rights nugatory. If any right can be completely expressed as a more or less complex set of duties on other people towards the possessor of the right, and those duties can in turn be explained in terms of some higher-order moral principle, then the point of a separate language of rights seems to have been lost, and with it the explanatory or justificatory force possessed by references to rights.

Many political philosophers, says Tuck, have been willing to affirm just this, while others (such as H. L. A. Hart) have expressed some concern,

> feeling . . . that the point of attributing rights to people is to attribute to them some kind of "sovereignty" over their moral world. According to this view, to have a right to something is more than to be in a position where one's expressed or understood want is the occasion for the operation of a duty imposed upon someone else: it is actually in some way to impose that duty upon them, and to determine how they ought to act towards the possessor of a right.

According to Tuck, "any theory that stresses the idea of an active right will tend to have at its heart the idea of the individual's sovereignty within the relevant section of his moral world. It will also tend as a consequence to stress the importance of the individual's own capacity to make moral choices, that is to say his *liberty*." In other words, "if active rights are paradigmatic, then to attribute rights to someone *is* to attribute some kind of liberty to them."[5]

The Hart-Tuck thesis (to borrow a term from Michael Zuckert), is not unproblematic.[6] If the passive-rights paradigm renders talk of and justificatory

---

5. Tuck, *Natural Rights Theories: Their Origin and Development*, 6–7 (original emphasis).

6. Hart's presentation of the position has received insightful criticism from William Frankena. See Frankena's "Natural and Inalienable Rights," which is a response to H. L. A. Hart's "Are There Any Natural Rights." Frankena poses some rather challenging questions to Hart, which I think Hart is hard pressed to answer.

appeals to rights superfluous, the active-rights paradigm seems to as well. For that paradigm reduces rights to liberty, in which case we need only to speak of the liberties of persons and not at all of their rights. But there is a clear analytic distinction between having the liberty to do something and having a right to that liberty. Suppose we examine this from the standpoint of positive law. Let us consider two different states, Q and R, each with its own laws and constitution. In both Q and R people have the liberty to speak their mind freely without interference and restrictions by the state. In Q, however, this is simply a function of the tacit permission of the laws. That is, in Q the laws simply refrain from interfering with the physical ability of each person to speak his mind. The laws in Q impose no coercive sanction for stating for any position whatsoever on politics, religion, etc. But neither do the laws expressly give permission to each citizen of Q to maintain whatever position they want. The laws are simply silent. It is manifest that each citizen in Q possesses both the physical ability, the *potentia,* and the political liberty to speak his mind. But if we consider only positive law, it would be something of a leap, pace Hobbes, to maintain that what Q's citizens have is a right. For the citizens of Q don't really *have* anything when it comes to speaking their mind freely. If ever terminology constituted excess baggage, referring to a liberty due entirely to the silence of the laws as a right seems to be the paradigm case.

By way of contrast, consider the positive laws of R. In R the ordinary laws say nothing whatsoever about the right of each citizen to speak his mind freely. But R also has a fundamental law, a written constitution, that precludes the national assembly as well as every provincial assembly, city council, and town meeting from drafting any ordinance that infringes upon the right, granted by the constitution of R, of every citizen to speak his mind without interference from the government. The situation in R is manifestly different from the situation in Q. Each citizen in R has been given something by the Constitution that no law has granted to any citizen in Q—namely, the permission to act in a certain way as well as protection for acting in that way. Furthermore, citizens in R have been given a legal basis to seek redress against governmental infringement upon their ability to speak freely. To call such a thing a right rather than a liberty is not superfluous, because the citizens of R have the protection of a liberty rather than just the liberty itself.

The above does away with the idea that to have a right is to have a liberty *simpliciter.* Even if it is *necessary* to have a liberty in order to have a right, it is clearly not a *sufficient* condition. Put another way, while a right may entail a liberty (in some sense of the word), there doesn't seem to be any reason to say, beyond mere assertion, that a liberty entails a right. Is there then some way to define a right in which the word retains a distinct meaning of its own—one that doesn't reduce to duty or liberty? I think Anscombe presents us with just such a way. I must note that some may find her turn of phrase difficult or cumbersome. I retain it here because it is precise.

According to Anscombe, any right can be explained as a specific instance of a certain kind of modal. Modal propositions express possibility or necessity and employ words and phrases such as *must, have to, can, cannot,* and *able to.* The following are examples of modal propositions: God must exist (that is, he exists necessarily; he can't not exist); or Jim didn't have to mow the lawn Thursday at four o'clock (that is, he might have failed to do so). Now, says Anscombe, a right is best explained as a stopping modal (which is not to say that all stopping modals involve rights): "Among the many many uses of modals we notice a range which may be brought under the heading: 'stopping from doing something.'" To borrow her example, suppose that Joe and Jane are playing chess, and Joe moves his king three spaces forward. Jane replies with a stopping modal: "You can't move your king like that." Some may claim, perhaps, that this only means "'Moving your king in this situation is against the rules'. So it does. But one may equally well say: 'That's against the rules' is a special form of 'you can't do that.'" Anscombe continues, "Now in the practice of human language and life stopping modals are often used with special mention of persons. 'You can't do that, it might hurt Mary'; 'You can't sit there, it's John's place'; 'You can't eat that, it's for N.'"[7] Take, as an example, the following stopping modal: You can't do that, it's for N to do. According to Anscombe, the speaker may be expressing contempt for N by suggesting that he do some degrading task, or the speaker might be expressing praise for N's remarkable abilities because he knows N will do the job right. But the speaker may also be asserting that while others experience a "stopping cannot" with respect to the task in view, N does not. Therefore, part of what it means to say that N has a right to some action, Z, is to say that N has no "stopping cannot" with respect to Z. That is, N has permission to do Z; N may do Z. To say that N has a right to Z, however, is to say more. It is also to say that, with respect to Z, others, like X, do experience such "stopping cannots" *for the reason* that Z is for N *to do.* Anscombe infers from this that the generation of the idea of a right is found in a "stopping cannot" together with a special reason, or logos, for the "stopping cannot." To translate Anscombe's thought into ordinary lan-

---

7. Anscombe, "On the Source of the Authority of the State," 139–40.

guage, to say that N has a right to do Z is to say that N may do Z, that others may not interfere with N performing Z, and that the permission for N and proscription for others are both grounded by a special reason.[8]

Notice how saying that X can't do Z because it's for N to do, as a special logos, grounds N's right in a task he is to do. We speak of rights in this sort of way all the time. But upon examination, the relation between the stopping modal and the special logos seems rather mysterious and inexplicable. How can a task constitute a special logos grounding a right? Anscombe answers as follows: "If someone has a role or function which he 'must' perform, or anything that he 'has' to do, then you 'cannot' impede him" and "If something is necessary, if it is for example a necessary task in human life, then a right arises in those whose task it is, to have what belongs to the performance of the task." This provides us with an explanation of the nature of a right. "'A right' is of course to be explained . . . by reference to a certain sort of stopping modal, a set of 'you cannots' which surrounds, fixes and protects a 'can' on the part of the one who is thereby said to have a right." That "can," again, is grounded in a task. The reason is this: the "stopping cannots" restricting the actions of others must be rationally grounded to be something more than just arbitrary constraints. They are allegedly grounded in the "can" of N. But why should the fact that N can do Z entail anything about what others cannot do? It doesn't seem to unless the action is something that N in some sense must (morally) do.[9] But it seems perfectly coherent to say that N has a right to do Z *if* Z is something N *must do* (say, to live or function as a human) and to say that others cannot reasonably interfere with some action that is necessary for N. Of course, for this to make sense, it is perhaps the case that any right must be grounded in a

---

8. I owe the ordinary language translation of Anscombe to J. Budziszewski.

9. Some might wonder why the qualifier *morally* appears here. Well, it seems odd to suggest that one has a right, one that imposes "stopping cannots" upon others, where the only sort of necessity is physical. Suppose N is being forced to do something truly horrible. Perhaps someone has planted a chip inside his brain and is controlling him by sending various electronic pulses to impulse-control places in the brain. Now suppose that our evil controller is forcing N to go about harming others. N must do this. He cannot help but do it. There is clearly a kind of necessity here. Most of us don't consider N blameworthy for his actions (though compatibilists must at some level think that he is). Nevertheless, no one thinks that just because N is under a physical necessity to act in this way that this necessity imposes "stopping cannots" on others such that they must let N harm others just because he is being forced to. But if the necessity in question is not physical, it is hard to see how it can be anything other than moral. Consider, in this context, the words of Hugo Grotius: "In this sense, a right is a moral quality annexed to a person, entitling him lawfully to possess some particular thing, or to perform some particular act" (*De iure belli ac pacis*, bk. 1, chap. 1, 18). In short, a right might be defined as a moral ability or moral faculty or power to act in some way or other. We will elaborate this later in this chapter.

prior rule to the effect that no person x can interfere with any person y's performance of a task if that task is (morally) necessary for y.[10]

Now, I can hear various objections to the Anscombe approach. After all, should all rights be understood of "stopping cannots"? Suppose there are at least some rights-claims that amount to this: N must do Z for X, thereby producing for X a right to receive Z from N? How are "stopping cannots" relevant to rights established by "musts"? Further, consider active rights. Aren't these just a matter of saying that X is free to do or refrain from doing some action Z? How do "stopping cannots" come into play in this situation? We might reply in the following manner. If the language of rights is not entirely reducible to the duties of some individuals to others or the liberty possessed by an individual, it seems to follow that rights must involve or entail some sort of limits upon the action of others vis-à-vis the bearer of a right. This idea of behavioral limitation underlies both the active and the passive conception of rights inasmuch as those, such as Tuck and Hart, who speak of active rights speak of more than just liberty and freedom but also of a right to freedom. Thus, for N to possess a right is to imply some sort of limitation with respect to the behavior of all others. And all limitations can be expressed in terms of "cannots." Suppose a right is somehow generated by a "must," such that N has a right to receive some benefit resultant from some action that some law stipulates X must perform with respect to N. If a right can be so generated, the "must" still amounts to a limitation that can be expressed as a stopping modal. For in this case, it means that there is some action Z with respect to N that X cannot refrain from performing (where the "cannot" in question is moral or legal rather than physical). To say someone must do something is to say that they cannot refrain from doing it. In the case of a moral right, such an expression means that X lacks the moral authority to refrain from performing Z.[11]

In Anscombe's scheme, the limitation is imposed upon X for the sake of protecting the ability (or "can") of N with respect to Z. But what does it mean to say that N can perform Z? The whole point of the Hart-Tuck thesis is to define a right as a kind of moral sovereignty, such that N is free with respect to performing Z. If N has a right to Z, it is a right to perform or to refrain from

10. The last sentence is mine and not an elaboration or summary of Anscombe's argument. I am using capital letters in place of names for particular persons and in place of particular actions, whereas I am using lower case letters to express universal generalizations.

11. But what about the enabling "can" with respect to the passive right? N is being enabled to experience the benefit that results from X doing Z, and this enablement results from the "stopping cannot" to the effect that X cannot not perform Z.

performing Z. But to say that N can perform Z is not to say that he can refrain from performing Z. In Anscombe's terms, to say that N has a right to Z where the right consists in "stopping cannots" binding upon others to protect N's "can" *does not entail N's freedom to refrain from performing Z.* In fact, so long as we are not talking about mere physical possibility or freedom of will, to say that N is at *liberty* to do Z does not entail that he is at *liberty* to refrain from doing Z. Moreover, to say that N must perform Z, where "must" refers to a moral requirement, entails that N can perform Z, where "can" means "has the moral authority or moral ability to perform Z." It also entails that N cannot refrain from performing Z, where "cannot" refers to the lack of moral right to refrain from performing the action. In short, one may have a right to do some action Z and simultaneously have a duty not to refrain from Z.

The Anscombe thesis seems to fare better than the Hart-Tuck thesis, for Anscombe maintains that rights must be justified by a reason, a logos, and that the reason must be the sort that can give rise to a right. The sorts of reasons that can ground rights are necessary tasks. Of course, if one has a right to perform a (morally) necessary task, one also has a right to the means of performing that task. Therefore, the fact that some thing p is necessary for some person x to perform some task z that is particularly or essentially human entails that x has a right to p.

I concur with Anscombe's description of a right. But for the time being I want to set that aside and simply say that a right is N's "can" protected by "stopping cannots" placed upon other people with respect to some action or task Z that is for N to do, where the moral "can" for N to do Z does not entail a right to refrain from doing Z (though I will not here posit that it entails that N cannot refrain from Z). Such a definition of a right brackets the readily apparent dispute between the Hart-Tuck thesis and the Anscombe thesis about whether or not a right with respect to Z follows from the (nonphysical) necessity that N must do Z or from the liberty of N to do or refrain from doing Z.

Does the foregoing discussion help us better understand what a natural right is? I think so. A natural right is a "stopping cannot" with a logos protecting a "can" that a person possesses in virtue of human nature. That is, if N has a natural right to do Z, then something about N's nature as a human being morally enables N to do Z and morally restricts others (whether individuals or the government) from preventing N from doing Z. But how do passive rights, construed as claim rights, fit in? One might explain passive rights in this way: to say any person x has a right to some thing r means that some person y has an obligation to provide r to x. That is, on the passive-rights paradigm,

N's right to benefit from X doing Z arises from X's obligation to do Z. X's obligation to perform some duty, some action Z, that benefits N, leads to N's right. I cannot see what sense it makes to say that these sorts of rights are natural. The duties of X may be natural. And if the duty of X with respect to N gives N a claim or right, then natural duties would seem to lead to, at the very least, prepolitical, and even presocial, rights. Still, although the obligations of any person y, on the passive view, may result directly from y's nature, it doesn't seem that any person x's rights result directly from x's nature. At best, N's right is to an action X is bound to perform because of X's nature. Suppose an objector poses this dilemma: couldn't something about N's nature give rise to X's obligation? The difficulty is that on the passive view this something about N's nature couldn't be a right, for, on the passive view, the right or claim results from X's obligation and not the other way around. Moreover, it seems strange to say that something about N imposes an obligation on X that thereby gives N a right to some action or some thing from X where the *right* is founded only on X's obligation (as our objector must maintain). Is this really different from saying that something about N gives rise to a right of N to R that thereby imposes an obligation upon X to provide R or at least to let N have it? If it is not, then the sorts of rights in question are not passive after all. This consideration need not be taken to suggest the correctness of the active-rights paradigm as construed by Hart and Tuck in order to make sense of natural rights. There is another paradigm—one in which the natural rights of N are grounded in the natural duties of N rather than in the liberty of N to act or refrain from acting in some manner or in the duty of X to render N some benefit.

There Are No Natural Rights

Given the foregoing discussion, the denier of natural rights might take one of two different strategies: he might deny that there are any such things as rights at all, or he might admit that there are rights but deny that these have any connection to human nature (conversely, he might affirm that the only rights are purely positive). If he denies that there are any rights, he might mean to say that the notion of rights is an incoherent concept, that the language of rights is entirely nugatory, and that there are no rights in any possible world. Or the denier of rights from this direction might mean to say that while some states or constitutions might grant rights to citizens, the state or constitution currently under consideration does not. Alternatively, the denier of rights might concede that there are plenty of legal and constitutional rights, but that these have no grounding in human nature. Instead, any of the rights you can point to in any political system are entirely a matter of human law and therefore the creations of human will. Suppose the idea of purely positive rights somehow (magically) makes sense. Even so, we can conceive of a state or constitution that grants such rights and one does not. The thoroughgoing positivist (who is both a legal and a normative positivist) will be unable to provide any rational ground for preferring one of these states over the other. The state that grants no rights must, assuming normative positivism, be as good as the state that does. Any preference of one over the other will be, therefore, purely arbitrary. The same will be true of the laws of a particular state. Whether the laws of a particular state create or uphold rights or whether they do not is a matter of indifference. These are equally good (or equally bad) alternatives.

More is entailed by a denial of natural rights. If there are no natural rights, then there seems to be no such thing as tyranny. For tyranny seems to presuppose not only moral realism and natural law but also the existence of natural rights. When we say someone has been tyrannized, we mean that they have been treated unjustly. And by that we seem to mean that someone has not been rendered the behavior they were due from the government, even if the required behavior was simply that the government refrain from treating citizens in a certain manner. But if there is no such thing as tyranny, then it becomes quite difficult to make sense of constraints upon governmental action, whether legal or institutional. Furthermore, if there are no nonpositive rights, then the whole notion of the state's authority collapses. Anscombe observes, "Authority on the part of those who give orders and make regulations is: a right to be obeyed." Without such a right, government collapses into "sophisticated banditry." Even if one disagrees with Anscombe's definition, it certainly seems to be the case that the authority to act (and in the case of government to compel others to act) entails a right to act. Thus, we might think of a right to act as a necessary condition of the authority to act. We cannot, without collapsing into incoherency, suggest that this right of the state to be obeyed emerges from positive law, for we are considering our obligation to obey the state's commands—that is, to the positive law itself.[12] The whole notion of political or legal obligation therefore collapses to the ground unless the notion of a right is coherent and unless we can sensibly speak of rights founded on

12. That is to say, our obligation to obey positive law must come from some source outside of positive law. Therefore the claim of the state upon our obedience, if indeed it possesses such a claim, must also come from outside of the positive law.

something other than positive law. Indeed, obligation itself falls to the ground if there is no such thing as a right. I have argued (in agreement with philosophers as diverse as Immanuel Kant, Morton White, and G. E. M. Anscombe) that moral necessity (which is another way of saying moral obligation) entails moral right. I am morally empowered to do that which I morally must do. More formally, if a person x falls under a natural or moral obligation (that is necessity) to do y, then x has a natural or moral right to do y. But, per *modus tollens*, if there are no natural or moral rights, then there is no obligation (i.e., no moral necessity) either.

Natural Rights Precede Natural Law: The Unlimited View

If there are natural rights, then there is a prima facie possibility that Thomas Hobbes has correctly described them. Here we must again consider the Hobbesian state of nature. In the state of nature, says Hobbes, there is no sovereign, no law, and, consequently, no justice or injustice, no right or wrong. Each person is therefore free to do anything that he deems conducive to his survival (Hobbes readily points out that things people in society call vices are virtues in a state of war). Furthermore, there is no property in the state of nature. Therefore, everyone has a right to everything, including the bodies of other people (should one need to put them to use for one's own survival in that nasty and brutish state). Put another way, in the state of nature, one doesn't even have property in or ownership of one's own body. This right to everything and to do anything perceived as conducive to survival Hobbes labels the *right of nature*. He says, "The right of nature, which writers commonly call *jus naturale*, is the liberty each man hath to use his own power, as he will himself, for the preservation of his own nature, that is to say, of his own life, and consequently of doing anything which, in his own judgment and reason, he shall conceive the aptest means thereunto."[13] Because individuals possess an absolute right to everything and to do anything in the state of nature, there is no justice or injustice in that state. That is, in the state of nature no one is due any sort of behavior from anyone else and no one has a claim upon another or upon another's behavior with respect to him. That some person N, therefore, possesses the right of nature places no limitation on the behavior of others with respect to N. N's natural right is an unrestricted "can" (or a "can" limit-

---

13. Hobbes, *Leviathan*, 79.

ed only by the goal of survival) that involves no "stopping cannots" with respect to anyone else, making it also unprotected. Hobbesian natural right therefore grounds a kind of absolute permission. The very fact that individuals possess the right of nature within the state of nature entails that in their natural state, human beings are not subject to a real natural law that prescribes some actions and proscribes others absolutely. Such a state is, of course, unbearable. So, says Hobbes, the laws of nature point people away from the state of nature by telling each person to seek peace with others insofar as others are willing to seek peace with him. Seeking peace with others entails each person transferring his right of nature from himself and to an absolute sovereign, given absolute (i.e, unlimited) authority in order to secure peace. But in establishing the sovereign and in transferring the right of nature from oneself to the sovereign, one does not surrender the ability to act in self-defense whenever one's life is jeopardized by another, even if that other turns out to be the sovereign (and even if the sovereign is seeking to impose a just punishment). One's right to act to preserve oneself, however, places no obligation upon the sovereign (and for that matter doesn't seem to place any obligations upon anyone else). The Hobbesian sovereign may act wrongly with respect to a subject (he may fail to take the best course of action for securing the survival of his subjects by trying, say, to kill a particular subject) but never unjustly.[14] Even so, for Hobbes, the right of self-defense is inalienable.

What does it mean to say, on this view, that natural rights (or natural right) precede natural law? If Hobbes thought the state of nature was historical, which he did not, then living by the right of nature would precede living according to the law of nature. But even then the former would not precede the latter in historical existence. The sort of priority or precedence in view here is logical and even metaphysical. Hobbes constructs his state of nature so that we can consider the logical origins of sovereignty (or, in our parlance, the state). He locates this origin in acts of human willing—each person wills to lay down his right of nature (by transfer rather than renunciation). This is dictated by the law of nature, which is instrumental or conditional, telling people that if they want peace, then they must surrender this right (insofar as others are willing to surrender it too). Because the law of nature dictates the laying down of the right of nature, the law of nature is actually parasitic upon the right of nature. Furthermore, the law of nature is actually generated by the special logos of the right of nature. The reason grounding the right of nature, ac-

14. Ibid., 112–13.

cording to Hobbes, is self-preservation. Because the state of nature is a state of war, this goal can be obtained only if people seek peace with one another. And this requires each person giving up the right of nature, by transfer to an absolute sovereign.[15] Hobbes's first and second laws of nature, discussed in the chapter 5, are derived, expressly, from the special logos, or the reason grounding, the right of nature. Therefore, for Hobbes, it seems as if the right of nature comes first. Men in their natural state have the right of nature and are not under the law of nature. But if they want to go on living, they must follow the law of nature by, first, laying aside the right of nature.

Hobbes's view seems to entail that the sovereign cannot be constrained in any way. After all, the sovereign is established by a transfer of the right of nature from individuals to a particular person or assembly set up as sovereign. To receive this right in a transfer is to receive the sort of unrestricted permission (a "can" with no "stopping cannots"), the right to everything, that individuals had in the state of nature. Hobbes affirms as much when he says that "whatsoever he [the sovereign] doth, it can be no injury to any of his subjects, nor ought he to be by any of them accused of injustice" and that "It is true that they that have sovereign power may commit iniquity, but not injustice, or injury in the proper signification."[16] The essence of sovereign power established by the Hobbesian right of nature is therefore absolute or unlimited. The sovereign faces no outside constraints (moral or legal) upon his actions. We might say that a Hobbesian sovereign never seems to lack *potestas*. Speaking of monarchy, Hobbes argues that "that king whose power is limited is not superior to him or them that have the power to limit it; and he that is not superior is not supreme, that is to say not sovereign."[17] Entailed here is the underlying idea that the true sovereign is by definition, for Hobbes, unlimited or unrestricted. And, at day's end, this is just the sort of sovereignty Hobbes's theory entails. Hobbesian natural right implies unlimited government.

Natural Rights Precede Natural Law: The Limited View

When it comes to the idea that natural rights precede and even ground natural obligations, the Hobbesian view is not the only game in town. There are

---

15. For "as long as this natural right of every man to everything endureth, there can be no security to any man (how strong or wise soever he be) of living out the time which nature ordinarily alloweth men to live" (ibid., 80).

16. Ibid., 112–13.

17. Ibid., 123.

some who subscribe to the priority of natural rights but who do not subscribe to Hobbes's right of nature. Some think that natural rights impose natural duties upon others, such that N's natural right requires of X that X act in some way or other with respect to N (perhaps that X not impede N's right to speak his mind freely). That is, there are some who think that natural rights limit behavior, and are prior to natural duties, and that natural duties actually derive from natural rights. If such rights are not grounded in natural law, then they must be held in virtue of something. Speaking about this very thing, Thomas Paine says, "Natural rights are those which appertain to man in right of his existence. Of this kind are all the intellectual rights, or rights of the mind, and also all those rights of acting as an individual for his own comfort and happiness, which are not injurious to the rights of others."[18] By "in right of his existence," Paine seems to mean "in virtue of his essence." If this is the case, then one can readily take Paine to mean that there is something about human nature that simply produces these rights, which then impose obligations upon others not to infringe on these rights.

But why can't these rights be infringed upon? Paine refers to humanity's right of existence, while the Declaration says that the Creator endowed man with inalienable rights. Various thinkers in the Judeo-Christian tradition have tied natural and inalienable rights to humanity's creation in the *imago dei*. One might think of God as imparting to his human creations an inviolable value sewn into the fabric of their beings. A Kantian, translating this idea into more abstract terms, might derive natural and inalienable from the fact that every human being is an end rather than a means and therefore ought to be treated as such. Rights preceding natural law might also be grounded in self-ownership, something Michael Zuckert thinks Locke believed. Because Zuck-

---

18. Paine, *The Rights of Man*, in *The Thomas Paine Reader*, 217. Paine distinguishes between natural rights that a person surrenders upon entering civil society and those that the person retains. He maintains,

> The natural rights which he retains, are all those in which the *power* to execute is as perfect in the individual as the right itself. Among this class, as is before mentioned, are all the intellectual rights, or rights of mind: consequently, religion is one of those rights. The natural rights which are not retained, are all those in which, though the right is perfect in the individual, the power to execute them is defective. They answer not his purpose. A man, by natural right, has a right to judge in his own cause; and so far as the right of mind is concerned, he never surrenders it: But what availeth it him to judge, if he has not power to redress? He therefore deposits this right in the common stock of society, and takes the arm of society, of which he is a part, in preference and in addition to his own. Society grants him nothing. Every man is a proprietor in society, and draws on the capital as a matter of right. (218)

ert seems to share the view he ascribes to Locke, I want to use his construction of Locke to elaborate this view.[19]

In contrast to Hobbes, who denies the existence of justice and injustice in the state of nature *because* there is no property there, Zuckert says Locke affirms the existence of property in the state of nature, thereby laying a foundation for justice in that state. Locke himself says, "every Man has a Property in his own Person. This no Body has any Right to but himself. The Labour of his Body, and the Work of his Hands, we may say, are properly his."[20] Thus, on this view, there is property in the state of nature because in that state each person owns himself. But how does this get us to the notion of limiting rights that impose obligations prior to positive law?

According to Zuckert, Locke has defined natural rights in terms of property, and property "implies an exclusivity: to say A has property in his life is to say B does not have a right to it. Property is a right-claim, which necessarily implies a correlative duty of forebearance."[21] As Zuckert notes,

> By using the term property to refer to the realm of natural rights, Locke very concisely said at least these three things. First, he said that he meant "right" to be that sort of moral claim that carries along with it claims to exclusivity. Second, Locke said that he meant there is such property in or by nature; that is, human beings possess natural rights of the sort that imply natural duties. Finally, he concluded that justice is, therefore, by nature. This last claim can be readily understood in terms of the point Hobbes made: if human beings

19. In what follows I will be drawing on chapter 7, "Do Natural Rights Derive from Natural Law? Aquinas, Hobbes, and Locke on Natural Rights," in Zuckert's *Launching Liberalism: On Lockean Political Philosophy.*

20. Locke, *Second Treatise*, 287–88. On the other hand, this same Locke maintained, in the opening pages of the *Second Treatise,* that human beings are the property of the Creator. He also inferred that, for this very reason, human beings were obligated to preserve themselves and refrain from suicide. Doesn't this present a problem for Zuckert's understanding? Well, says Zuckert, Locke meant the bit about each person being his own property rather than the bit about each person being the property of the Maker. After all, every behavioral limit Locke introduces with his weakly grounded, transcendent natural law is repudiated later in the treatise.

21. Zuckert, *Launching Liberalism,* 194. Zuckert appears to have begged the question. After all, does the fact that B is the property of A entail that anyone who is not A must refrain from using B? Might not B be held in common between A, C, and D? Further, what about the fact that B is not the property of E and F leads to the requirement that they must refrain from using B? Is it self-evident? Is this true by definition? Where is the connection between the "can use B" of his or those whose property it is and the "cannot use B" of everyone else? In short, how does the fact that something is exclusively the property of someone generate a correlative duty in others such that they must refrain from using it? The connection is altogether mysterious unless there is first some universally known rule of justice that says "render to each his due." But that would entail something Zuckert utterly rejects— that natural law comes before natural rights.

have an "own" by nature, there is justice by nature. Justice, as Locke saw it, implies and requires the establishment of "ownness," of claim inhering individuals.[22]

Thus, "The foundation or ground of rights, is, according to Locke, self-ownership." In saying this, Zuckert's Locke derives "the 'ought' of moral inviolability" from the "is" of self-ownership. "Locke's point is that if human beings are indeed self-owners, then they are inviolable, for inviolability (exclusive right) is precisely what ownership means or implies." But just what is a self, and what does it mean to own one (as opposed, say, to a Honda or a Ford)? Human identity, for Zuckert's Locke, is found not in being created in the *imago dei* or from being a rational soul, not in any of the traditional places, but, rather, in self-consciousness. "The 'I' is not, Locke argues, anything given in nature. It is made by the self in the course of its operations of sensation and reflection." For Zuckert's Locke, the human person must be a body with pains and pleasures if the self is ever to emerge. "At the same time, the self is most intimately concerned with (attached with care to) its pleasures and pains, its happiness and misery. Human beings are unique in that as selves they can seize on their entire lives as wholes, seeing them as unities or potential unities spread over the dimensions of time and aiming toward happiness or misery as such." Furthermore, "The self not only possesses its data of consciousness but also its body, which is the source of most of these data of consciousness. The self appropriates the body and makes it its own, that is to say, makes it the instrument of its intentional actions in relation to its broader purposes in life. . . . Self-ownership procures ownership of body and action." Zuckert concludes,

> My self, my happiness and misery, my body and its action, are all mine in such a way that my sovereignty over them necessarily and ipso facto excludes similar claims to them by others. In the first instance, this ownership has nothing moral about it; it is merely a fact of the structure of self-consciousness. Yet it has moral implications, for the "I" necessarily is concerned with its own happiness and misery. So far as it accurately understands its situation, it necessarily raises rights claims over its body, actions, and road to happiness. The self posits itself as possessor of rights to life, liberty, and the pursuit of happiness. Its very claim for itself as a self contains a claim to exclusivity vis-à-vis others.

22. Ibid.

This claim of exclusivity does not derive from some preexisting law or duty, natural or otherwise, but it does imply a subsequent duty—a duty of forbearance. Each claims a right that others forbear from interfering with what is the self's own, and logic (although not the practical conditions of existence) requires that each self raising such a claim recognize that every other self raises ipso facto the very same claim on the very same ground. This is a very imperfect duty, however, in that there is very little to require that it actually be honored. Although an observer such as Locke can notice standards of natural right and wrong, of natural justice, in nature human beings are apt to overlook the claims of others. The result is war. The solution, of course, is government and law, which, if properly made, recognize each person as a self with rights and take their bearings from the natural standards of justice—to respect what is each one's own, or to respect their "property" or their rights to life, liberty, and the pursuit of happiness.[23]

We cannot pass from this section without noting that a coherency problem stalks this view. But it better serves my purposes to address the coherency problem in the section on the Constitution's presupposition.

Natural Rights Derive from Natural Law

One of the foremost proponents of the idea that rights result from prior duties imposed by natural law was Samuel Pufendorf. He argued, "*moral* power in a man is that whereby he is able to perform a voluntary action legitimately and with a moral effect, that is to say, so that his action shall harmonize with the laws, or at least be not repugnant to them."[24] According to Knud Haakonssen, Pufendorf thought of rights as generated by natural law obligations in two senses. In the first sense,

Pufendorf uses *ius* in the sense of subjective rights to refer to four different categories of deontic powers: power over one's own actions termed *libertas;* power over another person's actions, termed *imperium,* power over one's own things—property, termed *dominium;* and power over another person's property, termed *servitus.* The three last are "adventitious," that is, they are instituted by men through contractual and quasi-contractual arrangements, and they thus presuppose the first power. *Libertas* encompasses the absence of subjection in a human being's command of his physical and moral personality—his life, actions, body, honour, and reputation. This right, or clus-

---

23. The preceding quotations in this paragraph are from ibid., 94–96.
24. Cited in White, *Philosophy of the American Revolution,* 188.

ter of rights, does not depend on the agreement of others; it exists in a person by nature or innately. . . . The natural or innate character of *libertas* does not, however, mean that it is sui generis and independent of natural law. A clue is given in a passage concerning the rights of the foetus. There Pufendorf makes it quite clear that such rights exist as a result of the fact that other people have duties, imposed by natural law, to respect such rights. To appreciate Pufendorf's way of thinking, we must distinguish between the "obligator," who is the person to whom one is bound in obligation, and the "obligee," who is the person thus bound, and the beneficiary of the obligation. The obligator and the beneficiary can be one person, as when A promises B to do something for him or her. However, in the case of *libertas* the obligator is God, to whom we are obligated to obey the law of nature by, among other things, respecting the *libertas* of our neighbour, but it is the neighbour who is the beneficiary of this obligation, his benefit being his *libertas*.[25]

In this sense of "right," "a right is that which there is duty to yield, whether to oneself or others."[26]

Pufendorf's second sense of the word *right* can be understood as follows: "That which we have a duty to do, we must have a right to do, and in this sense, a 'right' is a moral power to act, granted by the basic law of nature in order to fulfill duties imposed by this law." In other words, rights "have a positive as well as a negative side, both of which are derived from duties conceived as impositions of natural law."[27] Morton White elaborates this idea by considering Pufendorf's (and Burlamaqui's) distinction between natural (physical) ability and moral ability. A person has the natural ability or power to do those things for which he has the physical strength. From this it follows that through their natural power, individuals can fail to conform their actions to the precepts of law (including natural law). In contrast, the moral power to act *derives* from conformity to or harmonization with moral law. This idea of conformity to moral law brings us back to the notion of natural rights grounded in natural duties or tasks set for human beings by natural law. After all, Pufendorf understands laws as precepts that enjoin or forbid certain actions. In short, natural law sets tasks for human beings that thereby give rise to rights.

Many scholars believe that Locke, pace Zuckert, shared the Pufendorfian understanding of natural rights. According to Haakonssen, "For Locke, as for Pufendorf, natural rights are powers to fulfill the fundamental duty of natur-

---

25. Haakonssen, *Natural Law and Moral Philosophy*, 40.
26. Ibid., 41
27. Ibid. See also White's *Philosophy of the American Revolution*, 188–89

al law."[28] There is at least something to Haakonssen's claim. Locke speaks first of the law of nature and the duty to self-preservation before he speaks of the right to self-preservation. Furthermore, this duty is grounded in the law of nature: "Every one as he is *bound to preserve himself*, and not quit his station willfully; so by the like reason when his own Preservation comes not in competition, ought he, as much as he can, *to preserve the rest of Mankind*, and may not unless it be to do Justice on an Offender, take away, or impair the life, or what tends to the Preservation of Life, the Liberty, Health, Limb or Goods of another"; "And Reason, which is that Law, teaches all Mankind, who will but consult it, that being all equal and independent, no one ought to harm another in his Life, Health, Liberty, or Possessions."[29] Before saying that each person has property in himself (as noted before), Locke says that humans are God's property.[30] This fact seems to ground the prohibition on suicide. But can Locke affirm both that human persons are God's property, subject to the duties he imposes upon them, and that humans are simultaneously self-owners? Some (e.g., Zuckert) will say that if someone has property in a thing, then no one else can have property in that thing at the same time, and, consequently, that if any person x is the property of God, then x cannot be the property of anyone else—least of all x. This argument seeks to show a contradiction between the propositions "N belongs to God" and "N owns himself." But where is the contradiction? Locating it is a thornier matter than some would have us believe. Affirming a contradiction requires saying that any good y cannot be the property of more than one person simultaneously—that is, property entails absolute exclusivity to one and only one person. But why should this be the case? Perhaps some things are, for whatever reason, the property of more than one person at the same time. In that case there's at least a prima facie possibility that God and N both have property in N in some sense (i.e., that for any person x, both God and x have property in x). Of course, even if property implies exclusivity to one and only one person, there is no contradiction between "God has property in N" and "N has property in himself," unless property has precisely the same sense in both statements. But there's no reason to think Locke intended *property* to have just the same sense in both these instances. It is possible, as A. John Simmons suggests, to see Locke as saying that "our property in ourselves" is "a trust from God."[31] There are various ways to make sense

28. Haakonssen, *Natural Law and Moral Philosophy*, 55

29. Locke, *Second Treatise*, 271.

30. Ibid.

31. Simmons, *The Lockean Theory of Rights*, 101–2; see also chapter 5.

of this idea. Here's one way: for Locke we are self-owners proximately speaking, that is, vis-à-vis others, whereas we are not self-owners ultimately speaking, that is, vis-à-vis God. Put another way, we own ourselves and our actions as stewards but not as proprietors. We are given something in trust, and the trust is ours while we have it. But ultimately we do not have final ownership. Or we might consider it this way: "each person has property in himself" is really just a way of saying "no human person is such that they are owned by another human person."

In the American political tradition, James Madison represents the clearest version of the idea that natural law or natural duties precede and ground natural rights.[32] This is best seen in his discussion of religious liberty. In *Memorial and Remonstrance against Religious Assessments*, Madison holds that as religion is a duty that can only be directed by reason and conscience and not by force, religion must be left to every individual's conscience and conviction.[33] It is therefore a right to exercise one's religious convictions in accord with the dictates of one's conscience. This right is also inalienable. "It is unalienable, because the opinions of men, depending only on the evidence contemplated by their own minds cannot follow the dictates of other men: It is unalienable also, because what is here a right towards men, is a duty towards the Creator." Every person has a duty to "render to the Creator such homage and such only as he believes to be acceptable to him." Inalienable rights are powers for fulfilling natural duties or obligations that come prior to civil society. "This duty is precedent, both in order of time and degree of obligation, to the claims of Civil Society. Before any man can be considered as a member of Civil Society, he must be considered as a subject of the governor of the Universe." As a subject of the governor of the universe, a person is not free to transfer the attendant obligations of being such a subject when one enters civil society. "[I]f a member of Civil Society, who enters into any subordinate Association must always do it with a reservation of his duty to the General Authority; much more must every man who becomes a member of any particular Civil Society,

32. I have adopted this paragraph with slight modification from a paper I presented at the annual meeting of the Western Political Science Association, entitled "Natural Law Democracy: The Enduring Relevance of Classical Natural Law to American Constitutional Thought," held in Long Beach, CA, March 2002.

33. Madison, *Memorial and Remonstrance against Religious Assessments*, June 20, 1785. My interpretation follows the traditional understanding of *Memorial and Remonstrance*. See Eva T. H. Brann, "Madison's *Memorial and Remonstrance*: A Model of American Eloquence," and Peter Augustine Lawler, "James Madison and the Metaphysics of Modern Politics." In "James Madison on Religion and Politics: Rhetoric and Reality," Thomas Lindsay takes a very different perspective, suggesting *Memorial and Remonstrance* is rhetoric rather than reality.

do it with a saving of his allegiance to the Universal Sovereign." Thus, for example, religion is "wholly exempt" from the cognizance of civil society and is not "subject to that of the Legislative Body."[34]

The Constitution on Natural Rights

Inference to the Best Explanation, Stage 1: Eliminating Alternative Explanations

If there are no natural rights, then one of two things follows: either there are no rights at all, or there are rights, but they are purely positive. Clearly, the Bill of Rights (and perhaps Article I, Section 9) rules out the first alternative. Our Constitution recognizes the rights of citizens vis-à-vis the national government. Furthermore, the Fourteenth Amendment recognizes the rights of citizens vis-à-vis their respective states. Therefore, the Constitution recognizes rights. The only questions are as to whether the rights it recognizes are purely positive and whether these are the only rights it presumes that people possess. There is at least a prima facie case for extraconstitutional rights found in the Ninth Amendment: "The enumeration in the Constitution, of certain rights, shall not be construed to deny or disparage others retained by the people." This refers to rights not contained in the Constitution but retained by the people. And it doesn't say that people hold these rights in virtue of their respective state constitutions. Thus, the thesis that there are no natural rights will likely have a hard time coming to terms with the Ninth Amendment. But this is just a peripheral and rather small problem for the thesis that the Constitution does not presuppose the existence of natural rights.

Consider what must follow if there are no natural rights and the only rights that exist are therefore nothing but determinations of positive law. For a citizen of R, the only rights he has are those expressly granted in fundamental law (say, a written constitution) or by ordinary acts of the legislative power. But if there are no natural rights, where do these positive rights come from? They come from acts of human willing. And the power whose will establishes these legal rights is the sovereign. In a thoroughgoing positivistic framework, the unconstrained will of the sovereign is the generator of rights. We established in chapter 3 that the sovereign in the U.S. constitutional system is the people.

---

34. Madison, *Memorial and Remonstrance*, 299.

But the people are not an unconstrained sovereign. Constraints upon the popular sovereign amount to institutionally effected "stopping cannots." The reason for the "stopping cannots" is clearly the protection of the life and liberty of the individual. But this is just another way of saying that the "stopping cannots" imposed upon the sovereign are for the sake of the "can" of the individual citizen or of groups of citizens. In this context, consider Madison's defense of the extended sphere in *The Federalist* No. 10. It is clear from this essay, taken together with *The Federalist* Nos. 51 and 63, that Madison subscribes to majoritarian government. But he also thinks constraints should be placed upon the majority (which constitutes the effective will of the popular sovereign) in order to prevent a majority faction from determining the popular will. A faction is a group that is adverse either to the permanent and aggregate interests of the community or to the rights of minorities. In effect, Madison argues for a large republic rather than a small one in order to protect minority rights (as well as the common interest) by constraining or directing the will of the popular sovereign. This, in turn, seems to lead to a contradiction between the following propositions: (1) as there are no natural rights, the sovereign, in this case the people, is unconstrained in the granting and preserving of rights; and (2) the popular sovereign is constrained. And the reason seems to be just this: an unconstrained popular sovereign will is faced with no "stopping cannots," but a constrained popular sovereign rather clearly has "stopping cannots" limiting its behavior.

In sum, if there are no natural rights and therefore only positive rights, there is no obligation upon or "stopping cannots" restraining the sovereign. It follows that the sovereign is free to grant whatever rights he sees fit in the making of law. But the Constitution places constraints upon the will of the popular sovereign precluding the people from doing whatever they want in this matter. Majority will cannot form and act outside of a process that favors long-term, broadly distributed majorities. And such majorities arguably have goals and arrive at conclusions about what rights a constitution should recognize that are different from the goals pursued and the conclusions about rights reached by factitious majorities. Furthermore, the Bill of Rights restricts the popular sovereign in the making of law. But if the people are sovereign, and therefore the makers of law, and if law is determined only by human will as expressed through the sovereign's decree, then such an arrangement doesn't seem to make sense.[35]

---

35. Just as we reach this conclusion a cunning objector might point out that the popular sovereign faces no significant constraints. After all, our objector tells us, the popular sovereign can amend near-

As I argued earlier, the Constitution is prescriptive in that it imposes obligations upon people. Because mere exercises of force do not obligate, it follows that prescription (and legal obligation) presupposes a source of obligation external and antecedent to human law. Therefore, the Constitution, because it is prescriptive, must presuppose an external source of obligation normative for human willing. This means that human beings, in some of their actions, are under obligations that do not derive from positive law. To say this is to say that human persons fall under moral necessity (or obligation) in some of their actions. There are some things that human persons must do. But that which a person must do, he has a right to do. If any person x must (is obligated to) do something, then he can do it. If that obligation is antecedent to human enactment, then so is the concomitant right. Given *modus tollens,* to deny the right is to deny the obligation. Therefore, if the Constitution presupposes that there are no "natural" rights antecedent to human law, then it presupposes that there is no obligation antecedent to human law capable of grounding a duty to obey the law. The prescriptiveness of the Constitution entails obligation antecedent to the Constitution (and therefore to human willing); the presupposition "there are no natural rights" entails that there is no such thing as obligation antecedent to human willing. Given the law of noncontradiction, it cannot presuppose both that there is and that there is not obligation. If we have independent reason for thinking it presupposes obligation, antecedent to human law, then we have reason to say that it also presupposes rights prior to human law. We do have such reason: the prescriptive character of the Constitution.

The view that the unlimited permission of the right of nature precedes natural law is easier to eliminate as a possible constitutional presupposition than either the denial of natural rights or the view that natural rights precede nat-

---

ly anything in the Constitution. The careful reader will recall that we faced this very objection in chapter 3. The reply in that chapter suffices here as well: The amendment process is subject to constraints that, like the policy process, favor long-term and broadly (i.e., nationally) distributed majorities. But if positive law and rights are all there are, then no reason can be given for constraining the popular sovereign in the amendment process. Such constraints would be arbitrary and therefore unintelligible. To be sure, our objector would be right to point out that the popular sovereign could use the amendment process to remove any constitutional constraints upon popular sovereignty. But should this be done, it seems to me that the Constitution will have been replaced rather than simply amended. This new constitution will stand in relation to the present Constitution as that Constitution stands in relation to the Articles of Confederation—as a new and different regime design replacing an older one. The fact that some person or group in a polity is possessed of the ability to replace the current institutional arrangement with a new and different one, however, does not imply that the person or group that can do this has always been possessed of absolute sovereignty—or else revolutions the world over have never effected a change in sovereignty anywhere at all and hence have not truly been revolutions.

ural law but also impose real limits upon individuals. As I hope is sufficiently clear from the section that elaborates this interesting notion, Hobbesian natural right provides the foundation for an unlimited sovereign. When Hobbes defines an unlimited sovereign, he defines it as unconstrained—for that which has the power to limit or constrain an apparent sovereign is the actual sovereign. All the constraining features of the Constitution are therefore inconsistent with this idea of Hobbesian natural right. Accordingly, as I argued in chapter 3, any possible sovereign (whether the government or some branch of the government or whether the people) under our Constitution is very limited. Thus we find a contradiction: the unlimited version of rights-precedence requires an unconstrained sovereign; our Constitution instantiates a constrained one. Therefore, the possibility that the Constitution presupposes Hobbesian natural right falls to the ground rather quickly.

This limited version of the view that natural rights precede natural law also arguably stands in tension with the Constitution's presupposition of a real natural law. It is difficult, after all, to see how natural law (or how obligation) can be generated by natural rights. Suppose, for a moment, we take the view that natural rights precede natural obligations and that these rights are founded on ownership or property. On this view, N's natural rights derive from the fact that N has property in himself. And Locke is alleged to say that property implies exclusivity such that to say N has property in some thing O is to say everyone else has an obligation not to interfere with N's use of O and no one can take O from N. If N has property in his acts, then others have an obligation not to prevent N from doing those actions in which he has property. And N has the same obligation toward everyone else. But from where does this obligation come? Why should the fact that N has some property in a thing or an act entail anything about what others are obliged to do with respect to N?[36] There is a huge gaping hole left by a missing premise in the move from N's property to everyone else's mysteriously generated obligation to respect N's property. In fact, the obligation of others to respect N's property doesn't exist unless there is first a rule or law such that if some thing or act O is the property of N, then others must respect N's property and not interfere with his use of O or

---

36. We have at least one instance (namely, Thomas Hobbes) of someone who thinks that N's natural rights say nothing about the obligations of others with respect to N. It's hard to see why he's wrong on this count. Harry Jaffa argues, "if we conceive these rights as operative within the Lockean state of nature, we will immediately see that no man is under any necessary obligation to respect any other man's rights" (*The Crisis of the House Divided: An Interpretation of the Issues in the Lincoln-Douglas Debates*, 324). Of course, we might think, and with good reason, that Jaffa should have identified this state of nature as Hobbesian rather than Lockean.

doing of O. The right cannot generate (or impose) that rule by itself, because the rule imposing the obligation to respect property is either external to and transcendent of human will or reducible to it, in which case it really isn't obligatory at all. In short, the "stopping cannots" imposed upon others cannot be imposed simply by virtue of the fact that N has property in a thing. The ground of the right must be an ontologically prior law imposing an obligation upon individuals to respect the property of others. Put another way, the idea that rights, by themselves, generate obligations seems self-referentially incoherent. To make the position go, it presupposes a general rule to the effect that each person is to be rendered his due and that what is due him is respect for his property. Of course, proponents of the position, such as Zuckert, admit no such prior rule. But the absence of such a rule seems, at day's end, to rob proponents of this view of any kind of obligation prior to and normative for human willing.

How does the Constitution come into all of this? I have argued that prescription presupposes obligation antecedent to prescription and that obligation therefore requires some nonpositive source. If there is no such source, then all so-called law is simply a command imposed by force, whether by the community or by some sovereign who rules over the community. The Constitution is prescriptive, and so it presupposes real obligation external to and normative for human willing. But the version of the limited view in which the obligation that property is to be respected is generated by the sheer fact of ownership (the Zuckert view) seems to undo obligation by rendering the relationship of property to duty altogether mysterious.

Just here an objector seizes upon the argument. The argument, he says, turns entirely upon the inability of the limited-rights-first view to account for obligation. But, he tells us, he really must insist that there is a purely analytic connection between rights and obligations. What are we to make of this? Our objector seems to think that rights by definition impose obligations or that it is self-evident that they do. But we have already seen that this is false, for we have one theory—the Hobbesian theory of the right of nature—in which rights (or the right of nature) impose no obligations whatsoever upon others. This suggests that it is not self-evident that rights impose obligations. Furthermore, the presence of the Hobbesian theory means that the objector cannot settle the matter by definition (as he is trying to do) without viciously begging the question. In short, if the idea that rights impose obligations can be disputed, then there can't be a purely analytic connection between rights and obligations. We might add that if there is a purely analytic connection here such that rights impose duties as a matter of definition, then it begins to look as if rights are rules rather than simply property or *dominium*. In this case, while declaiming the idea that rights depend on natural law, the objector has defined rights as rules that impose duties—he bolted the front door to the priority of natural law only to let it right back in through the back door.

The foregoing seems to leave us with one alternative on the table: natural rights derive from or are grounded in a prior natural law. Natural law may ground natural rights in one of the two ways described by Pufendorf; but, however the case may be, natural law has a logical or ontological priority in grounding obligation. How does natural law ground natural rights? It seems to me that this works much like Anscombe described. Natural law sets for human beings some essentially human task that (morally) must be done. This "must" logically implies a "can" or moral power to carry out or fulfill the "must." A person therefore has the moral power or ability to fulfill his obligations. This moral permission is the first part of what constitutes a right. We should note that, on this view, a person also has a right to the means necessary to fulfilling his obligations. As for the second part of a right, the same law that imposes obligations upon someone also proscribes others from doing anything to keep him from fulfilling his obligations. That is, the same moral necessity that invests any person *x* with moral ability or permission to fulfill his obligations also imposes "stopping cannots" on any person *y*, making it morally impermissible for any person *y* then to interfere with any person *x*'s performance of his duty. There doesn't seem to be anything in the Constitution to contradict this notion. And this view harmonizes with the Constitution's presupposition concerning obligation.

Inference to the Best Explanation, Stage 2: Consilience and Simplicity

In this section I will move swiftly at times as much said here is simply an application of arguments made elsewhere. The denial of natural rights and the unlimited version of rights-precedence both fail to explain all the constraining features within the Constitution. I have argued that if there are no natural rights morally enabling individuals to do certain things, then, via *modus tollens*, there is no such thing as obligation normative for human willing. In this case all law is just an exercise of will. And any act of will is as good as any other. Moreover, the constraining features of the Constitution, as I have argued, do distinguish between acts of will, favoring long-term will over immediate will. It follows, therefore, that the denial of natural rights is unable to explain all of the Constitution's constraining features. The same point can be made in a different way. As I have suggested, if there are no natural rights, then it is impossible for government or for a sovereign to act unjustly vis-à-vis citizens. If government or the sovereign cannot wrong citizens, then there is no reason to constrain the actions of the government or the sovereign with respect to the citizens. But, any way you slice it, government under the Constitution is greatly constrained vis-à-vis the citizens. And the popular sovereign, acting through the institutions established under the Constitution, is likewise constrained. Of particular relevance here are the Bill of Rights and the limited delegation of powers (or governmental ends) in Article 1, Section 8. These constrain government and the will of the people insomuch as popular will must conform to these constraints in the making of law.

As for the unlimited-rights view, we have a rather strong argument that this view entails an unlimited or an unconstrained sovereign. There is no need to rehash our argument for this position. Nor is there any need to rehash the argument from chapter 3 that there is no such sovereign under the Constitution (no possible candidate for sovereignty even came close). Therefore, the denial of natural rights and unlimited rights-precedence leave many features of the Constitution unexplained—all the constraining features and things such as a limited delegation of powers—and will therefore require auxiliary hypotheses in all these instances. It would be strange if one of our remaining alternatives wasn't more simple and consilient.

Both the limited version of the idea that rights precede natural law and the idea that natural law precedes natural rights successfully explain a limited delegation of power and all of the Constitution's constraining features. For they both entail limits upon what any person, any sovereign, and any government can rightly do. In fact, both propositions explain many constitutional features. But the limited-rights-first view fails to explain some facts explained by the natural-law-first view. The limited-rights-first view has a major failing and then some lesser failings. Concerning the major failing, the arguments advanced in this chapter have suggested that limited rights-precedence is unable to explain *obligation* in general.[37] The generation of the obligation of others to observe rights-claims, to respect property, or to render to each person his due is (protests notwithstanding) unexplained by adherents of limited rights-

---

37. Sometimes people say rights can generate obligations or claims upon the actions of others. But how this can be without a logically prior rule that just claims are to be honored or that justice is to be done is never shown.

precedence. But, per our arguments in chapters 1–5, obligation is a major constitutional feature. By virtue of its prescriptiveness, the Constitution presupposes a source of obligation to obey (just) human law that must come from outside human law. This suggests that natural law–precedence explains at least one more major constitutional feature than limited rights-precedence, making natural law–precedence more consilient, and that it therefore requires one less auxiliary hypothesis, making it simpler. If I am right, then the idea that natural law precedes natural rights and gives them what grounding they have provides a better explanation of our constitutional system than the denial of natural rights and limited or unlimited rights-precedence.

As to the lesser failings, there seem to be specific constitutional provisions explained by the priority of obligation to rights but not by the priority of rights to obligation. Such provisions have something in common: they all seem to recognize an obligation to do something where the obligation cannot be reduced to an obligation to respect individual rights. Are there any such obligations? Well, the delegation of powers in Article 1, Section 8, seems to contain some. Under the delegation of powers, Congress is delegated the power to declare war. The thesis that natural rights precede obligation provides no immediate explanation of this. But the priority of natural law has an explanation generated from the theory. The natural law prescribes justice even in war, and the delegation of the power to declare war to Congress "seems predicated on the idea that there is something unjust about undeclared war (what else does the declaration accomplish?)."[38] The delegation of powers also contains other provisions arguably inexplicable in terms of obligations arising from individual rights or individual autonomy. Congress is given certain powers that seem better explained as powers to promote the general welfare than as powers to protect individual rights (e.g., the power to regulate commerce among the states, to establish post roads, or to declare war).[39] If one concedes the ex-

---

38. Robert Koons, personal correspondence.

39. The power "To promote the progress of science and useful arts" seems an obvious candidate here. But the power to promote these is a power to do so "by securing for limited times to authors and inventors the exclusive *right* to their respective writings and discoveries" (*italics* mine). Some might say this means that the protection of rights is what this delegation is all about. But the wording of the power grant precludes the interpretation that the power to promote art and science is generated by an obligation to protect individual rights. For the priority of rights would mean that these things are promoted *in order* to protect the rights of authors and inventors. Instead, the delegation says that these rights are protected *in order* to promote the progress of science and useful arts. And just here we can add that the promotion of these is a promotion of the general welfare rather than a protection of individual rights. Put another way, the protection of rights in the delegation seems to be a means rather than an end, which makes no sense if the reason for the provision is the protection of the rights mentioned.

istence of any constitutional provisions of this sort, then a problem emerges for the limited-rights-first view. For the laws produced as a result of such delegations will be prescriptive, presupposing a source of obligation to ground them. But, even if, *per impossible,* rights could ground obligation, they could only ground the obligation to respect individual rights. They cannot underwrite any obligation to pursue the general welfare. The priority of natural law, however, can explain all provisions that go beyond the protection of individual rights or autonomy and that promote the general welfare, for the pursuit of the general welfare is a prescription of the natural law.

Inference to the Best Explanation, Stage 3: Teleological Fitness

The Constitution aims to preserve natural rights in two respects. First, it aims to do so by constraining the government vis-à-vis the people in order to prevent tyranny. Second, it constrains the majority (i.e., the popular will) in order to protect individuals or groups from the popular sovereign.

One might argue that tyranny amounts to the sovereign or governing power treating citizens or subjects in a way that they do not deserve. That is, tyranny is a failure on the part of the sovereign or of the government to render to the polity as a whole (or to some group or individual within the polity) its due. Consider the case in which the wicked Queen Jezebel decides to take the righteous Naboth's vineyard against his will and without compensation just to show Naboth who's boss and to stop Ahab's inane complaints. Suppose, with the author of the story, we deem this action tyrannical (it doesn't really seem much of a leap). Why was this act tyrannical? Well, Jezebel took something from Naboth that belonged to him, something that was his to give or keep according to his good pleasure. In other words, the sovereign committed an act of thievery. I suggest that in every case where we label something tyrannical and then look to see why, we will always end up saying that the misbehaving sovereign (or governmental official) was depriving some citizen or subject of that which was the citizen's or the subject's by right. It also seems as if the popular checks on governments, a limited delegation of powers, a Bill of Rights, and the separation of powers together with checks that give the people's branch a kind of end-of-the-day sovereignty (or final say) are all best explained as efforts to control the government. But what does it mean to control the government? It means to prevent the government from tyrannizing its citizens. Therefore, if these features of the Constitution in fact constrain governmental behavior, then there is a constitutional tendency to protect rights.

Can these rights be mere artifacts of human construction? Such a view would be unreasonable. But before the thought is finished, an objector pipes up and says, "Now see here, these are all constraints upon the government. But the government isn't sovereign; the people are. All these constraints upon the government are just ways of protecting the people's final and absolute say about what shall be law. So there are no rights but what the people grant; the people as sovereign have granted these and taken steps to ensure, through a constitution, that their sovereignty supervenes over the ordinary operations of the government." That might be the end of the matter except for the fact that, as I've argued, our system works so as to constrain not only the government, but the people as well. First, the popular sovereign exercises its will through the instrument of government. If there are constraints upon government, then there are constraints upon how the popular will can employ the instrument of government. Second, the popular sovereign is greatly constrained through the republic's extent of territory. Madison provides us with a structuralist account, in *The Federalist* No. 10, of how the extended sphere works to protect minority rights from abuses by a popular sovereign (though this is not all he does in the essay). To recapitulate the argument, the disease most incident to popular government is faction. Factions pursue narrow interests (or selfish passions) at the expense of the permanent and aggregate interest of the whole polity or at the expense of minority rights. The fear in a republic is that some such group will constitute a majority of the whole. In order to prevent government by a majority that will pursue selfish interest at the expense of the common good or minority rights, the Constitution establishes an extended or large republic, thereby flipping the wisdom of antiquity, on this particular, on its head. The extended sphere fosters the protection of natural rights by resisting factitious government. How does it do this? In Madison's oft-quoted words,

> The smaller the society, the fewer probably will be the distinct parties and interests composing it; the fewer the distinct parties and interests, the more frequently will a majority be found of the same party; and the smaller the number of individuals composing a majority, and the smaller the compass within which they are placed, the more easily will they concert and execute their plans of oppression. Extend the sphere, and you take in a greater variety of parties and interests; you make it less probable that a majority of the whole will have a common to invade the rights of other citizens; or if such a common motive exists, it will be more difficult for all who feel it to discover their own strength, and to act in unison with each other. Besides other impedi-

ments, it may be remarked, that where there is a consciousness of unjust or dishonorable purposes, communication is always checked by distrust, in proportion to the number whose concurrence is necessary.[40]

But granting that the extended sphere fosters or tends to the protection of minority rights by suppressing majority faction, how does this reveal a constitutional tendency to protect *natural* rights? Suppose Madison's argument holds, as I think it does. Then, for any group *x*, their rights are more likely to be protected in an extended republic than in a small republic because factitious majorities likely to oppress *x* are less likely to exist or, at least, to govern in an extended republic than in a small one. In a republic the people are sovereign and the sovereign's will is determined by the majority; therefore, the impact of the extended sphere is upon the will of the sovereign. If the goal is to protect minority rights from a majority faction, then, in fact, the goal is to protect minority rights from the sovereign. But what sense can this possibly make if the only rights in view are determinations of positive law? For in that case all rights are determinations of the sovereign will. And because the majority determines the sovereign will, the existence of rights is determined by the majority. Furthermore, if there are no rights antecedent to positive law, then the will of the majority cannot go wrong vis-à-vis individual citizens or minority groups. Consequently, it makes no sense to try to protect minority rights from the acts of "factitious" majorities if rights are created by positive law. For then there is no such thing as a wrongly directed majority will.

Conclusion

I have argued that if human "laws" are really nothing other than sheer exercises of force, then they are not obligatory. The power to bind comes not from force alone, however strong or irresistible the force be upon another. A person compelled by force is simply that—compelled or forced. Calling this obligation is to render all such talk nugatory. It follows that binding human laws must receive what power they have to bind from outside of themselves. I have also argued that, for like reason, prescription presupposes obligation antecedent to the prescription. If there is no obligation antecedent to prescription, then so-called prescriptions are just exercises of force and therefore not obligatory. But nonobligatory prescriptions do not prescribe in any meaning-

---

40. *The Federalist* No. 10, 48.

ful sense of the word. Furthermore, I have contended that the Constitution is indeed prescriptive (as rules about rules must be) and that the laws produced by it are prescriptive. As prescription, the Constitution must presuppose obligation that is outside and normative for it. The Constitution, however, is a contrivance of human will. Therefore, to say that our prescriptive Constitution presupposes obligation that is antecedent and external to it seems, rather clearly, to entail saying that it also presupposes that obligation is antecedent to human willing. Or, we might argue, that the Constitution can't reduce to human willing on the ground that if it does, then it just becomes a nonbinding exercise of force. In which case it doesn't really prescribe anything at all. All of this seems to mean that humans are under an obligation that does not derive from the Constitution or from any other acts of human willing. To say humans are under such obligation is to say they are obliged or morally bound. It doesn't make sense to say they are morally bound to do anything and everything. In fact, to say that would be to admit something of a contradiction (one would be bound both to do and not to do x; but, then, how is one morally compelled to one action or the other?). Thus, the admission of obligation as external to the Constitution seems to amount to the admission that there are some acts that human persons are under a moral necessity to do or that human persons are under a moral necessity to refrain from doing. But, as we have seen (and as virtually everyone admits), that which one must do, morally speaking, one has a moral right to do (or can do). That is, that which one must do, one has the *potestas* or moral authority or moral power to do. Therefore, the very idea of obligation antecedent to human law seems to entail some sort of right (whether we choose to call it natural or not) antecedent to human law. Thus we move from the prescriptive nature of the Constitution and the laws it produces to the presupposition of something like natural rights or a morally enabling "can."

Would such rights be inalienable? Well, if the obligations under which humans fall are truly binding, then they cannot alienate or transfer away the duties imposed upon them. But if this is the case, then rights necessarily entailed by those duties cannot be alienated either. Does the morally enabling "can," however, entail "stopping cannots" for others? It would at least seem to. Consider the following case: transcendent moral obligation entails that any person x (perhaps they must find themselves in certain circumstances first) do z. Why would this be required? So that z would be done—perhaps because z is good, etc. But now suppose no "stopping cannots" were erected for any other person y such that y could prevent x from doing z. What seems to follow is that there is and is not a moral necessity that z be done, which is clearly contradictory. Therefore, the Constitution's presupposition of obligation antecedent to human willing seems to entail rights in the full sense (both as enabling "cans" for the person with the right and as "stopping cannots" for the person not in possession of the rights) that are antecedent to and normative for human willing. It also seems to presuppose that these rights are inalienable.

— 7 —

Is the Constitution
Any Good?

W E B E G A N   T H I S   S T U D Y with a specific question: is the Constitution any good? But in order to answer that question, we needed to first elaborate the Constitution's moral framework. The bulk of our work has been uncovering the Constitution's normative framework. And having done that, we are now in a position to evaluate it. It would take an additional book to defend all the Constitution's normative presuppositions vis-à-vis the rejected propositions. Fortunately, much that is evaluative has already been said concerning the coherence of rejected propositions. In what follows I will draw on that work.

Evaluating the Constitution's Normative Structure

The preceding argument enables us to say that the Constitution presupposes (1) a constrained popular sovereign; (2) a real, teleological, and thick common good; (3) a natural law that provides a standard to which human laws must conform in order to obligate, which is known through noninstrumental reason and which is known at least to most; and (4) that natural rights are log-

242

ically dependent on a prior natural law, and that natural rights are moral abilities to fulfill the duties imposed by natural law. This looks a good deal like the description of classical moral theory outlined in chapter 1, but we have not arrived at this conclusion in the usual way.

The Constitution on Sovereignty

In chapter 3, I argued, first, that sovereignty does not consist in administering what Pufendorf terms the parts of sovereign power (what we might also call the functions of government). Rather, sovereignty consists in a *final say* about what human enactments attain to the status of law. Furthermore, I maintained that constrained sovereignty, pace Hobbes, is a perfectly sensible idea. Second, I argued that any conceivable sovereign under the Constitution could be nothing but constrained. That is, under the Constitution, no person or group possesses Hobbes's supreme sovereignty. Third, I argued that the Constitution promotes popular sovereignty by giving the branch closest to the people a great deal of final say, by turning the eyes of the other branches toward public opinion in various ways (including by giving the people's branch an end-of-the-day final say), and by giving the people a final say through the amendment process. In short, I maintained that the Constitution promotes popular sovereignty, but that the popular sovereign is greatly constrained by various mechanisms that distinguish among exercises of sovereign will, favoring some exercises of will (those that comport with long-term preferences) over others (those that comport with immediate desires). The constitutional framework favors long-term preferences, desires, sentiments, and will over short-term or immediate ones. It favors broadly shared preferences, desires, and sentiments over narrow ones.

I think the critic is most likely to seize upon the Constitution's establishment of *constrained* sovereignty. Two Hobbesian arguments come to mind. First, in chapter 6 we saw how Hobbesian natural right establishes an unlimited sovereignty. People in a state of nature have a right to everything and to do anything that they think furthers their survival. This right is a permission to act that, on Hobbes's view, entails no limitations on the behavior of others. The sovereign is established by a transfer of this right of nature from individuals to the sovereign. But then the sovereign possesses the right of nature. Because the right of nature does not limit behavior, the sovereign is set up by an absolute power without limitation. Second, recall Hobbes's argument that a limited monarch does not possess supreme sovereignty. The real sovereign is the person or group with the power to limit the monarch. Well, this argument can be applied to any sovereign. Whoever the apparent sovereign is, if that person or group is limited, then the person or group imposing the limit is the real sovereign. But what if the sovereign chooses to limit himself? A good Hobbesian will reply that the notion of self-limitation is incoherent. Any limit the sovereign imposes upon himself (or upon themselves) can be lifted by him. It is not, therefore, a true limit.

Let's take the arguments above in order. The first argument depends on the highly dubious assumption that individuals in the state of nature only possess the right of nature. But why think that? Some who recommend a constrained sovereign maintain that no one ever possesses the right of nature. Such people hold that individuals in the state of nature fall under the jurisdiction of a law of nature that imposes obligations upon them to behave and to refrain from behaving in certain ways. Perhaps individuals in the state of nature, on this view, possess what Locke calls the executive power of the law of nature.[1] But such power (or right) is nothing like the unlimited and absolute permission of the right of nature, for it is restricted to the power to enforce the requirements of the natural law. If this is the case, as Locke argues, when individuals compact together to create a society, they transfer to that society the executive right of the law of nature. When that society eventually establishes a government, the power the society transfers to the government is the right to enforce the natural law. On this view, both the right of the sovereign and the government are circumscribed by requirements of the natural law. I see nothing problematic with the view that the law of nature imposes moral constraints upon people in a state of nature. But in that case, there is nothing problematic with denying that any person possesses the right of nature and therefore with denying that a sovereign receives such power from covenanting or compacting individuals. To maintain that constrained sovereignty is incoherent, in terms of the Hobbesian argument just advanced, however, one must maintain that people in the state of nature must, as a matter of necessity, possess the right of nature and, consequently, that they cannot be limited by a law of nature, while in the state of nature, in any possible world.

It's hard to tell what to make of the second argument that a limited sovereign does not possess supreme sovereignty. A limited sovereign isn't a supreme sovereign in the Hobbesian sense. But so what? Why think that possessing sov-

---

1. Locke, *Second Treatise*, 271.

ereignty requires anything like possessing unlimited power (i.e., supreme sovereignty)? Why not just admit that sovereignty doesn't entail supreme sovereignty? As I suggested, a Hobbesian can retort that a limited sovereign has been limited by someone and that the someone doing the limiting is therefore the real sovereign. But what if the someone doing the limiting is none other than the sovereign himself? Then the sovereign would be limited but not by anyone possessing a greater sovereignty. The Hobbesian must reply that the sovereign cannot impose real limits upon himself *for the reason* that he is able to remove any limit he imposes *whenever he wants*. If that's the case, the limits aren't really limits at all. Animating this argument is the suggestion that the very notion of self-limitation is incoherent. For any person, *x*, any limit *x* imposes upon himself can be removed by *x* whenever *x* wants. To make a go of it, the Hobbesian argument requires that this premise is true. But it clearly isn't. There are all sorts of limits that any person *x* can impose upon himself that he cannot remove any time he wants (e.g., a person who promises is not able to free himself of the obligation to keep the promise just because he so desires). So long as there are *any* such limits at all, the notion of self-limitation is perfectly coherent. That being the case, the sovereign can limit himself. But suppose the sovereign is some group of people. Well, groups of people can impose limits upon themselves that they can't remove any time they want as easily as individuals can. Arguably, the colonists imposed real limitations upon themselves when they created political societies by covenants, adopted frames of government for the purpose of attaining the goals specified in the covenants, and appointed officials to administer those same governments. Once they brought those governments into being, the colonists couldn't get rid of them whenever and just because they wanted to. In short, the notion of self-limitation is entirely coherent. But if that's the case, the notion of constrained sovereignty, popular or otherwise, is unproblematic. Therefore, the Constitution's institutionalization of constrained popular sovereignty makes perfect sense.

I want to drive home a point alluded to above. If there is a natural law, obligatory for all persons, overarching ruler and ruled alike (as well as all societies), placing them on a par before the moral law, then no sovereign can be called unlimited or absolute in any meaningful sense. The sovereign will always be subject to a higher law. Rulers possess in this case a proximate sovereignty that is governed by the ultimate sovereignty of the natural law (or the one who made that law). That no one can possess supreme sovereignty in such a case doesn't seem problematic in the least.

The Constitution on the Common Good,
Natural Law, and Moral Obligation

In this section I want to address what the Constitution has to say about moral obligation (and address the nature and extent of moral knowledge in the next). In chapter 4 I argued three main things. First, I argued that the Constitution presupposes a common good that is *real* rather than nonexistent or constructed by convention. The good, I maintained, is independent of human willing, preferences, and desires and normative for human behavior. The Constitution presupposes neither moral anarchy nor preferential or procedural conventionalism. These accounts of the reality and nature of the good are ruled out because they provide no basis for distinguishing among preferences, desires, and acts of will. But the Constitution's delay mechanisms favor long-term desires, preferences, and exercises of popular will over immediate ones. The Constitution's constraining features entail a presupposition of a real good. Second, I argued that the good is teleological rather than deontic. If the Constitution presupposed a deontic view of the good, then it should not aim at particular outcomes or certain goods. But the Constitution's constraining features favor policy outcomes (and the pursuit of goods) corresponding to long-term, broadly shared interests, desires, and preferences over immediate ones. Third, I argued that the Constitution presupposes a thick, rather than a thin, teleological common good. Each of the candidates for a thin good—wealth, pleasure, and fame—fails to explain many things about the Constitution. Furthermore, these goods are so minimally substantial that just about any sort of action is compatible with most of them. As well, wealth seems an utterly implausible candidate for a real good. For wealth is a means rather than an end; it is only ever pursued for the sake of something else rather than for its own sake. In the end, I suggested that the Constitution aims at a thick common good having something to do with reason's governance over persons. The parts of chapter 5 relevant to our considerations here are (1) that a real good is not obligatory until prescribed and so the natural law is what adds prescription to the common good; (2) that human law requires an external source of obligation giving it what power it has to obligate citizens if it is to be more than mere force; and (3) that the prescriptiveness of the Constitution presupposes the existence of this external source of obligation. Chapters 4 and 5 together entail that the Constitution presupposes a real common good that provides a measure of human actions that is also binding upon human persons such that they ought to pursue or preserve the common good and ought not to act contrary to it.

Therefore, the Constitution presupposes a real thick teleological good, and each of these descriptive terms is controversial. Let's begin with the first—real rather than nonexistent. I have already argued that moral nihilism is the animating assumption of moral anarchism as well as of preferential and procedural conventionalism (and for normative positivism as well). But there is at least one argument, made by realism's opponents, that is perfectly incoherent: there is no truth about morality because there is no such thing as truth at all. Or, put another way, there is no moral reality independent of the perception of individuals for the reason that there is no reality independent of the perception of individuals. But the claim that there is no truth at all is complete nonsense. If there is no truth, then at least one thing is true—namely, that there is no truth. This is absurd. Moreover, if all reality depends entirely upon the perception of individuals, then something about reality is not dependent upon individual perception—namely, that all reality depends on individual perception. One cannot deny the existence of a moral reality independent of individual perception on the ground that all reality is determined by individual perception simply because the ground is incoherent.

Many who deny a moral reality transcendent of individual perception do not mean to say there is no reality at all. It's just that some believe physical reality is all there is. Or they believe, as that dated school of logical positivism did, for something to be true it must first be empirically verifiable. But moral reality is not part of our sense data. Moral reality is intangible and therefore unverifiable and therefore not capable of being true according to logical positivism. Logical positivism, however, committed a considerable error. The criterion of verifiability is itself not empirically verifiable and therefore, according to the canons of logical positivism, not true.[2] The local positivists' house of cards came crashing down. Because the criterion of verifiability is incoherent, it cannot be used to rule out the existence of moral reality.

Materialism fares little better here. There is no reason to think that matter is all there is or that the universe is a closed causal nexus (things like the observed regular operations of the laws of physics in no way entail a closed causal nexus). Even if human experience were restricted to material reality, this would not prove materialism true. At day's end, other than a personal bias for materialism, there is little by way of reason to accept it. As the well-regarded physicist Steven M. Barr points out, all the arguments for materialism "seem

---

2. On the criterion of verifiability, see Alvin Plantinga, *God and Other Minds: A Study of the Rational Justification of Belief in God*, chap. 7, and *God, Freedom, and Evil*, 55–56. Oddly enough, one still runs across variants of logical positivism and presuppositions derived from it in political science and in constitutional theory. But, as Plantinga observes, "By now, logical positivism has retreated into the obscurity it so richly deserves" (*Warranted Christian Belief*, 8).

to boil down in the end to 'materialism is true, because materialism must be true.' The fact seems to be that the philosophy of materialism is completely fideistic in character."[3] Furthermore, if the physical universe is all there is, how can anyone know that this is the case? The reality of matter is not a directly sensed fact but an inference premised on the reliability of our senses and our faculty of inference (i.e., reason). But the inference from sense data to material reality is not itself something that admits of empirical verification. Even worse for the modern materialist is a damning argument developed by Plantinga.[4] If our faculties of inference evolved randomly according to such Darwinian mechanisms as survival of the fittest, then the aim of such faculties will be survival rather than the production of true beliefs. If our belief-producing faculties aim at survival rather than the production of true belief, then, while they may produce true beliefs, we have no warrant for thinking that they do so reliably. The lack of warrant results from the fact that true beliefs are, at best, an unintended by-product of the human design plan. If the conjunction of Darwinian evolution and naturalism is accepted, then there is no warrant for the beliefs "evolution" and "naturalism," for in that case they will have been produced by faculties aimed at survival rather than at truth. The Darwinian materialist has cut himself off at the pass. In the end, there seems no reason for those not persuaded of materialism to adopt the position. But then there is little reason to reject moral realism because of materialism.

If someone nevertheless chooses to maintain that moral realism is false, then, to be consistent, he must hold to subjectivism (which I labeled moral anarchism) or conventionalism (which is the same as normative positivism). "Subjectivism is the theory of meaning maintaining that ethical expressions describe an ordinary, factual reality, but also that this reality is subjective and not objective. More particularly, ethical expressions do refer to something and thus have a descriptive function, but that to which they refer is the speaker's own feelings, thoughts or attitudes."[5] Normative positivism "denies the existence of transcendent standards and principles" and "accepts only the norms and rules established by the positive laws and conventions of each society." In which case, "There can be no standards and principles apart from, or prior to, the emergence of positive laws and conventions."[6]

---

3. Barr, *Modern Physics and Ancient Faith*, 16.
4. See Plantinga, *Warrant and Proper Function*, chaps. 11 and 12.
5. Michael Moore, "Moral Reality," 1075.
6. T. K. Seung, *Plato Rediscovered: Human Value and Social Order*, 293–94.

Subjectivism as a theory of meaning in general, and therefore as a theory of moral meaning, falls prey to a number of objections. Legal theorist Michael Moore has aptly summarized those objections:

> First, the most popular form of subjectivism cannot even be coherently stated. The subjectivist who urges that some ethical statement "p" has no meaning beyond that contained in the statement "I believe that p" violates what we mean by "believe." "Belief," like most words describing mental activity requires an object. One does not simply "believe" any more than one simply "intends," "desires," etc. One believes something, intends something, desires something. The thing that is believed must itself be a coherent proposition. What does one believe when one believes that round squares sleep furiously? The answer is "nothing," but this answer collapses subjectivism from a theory of meaning of ethical expressions into a theory of asserting that such expressions have no meaning. While one might assert this, this is not subjectivism.
>
> The subjectivist who analyzes moral statements in this fashion is also vulnerable to an infinite regress objection, as G. E. Moore noted long ago. If one asserts that the proposition "slavery is unjust" really means, "I believe that slavery is unjust," then this latter statement by the same reasoning must mean, "I believe that I believe that slavery is unjust" and that last statement must mean, "I believe that I believe that I believe that slavery is unjust." And so on. The short of it is that "belief" requires a propositional object that is not meaningless and does not contain another belief operator in it.
>
> Finally, subjectivism has the startling consequence that disagreement over ethical matters is impossible because there can be no contradiction in ethical discourse. If saying, "slavery is wrong," is to say "I believe slavery is wrong," and if saying "slavery is not wrong" is to say "I believe slavery is not wrong," there is no disagreement possible between two people who think they are disputing the moral merits of slavery. Neither disputant would be talking about slavery at all, but only about his own state of mind. If one wishes truly to disagree on such matters, one would have to argue that the other person is wrong about his own state of mind—which is not, of course, at all what one wishes to argue about.[7]

What about normative positivism (or conventionalism)? Normative positivism is subjectivism at the level of society or culture rather than at the level of the individual. According to T. K. Seung,

7. Moore, "Moral Reality," 1076–77

Normative positivism allows no external perspective. If we want to compare Hitler's Third Reich with the Weimar Republic, we have to make the comparison from the perspective either of the Third Reich or the Weimar Republic, or of a third country such as imperial Japan. There is no perspective that can transcend all these particular normative systems. This is the distasteful consequence of normative positivism.

For normative positivism, the absence of a transcendent perspective presents the serious problem of justification. In any normative system, the lower norms can be justified by the higher ones. But how can the higher norms, especially the highest ones (for example, Hans Kelsen's *Grundnorm* or John Rawls's basic principles of society), be justified? There is no way to justify the highest norms in a positivist system. It makes no sense even to raise the question of the justification for the highest norms, because they owe their existence to nothing higher than themselves. They stand on *nothing* but themselves; normative positivism turns out to be normative nihilism. To be sure, some positivists claim to give the internal justification of a normative system by demonstrating its internal coherence. Two salient examples are John Rawls's theory of reflective equilibrium and Ronald Dworkin's theory of law as integrity. But the internal coherence of a normative system cannot tell whether the whole system is just or unjust. Even the legal system of the Third Reich can be as coherent internally as any liberal democratic system.[8]

Seung concludes that "The only way to avoid the relativistic and nihilistic consequence of normative positivism is to accept transcendent normative standards."[9] C. S. Lewis drives this point home:

Everyone is indignant when he hears the Germans define justice as that which is to the interest of the Third Reich. But is not always remembered that this indignation is perfectly groundless if we ourselves regard morality as a subjective sentiment to be altered at will. Unless there is some objective standard of good, over-arching Germans, Japanese and ourselves alike whether any of us obey it or no, then of course the Germans are as competent to create their ideology as we are ours. If "good" and "better" are terms deriving their sole meaning from the ideology of each people, then of course ideologies themselves cannot be better or worse than one another. Unless the measuring rod is independent of the thing measured, we can do no measuring. For the same reason it is useless to compare the moral ideas of one age with those of another: progress and decadence are alike meaningless words.[10]

8. Seung, *Plato Rediscovered,* 294.
9. Ibid., 295.
10. Lewis, "The Poison of Subjectivism," 73.

The foregoing considerations should be enough for anyone to reject moral anarchism (or subjectivism) or normative positivism or, what amounts to the same thing as both of these, moral nihilism. For clearly moral realism (and natural law) is more consistent with our basic intuition that some actions are better than others and some worse, that some regimes are good and some wicked, and that some laws are just and others unjust. Yet despite these considerations, proponents of realism, and especially of natural law, are always presented with several nonsensical objections. Such objections must be addressed because they are frequently made, their wrongheadedness notwithstanding. First, moral realism (and natural law) is *criticized* because it allegedly fosters intolerance (which leads to tyranny). The reason for this is supposed to be that moral realism (or absolutism) fosters a sense of "I am right; and those who disagree are wrong." This statement is taken to be intolerant. Second, absolute morality is blamed for underwriting absolute government. The reason is usually unclear. I suspect the critics of moral realism and natural law simply assume that absolutism in one area (moral philosophy) entails absolutism in another (political rule). Therefore, moral realism is criticized for encouraging tyranny. If someone thinks he is right and others are wrong, then this is said to underwrite, psychologically, his taking action to enforce his mere opinion upon others. Third, moral realism is said to be incompatible with democracy because moral realism is inegalitarian. Moral realism is hierarchical and therefore said to promote hierarchical political regimes—the fact that some beliefs are better than others is said to underwrite the idea that some people are better than others and therefore more fit to rule. Fourth, moral realism is said to be discredited by the discovery of great variety in moral belief.

These objections to moral realism and to natural law are readily met. As to the first, recall the quotation from Mussolini in chapter 5. If moral relativism is true (i.e., moral nihilism, which underlies subjectivism and conventionalism or normative positivism), then tolerance is no better or worse than intolerance. In the case of moral nihilism, tolerance and intolerance are on the same footing, and one can neither be praised nor blamed for choosing one over the other. If one *ought* to be tolerant rather than intolerant, then there is a standard independent of human willing and normative for human behavior. In short, for tolerance to be obligatory, some form of realism must obtain. The second objection is based on a false inference. The idea that some moral absolutes exist in no way entails political absolutism (i.e. absolute government). It's quite difficult to see how anyone can think that it does. I suspect this is why the objection is so often voiced and so seldom written. Even worse for the second objection, moral nihilism, or relativism, is a doctrine well suited to the tyrant. Tyranny occurs when a sovereign treats his subjects or citizens wrongly. But if moral nihilism is true, then, necessarily, nothing is morally right or wrong. And if nothing is morally right or wrong, then there is no right or wrong way to treat other people. Given moral nihilism any person or group of persons x can never act wrongly with respect to any person or group of persons y. It follows that on moral nihilism, the sovereign can never act wrongly toward any individual or group of citizens or subjects. Because moral nihilism means that no actions are right or wrong, if some actions (e.g., tyranny) are wrong or blameworthy, then moral nihilism must be false. Because moral nihilism is a denial of moral reality, denying moral nihilism is a denial of the denial of moral reality—which is to say, an affirmation of moral reality. To put it another way, for the word *wrong* to make any sense, it must refer to a moral standard independent of human willing and normative for human behavior. It is therefore impossible to treat someone wrongly if moral realism is false. The very possibility of tyranny, therefore, depends upon the truth of moral realism. Hence, it is false to claim that moral realism promotes tyranny whereas relativism does not. The Mussolinis of the world always knew better.

The second objection, like the first, is self-referentially incoherent. This objection criticizes believers of moral reality for promoting political absolutism or absolute government. Suppose, against the evidence, that proponents of moral realism and natural law also advocated absolutism. What possible criticism can the denier of realism make? If realism is false, then there is no sense in which absolutism is wrong and there is no basis for rational criticism of the political absolutist. In short, the second objection is premised on the wrongness of political absolutism and the promotion of absolute regimes. But political absolutism and the promotion of it can only be wrong or bad if moral realism is true. Consequently, for this objection of moral realism to make any sense, moral realism must first be true.

Just here we must note the commitment of natural law theorists to limited government (in marked contrast to antirealists like Mussolini). According to John Finnis, "In any sound theory of natural law, the authority of government is explained and justified as an authority limited by positive law (especially but not only constitutional law), by the moral principles and norms of justice which apply to all human action (whether private or public), and by the common good of political communities." Finnis adds, "The first theorist of government to articulate as a specific concept the desideratum that governmental authority be legally 'limited' seems to have been Thomas Aquinas." As

Finnis contends, Aquinas thinks government should be limited because "right government does not tolerate an unregulated rule by rulers ('rule of men'), but calls for rulers to be ruled by law, precisely because law is a dictate of *reason,* while what threatens to turn government into tyranny (rule in the interests of rulers) is their human *passions,* inclining them to attribute to themselves more of the good things, and fewer of the bad things, than is their fair share."[11] Thus, proponents of moral realism and natural law are not proponents of absolute government and, in fact, have good reason for being against it. If moral realism and natural law are true, then only certain acts of government can be legitimately binding. Natural law theorists favor governmental constraints as part of an attempt to keep government within the bounds of the natural law.

Self-referential incoherency also stalks the third objection, for if moral realism is false, hierarchical regimes cannot be bad. As should be obvious to all thoughtful persons, moral realism cannot be criticized for its consequences unless moral realism is in fact true—in which case the criticism fails. There are no bad consequences if moral realism is false. No consequence is better or worse than any other in such a case. Of course, I am doubtful that moral realism and natural law thinking do underwrite hierarchical regimes while undercutting democracy. First, this very suggestion is premised on the fallacy of equivocation. The hierarchy in moral realism and natural law is a hierarchy of ideas. In contrast, political hierarchy is a hierarchy of persons. The third objection follows from a failure to distinguish these two very different senses of the word. Moreover, these different senses in no way entail each other (if objectors of this sort think otherwise, it would be nice if at least one would provide an argument for this rather than simply saying so; one explanation of the fact that they do not is that they cannot).[12] Second, even if moral realism and natural law don't entail democracy, democracy may nevertheless entail moral realism and natural law. In his Walgreen Lectures at the University of Chicago, John H. Hallowell suggested that "it is these two doctrines—the doctrine of natural law and the equality of men—which lie at the foundation of what today we call 'democracy.'"[13] He quoted John Middleton Murray to the effect that "If the validity of moral law is an illusion, so is the validity of democracy."[14] To put this in terms of the foregoing chapters, democratic laws, in order

---

11. Finnis, "Natural Law Theory and Limited Government," 1–2.

12. I owe this point concerning the fallacy of equivocation involved in the objection to J. Budziszewski.

13. Hallowell, *The Moral Foundation of Democracy,* 114.

14. Ibid., 124.

to be obligatory, rely on a source of obligation external to them. Otherwise they are merely exercises of force and consequently not binding. But democracy may entail natural law (and realism) in another respect. The famed Oxford-trained philosopher and literary critic C. S. Lewis argued, "Subjectivism about values is eternally incompatible with democracy. We and our rulers are of one kind only so long as we are subject to one law. But if there is no Law of Nature, the *ethos* of any society is the creation of its rulers, educators and conditioners; and every creator stands above and outside his own creation."[15] If there is no moral reality, then the likes of Thrasymachus, Pindar, and Carneades are right in the most basic respect—the rule of some by others can only be a function of differing strength. Pace Hobbes, strength is not all that equally distributed. Denial of moral realism and natural law actually sets up domination of the weak by the strong, because there is no sense in which the strong can go wrong in their treatment of the weak. But domination of the strong by the weak is as inegalitarian as can be. Moral realism holds that all persons fall under shared obligations because they are all of one kind. This is a true equality capable of grounding egalitarian regimes. Furthermore, Aquinas, the *locus classicus* of natural law theory, didn't think that regimes dedicated to equality and founded upon popular consent (i.e., modern democracy) are inconsistent with natural law. He described the best regime in this way:

> the best form of government is in a state or kingdom, wherein one is given the power to preside over all; while under him are others having governing powers: and yet a government of this kind is shared by all, both because all are eligible to govern, and because the rulers are chosen by all. For this is the best form of polity, being partly kingdom, since there is one at the head of all; partly aristocracy, in so far as a number of persons are set in authority; partly democracy, i.e., government by the people, in so far as the rulers can be chosen from the people, and the people have a right to choose their rulers.[16]

In his commentary on Aristotle's *Politics*, Aquinas maintained, "Political [as opposed to despotic government] is the leadership of free and equal people; and so the role of leader and led (ruler and ruled) are swapped about for the

---

15. Lewis, "Poison of Subjectivism," 81.
16. Aquinas, *Summa*, I–II, q. 105, art. 1.

sake of equality, and many people get to be constituted ruler either in one position of responsibility or in a number of such positions."[17] As I said, all of this looks a great deal like "modern" representative democracy and betrays a deep commitment to political equality. If there is a contradiction between natural law and such a regime, Aquinas likely would have detected it and realized the need to reject either democracy or natural law. But he didn't. The contemporary scholar who wishes to suggest that democracy and natural law are necessarily incompatible will have to demonstrate a formal contradiction between the two. This has yet to be done. It is hard even to conceive the sort of premises that would produce a necessary contradiction here.

Nevertheless, it is nearly always pointed out that Aristotle—sometimes considered the fountainhead of natural law theory—believed in natural slavery (and, concomitantly, natural rulership) and that such belief is inegalitarian to the extreme and most certainly incompatible with democracy, which is committed to the equality of all. Aristotle called the slave "a sort of living property." He defended the concept of natural slavery theoretically by arguing "That one should command and another obey is both necessary and expedient. Indeed some things are divided right from birth, some to rule, some to be ruled." The ruler-ruled relationship "takes many different forms." One such division occurs within the individual. "The living creature consists in the first place of mind and body, and of these the former is ruler by nature, latter ruled," and "The rule of soul over body is like a master's rule, while the rule of intelligence over desire is like a statesman's or a king's. In these relationships it is clear that it is both natural and expedient for the body to be ruled by the soul, and for the emotional part of our natures to be ruled by the mind, the part which possesses reason." Aristotle also thought that this relationship obtains across people as well:

> Therefore whenever there is the same wide discrepancy between human beings as there is between soul and body or between man and beast, then those whose condition is such that their function is the use of their bodies and nothing better can be expected of them, those I say, are slaves by nature. It is better for them, just as in the cases mentioned, to be ruled thus. For the "slave by nature" is he that can and therefore does belong to another, and he that participates in reason so far as to recognize it but not so far as to possess it.[18]

17. Cited in Finnis, "Natural Law Theory and Limited Government," 2.
18. Aristotle *The Politics* bk. 1, chap. 4, 65, 67; bk. 1, chap. 5, 68, 68–69.

This idea of slavery by nature is said then to flow from Aristotle's doctrine of natural right.

Two points made above immediately jump to mind. First, the denier of moral realism or natural law (i.e., the moral nihilist) cannot on this *ground* offer criticism of Aristotle. If moral realism is false and moral nihilism true, then slavery cannot be wrong and Aristotle cannot be wrong for holding a doctrine of slavery by nature.[19] Indeed, for slavery to be wrong, there must first be a prescription of natural law stating that people ought not enslave one another. Aristotle's critics on this point, therefore, always implicitly affirm that which they mean to deny—a real moral standard and law that provides a foundation for their criticism. Second, the very validity and goodness of democracy, democratic laws, and even equality under the law presuppose the truth of realism. As has been noted, people differ sufficiently in strength (and in Hobbesian prudence) to dominate one another. If there is no transcendent moral law grounded in a real good, then political rule can only be a function of differences in strength. And this is inegalitarian. The denier of moral realism and natural law, as a consequence of his principles, affirms that inegalitarian regimes are no better or worse than ones premised on equality. There is therefore no reason, on the denier's view, to favor one over the other or to reject one in favor of the other. Consequently, the one who criticizes moral realism and natural law for the reason that they advance inegalitarian regimes and are therefore incompatible with democracy, which the critic wishes to commend, has deprived himself of the ability to condemn inegalitarian regimes and to commend ones dedicated to equality. It is at least mildly shocking that such criticism has ever been advanced.

Moreover, Aristotle's doctrine of mastery within the self has no necessary entailment such that some individuals are to be ruled by others. To find out whether a similar natural hierarchy obtains among human persons or whether all persons are in fact naturally equal, a natural lawyer will recommend an examination of human nature. And what will that natural lawyer find when he examines human nature? I think he will find just what the natural lawyer Locke found:

> there being nothing more evident, than that Creatures of the same species and rank promiscuously born to all the same advantages of Nature, and the

19. I am arguing that the wrongness of slavery entails moral realism (i.e., that moral realism is a necessary condition of the wrongness of slavery), not that moral realism or natural law entail the wrongness of slavery, though I in fact think that they do.

use of the same faculties, should also be equal one amongst another without Subordination or Subjection, unless the Lord and Mast of them all, should by any manifest Declaration of his Will set one above another, and confer on him by an evident and clear appointment an undoubted right to Dominion and Sovereignty.[20]

And Locke thinks that neither God nor nature (i.e., God promulgating through nature) has done anything of the sort:

> For Men being all the Workmanship of one Omnipotent, and infinitely wise Maker; all the Servants of one Sovereign Master, sent into the World by his order and about his business, they are his Property, whose Workmanship they are, made to last during his, not one anothers Pleasure. And being furnished with like Faculties, sharing all in one Community of Nature, there cannot be supposed any *Subordination* among us, that may Authorize us to destroy one another, as if we were made for one anothers uses, as the inferior ranks of Creatures are for ours. Every one as he is *bound to preserve himself,* and not to quit his station willfully; so by the like reason when his own Preservation come not in competition, ought he, as much as he can, *to preserve the rest of Mankind,* and may not unless it be to do justice to an Offender, take away, or impair the life, or what tends to the Preservation of the Life, the Liberty, Health, Limb or Goods of another.[21]

Locke concludes, based on the foregoing (though later in the text), that no person can, of his own free will, enslave himself to another. "For a Man, not having the Power of his own Life, *cannot,* by Compact, or his own Consent, *enslave himself* to any one, nor put himself under the Absolute, Arbitrary power of another, to take away his Life when he pleases. No body can give more Power than he has himself; and he that cannot take away his own Life, cannot give another power over it."[22] Not only does the poser of the third objection fail to notice his implicit acceptance of moral realism and even natural law, he also fails to notice that the natural lawyer's examination of human nature can (and I think should) come out just where Locke's does. After all, the theories of the moral realist and the natural lawyer are premised on a shared human nature. They hold that all persons—ruled and rulers alike—share the same good because they share the same nature. Furthermore, natural lawyers think that all

20. Locke, *Second Treatise,* 269.
21. Ibid., 271.
22. Ibid., 284.

persons fall under the same obligations because of a shared humanness, and many hold that all persons know the basics of the moral law. These are all fundamental equalities. But what sense does it even make for the antirealist to speak of a shared humanness? If it makes no sense, then what sense does it make to rail against slavery by nature? It seems that Thrasymachus, Pindar, and Carneades lay the foundation for all enslavement by reducing all politics to contests of strength.

This leaves us with the fourth objection. According to this objection, moral realism and natural law are to be rejected because of the tremendous variation of moral belief across cultures and time. The first thing to note is that while this might pose a dilemma for certain kinds of natural law thinking, it poses no threat to moral realism or even to the idea that the moral good is obligatory for individuals. It is theoretically possible that the good really exists and that people fail, for whatever reason, to apprehend it correctly.[23] Failure to apprehend the good suffices to explain moral variation. Moreover, as Leo Strauss says, "the indefinitely large variety of notions of right and wrong is so far from being incompatible with the idea of natural right that it is the essential condition for the emergence of that idea: realization of the variety of notions of right is *the* incentive for the quest for natural right."[24] Heinrich Rommen concurs:

> The idea of natural law can emerge only when men come to perceive that not all law is unalterable and unchanging divine law. It can emerge only when critical reason, looking back over history, notes profound changes that have occurred in the realm of law and mores and becomes aware of the diversity of the legal and moral institutions of its own people in the course of its history; and when, furthermore, gazing beyond the confines of its own city-state or tribe, it notices the dissimilarity of the institutions of neighboring peoples.[25]

Rommen maintains that knowledge of moral diversity is essential to distinguishing changeless divine or natural law from human law. The second point is that the alleged variation in moral belief is not as variable as suggested. But

23. Moore observes, "The first and crudest version of the argument [against realism from anthropology] takes the fact of widespread disagreement as itself showing that there is no moral reality, moral truth, or moral knowledge. In this version, relativism is subject to the crushing rejoinder that the mere fact of disagreement among the judgments of people hardly shows there is no fact of the matter to be agreed upon" ("Moral Reality," 1089–90).

24. Strauss, *Natural Right and History,* 10. See also chapter 3 of this volume.

25. Rommen, *The Natural Law,* 4.

I will address this in the next section, which concerns the Constitution's presuppositions about how the natural law is known and the extent of that knowledge. The third, and most important point, is that this objection is, as Hadley Arkes has shown, self-refuting. According to Arkes,

> the variety of opinion which exists on the nature of virtue and vice is usually taken in itself as proof of the proposition that there are no understandings of morals that are universally true. On this undefended premise, as far as I can see, rests much of modern social science. It remains undefended in part because it is never brought to the level of an explicit proposition, and in part because it is at root indefensible. If it were stated in the form of a proposition, it would probably look something like this: "The presence of disagreement on matters of moral judgment—the sheer variety of opinion that exists in the world on these questions—is sufficient to indicate the absence of universal moral truths." . . . [T]hat is a proposition I cannot endorse, and the critical question may be how my own refusal to agree with this proposition would affect its validity. My disagreement establishes that the proposition does not enjoy a universal assent, and by the very terms of the proposition, that should be quite sufficient to determine *its own invalidity*.[26]

The idea that anyone ever supposed variation in moral belief could be counted as evidence against moral realism and natural law is quite extraordinary. In addition to the difficulty Arkes addresses, the proposition assumes that disagreement on some matter means that there is no truth of the matter. This suggestion is false *reductio ad absurdum*. Suppose the proposition is true. Then if some people asserted that the earth is flat and others maintained that it is round, it would follow that the earth has no shape—but this inference would be absurd.[27]

Once one enters the realist camp, one faces the dilemma of which realism to choose. The first choice is between deontic and teleological realism. Deontic realism falls prey to several objections already discussed in chapter 4. No rules are truly indifferent to ends or outcomes, but a fully deontic morality requires that they be. Kant himself fails miserably to produce a purely deontic ethic. He distinguishes a good will from a bad one. But this distinction cannot be made on the basis of will alone; rather, it must be made by recourse to some standard external to the will. But, then, for the will to be good, it must aim at

---

26. Arkes, *First Things*, 132 (original emphasis).
27. I borrow this example from Francis J. Beckwith, "A Critique of Moral Relativism," 14.

something external to it, something more than conformity to a mere rule. Even Kant seems to acknowledge this, albeit tacitly. For all of Kant's formulations of the hypothetical imperative aim at a good external to the will that is not reducible to conformity to a rule. He condemns willing certain things (such as committing suicide because one is no longer happy) for the reason that to will these, if one's will is universalized, is to will a contradiction. But there is no reason to care about this unless rational consistency is actually a good. But the good of rational consistency is not itself a rule; rather, it is an outcome or end or state of being aimed at by the rule "be rationally consistent." But this means Kantian rules are teleological. Kant unmasks his usually veiled teleology when he notes, "If then there is to be a supreme practical principle and, as far as the human will is concerned, a categorical imperative, then it must be such that from the conception of what is necessarily an end for everyone because this end is an end in itself it constitutes an objective principle of the will and can hence serve as a practical law. The ground of such a principle is this: rational nature exists as an end in itself." From this he deduces the practical imperative "Act in such a way that you treat humanity, whether in your own person or in the person of another, always as an end and never simply as a means."[28] Rational nature is an end in itself, and the will should aim at the preservation of this end. This is all very teleological. Finally, the purely deontic ethic can be criticized on the grounds that no will functions in this way. As I said before, no one wills more will. Every will aims to attain something—some object or state of affairs. One might conclude that this is what it means to will—to act so as to attain something—and that Kantian deontology promotes an impossible standard.

This brings us to teleological realism. Some have proposed that teleological realism is untenable because the teleological understanding of any sort of nature has been rendered impossible by modern science. Leo Strauss presented the "difficulty" as follows:

> The issue of natural right presents itself today as a matter of party allegiance. Looking around us, we see two hostile camps, heavily fortified and strictly guarded. One is occupied by the liberals of various descriptions, the other by the Catholic and non-Catholic disciples of Thomas Aquinas. But both armies and, in addition, those who prefer to sit on the fences or hide their heads in the sand are, to heap metaphor upon metaphor, in the same boat. They all

---

28. Kant, *Grounding for the Metaphysics of Morals,* line 429, 36.

are modern men. We all are in the grip of the same difficulty. Natural right in its classic form is connected with a teleological view of the universe. All natural beings have a natural end, a natural destiny, which determines what kind of operation is good for them. In the case of man, reason is required for discerning these operations: reason determines what is right by nature with ultimate regard to man's natural end. The teleological view of the universe, of which the teleological view of man forms a part, would seem to have been destroyed by modern natural science. . . . The fundamental dilemma, in whose grip we are, is caused by the victory of modern natural science. An adequate solution to the problem of natural right cannot be found before this basic problem has been solved.[29]

I doubt that if we consider only the empirical observations of modern science that teleology was ever in any serious danger. It was more an ideological posture of the "scientific" community that challenged teleological thinking than sober scientific evidence or analysis. But there have always been prominent scientists and philosophers who demurred from this posture. Today antiteleological thinking has come under serious attack, and those at the forefront have been physicists and philosophers. As for philosophers, Plantinga demonstrated that the proper functioning of our cognitive faculties is *essential* to our having any knowledge. Proper function is, of course, a thoroughly teleological notion. Koons argued for the necessity of a teleological account of causation. Assessing the case for teleology in the sciences, physicists John D. Barrow and Frank J. Tipler wrote, "living creatures *do* exhibit purpose in their behavior, and it is also obvious that bodily organs are most easily described in terms of the bodily purposes (functions) they serve. It is simply not possible to avoid using teleological concepts in biology."[30] According to developmental biologist Michael Denton, there is "scientific evidence for believing that the cosmos is uniquely fit for life as it exists on earth and for organisms of design and biology very similar to our own species" and "that this 'unique fitness' of the laws of nature for life is entirely consistent with the older teleological religious concept of the cosmos as a specially designed whole, with life and mankind as its primary goal and purpose."[31] Physicist Stephen Barr argued that modern physics is perfectly compatible with ancient religious faith (meaning Judeo-Christian faith), which is deeply teleological, and Great Britain's physicist of

29. Strauss, *Natural Right and History,* 8–9.
30. Barrow and Tipler, *The Anthropic Cosmological Principle,* 124.
31. Denton, *Nature's Destiny: How the Laws of Biology Reveal Purpose in the Universe,* 1.

note, John Polkinghorne (who is also, now, a theologian), concurred.[32] To be sure, not all scientists and philosophers agree. But there is good reason to say that the antiteleological posture is now open to question and even philosophical attack from the direction of science and philosophy.

Beyond the foregoing, there has always been a deeper problem with the suggestion that modern science discredits ancient teleology or even arguments of cosmic design. The successful attack on teleology is allegedly leveled by the Darwinian account of life. Darwin, some say, demolished design (and teleology along with it) by showing how the nonpurposive mechanism of survival of the fittest operating upon random, hereditable genetic mutations explains the variety of life. This was thought, via Occam's razor, to cut away the need for divine design and therefore for purpose (or final cause) in explaining natural organisms. But Darwin showed no such thing. When scientists and philosophers explain random mutations they say they occur randomly or by chance. As Peter van Inwagen, a leading philosophical light, argues, this seems to mean *chance* in the Aristotelian sense (where chance is defined in terms of radical contingency, such that something due to chance can be explained as "arising from the coincidence of independent lines of causation").[33] Some Darwinians make this their express definition of chance and randomness (e.g., Monod). In this case, genetic mutations are radically contingent. But radical contingency in the evolutionary process does nothing to rule out purposive divine agency. As van Inwagen contends,3

> It is . . . consistent with the thesis that all mutations (and, more generally, all events of evolutionary significance) are due to chance in this Aristotelian sense that God has been guiding evolution—by deliberately causing certain mutations (and other events of evolutionary significance). If God has been doing this, it does not follow that the history of terrestrial life would reveal anything inconsistent with the Darwinian thesis that all mutations are due to chance.

If the course of Darwinian evolution would indeed have to be radically contingent, then a theist who accepts Darwinism (and who accepts the thesis that

32. Barr, *Modern Physics and Ancient Faith;* Polkinghorne, *The Faith of a Physicist* and *Belief in God in an Age of Science.* See also Paul Davies, *The Cosmic Blueprint: New Discoveries in Nature's Creative Ability to Order the Universe* and "The Appearance of Design in Physics and Cosmology," in *God and Design: The Teleological Argument and Modern Science,* and essays by Richard Swinburne, William Lane Craig, and Robin Collins in this same volume.

33. Van Inwagen, "The Compatibility of Darwinism and Design," 354.

radical contingency is a consequence of Darwinism) might speculate that God has directed it down the path it has in fact taken by a judicious choice of mutations (and of climatic changes and of events of many other types). And the atheistic Darwinian will have to admit that nothing in the history of life, no possible paleontological discovery, could be inconsistent with, or even cast doubt on, this thesis. After all, the atheistic Darwinian thinks that the actual course of evolutionary history *was* produced by a sequence of events that was due to chance in the Aristotelian sense. Therefore, he must admit that if God chose the actual course of evolutionary history, God chose—produced, created—a course of events that was due to chance in the Aristotelian sense. And this is something that an omnipotent and omniscient being would find no more difficulty in doing than He would in creating a table of random numbers.[34]

In other words, Darwinian mechanisms can be used in purposive ways, in which case the attempt to use Darwin to brush aside teleology is a complete failure. But in this case, teleological accounts of human nature cannot be rejected on Darwinian grounds.

If science doesn't discredit teleology, which sort of teleology shall we choose? Thin teleological realism offers four candidates: fame, wealth, peace (survival), or pleasure. But an ethic is only of value to the extent that it provides a real standard for guiding action and for ascribing praise or blame to the actions of individuals, to the laws of various states, or to political systems taken as a whole. Yet if we take the thin teleological goods individually, they are so minimally substantial as to provide almost no specific guidance for our actions. Furthermore, some of them seem not to be real goods at all.

Let's start with fame. If fame means simply recognition or attention, then just about any act one can think of might procure the recognition or attention of others. One can be recognized for being a skilled athlete, a skilled thief, an honest man, a brutal dictator, or an exceptionally gifted serial killer. Clearly, there are things in such a list that no one considers good. We think a properly functioning person desires recognition for doing well. But if that's the case, then we don't think of fame as the good at all—for it is only good in reference to a higher good (i.e., doing well).

Wealth also is minimally substantial. One might gain wealth by honest or dishonest means. Furthermore, a wealthy person could be either a humani-

34. Ibid., 361.

tarian or a miser, like Scrooge. Wealth doesn't tell us whether to be honest or dishonest, just or a thief, generous or entirely selfish. In addition, as we've previously observed, wealth isn't a good at all. As Aristotle says, wealth has the character of a means rather than an end.[35] Rightly ordered desires don't desire means as an end.

Even Hobbes, who thought traditional morality to be in people's self-interest, seems to understand that peace (or survival) is minimally substantial. Any good supported by as wide-ranging a permission as the right of nature (even if this is only in the state of nature) provides little guidance for action at crucial moments. To maximize safety from invaders outside of the society and to secure domestic tranquility within it, we need a sovereign as strong as can be, one without constraints or limits—Leviathan unleashed. But if we have such a sovereign, then our very survival is threatened by the unleashed Leviathan. To maximize our safety from Leviathan, we must maximally constrain the Leviathan or we must tighten the leash as tight as can be. But this minimizes our safety vis-à-vis others within and outside of our society. This seems to create a considerable dilemma. But someone will surely suggest that it may be possible for a society both to increase the power of Leviathan so as to increase safety in terms of domestic tranquility and to tighten Leviathan's leash so as to increase the safety of the society from the government—a given society x may be at a place where it is capable of doing both. This may very well be true, but there will come a point where the leash has been tightened as far as it can be without choking the Leviathan (i.e., without diminishing the sovereign's power to ensure safety thereby reducing the safety of the people vis-à-vis one another and vis-à-vis external threat) and where the Leviathan has been strengthened as much as he can be without breaking the leash (i.e., without increasing the society's danger vis-à-vis the sovereign). That is, if safety vis-à-vis the sovereign is p and safety vis-à-vis others is q, there comes a point in which you have as much of p and q as you can have together such that you cannot act to increase p without diminishing q and you cannot act to increase q without diminishing p. This place is the possibility horizon. When we reach the possibility horizon, however, there is still safety to be had by either tightening or loosening Leviathan's leash. Shall we leave Leviathan's leash at its present tightness? Shall we gain safety from the sovereign by tightening it more? Shall we loosen the leash to ensure greater safety from domestic turmoil and

35. "As for the money-maker, his life is led under some kind of constraint: clearly wealth is not the good which we are trying to find, for it is only useful, i.e., it is a means to something else" (Aristotle *Nichomachean Ethics* 1096a).

external threat? There is no way to decide this question in terms of survival. We require recourse to a good or standard external to survival. If we are to know which of these options is best, we need recourse to a higher-order good. Survival itself is not much of a guide to action just when we need it most.[36]

As for pleasure, the old criticism of Jeremy Bentham's utilitarianism still rings true. There seems no way for the pleasure principle to avoid the consequence that it's better to be a pig satisfied than Socrates unsatisfied. That consequence is ridiculous. But the only way for the utilitarian to avoid it is to introduce some transcendent good or norm. John Stuart Mill's attempt to introduce qualitative distinctions into utilitarianism slips transcendent standards in under the radar, even as he loudly declaims doing any such thing.[37] Pace Mill, some pleasures cannot be better or higher than others in terms of pleasure alone. If we consider only pleasure, then quantity and intensity of enjoyable sensations is the only measure we have to use, in which case some pleasures are not better *or* worse or higher or lower than others. The only difference is that some produce more enjoyable sensations than others. If some pleasures are better or of a higher order than others, this can only be in reference to some rule or measure external to pleasure. Moreover, the pleasure principle is compatible with any action that brings pleasure to an individual or to a group. But just about anything can arouse pleasurable sensations in an individual or a group. Serial killers usually derive a very high degree of sexual satisfaction from their actions.[38] What if these individuals feel more intense pleasure than anyone else? What if the majority of a society is composed of serial killers? At day's end, the pleasure principle provides no basis for distinguishing between the intense pleasure the serial killer derives from murder and the pleasure Mother Theresa received from giving her life to help others.

Can a good that fails to distinguish between a serial killer and a Mother Theresa be considered a substantial good in any meaningful sense? There is another difficulty for the adherent to the pleasure principle. Great pleasure derives from love. But the utilitarian cannot access that pleasure. According to Michael Stocker, the utilitarian certainly *can* do "the various things calculated to bring about such pleasure: have absorbing talks, make love, eat delicious meals, see interesting films, and so on, and so on." And yet, "there is something

36. I owe the argument concerning the possibility horizon and the inability of survival to tell you what to do at that grand frontier to J. Budziszewski.

37. See Mill, *Utilitarianism,* chap. 2.

38. See Bressler, Burgess, and Douglas, *Sexual Homicide,* and Eric W. Hickey, *Serial Murderers and Their Victims.*

necessarily lacking in such a life: love. For it is essential to the very concept of love that one care for the beloved, that one be prepared to act for the sake of the beloved. More strongly, one must care for the beloved and act for that person's sake as a final goal; the beloved, or the beloved's welfare or interest, must be a final goal of one's concern and action." This poses a considerable problem for the utilitarian: "To the extent that my consideration for you—or even my trying to make you happy—comes from my desire to lead an untroubled life, a life that is personally pleasing for me, I do not act for your sake. In short, to the extent that I act in various ways towards you with the final goal of getting pleasure—or more generally, good—for myself, I do not act for your sake."[39] What then, is a poor utilitarian to do? Stocker suggests that for the utilitarian to maximize pleasure, he will have to give up maximizing pleasure. The utilitarian will have to cease to be a utilitarian in order to attain the good at which utilitarianism aims. An objector might say that this creates a difficulty for egoistic utilitarianism but not for social utilitarianism (i.e., not for the principle that the good is the most pleasure for the most people). But we can reply to the objection as follows. It is not clear that the person animated by the pleasure principle, where the good is increasing the pleasure for the most people, is able to enjoy the good of love in any deep or meaningful sense. Such a person, in doing the acts of love, is nevertheless motivated by the pleasure of society as a whole rather than by the good or even by the pleasure of his beloved. Surely this is not what we mean by love. Consequently, the pleasures attendant to true love do not follow upon acts so motivated. Social utilitarianism also fails, as I have suggested, to distinguish between a society of Mother Theresas and a society of serial killers—in fact, it might recommend the policy of aiding the serial killers rather than the Mother Theresas. But there is a graver difficulty, pleasure alone cannot tell anyone whether to prefer maximizing the pleasure of individuals or of society as a whole. To know which of these options is better, we require a standard external to pleasure.

What about the complex version of thin teleological realism? Surely this provides more guidance for actions. I am skeptical of this. What happens when the thin goods come into competition? If the good is thin and complex, then there is no way to choose among the goods of which it is composed. But the thinness of the goods involved makes such conflict quite likely and maybe inevitable. Each thin good is highly indeterminate and can be added to infinity. They are also minimally substantial. These considerations mean that most any

---

39. Stocker, "The Schizophrenia of Modern Ethical Theories," 68–69.

action might serve to further any one of the thin goods. It is therefore highly likely that some act or object *x* will increase pleasure at the expense of wealth or of increasing safety or even of fame. It is also likely that maximizing recognition and wealth or recognition and safety may come into conflict. And if these goods ever do come into conflict, as it seems they probably will, we cannot choose among them. If we do, we belie the fact that the good chosen was always of a higher order than the others, and, consequently, that the good is not truly complex. In the end, the possibility of such conflicts means that a complex thin teleological good may provide as little guidance as a thin good taken by itself. It doesn't seem that a coherent realism can admit such conflicts among basic goods or, for that matter, underwrite as many mutually exclusive (or contradictory) actions as each of the thin goods underwrites.

The Constitution on Natural Law

In chapter 5 I argued the Constitution presupposes (1) that the natural law adds prescription to real goodness (or the common good), such that good is to be done and its contrary avoided; (2) that the requirements of the natural law are known (rather than nonexistent) through noninstrumental (or substantive) reason rather than through sentiment or noninstrumental reason; and (3) that at a minimum the Constitution takes these commands to be known at least to most.

The preceding section provides most all the tools for addressing the first presupposition. After all, if there is some objective good *x*, but no prescription that *x* is to be pursued or preserved, then no one is obliged to pursue *x* or to refrain from acting contrary to *x*. In that case, things like brutal slavery and oppressive tyranny may represent failures to pursue the good, but they cannot be considered wrong or blameworthy in any deep sense. Without prescriptive natural law pointing out not only that something is good but also that good is to be pursued or preserved, there are no blameworthy actions. Tolerance and intolerance, absolute and limited government, tyranny and just rule, slavery and liberty are all on a par, in that no one is obligated to pursue some of these and refrain from pursuing others, and no one is morally praiseworthy for pursuing some or blameworthy for pursuing others, unless there is some external source of obligation normative for human willing that prescribes some of these and proscribes others. The criticisms of moral realism previously discussed, for this reason, also presuppose the truth of natural law.

The second point argued in chapter 5 requires further elaboration. Let's consider sentimentalism first. The primary problem with sentimentalism is that we have different and conflicting sentiments that seek to direct our actions in different ways. What are we to do when some sentiment *x* and some sentiment *y* that entails not-*x* both simultaneously seek to direct our action? We cannot choose between *x* and *y* on the basis of sentiment alone. But advocates of the theory of moral sentiment don't mean that we should listen to all our sentiments. Rather, they tell us that we should follow the *moral* sentiments. The distinction between *moral* sentiment and *mere* sentiment, however, cannot be made on the basis of sentiment. *Moral* sentiments must be distinguished by their conformity to a standard external to sentiment. As a realist, the sentimentalist readily concedes this. However, because our sentiments are in conflict and because we cannot tell which sentiments are moral and which are not by considering sentiment alone, we must have independent knowledge of the standard in order to know which sentiments to follow. In short, moral sentiments may be necessary to motivate right action, but they cannot by themselves serve as the basis for all moral knowledge.

Instrumental reason doesn't provide much of a guide either. For the instrumental theorist, reason is, as Hume maintains, the slave of the passions. Desire sets the end. Reason does nothing other than tell one how to attain the desired object. But if this is the case, says Hume, "'Tis as little contrary to reason to prefer the destruction of the whole world to the scratching of my finger. 'Tis not contrary to reason for me to chuse my total ruin, to prevent the least uneasiness of an *Indian* or person unknown to me. 'Tis as little contrary to reason to prefer even my own acknowledged lesser good to my greater."[40] According to Hampton, Hume's point is that the theorist of instrumental reason "will refuse to see that *any* preference for an object is contrary to reason, because reason does not, for such a theorist, have a goal of its own to oppose to the preference."[41] Advocates of instrumental reason seem to think the theory can provide a real ethic free of the baggage of noninstrumentalist or substantive conceptions of reason. But, given Hume's biting critique, it doesn't look as if instrumental reason is capable of serving as a reliable measure for human action—for anything at all might be preferred, in which case instrumental reason will have to tell us how to get there. Instrumental reason told Churchill that he ought to take certain steps because they were the best suited to preserve England and Paul Brand that he ought to adopt certain techniques

40. Cited in Hampton, *Hobbes and the Social Contract Tradition*, 36.
41. Ibid.

to attain his goal of providing medical aid to lepers. Instrumental reason also instructed Hitler and Stalin to take certain actions best ordered to helping them attain their strong desire to see certain individuals and groups exterminated. But an ethical system that can underwrite the actions of Churchill and Brand as well as of Hitler and Stalin is no ethical system worthy of the name. Churchill and Brand desired very different things than did Hitler and Stalin—the former desired the sorts of things conducive to the preservation of humanity, while the latter wanted the sorts of things contrary to the preservation of society, and instrumental reason does not discriminate between them. The only way around this difficulty is to posit, as Hobbes does, a fundamental strongest desire shared by all people—on his theory, survival. But people want different things the most. As Aristotle noted, most people want pleasure the most, the more civilized or refined want honor the most.[42] Some people want survival the most, while some willingly risk survival for fame, for love, or even for country. Finally, instrumental reason also suffers something of a coherence problem. According to Hampton,

> defining instrumental reason involves defining and defending a whole series of normative principles, so that a conception of instrumental reason is *constituted by* normative principles. That is . . . *a conception of instrumental reason is only a set of normative principles, related to one another by other normative principles* that involve not only how to reason with respect to ends, but also how to define what one's ends are. This set will also include a conception of how these norms are to be applied to a person's deliberations, or her planning, or her preference set, so that she can be considered to be fully rational. . . . So understood, any theory of instrumental reasoning is just as hip-deep in normativity as any moral theory.[43]

Given the problems with sentimentalism and instrumental reason, it appears we have the following conditional: if moral requirements are known, then they are known through noninstrumental (substantive) reason. Just here a question emerges. Doesn't the fact that moral beliefs vary across societies and over time rule out the idea of a universal, transcendent moral standard known or knowable to the practical reason of all? There are two reasons for thinking not. First, great variation in moral belief does nothing, by itself, to contradict the existence of a real natural law, knowable through noninstrumental reason.

---

42. Aristotle *Nichomachean Ethics* 1095a15.
43. Hampton, *Authority of Reason*, 206.

At best, variation in moral belief argues against conceptions of natural law that suggest that the moral law is known to all or very nearly all. The problem only emerges for the one who believes that promulgation is an essential ingredient of law. Of course, many natural lawyers hold just this, and so the objection must be addressed on their behalf.

Second, variation in moral belief is only half the story. Natural lawyers readily admit that there is variation in moral belief across societies and over time. No natural lawyer has ever seriously suggested that all people everywhere have precisely the same moral beliefs. As for the other half of the story, natural lawyers have maintained that there is shared knowledge of the basics of natural law. They have maintained this with rather than against the evidence. In 1931 John M. Cooper wrote,

> The peoples of the world, however much they differ as to details of morality, hold universally, or with practical universality, to at least the following basic precepts. Respect the Supreme Being or the benevolent being or beings who take his place. Do not "blaspheme." Care for your children. Malicious murder or maiming, stealing, deliberate slander or "black" lying, when committed against friend or unoffending clansman or tribesman, are reprehensible. Adultery proper is wrong, even though there be exceptional circumstances that permit or even enjoin it and even though sexual relations among the unmarried may be viewed leniently. Incest is a heinous offense.[44]

Cooper then notes, "This universal code agrees rather closely with our own Decalogue understood in a strictly literal sense. It inculcates worship of and reverence to the Supreme Being or to other superhuman beings. It protects the fundamental rights of life, limb, family, property, and good name."[45] Cooper is not generalizing from the moral codes of the great societies that have existed across history. Rather, he is making generalizations from the anthropological data of the time on *primitive* cultures. Finnis makes a similar point:

> Students of ethics and of human cultures very commonly assume that cultures manifest preferences, motivations, and evaluations so wide and chaotic in their variety that no values or practical principles can be said to be self-evident to human beings, since no value or practical principle is recognized in all times and all places. . . . But those philosophers who have recently

44. Cited in Rommen, *The Natural Law*, 201.
45. Ibid.

sought to test this assumption by surveying the anthropological literature (including the similar general surveys made by professional anthropologists), have found with striking unanimity that this assumption is unwarranted.

These surveys entitle us, indeed, to make some rather confident assertions. All human societies show a concern for the value of human life; in all, self-preservation is generally accepted as a proper motive for action, and in none is the killing of other human beings permitted without some fairly definite justification. All human societies regard the procreation of human life as in itself a good thing unless there are special circumstances. No human society fails to restrict sexual activity; in all societies there is some prohibition of incest, some opposition to boundless promiscuity and to rape, some favor for stability and permanence in sexual relations. All human societies display a concern for truth, through education of the young in matters not only practical (e.g., avoidance of dangers) but also speculative or theoretical (e.g., religion). Human beings, who can survive infancy only by nurture, live in or on the margins of some society which invariably extends beyond the nuclear family, and all societies display a favor for the values of cooperation, of common over individual good, of obligation between individuals, and of justice within groups. All know friendship. All have some conception of *meum* and *tuum,* title or property, and of reciprocity. All value play, serious and formalized, or relaxed and recreational. All treat the bodies of dead members of the group in some traditional and ritual fashion different from their procedures for rubbish disposal. All display a concern for powers or principles which are to be respected as superhuman; in one form another, religion is universal.[46]

Assessing the anthropological data, Oxford don and Cambridge professor C. S. Lewis wrote,

And what of the second modern objection [to the idea of natural law]—that the ethical standards of different cultures differ so widely that there is no common tradition at all? The answer is that this is a lie—a good, solid, resounding lie. If a man will go into a library and spend a few days with the *Encyclopedia of Religion and Ethics* he will soon discover the massive unanimity of the practical reason in man. From the Babylonian *Hymn to Samos,* from the Laws of Manu, the *Book of the Dead,* the Analects, the Stoics, the Platon-

46. Finnis, *Natural Law and Natural Rights,* 83–84.

ists, the Australian aborigines . . . he will discover the same triumphantly monotonous denunciations of oppression, murder, treachery and falsehood, the same injunctions of kindness to the aged, the young, and the weak, of almsgiving and impartiality and honesty. He may be a little surprised (I certainly was) to find that precepts of mercy are more frequent than precepts of justice; but he will no longer doubt that there is such a thing as the Law of Nature. There are, of course, differences. There are even blindnesses in particular cultures. . . . But the pretence that we are presented with a mere chaos—though no outline of universally accepted value shows through—is simply false and should be contradicted in season and out of season wherever it is met. Far from finding a chaos, we find exactly what we should expect if good is indeed something objective and reason the organ whereby it is apprehended—that is, a substantial agreement with considerable local differences of emphasis and, perhaps, no one code that includes everything.[47]

I want to note these last lines—the natural law thesis, properly understood predicts both similarity and variation in moral belief across cultures and over time. In short, what we observe anthropologically arguably fits quite well with the idea that, at least to some extent, the natural law's requirements are known to most or all.

The Constitution on Natural Rights

In chapter 6 I argued that the Constitution presupposes a view of natural rights, such that there are natural rights, which are derivative from rather than prior to natural duties. I maintained that natural rights are entailments of natural duties, such that if a person x finds himself under a moral necessity to do some act y, then it follows that x has the ability to do y and that others have a duty to refrain from preventing x from doing y. I also argued that because moral obligation antecedent to and normative for human willing entails rights antecedent to and normative for human willing, a denial of natural rights entails a denial of natural obligation. The Constitution, however, presupposes a nonpositive (and nonconventional) source of obligation that grounds the obligation of human law, an obligation presupposed in the prescriptive character of the Constitution and the laws it produces.

Is this view of natural rights a good one? Well, if it is good and unproblematic that the Constitution presupposes natural obligations, then there is no

47. Lewis, "Poison of Subjectivism," 77–78.

problem so far as natural rights are concerned. Natural rights are entailments of natural obligations, of duties flowing from human nature. One cannot affirm one without affirming the other. If one is not problematic, logical consistency says that neither is the other. Because natural rights are entailed by natural obligation, denying natural rights means denying natural obligation, i.e., a source of obligation external to and normative for human willing. But this returns us very quickly to moral nihilism, for if natural law does not exist, then no actions are obligatory. The designer of absolute political regimes, the tyrant, the slave owner, the thief, the dictator who commits genocide, none of these have failed in moral obligation if there is no natural law. They are all given moral free rein by the denial of natural law. We saw that certain critics of moral realism and natural law wish to criticize all of these. If they do, then they should affirm natural law. If these critics do that, they must, as matter of entailment, affirm natural rights. So doing, they will affirm the philosophy latent in the Constitution.

Conclusion

If moral realism and natural law are false and, concomitantly, moral nihilism true, then there is no basis for rendering moral judgment upon anything at all. The consequence of moral nihilism (or, in contemporary parlance, moral skepticism) is that morality amounts to nothing. But as King Lear reminds us, nothing comes from nothing. Moral anarchy (or subjectivism), conventionalism, normative positivism (even instrumental reason, at day's end) all presuppose the denial of moral realism and, consequently, affirm moral nihilism. If these are true, then there is no basis for criticizing the actions of individuals or the laws enacted by governments or legal systems as a whole. If moral nihilism is true, then there is no such thing as good or bad acts, good or bad laws, good or bad states. But our most fundamental and human moral intuition is that we can in fact distinguish between good and bad acts, laws, and states. Even the critic of moral realism and natural law knows this—otherwise he would never have criticized moral realism and natural law for promoting intolerance, political absolutism, tyranny, or hierarchical rather than democratic regimes. If these really are bad and therefore to be condemned, then realism must be true. The person who truly denied moral realism and natural law would not condemn intolerance (because it could not be worse than tolerance in any meaningful sense), tyranny (because there would be no such thing as tyranny if there is no real good prescribed by natural law), and political absolutism (because limited and unlimited sovereigns would be on a par). Nor would the denier of moral realism and natural law praise democracy, for he would recognize that democracy could not be good in any meaningful sense if moral realism is false. In fact, the true denier would recognize that if moral realism and natural law fall, then there is no political rule but only contests for power. In such contests, the strong will win and will dominate the weak. The denier of natural law will recognize, with Thrasymachus, Pindar, and Carneades, that strength is the basis of all rule and that this is inegalitarian indeed. The fact that critics of moral realism and natural law offer critiques of certain actions (intolerant ones), laws (tyrannical ones), and regime types (hierarchical ones) betrays the fact that they share with us a common intuition of a real goodness prescribed by the law of nature.

I suggest that it is a good thing that the Constitution embodies our most fundamental intuitions about the nature of moral reality. But is the Constitution any good? By now it should be obvious that this question asks us to distinguish between good and bad regimes. The poser of the question must affirm moral realism. The Constitution shares his affirmation that there is a real good. Therefore, if *good* has any meaning at all, then the answer is yes.

Bibliography

Ackerman, Bruce. *Social Justice and the Liberal State.* New Haven: Yale University Press, 1980.

———. *We the People: Foundations.* Cambridge: Harvard University Press, 1991.

Angeles, Peter A. *The HarperCollins Dictionary of Philosophy.* 2nd ed. New York: HarperCollins, 1992.

Anscombe, G. E. M. "On the Source of the Authority of the State." In *The Collected Philosophical Papers of G. E. M. Anscombe, Volume 3: Ethics, Religion and Politics.* Oxford: Basil Blackwell Publisher, 1981.

Aquinas, St. Thomas. *Summa Theologica.* Translated by the Fathers of the English Dominican Province. 5 vols. Allen, TX: Christian Classics, 1981.

Aristotle. *Nichomachean Ethics.* Translated by Martin Ostwald. Englewood Cliffs, NJ: Prentice Hall, 1962.

———. *On Rhetoric: A Theory of Civic Discourse.* Translated by George A. Kennedy. New York: Oxford University Press, 1991.

———. *Physics.* In *Introduction to Aristotle,* edited by Richard McKeon. Chicago: University of Chicago Press, 1974.

———. *The Politics.* Translated by T. A. Sinclair. Revised by Trevor J. Saunders. London: Penguin Books, 1992.

Arkes, Hadley. *Beyond the Constitution.* Princeton: Princeton University Press, 1990.

———. *First Things: An Inquiry into the First Principles of Morals and Justice.* Princeton: Princeton University Press, 1986.

Baltimore, David. "Limiting Science: A Biologist's Perspective." *Daedalus* (Summer 1988).

Banning, Lance. *The Sacred Fire of Liberty: James Madison and the Founding of the Federal Republic.* Ithaca: Cornell University Press, 1995.

Barber, Sotirios A. *On What the Constitution Means.* Baltimore: Johns Hopkins University Press, 1984.

———. *Welfare and the Constitution.* Princeton: Princeton University Press, 2003.

Barr, Stephen M. *Modern Physics and Ancient Faith.* Notre Dame: University of Notre Dame Press, 2003.

Barrow, John D., and Frank J. Tipler. *The Anthropic Cosmological Principle.* Oxford: Oxford University Press, 1988.

Beard, Charles A. *An Economic Interpretation of the Constitution of the United States.* New York: Macmillan Company, 1913.

Beckwith, Francis J. "A Critique of Moral Relativism." In *Do the Right Thing,* edited by Francis J. Beckwith. Belmont, CA: Wadsworth/Thomson Learning, 2002.

Bedeau, Mark. "Where's the Good in Teleology." *Philosophy and Phenomenological Research* 52, no. 4 (December 1992): 781–806.

Berns, Walter. "Judicial Review and the Rights and Laws of Nature." In *The Supreme Court Review: 1982,* edited by Philip B. Kurland, Gerhard Casper, and Dennis J. Hutchinson. Chicago: University of Chicago Press, 1982.

———. *Taking the Constitution Seriously.* New York: Simon and Schuster, 1987.

Bodin, Jean. *On Sovereignty.* Edited and Translated by Julian H. Franklin. Cambridge: Cambridge University Press, 1992.

Boyle, Joseph. "Natural Law and the Ethics of Tradition." In *Natural Law Theory: Contemporary Essays.* Oxford: Clarendon Press, 1992.

Brann, Eva T. H. "Madison's *Memorial and Remonstrance:* A Model of American Eloquence." In *Rhetoric and American Statesmanship,* edited by Glen E. Thurow and Jeffrey D. Wallin. Durham: Carolina Academic Press, 1982.

Bressler, Robert K., Ann W. Burgess, and John E. Douglas. *Sexual Homicide: Patterns and Motives.* New York: Free Press, 1988.

Budziszewski, J. *What We Can't Not Know.* Dallas: Spence Publishing Company, 2003.

———. *Written on the Heart: The Case for Natural Law.* Downers Grove, IL: IVP, 1997.

Cicero. *The Republic* and *The Laws.* Translated by Niall Rudd. Oxford: Oxford University Press, 1998.

Copleston, Frederick. *A History of Philosophy: Volume 1: Greece and Rome: From the Pre-Socratics to Plotinus.* New York: Image Books, 1985.

Corwin, Edwin S. *The Higher Law Background of American Constitutional Law.* Ithaca: Great Seal Books, 1955.

Davies, Paul. "The Appearance of Design in Physics and Cosmology." In *God and Design: The Teleological Argument and Modern Science,* edited by Neil A. Manson. London: Routledge, 2003.

———. *The Cosmic Blueprint: New Discoveries in Nature's Creative Ability to Order the Universe.* New York: Simon and Schuster, 1988.

DeHart, Paul R. "The Dangerous Life: Natural Justice and the Rightful Subversion of the State." *Polity* 38, no. 3 (July 2006): 369–93.

Denton, Michael. *Nature's Destiny: How the Laws of Biology Reveal Purpose in the Universe.* New York: Free Press, 1998.

Diamond, Martin. *As Far as Republican Principles Will Admit: Essays by Martin Diamond.* Edited by William A. Schambra. Washington, DC: AEI Press, 1992.

Dretske, Fred. *Explaining Behavior.* Cambridge: MIT Press, 1988.

Dry, Murray, ed. *The Anti-Federalist: An Abridgement by Murray Dry, of "The Complete Anti-Federalist,"* edited, with Commentary and Notes, *by Herbert J. Storing.* Chicago: University of Chicago Press, 1981.

Eidelberg, Paul. *The Philosophy of the American Constitution: A Reinterpretation of the Intentions of the Founding Fathers.* New York: Free Press, 1968.

Eisgruber, Christopher L. *Constitutional Self-Government.* Cambridge: Harvard University Press, 2001.

Elazar, Daniel J. *The American Constitutional Tradition.* Lincoln: University of Nebraska Press, 1988.

———. *The Covenant Tradition in Politics.* 4 vols. New Brunswick, NJ: Transaction Publishers, 1995–1998.

Ely, John Hart. *Democracy and Distrust: A Theory of Judicial Review.* Cambridge: Harvard University Press, 1980.

Finnis, John. *Aquinas: Moral, Political, and Legal Theory.* Oxford: Oxford University Press, 1998.

———. *Natural Law and Natural Rights.* Oxford: Clarendon Press, 1980.

———. "Natural Law Theory and Limited Government." In *Natural Law, Liberalism and Morality,* edited by Robert P. George. Oxford: Clarendon Press 1996.

Fiorina, Morris P., and Paul E. Peterson. *The New American Democracy.* Needham Heights, MA: Allyn and Bacon, 1998.

Fisher, Louis. *Constitutional Conflicts between Congress and the Presidency.* Princeton: Princeton University Press, 1985.

Flaumenhaft, Harvey. *The Effective Republic: Administration and Constitution in the Thought of Alexander Hamilton.* Durham: Duke University Press, 1992.

Frankena, William K. "Natural and Inalienable Rights." *Philosophical Review* 64, no. 2 (April 1955): 212–32.

George, Robert P. *In Defense of Natural Law.* Oxford: Oxford University Press, 1999.

———. "Natural Law and Human Nature." In *Natural Law Theory: Contemporary Essays,* edited by Robert P. George. Oxford: Clarendon Press, 1992.

Gilson, Etienne. *From Aristotle to Darwin and Back Again: A Journey in Final Causality, Species, and Evolution.* Translated by John Lyon. Notre Dame: University of Notre Dame Press, 1984.

Goldstein, Leslie Friedman. "Popular Sovereignty, the Origins of Judicial Review, and the Revival of Unwritten Law." *Journal of Politics* 48, no. 1 (February 1986): 51–71.

Grey, Thomas C. "Do We Have an Unwritten Constitution?" *Stanford Law Review* 27 (February 1975): 703–18.

———. "Origins of the Unwritten Constitution: Fundamental Law in American Revolutionary Thought." *Stanford Law Review* 30 (May 1978): 843–93.

Griffiths, Paul E. "Functional Analysis and Proper Functions." *British Journal for the Philosophy of Science* 44, no. 3 (September 1993): 409–22.

Grotius, Hugo. *De iure belli ac pacis.* Translated by Louise R. Loomis. Roslyn, NY: Walter J. Black, 1949.

Haakonssen, Knud. *Natural Law and Moral Philosophy: From Grotius to the Scottish Enlightenment.* New York: Cambridge University Press, 1996.

Hall, Mark David. *The Political and Legal Philosophy of James Wilson, 1742–1798.* Columbia: University of Missouri Press, 1997.

Hallowell, John H. *The Moral Foundation of Democracy.* Chicago: University of Chicago Press, 1954.

Hamilton, Alexander, James Madison, and John Jay. *The Federalist Papers.* Edited by Garry Wills. New York: Bantam Books, 1982.

Hampton, Jean. *The Authority of Reason.* Cambridge: Cambridge University Press, 1998.

———. *Hobbes and the Social Contract Tradition.* Cambridge: Cambridge University Press, 1987.

———. *Political Philosophy.* Boulder, CO: Westview Press, 1997.

Hankinson, R. J. "Philosophy of Science." In *The Cambridge Companion to Aristotle,* edited by Jonathan Barnes. Cambridge: Cambridge University Press, 1995.

Harman, Gilbert. "Enumerative Induction as Inference to the Best Explanation." *Journal of Philosophy* 65, no. 18 (September 1968): 529–33.

———. "The Inference to the Best Explanation." *Philosophical Review* 74, no. 1 (January 1965): 88–95.

Hart, H. L. A. "Are There Any Natural Rights?" *Philosophical Review* 64, no. 2 (April 1955): 175–91.

———. *The Concept of Law.* 2nd ed. Oxford: Oxford University Press, 1994.

Hickey, Eric W. *Serial Murderers and Their Victims.* Belmont, CA: Wadsworth Publishing, 1991.

Hobbes, Thomas. *On the Citizen.* Edited and Translated by Richard Tuck and Michael Silverthorne. Cambridge: Cambridge University Press, 1998.

———. *Leviathan.* Edited by Edwin Curley. Indianapolis: Hackett Publishing Company, 1994.

Hofstadter, Albert. "Objective Teleology." *Journal of Philosophy* 38, no. 2 (January 1941): 29–39.

Howe, Daniel Walker. *The Making of the American Self: Jonathan Edwards to Abraham Lincoln.* Cambridge: Harvard University Press, 1997.

———. "The Political Psychology of *The Federalist.*" *William and Mary Quarterly* 44, no. 3 (July 1987): 485–509.

Hurley, Patrick J. *A Concise Introduction to Logic.* 6th ed. Belmont, CA: Wadsworth Publishing, 1997.

Jaffa, Harry V. *The Crisis of the House Divided: An Interpretation of the Issues in the Lincoln-Douglas Debates.* Chicago: University of Chicago Press, 1982.

———. *A New Birth of Freedom: Abraham Lincoln and the Coming of the Civil War.* Lanham: Rowan and Littlefield, 2000.

Jones, Charles O. *The Presidency in a Separated System.* Washington, DC: Brookings Institution, 1994.

Kant, Immanuel. *Grounding for the Metaphysics of Morals; with, On a Supposed Right to Lie because of Philanthropic Concerns.* 3rd ed. Translated by James W. Ellington. Indianapolis: Hackett Publishing Company, 1993.

Ketcham, Ralph. *James Madison: A Biography.* Charlottesville: University Press of Virginia, 1990.

Koons, Robert C. *Realism Regained: An Exact Theory of Causation, Teleology, and the Mind.* Oxford: Oxford University Press, 2000.

Lawler, Peter Augustine. "James Madison and the Metaphysics of Modern Politics." *Review of Politics* 48 (1986): 92–115.

Leff, Arthur Allen. "Unspeakable Ethics; Unnatural Law." *Duke Law Journal*, no. 6 (December 1979): 1229–49.

Lewis, C. S. *Abolition of Man.* New York: Collier Books, 1955.

————. *Miracles: A Preliminary Study.* New York: Simon and Schuster, 1996.

————. "On Ethics." In *Christian Reflections,* edited by Walter Hooper. Grand Rapids, MI: Eerdmans, 1994.

————. "The Poison of Subjectivism." *Religion in Life* 12 (Summer 1943). Reprinted in *Christian Reflections,* edited by Walter Hooper. Grand Rapids, MI: Eerdmans, 1994.

Lewis, Ewart. "The Contributions of Medieval Thought to the American Political Tradition." *American Political Science Review* 50 (June 1956) 2: 462–74.

Lindsay, Thomas. "James Madison on Religion and Politics: Rhetoric and Reality." *American Political Science Review* 85 (1991): 1321–37.

Lipton, Peter. *Inference to the Best Explanation.* London: Routledge, 1993.

Lisska, Anthony. *Aquinas's Theory of Natural Law: An Analytic Reconstruction.* Oxford: Clarendon Press, 1997.

Locke, John. *Questions Concerning the Law of Nature.* Edited and Translated by Robert Horwitz, Jenny Strauss Clay, and Diskin Clay. Ithaca: Cornell University Press, 1990.

————. *Two Treatises of Government.* Edited by Peter Laslett. Cambridge: Cambridge University Press, 1960.

Lutz, Donald S. *The Origins of American Constitutionalism.* Baton Rouge: Louisiana State University Press, 1988.

MacIntyre, Alasdair. *Whose Justice? Which Rationality?* Notre Dame: University of Notre Dame Press, 1988.

Madison, James. *James Madison: Writings.* Edited by Jack N. Rakove. New York: Library of America, 1999.

————. *Memorial and Remonstrance against Religious Assessments,* June 20, 1785. In *The Papers of James Madison,* vol. 8, edited by Robert Rutland et al. 17 vols. Chicago: University of Chicago Press, 1973.

Maltz, Earl M. "Slavery, Federalism, and the Structure of the Constitution." *American Journal of Legal History* 36, no. 4 (October 1992): 466–98.

Martinich, A. P. *The Two Gods of Leviathan: Thomas Hobbes on Religion and Politics.* Cambridge: Cambridge University Press, 1992.

Mayr, Ernst. "The Idea of Teleology." *Journal of the History of Ideas* 53, no. 1 (January–March 1992): 117–35.

McCloskey, Robert G. *The American Supreme Court.* 2nd ed. Chicago: University of Chicago Press, 1994.

McCoy, Charles S., and J. Wayne Baker. *Fountainhead of Federalism: Heinrich Bullinger and the Covenantal Tradition.* Louisville, KY: Westminster/John Knox Press, 1991.

McDonald, Forrest. *Alexander Hamilton: A Biography.* New York: W. W. Norton, 1979.

————. *Novus Ordo Seclorum: The Intellectual Origins of the Constitution.* Lawrence: University Press of Kansas, 1985.

————. *States' Rights and the Union: Imperio in Imperio, 1776–1876.* Lawrence: University Press of Kansas, 2000.

————. *We the People: The Economic Origins of the Constitution.* Chicago: University of Chicago Press, 1958.

McDowell, Gary L. "Coke, Corwin, and the Constitution: The 'Higher Law Background' Reconsidered." *Review of Politics* (Summer 1993): 393–420.

Meyer, Susan Sauve. "Aristotle, Teleology, and Reduction." *Philosophical Review* 101, no. 4 (October 1992): 791–825.

Michael, Helen K. "The Role of Natural Law in Early American Constitutionalism: Did the Founders Contemplate Judicial Enforcement of 'Unwritten' Individual Rights?" *North Carolina Law Review* 69, no. 2 (January 1991): 421–90.

Mill, John Stuart. *Utilitarianism.* Edited by George Sher. Indianapolis: Hackett Publishing Company, 1979.

Millikan, Ruth Garrett. "In Defense of Proper Functions." *Philosophy of Science* 56, no. 2 (June 1989): 288–302.

————. *Language, Thought, and Other Biological Categories.* Cambridge: MIT Press, 1984.

Moore, Michael. "Moral Reality." *Wisconsin Law Review,* no. 6 (1982): 1061–1156.

Murphy, Jeffrie G., and Jules L. Coleman. *Philosophy of Law: An Introduction to Jurisprudence.* Rev. ed. Boulder, CO: Westview Press, 1990.

Murphy, Walter F. "The Art of Constitutional Interpretation: A Preliminary Showing." In *Essays on the Constitution of the United States,* edited by J. Judd Harmon. Port Washington, NY: Kennikat Press, 1978.

Nagel, Ernest. *Teleology Revisited and Other Essays in the Philosophy and History of Science.* New York: Columbia University Press, 1979.

Nathanson, Stephen. *Should We Consent To Be Governed: A Short Introduction to Political Philosophy.* 2nd ed. Belmont, CA: Wadsworth/Thomson Learning, 2001.

Neustadt, Richard E. *Presidential Power and the Modern Presidents: The Politics of Leadership from Roosevelt to Reagan.* New York: Free Press, 1990.

Nozick, Robert. *Anarchy, State, and Utopia.* New York: Basic Books, 1974.

Occam, William. *A Dialogue.* In *A Letter to the Friar's Minor and Other Writ-*

ings, translated by John Kilcullen. Cambridge: Cambridge University Press, 1995.

Paine, Thomas. *The Thomas Paine Reader.* Edited by Michael Foot and Isaac Kramnick. Middlesex, England: Penguin Books, 1987.

Pangle, Thomas. *The Spirit of Modern Republicanism: The Moral Vision of the American Founders and the Philosophy of John Locke.* Chicago: University of Chicago Press, 1988.

Plantinga, Alvin. *Does God Have a Nature?* Milwaukee: Marquette University Press, 1980.

———. *God, Freedom, and Evil.* Grand Rapids, MI: William B. Eerdmans Publishing Company, 1974.

———. *God and Other Minds: A Study of the Rational Justification of Belief in God.* Ithaca: Cornell University Press, 1967.

———. *The Nature of Necessity.* Oxford: Clarendon Press, 1974.

———. *Warrant and Proper Function.* New York: Oxford University Press, 1993.

———. *Warranted Christian Belief.* New York: Oxford University Press, 2000.

Plato. *The Laws.* Translated by Trevor J. Sanders. London: Penguin Books, 1970.

———. *The Republic of Plato.* 2nd ed. Translated by Allan Bloom. Basic Books, 1991.

Polkinghorne, John. *Belief in God in an Age of Science.* New Haven: Yale University Press, 1998.

———. *The Faith of a Physicist.* Princeton: Princeton University Press, 1994.

Powell, H. Jefferson. *The Moral Tradition of American Constitutionalism: A Theological Interpretation.* Durham: Duke University Press, 1992.

———. "The Original Understanding of Original Intent." In *Interpreting the Constitution: The Debate over Original Intent,* edited by Jack N. Rakove. Boston: Northeastern University Press, 1990.

Pufendorf, Samuel. *On the Law of Nature and of Nations in Eight Books.* In *The Political Writings of Samuel Pufendorf,* edited by Craig L. Carr and translated by Michael J. Seidler. Oxford: Oxford University Press, 1994.

Rahe, Paul A. *Republics Ancient and Modern: Classical Republicanism and the American Revolution.* Chapel Hill: University of North Carolina Press, 1992.

Rakove, Jack N. *Original Meanings: Politics and Ideas in the Making of the Constitution.* New York: Alfred A. Knopf, 1996.

Rappaport, Steven. "Inference to the Best Explanation: Is It Really Different from Mill's Methods?" *Philosophy of Science* 63, no. 1 (March 1996): 65–80.

Rawls, John. *A Theory of Justice*. Rev. ed. Cambridge: Harvard University Press, 1999.

Reppert, Victor. *C. S. Lewis's Dangerous Idea: In Defense of the Argument from Reason*. Downers Grove, IL: InterVarsity Press, 2003.

Rodgers, Daniel T. "Republicanism: The Career of a Concept." *Journal of American History* 79, no. 1 (June 1992): 11–38.

Rommen, Heinrich A. *The Natural Law: A Study in Legal and Social Philosophy*. Indianapolis: Liberty Fund, 1998.

Rosenberg, Gerald N. *The Hollow Hope: Can Courts Bring about Social Change?* Chicago: University of Chicago Press, 1993.

Rousseau, Jean-Jacques. *The Social Contract*. Translated by Maurice Cranston. London: Penguin Books.

Sandel, Michael J. *Democracy's Discontent: America in Search of a Public Philosophy*. Cambridge: Harvard University Press, 1996.

Schneewind, J. B. *The Invention of Autonomy: A History of Modern Moral Philosophy*. Cambridge: Cambridge University Press, 1998.

Searle, John R. *Speech Acts*. Cambridge: Cambridge University Press, 1969.

Seung, T. K. *Intuition and Construction: The Foundation of Normative Theory*. New Haven: Yale University Press, 1993.

———. *Plato Rediscovered: Human Value and Social Order*. Lanham: Rowman and Littlefield, 1996.

Sherry, Suzanna. "The Founders' Unwritten Constitution." *University of Chicago Law Review* 54, no. 4 (Fall 1987): 1127–77.

Sherwin-White, A. N. *Roman Society and Roman Law in the New Testament*. Oxford: Oxford Clarendon Press, 1963.

Simmons, A. John. *The Lockean Theory of Rights*. Princeton: Princeton University Press, 1992.

Smith, Adam. *The Theory of Moral Sentiments*. Edited by Knud Haakonssen. Cambridge: Cambridge University Press, 2002.

Sophocles. *Antigone*. Translated by David Greene. Chicago: University of Chicago Press, 1991.

Stocker, Michael. "The Schizophrenia of Modern Ethical Theories." In *Virtue Ethics*, edited by Roger Crisp and Michael Slote. Oxford: Oxford University Press, 1997.

Stockton, Constant Noble. "Are There Natural Rights in 'The Federalist.'" *Ethics* 82, no. 1 (October 1971): 72–82.

Storing, Herbert J. *What the Anti-Federalists Were For: The Political Thought of the Opponents of the Constitution.* Chicago: University of Chicago Press, 1981.

Strauss, Leo, *Natural Right and History.* Chicago: University of Chicago Press, 1965.

Stump, Eleonore. "Augustine on Free Will." In *The Cambridge Companion to Augustine,* edited by Eleonore Stump and Norman Kretzman. Cambridge: Cambridge University Press, 2001.

Suarez, Francisco. *De legibus.* In *Selections from Three Works of Francisco Suarez.* Classics of International Law. Oxford: Clarendon Press, 1994.

Taylor, Charles. *Sources of the Self: The Making of Modern Identity.* Cambridge: Harvard University Press, 1989.

Thagard, Paul R. "The Best Explanation: Criteria for Theory Choice." *Journal of Philosophy* 75, no. 2 (February 1978): 76–92.

Tinder, Glenn. *Political Thinking: The Perennial Questions.* 5th ed. New York: HarperCollins, 1991.

Tuck, Richard. *Natural Rights Theories: Their Origin and Development.* Cambridge: Cambridge University Press, 1979.

Tulis, Jeffrey K. "Panel 2: The Appointment Power: Constitutional Abdication: The Senate, the President, and Appointments to the Supreme Court." *Case Western Reserve Law Review* 47, no. 4 (Summer 1997): 1331–58.

Van Inwagen, Peter. "The Compatibility of Darwinism and Design." In *God and Design: The Teleological Argument and Modern Science,* edited by Neil A. Manson. London: Routledge, 2003.

Veatch, Henry B. *Rational Man: A Modern Interpretation of Aristotelian Ethics.* Indianapolis: Liberty Fund, 2003.

Walker, Graham. *Moral Foundations of Constitutional Thought: Current Problems, Augustinian Prospects.* Princeton: Princeton University Press, 1990.

White, Morton. *The Philosophy of the American Revolution.* New York: Oxford University Press, 1978.

———. *Philosophy, "The Federalist," and the Constitution.* New York: Oxford University Press, 1987.

Witherspoon, John. "Lectures on Moral Philosophy." In *The Selected Writings of John Witherspoon,* edited by Thomas Miller. Carbondale: Southern Illinois University Press, 1990.

Woodfield, Andrew. *Teleology.* Cambridge: Cambridge University Press, 1976.

Wright, Benjamin F. "American Interpretations of Natural Law." *American Political Science Review* 20, no. 3 (August 1926): 524–47.

————. *American Interpretations of Natural Law: A Study in the History of Political Thought.* Cambridge: Harvard University Press, 1931.

Wright, Larry. *Teleological Explanations: An Etiological Analysis of Goals and Functions.* Berkeley: University of California Press, 1976.

Zuckert, Michael P. *Launching Liberalism: On Lockean Political Philosophy.* Lawrence: University Press of Kansas, 2002.

————. *The Natural Rights Republic: Studies in the Foundation of the American Political Tradition.* Notre Dame: University of Notre Dame Press, 1996.

Index

Ackerman, Bruce: as a positivist, 16n43, 18n52, 25n66, 115n2; and dualist democracy, 17; as a regretful and tragic positivist, 19n56; on judicial review, 150n70

Amendment procedure: and constrained popular sovereignty, 86, 98–99, 108, 143, 192, 200, 231n35, 243

Amendments, to the Constitution. *See* Bill of Rights; specific amendments

Angeles, Peter A.: on the genetic fallacy, 82n16

Anarchy: moral, 116–17, 118, 121–22, 123n13, 138, 153, 160, 167, 168–69, 246, 273; political, 81, 138–39, 160, 167, 168–69; and the Constitution, 138–39, 190, 199, 206

Anscombe, G. E. M.: on defining "right," 209, 213–19; on the implications of denying the existence of natural rights, 218; moral necessity entails moral right, 219

Antigone: the unwritten laws of heaven, 9

Antirealism. *See* Relativism

Aquinas, St. Thomas: on natural law, 9, 162, 162–64n8, 163, 164, 164n9, 187–90; and self-evidence, 10–11n24, 13n32, 180–81, 188; and the common good, 118, 138; on Aristotle, 136n43; on the primary and secondary precepts of the natural law, 180–81, 180n52, 180–81n53, 188–90; and natural inclinations, 188–89, 188–89n76; on limited government, 252–53; and regimes premised on equality and popular consent, 254–55

Aristotle, 2n2, 8, 11n27, 12n30, 14, 19, 20, 21, 210, 255, 269; the unwritten laws, 9; influence of Aristotelian thought on framers, 21n58, 21–22n59; Hobbes's rejection of, 22n60; possible influence on Blackstone, 23n64; his causal theory in the *Physics*, 53n32, 60–65; and the common good, 118, 128; his view of the good rejected by Kant, 129n26; on the good and *eudaimonia*, 136, 136n43, 137n48, 137n49, 138; his view of dispositional essences, 188–89n76; and slavery by nature, 195, 255–56; and the necessity for consent among equals, 203, on wealth as a means, 264

Arkes, Hadley, 162n7; logical analysis of the Constitution, 4n4; and the classical interpretation of the Constitution, 12n30; on Rousseau and moral obligation, 169n21; on slavery and the Constitution, 198n83; on the self-refuting character of moral relativism, 259

Article I, Section 2: three-fifths compromise, 195, 196, 203

Article I, Section 8 (the delegation of powers), 85, 96n50, 102, 107, 236

Article I, Section 9 (limits on Congress), 85, 103, 144, 229; importation clause of, 195, 197, 203

Article I, Section 10 (limits on the States), 85, 96n48, 96n50

Article IV, Section 2: and the fugitive slave clause of, 195, 197–98, 203

Articles of Confederation, 25, 50, 51, 231n35; compared to the Constitution, 93–95, 103

Permissions

The author would like to express his gratitude to publishing houses and other copyright holders for permission to quote from the following sources: